An Uncertain Journey

Published in the United States by
Beckham Publications Co
13619 Cedar Creek Lane,
Silver Spring, MD 20904
ISBN: 978-0-9984870-5-2

An Uncertain Journey

A Memoir

William Louis Gross, Jr.
with T.A. Simmons

Beckham
Publications

Silver Spring

Table of Contents

Dedication iv

Prologue viii

CHAPTER 1 – EARLY SCHOOL YEARS 1

CHAPTER 2 – THE BEATINGS TAKE THEIR TOLL 10

CHAPTER 3 – CLAUDIA AND RUTH TO MY RESCUE 31

CHAPTER 4 – GRANDPA ROBERT'S HOUSE 38

CHAPTER 5 – BLOSSOMING UNDER MISS GIBBS 42

CHAPTER 6 – THE PERFORMANCE 48

CHAPTER 7 – TENDING THE FIELDS 50

CHAPTER 8 – THE FIRE 53

CHAPTER 9 – FOURTH GRADE 57

CHAPTER 10 – PEANUTS!!! 63

CHAPTER 11 – FIFTH GRADE 70

CHAPTER 12 – PEANUTS ARE FINALLY READY!! 76

CHAPTER 13 – ACHES, PAINS, AND SATISFACTION 83

CHAPTER 14 – THEODORE ROOSEVELT 91

CHAPTER 15 – GIVING MYSELF TO THE LORD 101

CHAPTER 16 – OUR PRESIDENTIAL PROJECTS 107

CHAPTER 17 – TRYING TO FORGIVE MISS BARNETT 115

CHAPTER 18 – THE MOURNER'S BENCH 120

CHAPTER 19 – MR. ARMSTRONG 131

CHAPTER 20 – NEW FARMERS OF AMERICA CONVENTION 137

CHAPTER 21 – THE PROJECT 147

CHAPTER 22 – FESTIVE TIME OF YEAR 154

CHAPTER 23 – BACK TO SCHOOL 164

CHAPTER 24 – KIMBERLY-CLARK 177

CHAPTER 25 – PREPARING FOR TUSKEGEE 191

CHAPTER 26 – THE ADVENTURE BEGINS 208

CHAPTER 27 – THE SPEECH 218
CHAPTER 28 - REAPING THE REWARDS 228
CHAPTER 29 – MY MILITARY DECISION 239
CHAPTER 30 – TELLING THE FAMILY 248
CHAPTER 31 – MILITARY LIFE BEGINS 252
CHAPTER 32 – BASIC TRAINING 266
CHAPTER 33 – HOME FOR A VISIT 279
CHAPTER 34 – AIRMAN GROSS, ADMINISTRATION 285
CHAPTER 35 – A TRIP DOWNTOWN 291
CHAPTER 36 – MORE TESTS!! 305
CHAPTER 37 – G.E.D. 312
CHAPTER 38 – DESEGREGATION 324
CHAPTER 39 – THE PHILIPPINES 332
CHAPTER 40 – MY FEET 346
CHAPTER 41 – CHICAGO 350
CHAPTER 42 – ELGIN AIR FORCE BASE 362
CHAPTER 43 – WASHINGTON, D.C., ROTC PROGRAM 380
CHAPTER 44 – VIETNAM 397
CHAPTER 45 – LOOKING TOWARD THE FUTURE 421
CHAPTER 46 – COMING HOME FROM WAR 437
CHAPTER 47 – TUSKEGEE INSTITUTE AT LAST!! 450
CHAPTER 48 – ME, A SPOKESPERSON 467
CHAPTER 49 - CERTAINTY ACCELERATES 479
CHAPTER 50 - CERTAINTY APPLAUDS 487
CHAPTER 51 - CERTAINTY REVEALED 488
CHAPTER 52 – A CULMINATION OF HIS LIFE'S JOURNEY 493
EPILOGUE 528

FIRST YEAR IN SCHOOL AS A SIX-YEAR-OLD BOY

Dedication

God, My Father

I dedicate this book to God, who is the author and finisher of my faith. He is the very essence of my being. He is the giver of knowledge through His Grace, and I will forever be appreciative of His existence.

God put my life on hold, protecting me from any captivity when trials and tribulations of society were imposing upon me without cause. Keeping harm away, God was cultivating me to be what He wanted me to be, and I'm thankful God always had a plan for me.

I always knew at a very young age, that there was someone in the universe bigger than my Father or Mother, or anyone else that I had ever seen. However, physically untouchable, yet capable of imposing His Will on people or things as he chose, I knew the presence of God was always there. As a child, I always longed to see this giant creator, along with His creations of this massive universe. Some portions I could see, yet there were innumerable amounts that I could not see.

I was stuck on physicality, with no one to "unstick" my thoughts. If you asked your elders questions that they could not answer, they would respond by telling you that you're too young, or go and play. God knew that I wanted to learn more about him. That is why, on many occasions during my childhood, He snatched me from the arms of death so that his son could save me spiritually. He even gave me the privilege to stand in the midst of one of His miracles, the virtual end of one of His rainbows, and witness the beautiful array of colors reflecting on my frail seven-year-old body. Because of these few miracles, I give Him all Praise, Honor, and Glory, and dedicate this book to Him.

My Wife, Patricia

You have been a pillow of strength. You have also been a citadel of protection and support in my life during some of the most difficult stages of my journey. I would have never made it through Vietnam without your unswerving devotion, love, and prayers, followed by lots of "care packages" filled with lemon pound cake, onions, and occasionally, canned chitterlings from my Mother-in-law, Mrs. Elizabeth Turner. Although you were well aware that I was in a combat zone, we never talked about it. We spent our thoughts on paper, expressing our love for each other and our love for our daughter Kim, who was a baby during my Vietnam service. We wrote each other love letters daily, many of which we still have. These love letters and the thought of Kim gave me hope and inspiration and aided me in getting through the War.

My Daughter, Kim

Kim, you have always been the cerebral one in the family. I always knew that you had a special gift, but in your childhood, I didn't know what that gift was. You have always been a leader, which could be seen in your playgroups as a child. You always had the ability to excel in whatever you do. Your teachers placed you in gifted classes, and along with them, your unique gift was finally revealed; the gift of singing. She can bring a church to its feet. You took the lead in encouraging me to write my memoirs. You and your brother, Karlton, have always had my back. If I become ill, both of you appear to become sick emotionally; that lets me know that somewhere during their lives, I did something right.

I recall going to Montgomery, Alabama, to move you back to Virginia after you graduated from Auburn University. We enjoyed the best Father/Daughter bonding that we had ever had. We talked and laughed for almost the entire way. You are always a joy to be around.

My Son, Karlton

Karlton, you have always been the artist, adventurer, and mechanic in the family. You have the talent to sketch and draw, and repair almost anything that malfunctioned around the house. Never have you felt reluctant to tackle anything that you wanted to do, including driving long distances to unfamiliar places alone. I have never asked you, but I always thought that you continuously feel God's presence around you.

When I think of you as a husband, I see you doing great things for your wife, Francisca, and your family. When I think of you as a father, you have molded, shaped, and outlined a wonderful life for your daughter, Maya.

I've recognized that you and Kim are gifts from God, and you both are so talented.

My Granddaughter, Maya Simone (The Sugar Plum) Gross

You have brought untold joy to my life since you came into this family. I admit to having spoiled you in every way that I can think of, and still looking for more ways, but they are all love-based. I believe that it was destined for me to spoil you because you reserved the privilege for me, and only me to see you take your first and second set of steps as a baby. You are a Godsend.

My friend, Temerial "T.A." Simmons

Were it not for your literary skills and your willingness to take on my life's story, organize it, and turn it into an exciting piece of work; this book probably would not exist. You are a Godsend T.A. Thank you very much.

Eboni Pearson and her son, Johannes

You both were indispensable contributors to the success of this book. Eboni, your software engineering knowledge and computer skills took most of the glitches out of the publication of this book. Johannes, your artistic talents and software engineering skills made the marketing of this book a real success. As I always do for every team member, I will always give God thanks for each one of you in my prayers. Thanks, Eboni and Johannes!

Prologue

There I was on the porch, arranging my marbles in a circle. I was ready to shoot the greenish cat-eyed colored one, but then I look out toward the field. This was a sight I had seen often, but not this close. Something was different. Without a sound, I could hear it calling me. I knew it was beckoning me to its presence. I peered closer, still no sound, but I knew it was calling me. Dropping my marbles, I went directly to it, and there I stood, astounded, and not even knowing the lasting effects of this experience.

I ran effortlessly through the fields, and I am obliged to God never to stop experiencing this feeling of joy. This joy only comes from Him. I turn around with both arms stretched wide as the breeze blows freely. If this were captured on a motion picture film, it would be shot in slow motion, accompanied by a melodic tune that justly tells the story. I would turn clockwise, counterclockwise, and back again, a dancing tribute to everything I see in God's Universe because I can hear the melody of all His Creation at this moment. My joy is perpendicular to the heavens, and my heart is parallel to the horizon. As far as I can see, God's creations are surrounding me, and they are enveloping me 360-degrees with an inspiring warmth only He could generate.

I stop dancing. I run now. Faster and faster. Not even a comet, meteor, or lightning can move at any rate to exceed my speed. I had seen something that I believed no one but me had ever experienced. The splendor and beauty of this phenomenon alone were captivating beyond my comprehension.

I was in the middle of the field, and my skin that was once a deep cacao brown was now reflecting a projection of colorful rays upon my entire body. Never had I seen my skin retain any other color but a "hated brown," where the hatred lay on top of my brown skin from those who despised its color. Upon my existence were colors reflecting the appearance of transparency and a colorful opaque presence beaming simultaneously. How the two could exist at the same time was a matter of divine intention.

After looking at my skin closely, I stood colored with warm sensations, as I was in the prism of God's love. I was directly in the middle of our field, yet it was a small distance from the porch. I recognized all the colors that Mama and my sisters had taught me, but it was the light reflecting within that captured me. It was brighter from within than it was before I stepped into its presence.

I don't know how long I was there, but I felt showered, bathed, cleansed, even baptized, like I was in some private changing room right there in the midst of our field. There was an energy that was all around me, and it felt like it was giving me a charge to "Go ye forth."

When the light moved and was no longer on my body, I turned as fast as I could back to the house and yelled, "Mama, Mama."

"Are you okay, Junior? Nothing was chasing you out there, was it? I saw you running faster than I've ever seen you run before."

"No, Mama, I'm fine. I've been in the rainbow!!! I walked right over to it and stepped right in it. My whole body was the same color as the rainbow. It turned my brown skin seven different colors."

"When did this happen?" Mama said with love in her heart, only a mother could say.

"I was on the porch shooting my marbles when I saw the rainbow. I had to go to it...it was like it was telling me to come," I replied.

"Rainbows show us God's promise to man. I'm glad you got a chance to see it so closely," Mama said.

"I was in it!" I said enthusiastically.

I looked at her face, and I could tell she knew what I had experienced. I went on to say to her even more details, and she took a break from cooking a pan of hoecakes she was making, so she could hear every word. On her face was a radiance that wasn't there before I began telling her about my encounter. Later, I saw her go into her room and kneel down to pray.

Not fully understanding it then, but realizing it decades later, when I was standing in the rainbow, it was a representation of my beginning, as well as my continuation. There were promises in perpetuity that would forever be surrounding me, and I would take a walk towards an uncertain journey.

CHAPTER 1 - EARLY SCHOOL YEARS

Clouds were moving across the Talladega sky like they had been directed to move away from the sun's rays. Seeing both of them together made for a beautiful scene that could easily be captured on an oil painting. But it was time for the clouds to leave and the sun to take center stage, as unique hues and pastel blues were finding their way to the sky. It was another Sunday morning, and I was merely happy, looking out of the window to see all that nature offered.

I don't know who told me I was born on Sunday, but it is the day of the week that mirrors the person I am. God choosing July 11, 1937, for me to arrive in this world, tells me He knew this would be the day of the week, I would begin my theories, hypotheses, and observations.

Everyone was happier, freer, and without the worry of dotted "I's" and crossed "T's." People wore their best clothes, even if they were wearing the same black suits or the same patterned dresses. They seemed to have some sort of expectation to receive something great on Sunday. However, seeing shoes shined, revived from old worn leather mixed with dust from dirt roads, was evident that Sunday's meant something special to the people of Talladega, Alabama.

Maybe it wasn't just Talladega, perhaps it was worldwide, and I just saw this where I lived. I found it fascinating to see older people who had ailments during the week have steps peppered with what looked like tapping in their toes. They even spoke differently about their aches and pains, as I could hear "Honey chile I'm blessed," "I'm in the Master's Hand," and "God is workin' it out."

Born on a Sunday must have made things interesting for my mother, Grace Groce. She had delivered more children than the days of the weeks, ten to be exact, and I was the last one. There were seven girls and two boys ahead of me, and I was named after my father, William Louis Groce, Sr.

"Let's get ready for church," I heard, as my mother's voice was snapping me out of my thoughts by the window.

Mama was almost ready, putting an earring on, as she called to all of us: Velma, Lillie Mae, Eunice, Bertha, Claudia, Ruth, Margarite, Leon, and me. She had already cooked what little breakfast we had, and we were eating in shifts, as some of the siblings were getting ready.

"Aren't these some pretty dresses Mama made for us, Claudia?" Ruth said.

"They sure are," Claudia chimed in right after the words 'pretty dresses,' before Ruth could finish.

Claudia always had an eye for beauty and details. She was a little older than Ruth, and the two of them were buddy pals. Ruth was quite intellectual, and the two of them together made a dynamic duo. They were like most twosomes, with a lot in common, who knew how to access each other's strength for a favorable outcome.

Velma and Lillie Mae were the oldest, and they were like assistants to Mama, helping out around the house, seeing what was needed, and were very vigilant. Bertha enjoyed cooking but did not like the outside. Eunice liked fashion and beauty, where both of them were like a twosome who could have contributed to articles and magazines. Leon loved spending time with his friends and helping Papa, and Margarite could always tell when I intended to make observations. Margarite always wanted to know why I was looking at the sky. Our oldest brother, James, had passed and left a trail of sadness on the family, and he had also left a legacy of a hard worker in just his twenty years.

"Our ride is here," Mama said, yet I only remember Ruth, Claudia, Margarite, and me going. It was a tight squeeze in the car, but we all managed to fit in. As the car was leaving, I looked back and saw the garden – a place that featured some of my mother's many talents. She always had a big garden with tomatoes, pumpkins, okra, beans, and peas, but the tomatoes were my favorite. It was impossible to keep me out of the garden, as I was a prepared eater. I took salt in my hand whenever I went out there. Shortly after that, an ironic thing would happen. There was a blister on my right cheek, and that looked just like a tomato. One day it ruptured.

There was so much blood that I thought I was going to bleed to death, but the was able to cauterize it.

Before we knew it, we had arrived at church, and everyone was walking in the door. Ushers were standing at the back door greeting and seating members and also guests. Big hats, patent leather shoes, and ties for men were the normal wear on Sundays, like scenes waiting to be sketched by an up and coming painter. With an eye for detail, the love of colors, and the art of storytelling, I presumed a painter could capture the "Prelude to Worship in the Black Church." I was beginning to believe that Talladega had lots to capture from a mind's eye on canvas.

Church was about to begin. We didn't make it in time for Sunday School, but hopefully, we would make it next Sunday.

I hurried to get next to Mama, where I was seated to her right. I buried the side of my face in her arm, where I had landed in a safe lagoon, and sucked my tongue in concert. This scene was one of my first memories of Mama, massaging her arms. They were soft and warm, with what was seemingly a preset thermostat. I could always count on them being cool in the summer and warm in the winter, where the gauge was always accommodating to me. Like a child's stuffed animal, or an inseparable blanket, her arms were my refuge, and I adored them.

I didn't understand everything that was said, but seeing the people jump up like springs lifting them from the chairs, waving their hands, and shouting "Thank you, Lord," made for an ornamental atmosphere. It was more like hot grease popping up in a pan, and where you couldn't predict where the oil was going to jump up next.

It was exciting to watch, especially if the churchgoers were "regulars." You could count on them jumping around and even running when they heard something spoken as they agreed.

I guess I would have to say that the pastor must have been doing a good job because there was a time when everyone was on their feet. They must have all agreed, so much so that I saw some hats fall off, and those with both hands raised. When the music joined in, it was like a wave that carried just about everyone to their own style of praise.

Soon it was time for the benediction, and we exited the sanctuary to the annex, and Mama nodded, letting me know it was okay to have lemonade afterward. Nothing could have topped off a Sunday service like that refreshing cup of freshly squeezed lemons, sugar, and water — three ingredients that added to Sunday happiness.

****

I could see the school bus coming down the road, and the smile on my face could light up the darkest of nights. Just hearing the bus coming tickled my senses, and I was ready to go. I had seen my brothers and sisters leave in the mornings and return in the afternoon. Now, as the last child, it was finally my turn to go to school.

My galaxy overalls were fitting me just fine. Yet, I could tell that in just a few months, they might be getting shorter. I didn't know how I would feel then, but it didn't bother me now. My shirt had a little hole in it, but I didn't think it was going to show inside my overalls. I was finally going to school, and I would have worn just about anything to see what this school business was all about.

When the bus stopped, the doors opened like outstretched arms, and the brakes hissed. I step on, looked back, and waved to Mama, and I was off to Talladega County Training School.

When the bus arrived at school, I could see the outside of the white stone building with words on it. I knew it meant school with our town's name and some other words in front of it. Kids were walking in, and I curiously observed everything from teachers standing in the halls to seeing kids from different parts of the city.

We went to our classes, and that feeling of excitement intensified. I couldn't wait to walk in my classroom, sit at my desk, and learn. My sisters had taught me colors, my mother had taught me alphabets, and I knew a few words like "cat," "dog," "and," "this," and "is." Additionally, I could read a little. Overall, I felt prepared for the first day.

"Boys and girls, I'm Miss Barnett."

My eyes glistened, and I repeated her name to make sure I would remember it.

Miss Barnett wanted to know our names, and when she got to me, I said, "William."

She wrote it down and went to the next student.

"Boys and girls, you are going to practice writing your name."

She gave us a sheet of cornbread paper and a big red pencil.

"After you write your name, you are going to write your A,B,C's," she said.

If I could have whistled in class, I would have. That's just how content I was while I was writing on my paper.

"William, I told you to hold your pencil with one finger and thumb, not two fingers," Miss Barnett yelled.

Before I knew it, I received a lashing with a whip.

"Ahh, ahh, ahh," I screamed.

"Hold your pencil as I told you," Miss Barnett yelled again.

Why, why was this happening? Nobody told me school was like this. My brothers and sisters always seemed happy. I couldn't believe this was happening. I was in this helpless place, and my escaping screams were covering my thoughts, a fear mangled place in my head. Nothing could begin to cover this physical pain, and my legs burned as she whipped them viciously.

I managed to do what I did best, and that was to observe. The thought of my sister Margarite who said I was always looking at the sky, came to my mind. However, I looked around the room and saw something that was becoming painfully obvious. The only children who were in trouble were the darker children, and those children's clothes were somewhat tattered, yet clean, like mine.

As the switch was high, and the humiliation near, I experienced pain that lighter-skinned children did not, and it was clear. On this first day of school, I, as a six-year-old, knew what discrimination was about by noon. It was staring me in the face, front and center.

I had heard the whispers of some White people not treating Black people with fairness. Mama and Papa would talk about it, but not directly to us. Never had I experienced this with White people, but I didn't know Black people mistreated Black people – what a lesson on the first day of school: Compliments of my first-grade teacher.

Throughout the whole day in class, I jumped every time I heard Miss Barnett's voice. I pre-prepared for a verbal stabbing and her switch on my leg. Nevertheless, I managed to hear her say that boys needed to wear ties to school.

My first day in the first grade left me with swollen eyes, welts on my skin, and a stain on my memory.

Finally, the bell rang, and it was the sound of freedom, at least until tomorrow. With just a few hours into the school day, I had my mind on nothing but going home.

When the school bus finally came to a halt, I could hear the brakes hiss, along with a screeching sound as the bus was getting ready to stop. I felt a great sense of relief as I arrived home. A balmy feeling surrounded me as I was preparing to get off the bus. With just one foot on the ground, I felt a sense of calm. With two feet on the ground, I knew I was in my sanctuary, where I was "Junior" and "June bug," names my family called me.

As I walked to the house, I could hear the wings of butterflies fluttering to their destinations, the croaking of the bullfrogs, and a late summer breeze passing by, playing tag with surrounding trees.

While in school, I had heard nothing but icy screams, which frightened my entire being and brought terror to the forefront. I had no memory of anything that was read or taught. No letters. No numbers. No colors. I didn't get to color. I didn't get to sing. I didn't get to learn a nursery rhyme or even see Dick and Jane run. This was a horrific unscripted scene, totally different from what I discerned from my brothers and sisters as they talked about school. I had to wonder if this was going to get better. I hated the thought that maybe it wouldn't.

I saw Mama in her garden, and I got a spring in my knees that made me take off and run. It seemed like her smile came and met me, as she took off her straw hat and waved it to me like I was on a ship ready to dock for home.

"June bug, I couldn't wait until you got home from school to see how your day was."

I could see that Mama was looking at me and saw that my eyes were swollen. She knew something wasn't exactly right. I immediately pepped up. I didn't want her to think anything had happened. I was okay with letting her think I was just a little scared on the first day of school and maybe got lost and couldn't find my class.

"Tomorrow, I'm going to take my teacher some flowers." Surely Mama wouldn't think anything was wrong now. I had thought about it actually, hoping this would help to get things on track with Miss Barnett.

"I think that's a good idea!" my mother said. I let the rhythm of her response give the idea that I had a good day at school as I hugged her, and she hugged me tighter.

I hadn't seen my mother smile like this in about a year and a half. I was glad to see her so happy. It wasn't so long ago that the entire house was sad because my brother, James, had departed our lives. He was the first son, and third child of my parents.

He was just twenty, and none of us saw his death coming. He had gone to work like any other day, where he had a job making ice blocks. He took immediately after high school and had maintained an excellent two-year work history with this company. Then, one unfortunate day, as everyone had gone to lunch, he had been locked in the ice house, only to be discovered when everyone returned. He was alive when found, but had experienced hypothermia. Eventually, pneumonia set in, and he never recovered. I remember the rides on his shoulders that made everything smaller when I looked down. However, when I looked up, I could touch the ceiling, where I was taller than all the adults.

On the day of James' funeral, Mama's face was smooth and stoic, void of emotion. I didn't see the Mama I always knew. In fact, the whole family was mournful, and it was evident that sadness would be near for some time with James gone.

When I saw Mama in the garden as I got off the bus, I saw the Mama I knew before James died. I wasn't going to let Miss Barnett's madness change the Mama I knew.

"Try one of these tomatoes, June bug," my mother said. Oh, how I loved tomatoes, and this one was just as I imagined, delicious.

****

I had a plan when I went back to school. I decided I was going to give Miss Barnett something I thought all teachers could appreciate. I walked up to her desk, and I presented her flowers. I picked them along the field where we had recess at school, and I was sure she would like them. There was no way to imagine what would come next.

Along with the petals fell my hope and my spirits. She tossed the flowers on the floor, and all the petals fell off individually. I began to cry, and her roar over my head was a haunting one.

"Where's your tie? I told you all boys need to wear ties. Where's yours?" That voice of hers was over my head like something that would come from a leviathan if it could talk.

I had gone into a crying-cough mode and couldn't respond. Tears were blurring my eyesight, and I couldn't answer.

"I forgot it today," I managed to get out with a trembling voice.

"I told you to wear a tie. Now let's see if you can remember from now on," Miss Barnett said with a growl.

I was picked up and slammed into a corner. Somehow, I managed to land into the designated dunce chair with my balance. As I rubbed my eyes, snot was running out of my nose, and she was placing something over my head.

This rough, black, scratchy material was being placed over me with a musty scent like it had been packed in a suitcase of a leaky house. To my surprise, it was a big black dress, no doubt once upon a time hers, and I had to wear that dress all day.

I don't know what was worse, wearing that dress or hearing the mocking sounds of my classmates. These taunting echoes made tears gush from my eyes. I held my hands over my ears to keep out most of these taunts, but a few still managed to come into my ears. I swung my legs back and forth as if to distract me from this neurotic abyss. As if this wasn't enough, she placed a woman's hat on my head to complete this look.

The more the tears came, the weaker I was getting. It was lunchtime, and I had no dime for lunch.

"Put your arms up, William," she hollered."

CHAPTER 2 – THE BEATINGS TAKE THEIR TOLL

I was so hungry by the time I reached home, I went straight to Mama's garden and ate three tomatoes. Mama was probably in the house, but I had to compose myself after another terrifying day of school. I wiped my hands on my overalls, and just as I looked up, I saw four men entering a car. I recognized the car and knew Papa from a distance by his hat. All four doors closed at once, almost ceremoniously, as the car pulled off, going to some sudden destination. I could see the dust flying up as if to salute the event I knew all too well. I could see the car getting smaller and smaller. There was Papa, and my lunch dimes headed down the road to buy the "good times."

****

I returned to school each day, continuing to take in the beauty of Talladega County Training School. Since there was no beauty in my classroom, I could at least appreciate the architecture of the school. It was an all-white brick building with a stone arch at the main gate, where the name was proudly displayed. The school was an L-shaped building all on one level, where students filed in ready to learn from first grade through twelfth grade.

The first part was brick, and a newer part had aluminum siding. My classes were in the newer part of the whole school, and this was very impressive to me.

I could not consciously hold this beautiful scene in my head as Miss Barnett's whip and her leviathan roar came toward me. Each time I tried to behold the beauty of the school, it escaped from me as I screamed with fear. However, I was determined to resume the feelings I had in the beginning about school despite her, but my happiness was short-lived. There was more and more of this leviathan's roar. It wasn't the tie this time, but she was savvy enough with her hatred to find something to whip me about and place me into a kind of submission that she felt was ideally suited for me.

I later learned Miss Barnett was raised on a plantation, where she had dodged harsh treatment. Her light skin had afforded her opportunities, where her other dark-skinned contemporaries were not able to access. She learned that her light skin was a badge of honor that came with a crown she wore upon her head. A finger was probably wagged in her face for emphasis to let her know she was above others, accompanied by "You are not like others ... and don't you ever forget it."

Now, with the power invested in her as a teacher, she was the one invoking these discriminatory practices. She was pointing to the faces of dark-skinned children, not letting them forget where they belonged.

It was time for recess, and for me, it was a retreat from Miss Barnett's wrath and a time to play. I found a stick and drew pictures on the ground. The ground still had a nice dew from the morning that made the soil moist and impressionable. I drew a smiley face on the ground, carefully making the circle and not some misshaped oval. At the first try, the circle was what I would consider perfect, and I was rather pleased with my drawings. I decided to make a family, drawing my own, starting with Mama and Papa. Some of the kids came to look, as some were pointing with admiration. Some decided to join in, drawing ground murals of their own.

The bell rang for us to go back inside, and I was pleased with my mural efforts. I took my seat, refreshed, and before I could settle . . .

"William, come here! Come here now!"

Before I could get out a "yes ma'am," Miss Barnett had grabbed me.

"I heard you were cussing outside," she said.

"No ma'am, I didn't say any cuss words." I could feel the tears coming.

"The children were standing right beside you and said you were cussing," she insisted. This was a story she said Ruthie Bell told her. Ruthie Bell was light-skinned with long hair. Her looks gave credence to the story.

Miss Barnett sent two students to get switches. I guess one student wasn't good enough. Maybe she wanted to have a collection of switches to select from, making sure she had a premium one just for me.

It was more of the same, just more intense. I believe this whipping was fiercer and more forceful than the other ones combined. The welts on my legs were raised and even more pronounced than before. the burning didn't subside for the rest of the day.

Yellow didn't look like yellow anymore, and "3's" didn't look like "3's." The alphabet seemed to jumble and even turn backward. I was in a lake of fear with nobody to rescue me. Every day I was afraid to learn, feeling every response was wrong. No matter what I would do, I was drowning in deeper waters, from the tears I cried myself, and from the "waters" Miss Barnett held me under.

This experience with Miss Barnett continued for weeks. The best I could do was look forward to Fridays, thankful it would be a two-day break from her. Although Fridays came once a week, it seemed like they came once a year.

The routine of going to school was pretty much the same. I knew what to expect, but it didn't make it better. Each day it was the bus ride to school, fear during the day, and the bus ride back home and to Mama's garden. I stood in the garden sometimes just to see the view all around. My sisters and brothers would get off the bus, go to the house, and start their chores. I would begin mine soon, but being in the garden, observing nature, was calming for me.

"Junior, Junior."

I saw my sister, Ruth, running with a look of panic on her face.

Her voice snapped me out of my gaze. When I looked back toward my father, the car that always carried him to his destination of "good times" was completely gone.

"Junior, something happened to the cow."

"Uh-huh, the cow, what happened?" I asked, not fully understanding.

"Go get Papa," Ruth said, panting.

"He just left."

"What do you mean he just left?"

I pointed in the direction the car went.

"He told me to move the cow to the other field, but the cow fell. I don't know what happened," she said in a panting voice.

I hadn't put my books in the house, so I left them outside on a tree stump and followed Ruth.

We ran through to the field over plowed soil, and sometimes unleveled soil that seemed to hinder our stride, but we kept going as fast as we could. When we arrived, it was evident that Ruth was right. Something was wrong with the cow. The chain was still attached when the cow fell into the ditch. The odd thing was that the cow's head was turned back further than I had ever seen before. The cow was panting, and we didn't know how many breaths the cow had left.

"Junior, I think the cow is dying!" Ruth said with a shrill.

"Maybe she's not," I said with hope.

I wondered what we should do next. Ruth had a bewildered look on her face that held a sense of sadness and anxiousness. I knew already that it wasn't Mama that she was worried about. She was concerned about Papa's reaction.

We walked back, and I picked up my books and took them into the house. Ruth looked nervous but attempted her homework while waiting for her sentencing. Even amid all the chaos, my mind traveled back to Talladega County Training School. I thought I would slip away for just a moment and lay my ties out for next week. I wanted to make sure I would not be in the line of Miss Barnett's leviathan roar.

****

The screen door slammed with the usual thud, and everybody was in bed. I was wide awake thinking about the lashes and roars from Miss Barnett. At least I didn't have to see her for two days, but she was still on my mind. Papa was just coming in, and something in Papa's footsteps seemed different. He had a pattern in his step like Step, step, step, stop, and turn. Repeat. Step, step, stop, and turn – pacing that went on for ten minutes. The house was so quiet around him; it seemed like a stage demanding a monologue, dialogue, or even a soliloquy. I wondered if he knew about the cow. Maybe he didn't notice that the cow wasn't where she usually stayed. But the walking became a quicker back and forth pace. The more I heard his pacing; I was almost sure he knew. What came next I did not expect. I heard a crash. I thought Mama was going to run out, thinking someone was breaking in, but she didn't get up.

I didn't know if the crash was deliberate or by accident, but I recognized the sound. It was a tin can where we kept odd objects, like keys and bolts. The pacing stopped, and Papa picked up the items. His pacing moved toward the living room, where there was more open space. This time he paced slower, as if not to bump into anything. Then, the pacing stopped. Just footsteps took place towards his destination, and the walking turned to whispers. I heard Ruth's voice, and I could hear her say words like "fell" and "accident," but I couldn't hear every word. Then I heard Papa say, "tomorrow," and "wood," but the rest of the conversation was muffled. Maybe the cow wasn't dead after all? I thought for a moment, and then Papa's footsteps went to his and Mama's bedroom.

****

Burning cow flesh hung in the air mixed with the scent of honeysuckles rising toward the Talladega sky. The mixture of wood and cow flesh made for a bad aroma. As the embers rose, the blackening cow's flesh etched indelible markings upon my memory that would last for decades. The cow's demise had been one that was purely accidental. Perhaps my sister, Ruth, was not familiar with the "lay of the land," or maybe the ditch where the cow fell, was hidden or simply unseen by her. Papa asked her to move the cow to another place to graze. In actuality, I always thought he should have done it, but he had places to go with his buddies and had drinks to consume. The task to handle an animal that size with a chain – then to tie it down – could have posed a danger for a fourteen-year-old girl.

Consequently, she had tied the cow too close to the ditch. As the cow grazed into the coveted area of honeysuckles, it fell, broke its neck, and broke the patience of my father.

When Papa discovered something had happened to the cow, Ruth was summoned by him to burn the cow's body the next day. If that wasn't enough, she had to cut all the wood needed to pull off this cremation.

Just when I thought Saturday would be a day of fun, I was met with this "disenchanting memorial."

I was too small to help Ruth cut the wood, yet my six years had given me enough compassion for my sister Ruth, and enough comprehension to see that my father's decisions were often made without logic. Why didn't he just let the buzzards eat the cow? Why was it so necessary that Ruth cut all the wood, in addition to burning the cow? Why couldn't we at least help Ruth cut the wood?

I toted wood for Ruth, as she continued to cut the wood to keep the fire going. Papa told her to put the wood on top of the cow. For some reason, the cow didn't burn well from the top down

I suppose it wasn't enough to wish for a great weekend to be without Miss Maude Barnett. Now, I had to pray that my father wouldn't add madness to the weekends.

****

Sunday morning came bringing beaming rays, spreading joy over the horizon of our farm. After such a saddening Saturday occurrence, it was a truly "Beauty for Ashes" beginning. I later learned that this farm was not really our farm but belonged to Mr. Thornton, and we would later always refer to it as the Thornton Place.

It was my "Coney Island," a place I could visit every day that allowed me to roam and explore nature and all it had to offer.

From the time I was three-to-six-years-old, my family lived and worked on this farm. It was 15 miles from Talladega County Training School, ten miles from town, and three miles from our church, Macedonia Baptist.

This farm gave me the first exposure to my childhood memories that I would forever remember. We had a barn that was ready to be filled with my endless imagination and theories. Inside was a hayloft where anyone could climb and pretend to be pirates and cowboys. However, for practical purposes, my family kept corn and other food crops in it.

One of the funniest things I can remember about the barn happened when my father planted so many rutabagas that he plowed them up and put them in the corn crib. We had so many that they started to sprout. After a little while, the greens could be picked from them, and they were just as good as the ones that came out of the field. By springtime, we picked a "mess of them," a phrase people say in the south, meaning a lot of them. This was convenient and good for us, for we could have them as a side dish or even the main dish.

As a child, I thought the "Inside Rutabaga Crop" was something that was done by my father's direct intention. Later, I discovered it was not his intention, but by accident. He was far too involved with his buddies care about the crops and the welfare of our lives.

My father was given the golden opportunity to buy all 500 acres of this farm where we lived. With his GI Bill, the farm could have been ours; but it appeared he was making his decisions from the inside of a "bottle." After seeing this and other missed opportunities he let pass by, I chose not to let any wise prospects go by in my life.

During our time at the Thornton Place, I saw science in everything. Since I wasn't observing and learning anything at school, I noticed how trees grew, the look of different branches, and the differences in the leaves. I found plants even more interesting, as they had leaves – some with buds that looked to me like they were signaling "beware." I noticed that two plants could look similar, but there would be a distinct feature that would reveal the "poisonous" or "non-poisonous" nature of the plant. I found this to be true as I heard the elders speak of what was poisonous, as it looked very different.

****

Monday came faster than a returning boomerang. I knew it was coming, but it came surprisingly faster than I imagined. I could hear the familiar sounds of the school buses passing, and Mama's salutations: "Have a good day, be good, and listen."

Yet, here, with this Monday morning, I was sandwiched between "What happened," and "Hope it won't happen again" thoughts, as a feeling of anxiousness washed over me.

I made sure I didn't dare forget my tie. I placed it in my bookbag Friday night just to make sure I had it. While I took it out, I retained the best outlook a six-year-old could take to school. I had observed birds and noticed there was something they did that was interesting. When looking for worms, they would peck in the ground, and keep nibbling the dirt, and keep going. Even though something might frighten or scare them away for a moment, they would return to the same spot and keep pecking until they got the worm.

****

A few weeks had passed, and the only thing different about school was the physical landscaping and the changing background. This was not a manmade effort, but a change of the season. Fall had marched upon the scene, arriving on cue, and trees were turning an array of colors – yellow, orange, burgundy, and brown. Leaves were falling, and I collected some, looking at the veins and lines in them, often comparing them to the lines in my hands. I wondered if there was a similarity between life in plants and life in humans. We had veins, they had veins, and We had both had blood running through our veins. I wondered what the leaves had running through their veins.

****

"William, Junior isn't walking too well," I heard Mama say to Papa. "He has some swelling. When he came home today from school, he mentioned he was hurting."

"What do you think is wrong with him?" Papa asked.

"I think he has a hernia that needs to be looked at by a ."

"I believe he will be alright; the swelling will go down. Many boys have that type of hernia, and it will leave," Papa said.

"I don't think this is going to go away immediately."

"Just put some salve on it. He's going to grow out of it," Papa replied, believing there was nothing serious.

To choose between the pain of Ms. Barnett and the internal physical pain I was experiencing was like asking me to swap the devil for the witch when both could cast down an evil spell. Mama tied me on the bed on some slats where I was tilted upside down to relieve the misery. I believe since I was sick, Mama took this time to attend to me and pre-treat the other siblings. She decided to give not only me but my sisters and brother some Polk salad, which was given to eliminate any worms from our stomach. My mother was savvy at knowing precisely the right time to pick these green leaves where they would be at their medicinal best.

I didn't go to school the next day, and even though my fate was set on "difficulty," I still didn't want to miss it. I was always willing to learn even if all the alphabets were turning backward, and all the vibrant colors were turning to pastels. I still wanted to be in an environment of learning.

As the days went by, I was still in pain, sore, and tender to the touch. Turning over and moving a certain way could cause excruciating pain. I could hear children outside playing, and I was sad to be in a place where I couldn't run or explore. I was used to seeing planes going by in the sky, watching the vapor trails come and go.

At once, the children's voices stopped. The running and laughter came to a halt. I couldn't determine what had happened, and I couldn't make any quick movements. Footsteps came in, like children in a single file line. I saw Papa pass by the room with his head looking toward the floor. Mama was right behind him. All the children were unusually quiet, unlike the normal rambunctious teenagers. Instead, there was a doleful cloud that hung above everyone.

We all found out that Papa's mother had been killed in a car accident. She was Grandma Fanny … Fanny Curry. She was a woman of Native American descent, with a long braid that I always noticed, and wondered if she wore it out of convenience or whether it was the style she loved. She would have to fight it back daily as it would have its own rhythm of movement. When she was at the pump, getting water for cooking, bathing, or watering animals, or even when she worked in the fields, there it was, swinging back countless times. Her hair seemed to want to come back forward to be near her heart, easing around her back, and sliding around her shoulder, where it would make it back toward the front.

She was married to Robert Groce, and she had a son when they met. He fathered this son like his own biological son, and not only did he give him a fatherly hand, but he gave him his last name "Groce" that would be present through the lineage, even though not by blood. This son she had was my father, William Louis. Together they had more children, where all the children were seamlessly blended together.

As a grandmother, her house had smelled of apple pies, cornbread, and stewed chicken. There would also be children running around and looking for adventures only a grandmother could give, and they would be given some privileges that grandchildren could get away with, where they couldn't with their own parents. She would wipe her hands on her apron and laugh with high pitch laughter that made us happy with cheer.

We later found out she was riding to town with one of her son's friends, and the car turned over. Somehow, upon impact, her neck was broken. I didn't know how my father was taking this. He didn't come out for the rest of the night, and I saw Mama take food to him. All of the children were quiet until the next morning, and I could hear the wind blowing into the cracks of the house that seemed to howl lonesome tune.

The next day I saw Papa. I didn't know what to say. The pain from my hernia had lessened, and I was able to move around. None of us went to school the next day, as we were pulling things together, seeing how we could help at Mama's orchestration.

I thought I would take Papa some food in place of my mother when it was time for his next meal. When I did, I saw his eyes, and I knew tear-fallen eyes all too well. I thought it best not to say anything but hug him, and when I did, he responded from there.

"I see you are out of bed," He said.

"Yes, sir. I'm still sore," I responded, but not wanting the emphasis to be on me.

"What's going to happen now?" I asked. I realized that I let the question come out of my mouth too quickly. I was hoping this was not too insensitive or too early to ask my father.

"We're going up there."

I knew where "up there" was. This was where his mother and step-father lived, and everything else would naturally unfold.

****

Things were getting back to normal. We were recovering from Grandma Fanny's death, Mama was back to gardening, cooking, and sewing, and Papa was with his buddies again, drinking and seeing the sights of Talladega.

I was glad it was Saturday, but something seemed strange. Mama was not up. Usually, she was up stirring around and fixing some portion of the breakfast, even if the girls, Eunice, Claudia, Ruth, Bertha, or Margarite, were told to fix something.

Something was wrong, and I knew it. This was as wrong as if the sky was green, and the grass was blue when Mama wasn't up. I could see my sisters had the same concern on their faces.

"Mama isn't up," I heard someone say. Everybody was in a blurry conference about Mama, when finally, Claudia just went to her room.

"Mama," Claudia called for her.

"Mama!" she said again.

She could faintly hear Mama answer and knew something was wrong. Claudia opened the door and found Mama in a pool of blood.

All I could hear were whispers from that point. Claudia directed the girls to different duties. She didn't ask Leon or me to do anything, and I wondered why. She did, however, tell us to go find Papa.

We left in haste, and Papa was where he always was, in the car with his friends. I told him something was wrong with Mama, and the girls were trying to help her. He turned and ran toward the house, while Leon and I told his friends what had happened. Words of "You don't say" returned to us, but not with one ounce of concern.

When Leon and I got back to the house, I saw Mama's color go from a mahogany brown to a pale, wilted grey. She had lost a lot of blood.

Mama was rushed to the hospital, and we waited. A few days went by, and we were under the directions of Claudia.

****

It was another day in the doldrums of first grade, and like usual, I played by myself at recess. Just showing up at school was in total opposition to Maude Barnett's wishes. Nevertheless, she was prepared to give me a punishment that she probably justified in her mind as discipline.

****

After school, when I got home, something was different. I couldn't explain it.

I had to admit Claudia had the house running just like Mama, as she enforced that everyone needed to pitch in and help.

But something had changed or entered the house. I looked around the kitchen and saw everything was the same. Something had moved within the invisibility of our home. It took over and gave a soothing demeanor to the atmosphere that was beyond my comprehension or Claudia's leadership.

And then I heard it. It was Mama. She was clearing her throat with that "ump um," which starts the beginning of a speech, address, or song. I ran to her room like I was after one of her hoecakes, as I once raced and slid under the bureau to get one.

"Hey, Junior," she said when she saw me. Her voice was sounding like a song composed and arranged for just those two words. Those two words were like being hugged tightly and never being turned loose. This moment melted all the dregs of dreadfulness away.

"Mama, how was your operation?" I asked, wondering if she could feel the knife cut into her.

"Oh, I didn't feel a thing," Mama said. She knew where my mind was going, and I could tell she was a little sore and was not ready to go out to do any fieldwork yet. She made a face when she sat up or turned to move and didn't move quickly.

"Well, Claudia did everything the way you would have wanted it," I spouted out like a fountain, thinking Mama would be relieved and appreciate the effort.

"I thought she would," she responded, and I could see she was glad everything was as close to normal as it could possibly be for her family.

****

All the joy that Mama re-established in the household was followed with news that caused us all to spiral into "wonder why?" Not too many weeks later, dishes were being packed, clothes were being moved, all the animals were rounded up, and I wondered what was going on? The look on Mama's face was a stoic one, not easy to crack or discern, but just one that was there. I kept trying to make my own predictions, but I didn't know what was happening.

All the rooms were empty, and all of our things were packed. We were headed to what was called 'The Walter Easley Place.' It turns out that Papa didn't pay the rent, and that sealed our fate to remain at this property, 'The Thornton Place.'

I had to say goodbye to the big barn, the corn crib, Mama's garden with all the tomatoes, and move to this abyss of the unknown.

In the six years I had lived, I had lived a lifetime. I had seen what few had seen in an entire lifespan, and this is how observing became second nature to me.

When I got to the Easley Place, it was another adventure waiting to happen. There was a great "environmental introduction" waiting for me. I had learned Environmental Lessons 100 from the Thornton Place; I was learning Environmental Lessons 300 at the Easley Place. On display was a range of bullfrogs, butterflies, and fish, to crawfish, bridges, beetles, and more. Yet there was one thing that lingered in the midst. The course of this enjoyment came with the deeds of Maude Barnett.

Like any other school day, I was on Maude Barnett's hit list. Nevertheless, my bodily functions had to go on as usual, and they could not be subjected to the actions of Miss Barnett. I can't say I had gotten used to her wrath, but I can say that I knew what to expect. Little did I know that my privileges to go to the bathroom would be revoked.

"Miss Barnett, may I go to the bathroom," I asked with all the politeness I had been taught.

She ignored me at first, or maybe she didn't hear me. I proceeded to ask again in the same manner of politeness. Nothing. Stark silence. Children talking. Chalk sounds on the board. Crayon-coloring and pencil-writing continued, but no answer from Miss Barnett.

"Miss Barnett, may I please use the bathroom!" I asked for the third time, but with more intensity, and still with the same politeness.

"No, William, you may not go to the bathroom," Miss Barnett said with all the rage that she had within her.

I sat hopeless and helpless, and a dizzying feeling came upon me. I turned and twisted in my chair, not knowing what to do. Contemplating running out and staying in class was at my forethoughts. But I couldn't run out. I couldn't run the risk of more consequences piling upon me. In an instance, there would be a heaping darkness upon me, and I couldn't imagine bearing more on me. I was becoming even more frightened of her, and I was in a pit where I slowly descended, and I could do nothing about it.

And then it happened. I couldn't hold it or control it anymore. It wasn't my choice, and I couldn't even help myself in the state that I was in. There was no way I could get on the bus. The humiliation from the children on the bus would be greater than what I had already experienced. I knew it was going to be a long walk home, but I had to take it. I held a book awkwardly behind me the entire way home, and it was just me and my embarrassment taking this lonely stroll home.

My life was going to be different the next day. Maude Barnett was going to be directly in front of William L. Groce, Sr. and Grace Groce. Miss Barnett was going to be in a conference room, subjected to some tough questions by my parents.

She was going to be required to give an account of what had happened and possibly every child was going to be questioned separately, if need be. Things were going to change. My days of her harassing, abusing, and neglecting me were going to be over. While walking home, these thoughts gave me hope that she was going to have to apologize to me. When my parents finished with her, she was going to be a new teacher to me, and my days as her whipping post were going to be over.

The next day came, and I was waiting for Mama and Papa to get ready to head to school. It seemed like everything was in slow motion. Papa walked outside, so I figured he must have been waiting to see if everything was in order outside on the farm before he left. I looked outside, and he was in the distance with his regular crew, his buddies, with more of the family dimes and my hopes that had been dashed for having better days with Miss Barnett.

I was sure my parents would appear at school, but no one showed up. I faced the prison of Maude Barnett, the warden, who injected fear into my being, making learning an impossibility. Just surviving the days of scolding, beatings, and intense hunger was all I could think about within a typical school day.

****

I could always count on the long arm of nature to reach out with loving attentiveness to soothe me. When I was down, it elevated me, and even when things were great, it would lift me higher. The environment around me was a wonderful place that I began to believe God had designed just for me.

Mama allowed me free range to roam and see the beauty of the environment and experience the lessons that nature taught.

"You need to wear a hat," Mama said.

I ran harder, as I was moving further from her words.

"You'll get sunstroke out there!" she said, somewhat worried and yet somewhat content, a fence she straddled with "oh well," as I was long in the distance.

Her words were faint now. I was further into the field, roaming farther out with no mind to wear a hat. Figuring it would interfere somehow, I was headed to what seemed like endless fields and peaceful meadows. I could see trees and plants, hear the bullfrogs croaking, and I would examine the wings of butterflies fluttering around.

What I wasn't learning – and couldn't learn – due to fear at school, nature was taking me by the hand to observe. Nature was shaping me into a scientist, and I didn't even know it at the time. My eyes were becoming microscopes, seeing simply intriguing things. This place was in a valley, with mountain-like features, where the surrounding backdrop sat up high. Hummingbirds buzzed by; it felt as if they were intentionally summoning my attention. These birds were building their nests in elm trees that were the size of quarters, and this totally mystified me. The nest was a tapestry of woven majestic patterns, so intricate and delicate that it seemed unreal that hummingbirds could form such a thing.

I couldn't help but compare the beauty of nature and the lack of it in our family's lives at the time. To see the hummingbirds prepare for their family showed me the lack of preparation in ours. Why was my father not caring about our welfare? Why was he always taking off going with his buddies to drink? Why was he not going to school to see why I was beaten every day like a wounded circus animal?

It was even harder to believe that he was once in the military, where he had at least seen what structure was and what it was like to partake in it.

Maybe it was just that, he hated partaking in it.

He went AWOL every weekend, traveling back to Talladega to see Mama when he was stationed in Georgia at Fort Stewart. Was it there that he was unraveling from a regimented course he couldn't successfully complete? Was caring for a family too regimented for him, and he was going AWOL on us as well? Had he decided that he could no longer live a life that was regimented with at least enough guts, where he could take care of a family?

I sometimes misunderstood my mother during these times and wondered why she withstood these conditions. Many a time we didn't have food, and my father didn't want additional help. His response was, "I don't want nobody giving me nothing." This was food from the USDA, food that consisted of cheese, powdered eggs, beef stew, peanut butter, and powdered milk. What I didn't understand was how we were basically starving, but my father didn't think we needed it or wanted us to have it, due to his pride.

Some seasons were really tough when Mama's garden was depleted. Food was scarce. Mama didn't sign off on his irresponsibility, but she somehow tolerated his irrationality. Maybe it was just her kind nature that she carried from her childhood to adulthood. Her father, Jim Houston, had carried a trait of irrationality, which I had often seen. He was belligerent, impatient, stingy, and wanted nothing great for us as his grandchildren. His comments about my sisters' future were less than "grandfatherly," and he didn't want us to have a single watermelon in his garden. However, his son, my Uncle Claude, would give us access to many watermelons and would later encourage us with exciting words, "Now go and bust your stomachs open."

I suppose Mama channeled her energies toward homemaking in the way that put her far ahead of her time. Everything she created could have been chronicled in a weekly magazine. She was a woman way ahead of her time with cooking, canning, baking, and mattress making.

****

Carrying on with my everyday life, I once sat on an earthen bridge over a brook, noticing some sunfish in a clear pool of water. They were swimming back and forth in a circular motion and finding food. Periodically, they were going into the dark recesses of the bank that floodwaters had created during heavy rains. I had an idea.

I headed back to the barn and fetched a bucket. It was evident I would need a rope to suspend the bucket downward.

I believed if the bucket was slanted to the side, there would be a better chance for the fish to swim inside because the bucket lying on its side would simulate the dark recesses of the earthen bank. Bingo! It worked. I was able to lure two large sunfish into the bucket, and I couldn't wait to show Mama. I ran to show her, with the bucket jingling and wind blowing through my galaxy overalls.

"Mama, Mama, look what I caught?" I said in between breaths.

Mama looked over in the bucket with surprise. "How did you catch them?" she asked. I explained my method. She was impressed.

"If you could come up with the idea to catch those fish, I will clean and cook them for you," she said with such tender love.

****

Maude Barnett had a gleam in her eye that twinkled more than any star I had seen in my six years. I guess the town had been talking, and she rendered her due diligence of listening. I felt she was glad of our misfortunes. We were moving again, not knowing why we were leaving presented another mystery for me to ponder. I continued to ask myself what happened, and if this was my father's choice or by some other force. Did his absence from us with his friends have anything to do with our leaving? Either way, my ecological and environmental adventures at the Easley Place were over, but from scene to scene, I would keep all the memories. At least it was time for school to end for the year, and I was looking forward to that.

We were heading to Grandpa Robert's and Grandma Fannie's place, but Grandma Fannie was no longer with us, and even though time had passed, we were still trying to balance and keep our feet on the ground. In her absence, there was at least one whipping that I didn't have to worry about getting. Grandma Fannie had a strange regiment in her household. When my brother James was living, if you failed to speak to him before going to other rooms in the house, you got a whipping. I would not have passed by brother James intentionally, but in the excitement of going in the house to see cousins to play with and have adventures, it was easy to be side-tracked. Yet, with Grandma Fanny, you didn't forget but one time.

Our time at Grandpa Robert's place moved quickly to the end of summer. There were more farming and gathering, which was a lot of the same that we had already experienced.

****

Going back to school meant back to the first grade, and Maude Barnett made sure of that. A year with Maude Barnett was all any human could take. I remember seeing my report card, and it said I would be held back. A sadness fell upon me, knowing the students in my class would go on, and I would not. Yes, I didn't learn the fundamentals that year. True, there was a lot I missed, but I never seemed to miss the switch of Maude Barnett and her desire to cut my skin – along with a cut in spirit. I was not where other kids were, or becoming what other kids were becoming – a well-rounded student.

Reluctantly, I entered the first day of school. What kind of start could this day have? I remembered my first day last year like it was yesterday, smiling with wonder and excited with hope. Today I am without both, for I am returning to the first grade again. I was seven now, a year older than the rest of the class, but maybe I'll get a chance to show what I know this year. Before I could finish the thought, I couldn't believe who I saw in my classroom. This had to be a big mistake. I knew I was retained, and I had the whole summer to come to terms with it, but I know this cannot be happening. How can I be back with Miss Barnett again? Who played this cruel joke on me? This couldn't be right, and if it is, how was this going to help me?

She towered over me in her disguise as a teacher, but she really was an obscured bully. That's exactly what she was. Not the overt type who knocks books out of kids' hands, or says, "Give me your lunch money?" but the kind that lurks in classrooms. She was the kind of bully that robs children of their dreams when nobody is looking. She demeaned children with grades that don't fit their effort. They find sneaky ways to say the projects weren't quite what they were looking for in the finished product while speaking hurtful words to kids. Yes, Maude Barnett was a bully in the disguise of an educator, and this was the kind of bullying teacher that was hurting a population of students, harming their spirits for years to come.

I had six months of the same treatment from Maude Barnett. Nothing was different. I could set a clock by her actions, as well as predict her diction and inflections in words when she came to me. I can still see the style of dresses she wore, and how it swayed with fury when she lashed the whip she asked my classmates to fetch for me. I'm sure if the trees could have boycotted growing whips, they would have. So many whips had come off on my behalf alone.

Nevertheless, God had given trees their own assignment, despite all that was happening to me. God knew all too well about trees. His son had been crucified on a cross made from a tree. That tree knew about sacrifice and "The One" that was sacrificed. I concluded the trees at school had been assigned, for a season, to me.

It was recess, and I blew smoke out of my mouth like smoke from a cigarette. The scene always fascinated me like most children. I could blow it straight out or make O's that were shaped like the capital letters. I was a second-year first-grader, and I had already learned how to turn my eyelids back, so I was having fun with meteorological fascinations that could only be experienced at specific temperatures. Cold weather wasn't always fun, but when you could stand out and blow what looked like smoke, it was as fun as shooting marbles. I must have been having too much fun and looked to be taking a retreat from Miss Barnett's brutality. She couldn't stand that I hadn't succumbed to her "A.M." featured whippings and wanted me to wallow in the pity of pain that she caused me for one and a half years.

Then, suddenly, like a motion picture film without the popcorn, I was featured as her object in her twisted desire to cause me pain beyond exception. She grabbed me and bent my hand back, which seemed like 90 degrees. Her dress moved up and down on cue, back and forth. It was also moving at the hem, while the meat on her body violently shook. Her face grimaced into a monstrous look, with a mission to make me submit. She was determined to keep me inside whatever the maddening fortress she was creating around me.

Her instrument of choice today was a ruler, and she held my four fingers hostage, along with my fear. Something about this act was more intense than I had ever experienced. When she came down on my hand, it burned, and I howled uncontrollably, and she continued hitting my hand without any mercy. My eyes filled with water that dripped to my hand as if it were trying to soothe the burning and stinging, but it could not. I went into a full-blown scream like I was calling someone from one end of the field to the other. The more I responded to her pain; the more something ignited her anger to continue. I twisted my hand, trying to get away from her grip, and it was tightening like the jaws of some wild animal hunting its prey.

She must have hit my hand to the tune of her vile anger to what seemed like fifty times. By the time I could wipe away the tears, my eyes were still blurry. I thought I saw blue hues in front of my hands. There was something wrong with my vision. So much water had passed my eyes that I assumed they must have been swollen as they usually were on these occasions. I couldn't see much, but when I looked at my hand, I saw blue hues inside. Miss Barnett had hit my hand so hard; it caused the inside of my hand to change to the color blue.

I got to the bus, and I couldn't touch anything with my right hand. It felt like someone had taken a meat tenderizer to it and never planned for me to use it again. I showed it to Claudia and Ruth, and I saw a look in their eyes that I had never seen before.

Their eyes were fueled with the same kind of anger that Maude Barnett had, and their anger had an address. Their anger had a direction. Their anger had an appointment.

CHAPTER 3 – CLAUDIA AND RUTH TO MY RESCUE

"Miss Barnett?" Claudia and Ruth were not speaking or making a good morning statement.

Claudia and Ruth called her name again, "Miss Barnett!!!" This time no question, it was a delivery, and there was something they wanted to present.

The children in our class stopped what they were doing. Miss Barnett told the class to get back to their work.

I had heard Claudia and Ruth whisper through the night, and I knew something was going to happen, but I didn't know what it was.

"Girls, it's been a long time since I have seen you," Miss Barnett said like she was some socialite welcoming guests to sit in a gazebo, surrounded by floral fragrances and punch in a goblet.

"It's great to see your sisters, William."

I couldn't believe what I was hearing. This was an about-face from the woman that bent my hand back to Creation.

Ruth and Claudia moved closer to her, and little did I know what was coming next.

"Miss Barnett?" Claudia and Ruth were not speaking or making a good morning statement. They were raising a question of "why" without saying the whole interrogative statement. Anybody who heard their feet coming to the classroom would have known they wanted answers. Their feet made sounds like soldiers marching together in sync. The weight of their intentions had made the sound vibrate through the halls of Talladega County Training School. It didn't sound like only two people walking, but a platoon marching under the command of a drill sergeant.

Miss Barnett had brought into her state of reasoning with her. It was evident she had mistreated kids so long without being addressed that she could do one thing and say another. She did believe she could be one thing to me, and this pedagogical duchess to my sisters.

This was the first time in my life I had seen a human have chameleon abilities. Less than twenty-four hours ago, she was a leviathan with a roar that could shatter every window in the Talladega County Training School. She raised her hand to mine with a ruler, as if her goal was to disconnect my fingers from my hand; marring the memories of my childhood forever.

I almost thought my own naked eyes were deceiving me. Was this real? Maude Barnett was appearing to be this inviting teacher to my sisters, glad to see them as former students, and then proceeding to tell them how I was progressing in her class.

A loud sound interrupted my thoughts. I saw a row of desks turned over like soldiers falling from enemy fire.

"You don't think we came to visit you, do you?" Ruth said with an authoritative voice. "Do you see this row of desks turned over? This is what you have done to our brother. You have turned his first years of school upside down."

"I...I...I...I...," Miss Barnett tried to get out.

"We ought to do to you what we did to George Floyd Kidd. He thought he was going to pick on Junior, but we stopped that," Claudia spit out the words without thinking.

This was one of the reasons I didn't talk about what Miss Barnett did to me to Ruth and Claudia because I knew they didn't have any respect for people when it came to revenge. Miss Maude Barnett would get that same version of a whipping they gave George on the playground. My sisters were brought up to be respectful, but they didn't mind taking the exit ramp off from that teaching. They had no problem avenging wrongdoing, wishing the opposition well, and making an appointment with God to ask for forgiveness at a later date.

"I wouldn't hurt William," Miss Barnett said with a face straight enough to cut glass.

"You need to reword that sentence," Ruth said, "to I will not hurt William again."

"Young ladies, you are both wrong and also out of line," Miss Barnett said, polishing her words like the silver she probably helped to shine on the plantation she came from. It was hard to believe she would be educated to teach, to disturb, and to infect the dark-skinned and impoverished children she didn't like with her poisonous practices.

"Out of line, did you say? Did you see what you did to Junior's hand? Claudia said, and Ruth chimed in at a slower pace. "Did you see his hand? Did you see what you did to his hand?"

Claudia reached for my hand and held it so Miss Barnett could see it. She looked and looked away, obviously not comfortable doing either. It was clear she was guilty, even if no one had ever seen her do it. Her facial expression had a sheepish look that didn't match her normal look. She tried to be composed, but she couldn't hold onto that look either.

"Yeah, Miss Barnett, it has passed by red, it turned blue because you beat Junior's hand unmercifully. He can't do anything with this hand. Sleeping on his hand last night was not comfortable one bit for him," Claudia said.

Ruth positioned herself to let Miss Barnett know her position on this matter. With one hand on one hip and a finger-pointing from the other, she proceeded with her address.

"We know what's going to happen. As soon as Junior comes in here, and he can't make an alphabet, a number, or something, which you know he won't be able to do, you'll be beating him. There will be another beating, and another beating, and another. What do you have against Junior? Huh, Miss Barnett?"

As Ruth continued, she kept looking deep inside Miss Barnett's eyes, knowing she wasn't going to get an answer. Miss Barnett looked away, holding onto the papers she had in her arms.

"What is it, Miss Barnett? We don't hear you talking now. We know what it is, and Junior knows what it is, too."

"I can't beli..." Miss Barnett tried to finish her sentence.

"Well, believe this Miss Barnett, if he cries another tear in this classroom as a result of another beating that you give him, we will open that window, let some fresh air in, and send you out, and we will send you out head first."

Miss Barnett's stature shrank. I saw a woman that was once standing tall, now trembling with fear, while her body fat was shaking uncontrollably and involuntarily. She was now the frightened one. She was standing amid her own classroom with her students looking on, feeling what I felt all those months in her class. From one conversation, one address, one ultimatum, she looked like she had been met by a firing squad right before the ammunition is released.

Before Claudia and Ruth left, she was staring into some stark, glaring space that existed only to her. Her perplexed face was far from the Miss Barnett I had seen for a year and a half. It was part frown, part surprise; like she had seen what old Black folk called a 'hant.' This was a ghost figure coming back, making good on a promise to take someone to hell. Miss Barnett dropped the papers she had in her hands, and Claudia and Ruth made their exit.

In a matter of minutes, I was in Miss Gibb's class. I was a second-grader with the fastest promotion to ever take place. When I took my seat, I caught a glimpse of the outside, and the sun never shined so brightly. In the presence of Miss Gibbs, I felt bathed in comfort, the kind where sucking my tongue and me rubbing Mama's arms was a place of relaxation. In Miss Gibbs's class, I was in a garden where I bloomed like a potted plant. I had been transplanted, where my roots could sprout freely. I could turn around and around and dance on the inside, for all of my fears were relieved. Miss Gibbs immediately put me at ease. I did have one fear. I wasn't sure this was real. What if this was some dream I was having? Did I pass out when Maude Barnett was beating me in my hand, and is this what I was wishing? Oh no, don't let this be a cruel trick that was arranged by Miss Barnett, that she could assemble my dreams. She could lead me down a valley of death, I finally get beside still waters and green pastures, and suddenly I hear her wicked laughter, and I would be directed back to her, under the bludgeoning of her switch.

I should ask to go to the bathroom, find Claudia and Ruth, and see if they really talked to Miss Barnett.

"William?"

I heard a voice like cool lather bubbling on the water with a fresh scent. I felt like I was running between sheets hanging on a clothesline, dancing in the wind.

I didn't answer; I wanted to hear my name again to make sure this time it wasn't a dream. So many pleasantries were present, for it was like every good memory had been revived to the tune of the eight letters I heard in my name. Suddenly, I knew it wasn't a dream. I felt Miss Gibbs's hand on my shoulder, and it was time for our arithmetic. Miss Gibbs took the time to help me and showed me how to use my fingers to count up and take away. I folded fingers down and extended them up one-by-one until I got the hang of it, and for a first-day second-grader, I could have added and subtracted until the sunset and came back up again.

From that day forth, the school looked like an architectural design that was built just for me. I actually fit in. This structure housed the hemispheres of my brain that would guide and anchor every decision that I would make in life. This structure now had an interior designer.

Miss Gibbs was the interior designer within this structure who knew where to place me and knew where I would thrive. Her teaching style was like a light fixture that complemented the entire classroom, illuminating the talents within me. She was able to put those lights on what seemed like select settings for each student, so they would be able to work toward their success with optimal results.

That light permeated the inside of my esteem and cast an ambiance that extended to my tomorrows of uncertainty. Indeed, now I had the chance to meet it with courage. It was all too clear to me that my fears were allayed. I had shed them like a snake that had left its skin behind because he had outgrown the old one. Miss Gibbs was the appointed person who helped me, and I grew to my next appointed phases.

The bus brakes squealed to the tune of my happiness. They even rejoiced in my new-found joy, and they made extra noises to cheer with me without the issue of a mechanical problem.

Upon returning home from school, the day was like déjà vu. I had seen this day before. It was "my" first day of school all over again. The similarities were uncanny, but there was one thing that troubled me. I saw my mother sad again. This was the sweet woman who I couldn't say enough words in the

English language to describe her goodness. She was looking into the room where James was sick, the place he had died, and she was standing there in a gaze. Moving to this house where he spent his last days could not have been good for the essence of who she was, nor for her own healing from her hysterectomy. We had moved twice since her operation, which had to be strenuous, even if she did delegate most of the duties. She still had to tell everyone what to pack, where to place it, and where to put what.

But now, Mama was standing like a willow tree, poised yet graceful, as the grief pulled her forward. She was looking at the bed where James heard a whisper to meet God in His eternity. Now, thinking about James brought a sense of sadness to Mama as she cried out, as no one was around.

I didn't go in for a while. I waited and looked, and I saw her tears fall like the last water drops falling from an old spigot after cutting it off – slower drops, some stead.

I looked at the marbles in my pocket and noticed one with a cat's eye. It was green, yellow, blue, and a dreamy color of the beach, where for a moment, I went far away. Turning it round and round, I could see the colors horizontally, diagonally, and vertically, giving a hypnotic look that mesmerized my mind for at least a second.

"Junior, how long have you been in from school?" Mama asked.

"I just got in," I said, not wanting her to know I had seen her cry. This time I could tell her what a good day I had and lift her spirits.

"Mama, I've been put in the second grade. I'm in Miss Gibb's class now." I smiled and could feel my ears move back, revealing all the teeth I had.

Wait a minute. Maybe I shouldn't have said that. I may have to tell how I got to the second grade and what happened. Maybe she wouldn't ask.

"Junior, I'm so proud of you."

I hurried up and cut in. "Miss Gibbs told me to do my fingers like this," I showed her, folding them down, extending them up. My fingers were like new buddies to me that helped me with my arithmetic, but unlike the buddies that Papa had, who helped him with a lot of "Take-Away." It seemed they were taking away stuff we essentially needed, or maybe it was Papa giving it away.

I didn't think Mama would approve of Claudia and Ruth threatening Miss Barnett, and I didn't want to be the one to tell on them. Mama believed in the biblical way of handling matters, and her anthem on most things were: "God will handle it." This was miles away from Claudia's and Ruth's premise on revenge: "We will handle it, God won't have to."

I was glad to see Mama's mind shift from James to my "second" first day of school.

CHAPTER 4 – GRANDPA ROBERT'S HOUSE

Winter quickly moved to spring, and Grandpa Robert's house had interesting surroundings. It was another day when God called me to one of his environmental treasures. On any given day, I could see bullfrogs, butterflies, and poisonous snakes, things that God carefully revealed at his own time, and I would see for the first time and marvel about them. There would be times that I would comb the woods, and it would be an adventure in itself, as I could find greens, garlic, or berries. In spring, it was the perfect time to go to the woods and find Huckleberry patches.

On a lot of these adventures, I would be alone, but one day my mother and I were outside in the spring air. I grabbed Mama's hand, and we were swinging our hands together up and down like a hammock moving back and forth. The blossoms were just beginning to bloom, and the air was a fragrant reminder of God's blooms.

We were out walking, looking for blueberry patches. We saw a tree that had fallen down across the stream. It functioned as a surface or a platform above the water where we could walk across. We basically would cross at the same place where the water recessed around some rocks. Down there, we would use those rocks as a platform, and there was a snake that made his home under those rocks. This snake would be there most of the time, but must not have been poisonous. Every time it would hear us coming, or feel the vibrations from our steps, the snake would extend its body above those rocks while sticking out its tongue. We weren't frightened, but if my mother and one of my sisters had seen the snake, they would have hit at the snake, making the snakes head go up and down until they got to the other side.

We walked along our fields and the woods, and we just let the sounds of the environment talk to us in between our conversations. We could hear birds singing and wind blowing through the leaves, making the perfect song, a melody of accompaniment.

We were making our way to Molly Pond, and it was a vibrant fixture adjacent to our land with rushing sounds of the water. The water moved against the rocks and soil, making for peaceful and interesting moments.

Something had to be pushing this water, it couldn't be going by rushing itself along by itself, and I was mesmerized by the movement. The pond was high, and my curiosity beckoned me to take a closer look.

I could see a bit better, but it wasn't the view I needed. I wanted a view that could answer the questions that were rushing through my mind. I thought about it, and my best bet was to go in a little closer to see if I could find the answers. I stepped further down, and my footing was uneven. I no longer felt the hardening of the earth, and I found myself moving downward, all while hearing my name being called. A shrilling pronunciation of 'Junior' that I had never heard before was repeated over and over. I had fallen in the pond, and my mother's call alerted me to all the love she had for me in the moments of her vocal screams.

I was rushing by in the waters. The scene that I had been so curious about, I was now becoming a part of it. My mother was coming toward me, and I was steadily moving with the current of the pond. My mother was not going to let the waters carry me, not her baby. Not the baby she had carried for nine months. I was reaching and still moving and becoming one with the pond. My mother was calling, still believing, and not planning to let the water win, and then something happened. Still moving through the waters, I felt something like a rope, but this couldn't be a rope. It didn't have a consistent pattern like a man-made rope. Surely, a rope couldn't have been growing in this slippery water. However, the more I felt it, it felt like a root – a root that had connected from one side of the bank, growing from one of the other trees. I truly believe that this root had to be divinely grown for a time such as this.

I was in the midst of Isaiah's prophecy when he wrote, "Then a shoot will spring from the stem of Jesse, and a branch from his roots will bear fruit. The Spirit of the LORD will rest on Him – the Spirit of wisdom and understanding, the Spirit of counsel and strength, the Spirit of knowledge, and the fear of the LORD." I had been rescued from the waters by this same Christ that Isaiah had spoken about. He had been prophesied to be a root, and now he made himself a root for my benefit.

As I held onto the root, my mother pulled me up. I knew things could have gone differently that day. My mother would have jumped in after me, no matter the cost, but God had a different outcome in mind. He had already sent His root – a second chance root.

God had actually saved me physically that day in the Molly Pond so he could later save me spiritually. Mama was definitely going to see to that. She always taught me to give God the glory, and I was thankful to Him for all He had done.

I had on a pair of overalls that day, which would have been heavy to maneuver through the rushing waters, especially if Mama had jumped in. As we went back to the house, I wondered if my mother thought about spanking me for looking too closely at the water. I believed she would have, but I do believe that Mama was so grateful and thankful that God had spared me, that she chose not to spank me.

After holding onto the root in the Molly pond, the rushing waters left me weighing at least twice my weight. My galaxy overalls were drenched, and the denim material held onto the water as I held onto the root. By the time Mama and I reached the house, she told me to pull them off immediately. She washed and rinsed them so they would be dry for school in the morning. She had to roll them very tight in a towel to get the excess water out. I saw her do this several times, and shake them out before hanging them up and holding them over a little fire she had made to dry them quicker. Just drying them in the overnight air wasn't going to have them dry by morning. However, the process Mama was using was going to have them ready.

With the same pair of overalls that were just wet, washed, and dried, I was getting ready for school, and happy at the same time under nuances of serenity. I was actually happy to think about going to school. Was this what school kids were feeling every night? Was this a feeling all children experienced? Was I the only one who hadn't experienced this type of happiness up to this point? Maybe this was like some rows in the fields I had seen when I was plowing. Some seemed to grow slower than others in the beginning stages, but when you looked a little later in the season, you couldn't tell which rows were once smaller than the others.

CHAPTER 5 – BLOSSOMING UNDER MISS GIBBS

As I went to school now, I had all the educational comforts that I could possibly need. There was Miss Gibbs's smile, her comforting disposition, and her perfume that enveloped my senses. This was all I needed. If the school had been in a shack with a leaking roof and a dirt floor, I would have been content with the climate Miss Gibbs brought alone.

As the days turned to months, I got some news that sounded like a thousand handbells on Christmas Eve. I would have Miss Gibbs as my third-grade teacher. She had taken me from a scared and scarred, two-time first-grader to a confident half-year second-grader. In that short half-year, she taught me the fundamentals I needed, which brought me up to a ready and steady third-grader.

What I didn't know or understand was how I had been chosen to have Miss Gibbs again as a teacher. I wondered if she requested me, or was she asked by the administration to teach both second and third grade. Maybe divine intervention put its wonderful hand into the process. No matter how it happened, I was elated. It was like going from midnight darkness to rising sun.

However, this didn't come without practice and hard work. Miss Gibbs helped me during lunchtime, where she gave me extra help. I could practice knowing that my mistakes were going to be a learning process instead of a death row sentence.

In the third grade, there was a change. Miss Gibbs' curriculum focus included an extra-curriculum area. She saw something in me; t I had no idea what it was at the time. Now that she had helped me with the fundamentals of reading, writing, and arithmetic, she was going to groom me for something that she said would last with me for years.

At the first lunch session, she gave me a poem. I read over it once, and I read it twice, all while pointing to each word.

"William, I want you to notice how each line ends with rhyming words," Miss Gibbs said softly, putting me at ease as she always did.

"It sure does!" I said with enthusiasm.

"Now, I want you to stand up straight and say it out loud," she encouraged.

I began to speak, and the words came out like wind in a whistle. Had I had wings, I believe I would have flown around the room.

"William, I knew I was right. You have a great speaking voice, and we will continue to work on your delivery."

If these words could have been converted into currency, I would have acquired a huge nest egg. I felt I had just received a million dollars by route of her encouragement alone.

Every week I was practicing with new poems, working on my delivery with pauses and inflections. What I didn't know was where these recitations were going to lead me.

"William, I will meet with you again tomorrow at lunchtime, and I will tell you what we are going to do."

"Yes, Ma'am," I said happily, with an assurance that my tomorrow would be great.

****

"Let me introduce you to Miss Slater," Miss Gibbs said with her normal voice of cheer.

"Good morning, Miss Slater," I said. I was no stranger speaking to Miss Slater, and Miss Slater was no stranger speaking to me. I had seen her in the hallway and knew that she and Miss Gibbs were some sort of cheerful "pedagogical twins." It was as if they were one and the same when it came to motivating students. She, like Miss Gibbs, had a great smile that extended from ear to ear. Additionally, she had eyes that looked like they had a focus only for me and the patience ready to cultivate me into a greater being.

"Now William, Miss Slater, and I are putting on a production, and we feel you will be a great addition to it," said Miss Gibbs.

I was wondering what a production was. Well, whatever it was, I knew it was something I wanted to be a part of more than ever.

With their double-team effort, I was going to be doing something I had never done before.

"Alright, William, we will have other students coming in soon," Miss Slater remarked.

Miss Slater passed out papers on the desks as other boys arrived.

I wondered what was on those papers. They were thick and printed with dark ink, and I wondered whether this was some sort of test. Even if it is was, I didn't feel defeated. For if I needed any help, I could count on Miss Gibbs and Miss Slater to definitely help me. Looking around the room, I saw the same perplexed faces that were identical to mine, until I heard a boy laugh out loud.

"We are going to be in a wedding?" a boy from sixth grade said.

"We are going to put on a dress?" another boy chimed in.

I didn't know his grade, but I had seen him in the halls before.

"We're going to do what?" the next voice said.

By the time I heard the last voice, a whole crop of voices had sprouted up, and I quickly looked into the booklet. In seconds, we were all laughing hysterically.

"That's the spirit," Miss Slater said.

"Just as you are all laughing now, is how I want the audience, comprised of your principal, teachers, and classmates laughing.

Stark silence descended upon the room.

"We are going to perform this in front of the school?" said the sixth grade boy, a hint of fear in his voice.

"Yes," Miss Gibbs said, but she assured him while telling all of us that we were chosen because we had great voices and stage presence. Both Miss Slater and Miss Gibbs felt we could give a performance that would entertain our school mates and the teachers.

It seemed like the word "training" stuck out in my mind. On this day, we were going to be "trained" as actors, and I was up for the challenge.

Miss Gibbs and Miss Slater assigned everyone their parts with her expectations and instructions.

"Everywhere you see the name of your character, you will have to memorize your part. We are going to all read it through first. Remember, it is like a big conversation. Each day we will practice during lunch and some other scheduled times. In the meantime, take your scripts home and practice each night."

"William," Miss Gibbs turned to me, "You are going to enjoy it. I know you will do well."

At the end of the day when the bus arrived home, I saw our mule, Will. I ran inside, spoke to Mama, put my books down, and got my script out.

"Junior," where are you going? Mama asked.

"Outside to do some homework," I yelled, moving ahead toward Will.

She didn't bother to question me further. I guess when she heard "homework," she was okay with me leaving.

Will was my friend. He was a mule my father bought that had been a wild, feisty animal. He evidently had been a tough one to tame due to the marking on his ear. The split on his ear was an indication to those that bought him should be beware of his mannerisms. However, he was nothing but gentle with me. He would always listen to me, tilting his head gently, as if he was interested in whatever I was talking about. Not only did it seem he was interested, but it seemed he understood everything I said also. I thought he would be the perfect one to hear the lines of the play, "The Womanless Wedding."

I had finished my rehearsal for the evening, and I had no other homework. Will seemed like he nodded in agreement that I had done a good job. Since I had finished, I decided I would shoot marbles on the porch, but first, I had to go in the house and get the can where I had all of them.

I arranged them in a way where they wouldn't shoot too far off the porch, and I would be able to retrieve them easily.

I was ready to shoot the greenish cat-eyed colored one when something caught my attention out toward the field. This was a sight I had seen often, but not this close. Something was different. Without a sound, I could hear it calling me. I knew it was beckoning me to its presence. I peered closer, still no sound, but I knew it was calling me. Dropping my marbles, I went directly to it, and there I stood, standing shocked, and not even knowing the lasting effects of this experience.

I was in the middle of the field, and my skin that was once a deep cacao brown was now reflecting a projection of colorful rays upon my entire body. Never had I seen my skin retain any other color but a "hated brown," where the hatred lay on top of my brown skin from those who despised its color. Inside this existence, there were colors reflecting the appearance of translucency and a colorful opaque presence beaming simultaneously. How the two could exist at the same time was a matter of divine intention.

After looking at my skin closely, I stood, colored with warm sensations, and I was in the prism of God's Love directly in the midst of our field, just one hundred feet from the porch. I recognized all the colors that Mama and my sisters had taught me, but it was the light – like none other – that I had never seen. It was brighter from within than it was before I stepped into its presence.

I don't know how long I was there, but I felt showered, bathed, cleansed, even baptized, like I was in some private changing room right there in the midst of our field. There was an energy that was all around me, and it felt like it was giving me a charge to "Go ye forth."

"Mama, Mama," I yelled while running as fast as I could back to the house without even thinking.

"Are you okay, Junior? Nothing was chasing you out there, was it? I saw you running faster than I've ever seen you run before."

"No Mama, I'm fine. I've been in the rainbow!!! I walked right over to it and stepped right in it. My whole body was the same color as the rainbow. It turned my brown skin seven different colors."

"When did this happen?" Mama said with love in her heart only a mother could say.

"I was on the porch shooting my marbles, when I saw the rainbow. I had to go to it, it was like it was telling me to come," I replied.

"Rainbows show us God's promise to man. I'm glad you got a chance see it so closely," Mama said.

CHAPTER 6 – THE PERFORMANCE

I was backstage, and the curtains were down in front of me. All the boys were getting ready, making sure their costumes were on. These costumes that Miss Gibbs and Miss Slater made were from some of their own personal wardrobe and some from parents' donations. We giggled as they looked at each other, anticipating what the audience was going to think.

As soon as the curtains were opening, I felt a few butterflies fluttering up and down within my stomach. Immediately I told myself I was going to move forward with all the courage that I had gained from the rays of the rainbow. I was going to present myself to the audience just like the rainbow had presented its rays upon my skin.

Just yards away, I could hear the anticipation. Whispering voices revealed the wonder of the students' minds. "What kind of play is this?" "I wonder what is this going to be about?" "What is a womanless wedding?" These were all questions that most kids would ask, all while being glad to attend an extra-curricular activity outside of class. Subsequently, there was restlessness among the audience. Students were shuffling their feet back and forth, moving restlessly in their seats, while anxiously waiting for the play to start.

When the curtains opened, the audience looked amused. Stunning looks were upon their faces, and there was no time to be afraid. We were well-prepared because we were under the direction of two educators, Miss Gibbs and Miss Slater. They believed in each one of us – a feeling I was grateful to experience.

As I took my place on the stage along with the other boys in the play, I sat down, crossed my legs very lady-like, and said my part with a thunderous, yet feminine delivery.

Something wasn't right; there was a roar of laughter that was disturbing. It didn't come in waves from one side of the room to the other. I knew this voice. I had heard it before. This laughter mushroomed over all other the laughter and was echoing in my ears. There was a burst of distinct laughter that I could distinguish from everyone else. Although I had never heard this person's laughter before, I knew the cadence of her voice. Her leviathan roars prepared me for any kind of sound that would come from the hole in her mouth. This was a cackle that was slightly above and slightly different from everyone else's laughter. It was a constant sound of rhythmic convolution. I couldn't believe she was laughing, for I had never even seen her smile. I guess it was evident that this springtime celebration brought everyone at Talladega County Training School ultimate enjoyment, and even this event could reach the humorous side of Miss Maude Barnett.

After being in "The Womanless Wedding," I was charged like a battery, ready to run. It was an exuberant feeling, stimulating everything in my being, making me feel as if I could conquer anything.

CHAPTER 7 – TENDING THE FIELDS

"Junior, I want you to plow the fields back over there," my father said.

I knew what Papa meant; no further explanation was needed. I knew the exact fields. This was not going to be one of my personal field trips, the kind where I would explore and see nature and all that it offered. This was work, and I was no stranger to it. Yet, to have a child plow these fields alone couldn't have been a good idea. The rows were long rows, lots of dry and dusty dirt flying everywhere, and I knew sweat would be coming down my face like rain. This was one of the hottest days in Talladega, but that could really be every day after April in Alabama, or at least it seemed.

I put on my clothes, my old standby overalls. My old work Galaxy overalls, not my school pair, but some I had outgrown. I tried to find something to eat, but I didn't find anything.

I went outside and hitched Will up to the plow. As a young boy, this was really a job for a man. After being on that stage with my courage intact, I didn't see why I wouldn't be able to plow the field.

Why was my father so satisfied leaving our home when there was no food in the house? I had seen this time after time. He was off with his buddies, spending our breakfast, lunch, and dinner money. We were seemingly always without something, yet the buddies my father rode off with were always meeting the needs of their families.

I got a jar of water and thought I would just go on. I had been behind so many mules and plows, that I had my own slogan. "If a mule's behind was a camera, I would be a movie star."

While I was plowing, I would hum to myself, sing songs, and I found myself saying some of the lines from "The Womanless Wedding." I had thoughts of my sisters and brothers and wondered what we all would be like when everyone grew up. I went up and down each row, just wondering what time it was. I couldn't tell whether time was going fast or standing still, because it seemed like one row was never going to end.

Then, a profuse sweat came over me. It was one of the last things I could remember. Things got blurry, and I thought it was just sweat running into my eyes. I kept wiping and wiping the sweat. Before I knew it, I was waking up in a strange place.

"Where am I?" I asked.

"William, William, can you hear me?" the Doctor kept repeating. "William, William."

It was hazy in the room, and I really couldn't figure out what had happened. The things I saw were kind of blurry, but the last thing I could remember was the sweat pouring down, and I was wiping my eyes.

Had it not been for Ruth going to get some water and passing through the fields, I'm unsure how long I would have been lying in the heat. Will was waiting right there beside me and didn't leave or trample over me. I wonder what he was thinking; I would have loved to been able to access his thoughts.

I was told that my Uncle Jack, Papa's brother, had come to the scene in haste when he had gotten word that I was passed out in the field. He was not a man that walked fast, or even got around quickly for that matter, due to his severe arthritis. Shockingly, it was a five-mile walk from where Uncle Jack was and where I was in the field. Instead of walking, he ran the whole way, while crying, unsure what he would find.

No one knew where Papa was, but I'm sure it was easy to determine who he was with instead of being in the field. I couldn't understand why Papa was so comfortable to let me, a young third-grader, be alone in the field. Why was it so important for him to be gone and have me plow with such a large animal in weather that was so hot, all by myself?

Papa didn't feel the need to have any further tests or exams run after I was examined. For two whole weeks, my head had a severe pain that was constant and would not leave. It was a persistent pain that didn't stop. This was just another example of my father's irrationality. It wasn't the first one, and it indeed wasn't the last one. Once, he got my Mama to help put some logs on a trailer with the mule. This was not a job that a woman should have been doing. While trying to steady the log on the trailer, Mama's little finger got caught in the link of the chain. It was broken. She had no medical attention because Papa thought it was something that could be attended to at home by wrapping it up and applying some sort of salve. Her finger from then on would always have a crook in it.

Why didn't he ask some of those same buddies that he drank with incessantly to help with this heavy manual labor instead of a child and a woman? It seems liked we were always bearing the brunt of our father's choices, and it didn't seem fair at all.

****

I don't know if what happened next in our lives had to do with Mama's finger, but we all benefited from her request to Papa. She told him she wanted electricity, and he got it. It had been a big help to my mother and a complete turnaround for me. It saved Mama a few steps she didn't have to take. However, she still had to cook on a wood-burning stove. As for me, I could do my homework without kerosene lamps, now that we had the benefit of lights.

Now that our house had electricity, one switch could illuminate an entire room. We weren't wasteful with it, but to see it from a distance gave the house an entirely different look.

Papa must have forgotten, or been so used to seeing the house with a dank and dark look, that seeing it with electricity ultimately frightened him one night. I heard him breathing heavily and moving at the pace of an Olympic runner, coming up to the house the first evening we had the lights on. In a panic, he opened the door, hardly being able to speak, and said, "I thought the house was burning down."

CHAPTER 8 – THE FIRE

The wind rustled through the trees as summer came in with bullfrogs croaking, butterflies fluttering, and whippoorwills hooting what seemed like cheerful, but lonely tunes. The sundogs were in the sky, which required me to look longer than I normally would. This peaceful scene was calming and inspiring, giving me another reason to appreciate nature.

It was a beautiful day, and just as Miss Gibbs had put me at ease to learn, there was something about this day that had put me at ease as well. It was only a few months ago that I had experienced my ordeal in the field, collapsing and falling into unconsciousness.

After taking my eyes from this scene, I turned and looked at my reality. I saw dark days of discontent, and we were in no shortage of those. Food was scarce, sometimes non-existent, and the clothes my siblings and I wore to school were a few levels below ordinary. There were even days when I looked at Will, and I was even jealous of him. There he was, taking crunchy, big mouthfuls of the greenest grass like it was absolutely the best. He had something to eat, and I didn't.

After getting beyond my thoughts, where it seemed I had many, there was something about this day that made for a suitable play date with nature. I counted the minutes until the sun rose with the plan to see it set. I had Will on a rope so he could graze a little out by the barn. Looking out for Will was important because when I fell unconscious in the field, he could have taken off running, which could have possibly killed me, but he stayed right there in front of me waiting.

I couldn't describe the placidity on this day. There were no assigned chores for me. Taking Will out to graze was something I always did without being asked, so for a few hours, I was able to run around in the fields; play, gallop, see the beetles, worms, and bumblebees on dandelions.

I was just so free and happy because a minute in nature could feel like an hour of enjoyment. This was my own formula for enjoying nature, as I would observe a little, play a little, and run around a little. It was the ultimate feeling of happiness within my own private amusement park.

I thought about my marbles. The cat-eye especially. It was a little larger than the others and my prized possession. Even if I wasn't going to shoot them, I still liked to have some of them in my pocket as I was walking around. Moving them around in my pocket in a circular motion, and hearing the clacking was calming and reassuring. I suppose it reassured me of some of the normalcy in my childhood, despite the unstableness things.

I headed back to the house, and I couldn't believe my eyes. A panic attempted to set in, but I couldn't and wouldn't let it grip me. I had to move quickly. I had to run. There was smoke on top of our roof, and something was wrong. The fire was starting to gather on top of the house.

Margarite, Bertha, Ruth, and Claudia were inside, and I had to get to them. Mama had gone to town, Papa was with his buddies, and my brother Leon was gone because he had found himself a group of buddies. Flooding thoughts poured through my mind as I got closer to the house.

"What if it was already burning on the inside?" I thought.

"Margarite, Bertha, Ruth, Claudia!" I yelled as loud as I could, but I didn't go inside.

I didn't hear anyone respond.

I hollered as loud as I could again, and still no answer. Where was everyone?

I ran around the house, and Claudia and Ruth were outside. Margarite and Bertha were on the other side of the house. They all were ringing out wet clothes and beating out rugs.

"The house is burning down," I yelled.

"The house is burning down," I yelled again as if they didn't hear me the first time.

"The roof is burning! The roof is burning!"

All I could think about was whether the roof would fall in.

"We got to get our stuff out," Margarite said.

We all peeked in, and it didn't look like the roof was going to fall in right away. I could hear the pops and crackles from the fires. We moved quickly. The five of us grabbed what we could. In actuality, we really didn't have much to save. Looking around at each other, we were the most precious "things" we had.

I began thinking about Mama. She was in town getting some groceries with what little money my father managed to give her. Now she would be coming back to a house that would possibly be engulfed in raging flames or completely gone. The thought put me in a sad place, not that we were losing a house to stay in, but Mama would be tasked to moving again. There would be nowhere to put the groceries she just brought. It was the third move since her operation, and sure, a couple of years had passed, but still. When was she going to have any stability as "the lady of the house?"

I seriously doubted that Mama's finger had correctly healed. She didn't go to the 's and now this. What would Mama be disappointed about most?

The best things we had were our God to pray to, our family we were blessed to have, finally getting electricity, and the hope of moving on to something better. Grandpa Robert's house was no more than a corn crib. It sheltered us, but barely.

I had planned to count the stars and examined the sky that night, but instead, I was counting our blessings.

If this house had not burned down, we would have been there our entire life. The house belonged to my father's father, Robert Groce. With it being his house, there would have been no demands at all for my father to leave. Just one winter here was harsh. It was so cold, for I could see my breath on cold days as soon as I woke up. Then there were cracks in the floor which revealed something I hadn't seen before. I happened to be on my hands and knees, crawling around on one of my adventures, and saw mice under the house.

Rainy days made for a melodic, yet chaotic sight. Several buckets were inside, catching water from the leaking roof. Many of the cracks were wide enough for not only a steady stream of waters, but it was a personal telescope where I could see the stars at night.

Although the condition of the house was less than desirable, we were still grateful. Yet, we were all without a complete understanding of why Papa wouldn't repair or restore things in the house to make our living conditions better. Many of us were sick in that house, but Mama treated us with her remedies of Pine Top for colds; Grandma Fanny's Coon Root for colds; and Poke Salad for parasites. Nonetheless, as for parasites, I didn't think we had many of those because we didn't have enough food in us for the parasites to want to hang around.

My mind was back to Mama. This was going to be another disappointment for her, and I sure wished she didn't have to face it.

When she did arrive, like always, she persevered. I looked at her face when she came to the house, and her look remained stoic – a look she had learned to master. We did, however, have an angel waiting in the wings. Mama's sister, Aunt Lillie Mae, took us in.

Papa, who seems to have a nose for shacks, would no doubt find us another one.

Here we go again.

CHAPTER 9 – FOURTH GRADE

The bus came around at its usual time, but it was the first time it came around to this residence. We were now at the Carl Leonard Place, and I was ready and excited to go back to school. The route to school was slightly different. We had been approximately twelve miles from school before when living at the Easley Place, not quite as far as the fifteen miles Grandpa Robert's Place or the Thornton Place. From either direction within the fifteen-mile radius, I was ready for the ride, which allowed me to observe the view and anticipate what I would experience in school this year.

It would be the first day of fourth grade, and I wondered what would be in store for me. I had done this a few times before, but this time I didn't find myself nervous or apprehensive. I knew the procedure now, and I knew the drill. If this was going to be a successful year, I needed to suit up with courage, walk in, and face whatever was before me. I was beginning to believe nothing could top my two first days of school with Maude Barnett – meaning: be worse. However, if it did, I had the assurance from my sisters, Ruth and Claudia, that they would go and fix it no matter how unorthodox they had to be to get it done.

Upon walking in, I saw old friends from the year before, some of them with new school clothes, but mine were not new. However, I told myself, you may not have new clothes, but you do have on your "newly-minted" courage.

I remembered what I was wearing on the stage in "The Womanless Wedding," and although I had on ladies' clothing, the most significant accessory I had on was the courageous act of moving ahead. I finally realized I had the same courage I had under the direction of Miss Gibbs and Miss Slater. Most knowingly, I also realized if I used this courage, I could move forward this school year.

Miss Gibbs and Miss Slater were directing more than a play; they were directing lives, at least mine anyway. From the day of the play, I got a new perspective on how to move forward.

I got closer to my classroom after all the students were shown where to go. I walked inside, saw my teacher, and uncertainty stood in front of me.

As the day went by, it was pretty evident that in this school year, I would need to add my creativity and my motivations to the year. I would continue with extra-curricular activities at school, make new friends, and just see more of what Talladega County Training School had to offer that could make the school year one of normalcy.

By the end of the day, I arrived at a theory. I had calculated all that I saw and all that I heard. Gratefully, it was not the year of Maude Barnett, and sorrowfully, it was not the year of Miss Gibbs. It was, however, the year of Mrs. Perkins, and I would be okay.

I was very fortunate to be able to count on the extra-curricular activities by God's ecological hand on the properties where we were now living. The Carl Leonard Place was around a place called the River Bend Community, and we were close to the Coosa River. Like many children, I loved rivers, creeks, and ponds. It was beautiful to be able to fish and swim and to see things I wouldn't usually see within the rows of crops on dry land. There was easy access to the river, a spring, and a branch that ran down towards the river. When looking downward while standing on a hill, you could see the spring starting to bubble up. This area served multiple purposes. My mother and sisters would go down to wash clothes, and sometimes where we would drink the water, which was more than refreshing.

In addition to fishing, there was excellent access to hunting, and the only place that my father would hunt. He had a bird dog that was a black and white pointer. Papa would mainly hunt quail, and when hunting was over, he would tie the dog at the back of our house.

A humorous turn of events came when the dog was sick. He had something happen to him that nearly exposed the bone on one of his hocks. Papa decided to treat him with turpentine. Mama would give us some with a little sugar on it for colds, so I suppose my father thought it was a good idea to treat the dog's skin with it. My father told me to treat the dog with turpentine while he was at work. The thickness of the dog's coat caused the chemical to move down toward the animal's rectum, and apparently, a tiny bit got in his rectum. The results were not exactly what my father planned. The dog yelped and ran so hard to the garden, looking for a sudden relief. He was burning so much that he scratched a hole – one foot deep – with dirt flying like he was the motor in a rotor rooter. He then sat down, allowing the cool earth to soothe his inflamed area.

****

"Kyser, you got your marbles? Let's go to the river," I said, panting and out of breath.

"Okay, you got yours?" Kyser said, also panting and running to keep up.

"Yeah!" I responded while thinking about the time I went to get them. It was when I thought I had them in my pocket, but I didn't. When I headed to the house to get them, I saw the roof on fire.

"So, how do you like it down here?" Kyser said.

"I like the river, the spring ... actually, I like a lot of things."

"Yeah, I like it down here too, but I'm so glad that you all are down here. We are just a short distance from each other. We can play together."

"Me too," Kyser responded.

Kyser was my Aunt Lillie Mae's son. Not only a great cousin but a great friend. He was right. Moving to the Carl Leonard Place allowed us to spend more time together than we ever had.

We looked at the spring and saw the bubbles rising, looking like a moving statue and a fountain at the same time. As time passed, we laughed, throwing our heads back with giggles that echoed throughout the Coosa River. We talked so much, we didn't even get the marbles out, but I still twirled them around in my pocket, as they gave me a sense of peace and stability.

The sun was beginning to go down, so we gathered our things and decided to head back home. We didn't want our mothers, who were sisters, to worry about us coming back to the house after dark.

****

I was getting my legs, so to speak. Muscles had formed. I was putting one leg in front of the other, standing and bending, strengthening my walk, readying myself for whatever was coming in the future. I was getting the grip I needed to plow through life. I had obtained more courage and confidence and was finally seeing how to manage life between school, home, and friendships.

Life at Talladega County Training School was everything I could predict as a fourth-grader. Fortunately, I was back with the "Gibbs-Slater Duo," as they were off to presenting another school-wide assembly. They got me ready for another production, as I practiced speaking, standing, and delivering beautiful poems, one which I particularly remember called, "The Children's Hour."

When the time came, we met during lunch with Miss Gibbs and Miss Slater, as did other boys and girls, and we practiced a variety of poetry pieces, steadily improving our deliveries. We raised our voices, paused, repeated, and annunciated where needed. Miss Gibbs smiled, Miss Slater smiled, but there was no particular order, just smiles that came with intermittent encouragement.

Then the moment had come after months of preparation. I was familiar with curtain time; only this was not a comedy. This was more of an uplifting, inspirational moment. We, as students, were serious and dignified, and Miss Slater and Miss Gibbs saw to that. They stressed poise, pace, and posture. We didn't dress in overalls or ordinary clothing, we dressed in our Sunday best. There was an audience to be in front of, and we had to look our best. We were not only giving recitations; we were giving Talladega County Training School a glimpse of what every student should look like, sound like, and become, as we brought to life various scenes using words, lines, and verses.

After we all spoke our parts, there was a resounding thunder of applause. Every clap was like a pat on our backs.

The students and teachers enjoyed seeing their students and former students become instruments of encouragement. With all the listening, there was something I didn't hear. I didn't hear echoes of laughter from Miss Barnett, nor was I supposed to hear it. However, I did wonder what she was thinking. Since I didn't hear her, this absence and silence stirred something within me that made me think if she ever thought I would be chosen to make such an impact. Did she ever think I would be good enough for any teacher to look upon me and choose me to be an inspiration to others? Part of me wanted to believe that she *did* know, and she *always* knew, and as a result, she hated me so much that she had to beat me to keep me down. Then, hopefully, this oppression would stop any intelligence I had within me to come forth. The other part of me knew that she hated dark-skinned children and saw all of us as less than. However, I had one more theory where intelligence was concerned. Perhaps she really couldn't accept that dark skin and intelligence could or should dwell within the same existence, and, if it did, she was going to see to it that it didn't.

In this year of school, I was right about focusing on extra-curricular activities. Making sure I was involved in them was a must. They were really a sustaining force for me during the year. They filled in the cracks and crevices, the distant moments that some teachers have with students when they teach out of what seems like an obligation. We, as students, may never know what that obligation really is, but we do recognize the hollowness that these teachers present.

I pretty much let the fourth-grade classroom serve me as a post office. I allowed it to deliver to me the knowledge I needed, along with what was required to complete all tasks. I sent it back with due diligence, and I saw it for what it was. It was an exchange, nothing more and nothing less. I knew the drill. I listened, learned, and lengthened my tolerance, and I accepted this was the way it was going to be. Maybe I had been so used to the "Gibbs-Slater Duo" teaching style that I knew when anything else was just different.

As the year went on, I made a friend named Charles McGee. Charles was the kind of guy people would call 'cool.' He was no trouble maker or class clown. Charles had the elements that some people think of as' cool,' yet he had an interesting side that made people want to be around him. He seemed to float along through class with an impenetrable shell. No matter what was thrown his way, it was okay with him. He didn't mind if he got an answer wrong. He could laugh it off and say, "I'll get it right next time." He also had a storytelling style that made him enjoyable. Maybe it was because he wasn't exactly a country boy, but not exactly a city boy. He was from Shocco Springs, a mountainous kind of area that was west of us. I somewhat imagined that had everything to do with his wording of stories. The homes were closer together, people probably gathered more frequently, and could hear a variety of things that happen in the course of a day, unlike the widespread homes of farm life.

His natural conversations were always peppered with details, and he could make comparisons that seemed to be off the top of his head. I wondered how it would have been for him to recite poems on stage, but I don't think he was inclined for it. Charles would probably have reworded his lines and said his part in a different way. He would not have meant to be defiant, but he would have said it to the tune of how he saw it.

CHAPTER 10 – PEANUTS!!!

Plowing through life and plowing the fields somewhat took the same steps. I knew all too well about the plowing in the fields and the mental and physical strength it took. I didn't know how many men had ever passed out behind a mule, but I could say I was one of them. After I survived to tell about it, I was in a place of wonder, yet, I couldn't let it paralyze me from moving forward. I often thought about whether I would ever pass out again, but I kept my mind on the positive side of matters.

I was now beginning to have agricultural ideas. We had always grown cotton, corn, and sorghum as our primary field crops, and I thought I would try my hand at peanuts on my own. I took an interest in peanuts due to my sisters' interests in them.

My sisters had an affinity for making candy with peanuts, and I saw the joy it gave them. With the molasses we had from the cane sorghum, it was a natural fit that they would make this into a hobby. However, the peanuts they had were not many. They used those that were given to us, and still put them to good use. What I saw in my sisters was a natural gift. In the midst of some of our hardest times, they had a way of making something out of virtually nothing.

So the idea came to me; why not plant about an acre of peanuts? My sisters would be able to have them without depending on when they would get some, and then they could focus on the candy making process that they seemed to love. Now, I was not a fan of peanut brittle, but to watch my sisters was like watching a T.V. show on a T.V. we didn't have. They were festive in their process, almost like an assembly line approach. Someone boiled the molasses, someone cooked the peanuts, someone mixed, and when it was all poured together and cooled, peanut brittle was formed. After watching this sisterly act of unity, I asked Papa to buy me some seeds, and he allowed me to plant about an acre.

I was happy that Papa obliged and said, "Yes" to buy the seeds. I lost no time getting everything in order. One thing I knew about peanuts, they didn't require a lot of maintenance. They did not need fertilizer like corn needed nitrogen; they had their own fertilizing system where they could be sustained from their own roots.

I planted them with a planter, using raw peanuts that had been shelled. The rows were as straight as they possibly could be. In no time, I had plants that were growing, and soon they needed to be weeded with a hoe.

What I didn't tell Papa was the actual reason I wanted the seeds. I didn't tell him I wanted to support my sisters' interests in candy making and the joyfulness it brought them. I couldn't be sure he wouldn't thwart my efforts, which would not give my sisters the opportunity to continue with what seemed like a festive hobby.

****

Mama told me once that he was planning to have Lillie Mae and Velma plow, and she vehemently protested. She didn't protest in a "blazing guns" way, but a simple "No," followed by an explanation that plowing was too strenuous an activity for young women. Why didn't Papa think of the fact? Will, the mule, weighed about a thousand pounds, and no young girls needed to be handling this animal.

My sisters really didn't have many interests outside of school. Some that may have been available had a nominal fee, but even small fees would add up, times the number of girls in our family. My father primarily took his money and was still subsidizing the "good times," using it with his friends, and my brother Leon rose to the occasion of the provider. It was noble that Leon provided, but I'm not sure it should have been at the expense of him leaving school. Maybe it wasn't. I was really uncertain about it because sometimes I pondered whether his providing for us was the out he needed to leave school, where he didn't want to be anyway. However, I thought Papa should have counseled him to stay in school if he didn't have a direct plan of action toward getting a job. Unfortunately, Leon was developing a posse of friends that were almost identical to Papa.

****

"Look what Papa bought me!" Kyser said with an excitement that could be seen lightyears away.

"Let me take a closer look," I said.

This was a beautiful object that signified Kyser was responsible. His father, my Uncle Ernest, would have in no way bought him this item had he not been responsible.

In the country where we lived, this item was used to acquire food and could be seen as the object of every young boy's eye. Young boys were taught this was not an item to play with and not to be used for some sport to pass the time away. We used this tool meaningfully, yet in the process, we enjoyed the act of peering and waiting. We also like deciding where to explore and when we would hunt.

I never had a BB gun, and this one was Kyser's first. It looked real. Real meaning, one that used bullets and not BB's. This was a Daisy Red Ryder BB gun, where the barrel was smooth, but not intimidating. I knew it wasn't harmful unless it was used in a harmful way. Kyser let me examine it and shared it with me, and I marveled at it.

"We'll have to go hunting!" Kyser said.

... And hunting we did.

Kyser and I made sure we did all our chores, and every possible chance we got, we headed out to hunt. We primarily hunted birds, but when we saw snakes crawling craftily, we shot at the heads, taking the steam out of their ambitions.

****

Before I knew it, school was out. My last day of school brought me joy that could not be contained.

"I got Miss Slater for fifth grade!" I yelled as they gave us our schedule. I was happy when we were told who our teachers were before we left school for the summer. It was only natural that I would have Miss Slater for fifth grade. I couldn't imagine a better fit. I had known her for two years, and she had helped my self-esteem go from the bottom to the top. She and Miss Gibbs had readied me for speaking and delivery, and now I would be in my own educational world, assured that a teacher wanted the best for their students.

I said goodbye to the students and saw Charles.

"Well, Charles, I guess I will see you next year when school begins."

"William, no doubt, I will see you before then."

"I wish you could go hunting with me and my cousin Kyser!"

"You all aren't out in the wood using sling shots, are you?" Charles said with a look on his face that told me he probably thought we really were.

"We use BB guns!" I replied

"You know you don't use a BB gun," he said, putting his hand to his side, summing up the comment.

"We do! Kyser's dad bought him one, and we go hunting for birds. My Mama cooks them, and they are delicious. I'm going to ask my dad if he will buy me a BB gun too."

"That sounds like fun," Charles said, but he wasn't so convincing in his response.

Maybe Charles hadn't ever gone hunting. If he hadn't, perhaps he could go with us.

"Why don't you ask your parents if you could come to Talladega and try hunting with us?" I thought I would ask to be friendly.

"Maybe so," Charles said. Again, he responded in a not so convincing way.

I didn't know his home story, and he didn't know mine. We were boys who played at school and didn't share stories about food scarcity and moving from home to home. Even if Charles couldn't hunt with Kyser and me, we still would have a good time whenever we saw him.

****

I was glad to see my peanut plants, and see what I could grow at the hand of my own agricultural touch. The plants were coming up nicely, and they looked healthy and vibrant green. The land which I had planted them on was just right –

a sandy loam which allowed the soil to move freely and not be hard for the roots to sprout. As much as I wanted to play, I saw grass come up between the plants. I knew exactly what that meant. It was time to weed them out with a hoe. Weeding was no small undertaking, but it would be okay if done early in the morning before the sun was shining or after the sun went down for the evening. I started working and got a little tune going right along, and hummed my way down to the end of the rows.

****

"I want everyone to come in and sit down," Papa said in a firm tone.

I was thinking, not now, please don't let it be that we are going to move again. Moving from house to house was one area among a few that was really hard to process. We had moved four times, and how could we leave now right in the middle of my peanut crop. I wanted to cry openly, but I didn't. Then, I thought about it. It's not like Papa ever called a meeting when we moved before. But what kind of news could this be that would require a setting like this. I felt a dull pain in my stomach, but I told it to go away by basically ignoring it.

I thought of how I at least had Miss Slater to go back to when the school opened. Please, no more deaths, and no more operations, and no more bad news.

"I just want to tell you all that we will all be going to church tomorrow ..." Papa said.

It seemed Papa left it open-ended as if he was going to say more, but the meeting was over as soon as it started. As a matter of fact, there was no time for more dialogue.

We all wanted to whisper and ask questions, but we had to get ready. I didn't know what to think. Everybody was getting out their Sunday best and preparing to go to Antioch Baptist. If there had been time, I would have run to the Coosa River and back with joy. I didn't know what Papa was going to say, but the idea that we were not moving, at least this summer, was as refreshing as the springs that were bubbling, where Mama and my sisters washed clothes.

All I could think of was, "Thank you, Lord."

Church was filled with the usual "Hallelujah's" and the usual "Preach on Preacher," but the real feature was Papa. Every one of his children's eyes was watchfully upon him. We didn't see anything different. No sudden movement or tears flowing. He just sat there, looking ahead very silently. We looked at Mama to see if she was looking at him also, but she wasn't. She, too, was also attentive to the service. However, there must have been a million thoughts moving through her mind. We didn't know what this sudden cause of going to church was all about. We didn't know whether God had talked to him through a drink he had on the previous Saturday night, or whether he really heard a convincing, self-governing voice that told him how much better life could be. I wondered whether it was a process, not just one day, but a reflection, where God had been speaking to him over time. Maybe God addressed him about the question I had asked him. I remember being so tired of how he wouldn't feed us or clothe us, yet his buddies that he drank with had the means to provide for their children. So, one day, I asked him directly, "Papa, why can't you feed us?"

There was a stark silence. No facial expression. No look of despair. There was a blank look that really couldn't be interpreted. I was looking for at least a hint of sorrowfulness or remorsefulness. Maybe even a look of embarrassment. I wasn't interested in embarrassing my father, but I was looking for him to say, "I'm sorry," or "I promise to do better." There was no response of any kind.

After his proclamation that we all would be attending church, we did notice in the weeks to come, Papa seemed to be a man who was more caring and was providing for his family. I did wonder if this change was due to the absence of his ever-present friends. None of his buddies had come around, and as a result, we all could see and feel the difference. Where we were once empty, we were filled with food. Where we were once without necessities, we were the recipient of things we so dearly needed. Maybe the absence of these buddies had something to do with this sudden change, but at the same time, I knew that we lived farther out, and perhaps those buddies didn't choose to drive out so far to meet and pick him up as they always had. We, however, were happy that this change had come.

Out of all these changes, I was happy about my personal navigation before this change. I was becoming resilient, learning how to take life as it came, with or without resources. I was learning how to make it. If I had to wear the same clothes, If I had to wear borrowed shoes, eat from the land, or eats the vegetable that we raised, that was all fine. If we had to eat the birds we shot, and if we had to eat the fish we caught, I would be fine, and I would make it.

God's timing had a precision to all of this. I had become confident and content before my father's sudden change, and I also could be content afterward. As a result, this positioned me to be even happier and more grateful when my father's change finally came.

****

It had been about ninety days since I planted my peanut crop, and I had been weeding them and carefully watching them. I noticed the sandy loam soil was a slightly darker color. Since the rain had come, the plants were coming up nicely. Yellow blossoms were appearing, giving the crop a nice uniformed color of yellows and greens, which could be seen from a distance.

I could hear birds hooting when I got out early each morning to attend to the peanut plants. It seemed like the sunshine was actually a little refreshing when it was shining, and I noticed something I had not paid attention to before. When the sun would go in and out, with clouds passing in front of it, I would count how many times that it took place per row. I found myself using it as a clock. As the sun would shine and retract, I could count on this happening about two times per row. Therefore, about every seven minutes, it would be a little cooler, then back to hot again. I was happy about the sun giving a little reprieve, for, within this time, I would be at the end of the row. By watching the sun, I knew that it would take about 14 minutes a row, non-stop.

CHAPTER 11 – FIFTH GRADE

Walking down the halls of Talladega County Training School on the first day of school was like the halls were giving me their own personal tour. My own footsteps were leading me around, without me even telling them where to go. I knew where I was going and was ecstatic. Today, I was walking in with the biggest smile upon my face, as I was off to my own educational world, and this time, the classroom had a welcome mat out for me with my name on it.

I felt as if I was basically going to be in bunny slippers and pajamas all day. I was in a comfortable zone beyond my understanding, as the comfort was already extended. When I walked into the door, there was Miss Slater with a smile, waiting for me as bright as any light in Times Square, and as wide as the Pacific Ocean. This was my home away from home.

"Good morning, William!"

"Good morning, Miss Slater!" I said quickly.

I don't even believe I even let her get it all out before I returned my "Good morning." It was like I was hearing handbells on Christmas Eve all over again.

The first day in Miss Slater's class was like something that was out of this world. It knitted me right back to where I was the last day of third-grade in Miss Gibbs's class.

During our first activity, we all stood up, and Miss Slater made sure we knew each other, as everybody stated their favorite thing. It was like the icebreaker we all needed to get to know each other. As the students went down the line, there he was! How glad I was to see that my friend, Charles McGee, was with me once again.

After the activity was over, I went to my desk and felt as if I had won a prize. It was great to sit in an atmosphere that was charged with positivity, and I was glad to be a part of it.

Miss Slater made sure we got a chance to know everybody's name. We wrote all the names down and something about the person that they wanted us to remember. It was already feeling like a little community was being built. We could all feel that in this "community," we all belonged, and we were given the hope we all needed on the first day.

She allowed about fifteen minutes for a class community activity, and then she was getting ready to pass out some papers. I raised my hand and thought maybe she would want me to help pass them out.

"Yes, William!"

"May I pass out the papers?"

"Sure, William," Miss Slater responded.

"Notice how William said, 'May.' That's the correct usage of the word, because 'may' means permission, 'can' implies ability."

I passed the papers out row-by-row, counting first how many students were there, and giving the papers to the first student to pass them back to the others. I had seen that done before in the fourth-grade class, and I thought, why not use it now. It did save a little time, and I didn't have to go desk to desk. I knew about rows, for I had been up and down them over the last three months tending to my peanut crop.

"Okay, boys and girls, I want to see exactly what it is you have been doing over the summer. After you finish answering the questions on the front, I want you to turn the papers over, and on the back, write a narrative about your summer. I want a full page on the back because I believe that everybody can tell us about their summer. Please include whether you traveled, people you saw, or whatever you did. No idea is too small. All activities are welcome. Make sure you include all of those things."

The first question on the front side of the paper stated: "Write the capital of Alabama." I knew this one. The second question asked, "Which number is closer to representing how many miles there are between Talladega and Montgomery." This was a multiple-choice question, and I knew it had to do with estimation. Estimation was a favorite of mine. My peanut crop had made me look at things from an exact standpoint. I had been estimating how many times the sun would go in and come out per row.

The whole page was a variety of questions about Alabama because in fourth grade, we studied Alabama history. Then there were questions about each of our core subjects: Math, English, and Science, and I answered each of those questions to the best of my ability. I couldn't guarantee all were correct, but I indeed did my best. There was no doubt I had been exposed to the material about each section, so I knew this was a test where Miss Slater wanted to see how much we had learned, as well as remembered from the previous year.

I couldn't wait to write about my summer. I led off with how I saw my sisters making their peanut candy in the spring and how that led me to plant my little peanut crop before fourth grade ended. I told about how I tended to it almost daily, either by looking at its growth, weeding it, or examining how the soil looked after it rained. I wrote about going to church, how we were all going every Sunday as a family, and how we could run to the Coosa River, see the springs of water that bubbled up to what seemed like a cool lather as we watched. This writing made me think about the summer in a totally new light as I penned it in this way.

I got a chance to take a look at what I had written. I edited it and looked at it again, being that we had a little more time. Miss Slater was good at letting us know how many minutes we had left and told us we should wrap up the last sentence. That's exactly what I did.

"Boys and girls, let's see if any of you would like to share," Miss Slater said.

It seems like the crowd was getting a little shy, but as one hand came up, it was like everyone was waiting for someone else to go first. In seconds, as I looked around again, it seems like everyone was ready to share.

"Oh, good! This is just great. We have a lot of students who want to participate. Well, we may not be able to get to everyone today. But, if we can just start off with a few, we can hear everyone's narrative by the end of the week," Miss Slater stated.

We thought that was a fair deal, as we would have something to look forward to, listening to everybody's summer each day we came in.

****

The next day went exactly according to plan. Miss Slater picked about five of us to read our summer adventures, and I was fortunate enough to be in the first group of the day. However, to hear what other kids had done was equally as thrilling. Some students said they had actually gone far away, some had gone to Birmingham, and some had gone to Montgomery. Others had visited their Grandmother's house just a holler's distance away. But the way Miss Slater received all of our adventures made us all feel we had really been somewhere. In actuality, we had. She was right; no summer adventure was too small. At the end of the presentations, we felt we were left on the edge of our seats, eagerly waiting for more adventures for the next day.

By the time recess came, everybody was thrilled that I was growing peanuts. It was the talk of recess. They wanted to know how I became interested, when did I decide to plant them, and was it my first time growing them? They wanted me to explain the entire process.

As recess turned into being a "play-tutorial" type of day, I answered questions for my classmates, and then we would play. However, it certainly wasn't long ago when I remembered recess being a dark and horrid place where, even when I played by myself, I had been lied on and punished. Gratefully, it was a new day, and when it was time to come back in, I was thrilled to be in the midst of whatever we were going to learn.

****

There was truth in the phrase, "Time flies when you are having fun." Before I knew it, a month of Sunday's had gone by, and we were in a steady stream of church attendance. I heard talks and whispers that Papa was interested in becoming a deacon. Sometimes, I would hear him and Mama talking. Other times I would hear some of my sisters talking.

Now, I had seen the deacons before. These were a group of men who usually sat together on one side of the church. I saw them talk together, make decisions, have meetings, take up collections at the end of services. *Does my father want to be a part of this group of men*? I thought to myself, trying to figure this out. My father was now going to be with another group of men. Was he replacing one group of buddies who were no longer coming around for another? I wondered whether this was a need or a sense of belonging, where he had to be a part of something outside himself? Didn't everybody really want that, and didn't everybody really need that? I couldn't fault my father if this was something that he needed, and maybe that was what he was attempting with his former buddies. The good part, I was sure that this group of men would not have the same effect on him as the last ones.

One thing was for sure; every group has the possibility of bringing its own kind of deficits, be it integrity or funding, and, unfortunately, the church wasn't any different in this particular case. Papa was going to have to face one deacon who was already positioned to be an opposition to him, and he was no stranger. He was Mama's dad, Old Man Jim Houston, his father-in-law. Jim Houston had already ruffled a few feathers with Papa when Papa was helping him weed his fields with Lillie Mae and Velma. Old Man Jim somehow thought it was fitting to tell Papa, "these girls are not going to amount up to much." Papa didn't try to determine why he said it, or ask him if the way they were weeding the crop had anything to do with this comment. Papa just simply made a quick decision. That's when Papa picked up his hoe, signaled to Lillie Mae and Velma that they were not going to chop another lick in this field anymore. The three of them turned and headed home.

As Papa was in the running for the next deacon's chair, Old Man Jim reared his head and decided to announce his thoughts, "We can't have him on the Deacon Board, Bill drinks liquor."

Other deacons quickly added to the conversation, "The only difference between you and him is that he lets it be known that he drinks his liquor. You drink it too, the only difference between you and Bill, he doesn't hide his, and you do!"

I'm sure the look on Old Man Jim's face suddenly changed, but his thoughts were probably the same. This was a man who didn't even want me or my brothers and sisters to have some watermelon, and had it not been for the intervention of his son, my Uncle Claude, we wouldn't have been able to have a seed from it. We were the children of his daughter, my mother, Grace, who had faithfully washed, cooked, and cleaned, and taken care of him, only to have to return to her own family and do the same thing all over again.

The next news we heard was that Papa was the newly minted deacon of Antioch Baptist Church, and probably much to the chagrin of Old Man Jim Houston.

CHAPTER 12 – PEANUTS ARE FINALLY READY!!

It was time. It was finally time. The peanuts were ready, and so was I. The sun, like usual, was always out, and it even seemed to have a gladness that the peanuts were ready. When it came to working on the farm, looking to the elements that would be in attendance with you always helped me move along better with the work. If you saw the sun as happy, you could actually deal with it better. If you saw the rain as helping, you could be refreshed by it when it brought cooler temperatures. If you saw the clouds as ornamental, you could appreciate them as they passed by the sun, bringing those moments of shade that were always welcome.

I knew the Friday before harvesting, what kind of day I might encounter, so I started out early. Hitching up Will to the middle buster plow was going to be a Friday evening job because the sun would have a little more mercy as it was going down. It had already shone its brightest, so the worst was over. To begin setting the plow, I could get started right at the beginning of the day.

When Saturday morning came, I was not only eager but ready. I shot a look over at Will, and he was ready too. That's another thing about working on the farm, if your animals are your friends, that makes the work easier. Will was definitely my friend, and I don't think it was just because I had given him handfuls of sugar but because we had bonded from the first time I had fed him and he bit me. Mama believed that when I fed him that he did not bite me, but gave me a love nip. Not understanding what he was doing, I "whopped" him one. That's when Mama told me he was just saying "thank you" with his bite. I was glad she was there to interpret, being equally glad Will did not break the skin on my arm.

Now, a few years later, Will knew the routine. He was there when I first put my hand to the plow, and when I began to get the hang of it. He was there when I was so weak from lack of nourishment and ultimately passed out.

I surmised that this was not going to be a fast process, because doing anything with a mule in the field never was. However, this process was different from traditional plowing. The plow was loosening the dirt around the plants, making it easier for me to pull them up. This process was working well. I got myself a little tune as I usually did when working, and got into a steady pace. I finally saw the fruit of my labor, and I rejoiced. Some of those Negro spirituals I was hearing in church every Sunday had gotten into my mind, and I was humming a few of those. For some reason, I heard *Wade in the Water*, so I starting humming that one. My mind switched from there to another hymn, which was *Amazing Grace*. I was in a good rhythm now, and by the time Will and I turned around, heading to the second row, I saw someone standing on the other end of the first row. He was standing in his galaxy overalls, waving, and then began pulling up the peanuts.

I didn't think I was seeing Papa, but it was someone I least expected. It was my brother, Leon. I was certainly glad that he had come to help pull up the peanuts. Finally, we met in the middle of the two rows, as he was coming and I was going. We stopped for a moment.

"Junior, the peanuts look real good. I think you did a great job raising these peanuts," Leon said.

"I'm glad Papa let me do it," I said. I had to admit I was glad Leon had noticed my first-time efforts.

"You know the sisters are going to enjoy making candy," I continued.

"Yeah, and I'm going to enjoy eating some of it," Leon said, rounding his comment with a big hearty laugh.

The laughter was refreshing in the field for those moments. It was a great brotherly moment that Leon and I shared.

We could have laughed longer, but we knew we better keep on going. One thing we didn't want was rain to come. It didn't look like it was coming our way, but sometimes a sudden downpour would come, and that would have canceled all the efforts of getting the peanuts out of the field.

I signaled to Will that we were moving on. I kept going down to the end of the row, and then we turned around. I was going back the other way, and by that time, I met Leon again; we stopped and talked a little bit, and then we kept on going. However, the next time I turned around I saw some others standing at the end of the row. Ruth, Claudia, and Margarite were standing there. Even Bertha, who was not fond of the outside, made an appearance.

I heard a series of "Junior, Junior, Junior" that sounded almost like a choral effect. "These peanuts look good." The laughter and the compliments gave more refreshing moments.

"Junior, you got a good-looking crop here!" Bertha said.

"Thank you," I responded, as I saw her touch the peanuts Leon had pulled up. She examined one closer and thought she would like to take a few in to show Mama.

"We knew she wouldn't be out here long," Ruth and Claudia said in a duet.

"She's showing Mama, alright," Margarite said. "That was her exit back to the house."

Within seconds everybody laughed; there was no malice, only a breeze of refreshment. This time, it came not from the wind outside, but from within the family.

Will and I turned around and headed down the third row, and behind me was a trail of laughter. I was in a verse of a new song, *Jesus Keep Me Near the Cross*, and the laughter became faint and distant. I was in my zone and going full speed ahead. I could hear the rhythm of Will blending right into my song. It wasn't too long that it was time to turn around to go back and head toward the other end.

When I was heading back, my brother Leon looked like a foreman running the labor assignments in the fields. Everybody was working like they were in an assembly line, some were pulling up peanuts, and some putting peanuts on racks in the field.

As I got to the end, we had someone else to join us. Her presence brought smiles to everyone who was already there. Here we stood, as she looked out into the cultivation of not only peanuts but the cultivation of a family.

"Junior looks like we are going to have some good peanuts this year. They look really good, and you did a good job with them. Bertha showed them to me," she said proudly.

"Thank you, Mama," I responded.

"Listen, I want you all to come in and get something to eat and get some water. I don't want you all to get too hot out here."

"Okay," we all said. Deep inside, I felt we all could have stayed a little longer, but we knew what dehydration could do under a "Talladega Sun." Mama didn't want any repeats of my passing out, mostly after it was never determined what the cause was when I fell over.

We all left the field, and Mama had some hoecakes waiting for us with some molasses on the side. Everyone was ahead of me because I lagged behind, looking at the work everyone had done, and I was grateful. I smiled and was happy as I looked back at the rows Will, and I made it through.

By the time everyone had gotten to the house, I could hear the clanking of dishes and the sops of the molasses.

"Bertha, did you help Mama with the hoecakes?" Claudia asked suspiciously.

I knew exactly where this was going. It was Claudia's way of asking Bertha if she had done any work since she shot out of the field.

"She did her fair share of work bringing the peanuts back to the house," Ruth chimed in.

I knew this was all in fun. They were not viciously setting Bertha up. Bertha just wasn't the outside, agricultural type.

Soon, it was time to return to the field, and everyone got up without any urging and started to walk outside.

"Mama, I'll do the dishes," Bertha said with an uplifting voice.

"Oh, let us guess …" Ruth started.

"… You'll be staying inside," Claudia finished the sentence.

"The dishes will be done when you arrive," Bertha said on cue like a Hollywood actress.

Everyone chuckled and expected as much. Bertha could always orchestrate how and where her chores would be – inside.

I didn't forget Will. He had worked hard too. Before we started, I took a bucket of water for him to drink. His gulps were loud and hearty as if he had no water for days. When he finished, he looked at me and knew it was time to start. I suppose he had a good memory too. He didn't bite me or give me a love nip, he just stood and flung his tail, and bowed his head.

****

When Papa finally came in for the day, he saw something that had totally shocked him. There was a look on his face, where his brows furrowed inward, and his mouth was open as he entered the house. Even though he had stepped inside, his head was still turned toward the direction of the field.

"When did you all do all of this? How did you all get all that done so fast? What ... happened?" he asked with a sense of shock and disbelief.

He had been gone all day, so he missed the entire harvesting process of my first peanut crop. When he arrived home, he saw two peanut shocks that had been loaded with peanuts. It was evident that seeing the peanut shocks caused a different kind of "shock" on his face and one within his voice.

"Junior started taking Will out to the field this morning. I saw him last evening switching the plows around, and I knew what that meant. When I got up, I saw Junior and Will heading down the first row," Margarite told Papa festively.

"I heard Leon stirring around. He was walking in what sounded like pacing back and forth like he was looking for something. I assumed he found it because quickly afterward, he walked out of the house, and I heard the door slam. I suppose he was rushing to get to the field to help Junior. Everybody was still getting up. We, however, were all moving a little slow, but when I told them to look outside at Junior, we all got a move on, got our clothes on, ate a little breakfast, and headed out," Margarite continued.

Papa hadn't responded. He was standing with his head turned back toward the direction of the field.

"Even Bertha went out!" Ruth and Claudia said, as they commonly spoke in a pair.

"I examined some peanuts to show Mama," Bertha chimed in, letting it be known how she contributed.

"That was her way of finding a way to go back inside," Claudia and Ruth added.

"William, everybody pitched in, inside and outside," Mama responded, throwing a glance at Claudia and Ruth as she was talking to Papa. "I couldn't have been prouder of the children today. They worked hard and saw exactly where they were needed. They were all working together as a unit."

Still silent; no response from Papa. He was just a statue, looking backward from the middle of the floor. Sounds of family conversations were in the background, where Claudia and Ruth were still joking with Bertha, inspecting the work she had done on the inside. Bertha was at the stove, ready to serve dinner, where she had carved out her inside job with Mama, and that was okay. Mama could undoubtedly use another pair of hands to help her in the house when she was inside. Yet often, Mama was a worker on the farm as well and could easily pick two hundred pounds of cotton on any given day. I figured Mama could use help with peeling, chopping, washing, cooking, and cleaning, so why not have Bertha work inside.

We were glad supper was coming, and while Papa was still standing here silent, Mama tried to call him out of his trance. She called him once, no response. She called him again, no response. She called him a third time and still no response. She tried again, and then the girls chimed in.

"Papa, it's time to eat," Claudia and Ruth yelled.

Papa slowly came out of his trance, and as he moved, his legs were like those of a tin man. He seemed to need oil. He commanded a stiffness that wasn't there when he came inside. When he finally moved his legs forward, they made sounds like thuds on the floor, a heaviness that I had not heard before. It was a zombie-like movement with no grace or composure, just a movement marching forward to one's destination. Papa finally made it to the back to wash up. We waited, throwing teasing looks at each other as we silently played around the table. Bertha had finished serving the food. Claudia and Ruth wouldn't dare miss an opportunity to thank her with their exaggerated manners like she was hired help. Eventually, Papa returned.

The heaviness in his legs did not sound as profound, but we could hear him coming. The thuds had been reduced by at least a fourth. On his way to the head of the table, he stopped where I was sitting. Had I been blind, the thud sounds would have told me exactly where he was. He put his hand on my shoulder for what seemed like an hour, but it couldn't have been more than a few mere seconds, and he said, "umm...uh-huh," or at least that's what I thought he was saying. After his hand left my shoulder, he went over to his chair. The sounds of his walk seemed to be telling, but I couldn't figure it out. He sat down, brought his chair closer to the table, and ate silently during the entire dinner.

CHAPTER 13 – ACHES, PAINS, AND SATISFACTION

When Monday morning came, I was walking with the same stiffness that Papa had. I was sore all over and was moving slowly.

"What's wrong with you, Bill?" Charles McGee asked.

"I'm just sore from harvesting peanuts," I said. I must have been walking differently than normal on the playground at recess. I didn't think it was that noticeable, but it must have been.

"Well, how long were the peanut rows, from here to the moon?" he said in his usual funny tone.

"It was a lot of rows, and I was walking with a mule in front of me."

"Wait a minute, a mule. What can a mule do?" Won't he stomp on the peanuts?" Charles asked seriously.

I laughed and laughed, and he joined in. Charles wasn't even offended that I laughed. Moments before he even knew that anything was wrong with his comment, he rode the wave of laughter like a surfer. Charles always had an ability to laugh at himself and take it on the chin, even when he got a problem or an answer wrong in class. My laughter alone must have tickled him because before we knew it, we had been laughing for what seemed like the rest of recess. I could tell some of the other kids wanted in. They wanted just a little bit of our laughter and to know what was so funny. We couldn't let up from laughing to tell them immediately. Water was coming from our eyes, and we were slapping our knees and bending over, moving only the way laughter could orchestrate.

It was time to go inside, and I promised Charles, I would tell him more about harvesting peanuts and how the mule didn't stomp the peanuts.

When we walked back inside, it seemed like my soreness wasn't as intense. Maybe the saying, "Laughter is the best medicine," was correct.

****

It was time for us to return inside from recess, and when we did, Miss Slater had an exciting activity waiting for us. She wanted us to be able to choose a president and research information about him. That was the beginning of our first research project, and actually, the first one I had ever done. Miss Slater pointed to the class set of encyclopedias that we would be using to look up the information. The encyclopedias were old and it was evident they had been passed down from other schools. We could see the name of White schools stamped inside, and we were the recipients of their old books, as new ones went to their schools first. Nevertheless, we could still use them to research needed information from them.

We would start using the encyclopedias later on in the week, but Miss Slater wanted to first talk about how to read information and then put it in our own words and not copy word for word. This reminded me of the scripture in the Bible. There were times when we could quote certain verses, and then there were parts of the Bible that we would put in our own words when we were sharing a story such as *Daniel in the Lion's Den.*

As we continued throughout the day, Miss Slater was gearing up our practice for the annual assembly. This time it seemed we were preparing early, but Miss Slater told us there were going to be lots of parts and more students from upper grades. She was letting us know early on that we were going to have an even more significant event.

The next day at school, I talked to Charles as promised. We were right back at recess in virtually the exact spot we were in when we were in a fit of laughter.

"Charles, you don't have the mule walking on top of the row, you have the mule walking in between the rows. The plow is in the middle, and its call a middle buster plow. It will plow on the sides of the plants, and the plants will be pushed upward – out of the ground – and can be easily pulled up."

I looked at Charles' face and I could tell he was visualizing it as best as he could. We knelt down and I put my fingers in the dirt. I saw some grass, as it was perfectly arranged to further explain this method.

"Let's pretend these are two rows of peanuts, the plow is going to go down the middle. The mule won't be here, but here," I said and pointed to the grass and the dirt in the middle. It appeared that Charles was beginning to understand.

"That seems like some hard work! It's no wonder you're sore," Charles said, part amazed and part withdrawn. "I don't know if I could do that," Charles continued.

"I think you could. Just like you work those arithmetic problems, and you have to do them again until you get them right, you could do this," I said encouragingly.

"How long have you been doing this...walking with a mule work, I mean?" Charles said.

I laughed a little, but thought that maybe I wouldn't laugh too long. I cut it off before Charles added his laughter. Since he appeared to be showing some genuine interest in farm work, I didn't want to kill his interests with laughter.

"I've been plowing with a mule since I was about seven. By the time I was eight, I could plow by myself," I said, but cautiously. I chose not to tell him about how I passed out at eight, and had to go to the .

"You really like this stuff?" Charles said eagerly.

"Well, I don't know about liking it, exactly. It is just something we have to do."

"So, you don't like it?" He asked, somewhat confused.

"I don't dislike farming, but it is hard work. You are outside most of the time, and the weather may or may not be in your favor. You know the "Talladega Sun." It's like it chooses nobody but you to shine on when you are out in it. But, you got to look at it like the sun is glad to be out and happy to be there with you. While out there, I hum a tune and focus on something good. I will say that I have enjoyed raising my peanuts the most. Maybe because it's something I did by myself, the planting and the weeding, and I can see how it turned out, according to the time and work I put in it."

"Well, now that you put it like that, it sounds like school. We got to do it, and some of it we like and some we don't, but if we focus on something good, it will be okay," Charles responded.

There we were, talking earnestly, comparing farming to school. This was far from the first time we talked about how sore I was harvesting the peanuts. We had turned into two old men, sounding like we were ready to give advice to our own children and their children.

I believe if Charles lived nearby, I would have had a plowing buddy. He would have been there every chance he could get to experience this new area of life he hadn't experienced called "farming." I could see him plowing every other row, as we switched off, and we would be laughing in between a great conversation. This is really how he was when Miss Slater taught us a new unit, no matter the subject. Charles would love to jump into things he didn't know about because change was never a problem for him. Change to Charles was like an address; if he went to it and showed up on the wrong street, it was fun for Charles to turn around and start all over again.

****

When the weekend came, I was up before the sun had gotten up. The day had a damp, clammy feeling, but I wasn't going to complain. It was much better than the scalding sun coming down. I thought about what I told Charles when it came to farming, the weather may or may not be in your favor, but adjusting your perspective would get you through the day.

I looked at the field where the peanuts once were. It was the place where my labor had once been. Now it was bare and ready to be plowed over and later prepared for another crop when the time came. I could really see what it meant, "You get out what you put in."

After the peanuts had been hanging on shocks outside, drying for about two weeks, it was time to place them in the barn.

"Junior!" A hand slapped on my shoulder, moving my mind from the field to this sudden moment.

"Leon!" I said, startled, but recovered once I saw it was him. I must have been so deep in thought that I didn't hear him walk up. Usually, he walked with a jangle, some clink or clank that was almost a mantra when he arrived. He was either keeping a beat with his hands or swinging them forward and backward. He had some rattling tune that he sang along. His fingers popped, adding a rhythm that gave his stride an added feature. But surely, I would have heard him. Something was different.

"Let's get those peanuts in the barn," Leon said. "I know this is why you came out here."

"Yeah, it seems like it's going to rain," I said.

"I think we are going to beat it," Leon replied.

We walked over to the shocks and began removing the peanuts. In tandem, we walked the peanuts toward the barn. Every step we made, made me feel like we were going across a finish line.

"Junior, are you going to plant another field of peanuts next year?" Leon asked.

"I think I will," I said.

"It's not every day fifth graders are doing what you are doing. You did this peanut crop by yourself." Leon said

"Well, you all helped," I said.

"We helped to get the peanuts out of the field, but you put them in the ground and tended to them. You weeded them and saw them come up," Leon said with a tone I hadn't ever heard. He was earnest and probably more serious than before.

"You ought to be proud of yourself, Junior," Leon said.

"Thanks, Leon," I said.

For a moment, it felt like a fatherly talk. I took it all in as we continued working.

When we got to the barn, the door opened with a creak, we flung it back, and the light flew in. Inside the barn was a musty odor that could only be driven out by a dose of hot sunshine, where the rays needed to continuously beam. The overnight dampness had set in, and it was reviving every trace of animal scent or whatever had once been packed inside. I could see the loft and the ladder rungs on the side of the barn that led to it. I felt them, testing them to see if they were still sturdy as the last time I had been on them.

I climbed up and signaled to Leon that I had made it up the loft. Looking around, I could see the area where we would place the peanuts.

"Alright, I'm ready," I said.

Leon passed up the first round of peanuts to me, and I placed them in the corner. We kept repeating the process until I heard some voices.

"Hey, Junior!" It was Ruth and Claudia. They passed some peanuts up to me.

"H..." I attempted to get out.

"Guess who ain't coming!" They said.

I didn't get a chance to get out the full "Hey" or "Good Morning," because they were ready with the report on Bertha.

I hurried to defend her. "She'll have our breakfast ready."

"She better," Claudia and Ruth said and laughed with a thunderous roar.

"We want to climb up there!" Claudia said, alone.

I wondered if Claudia was speaking for both of them. Perhaps, Ruth didn't want to come to up to the loft.

"Yeah, I'm right behind you," Ruth said.

My question was answered soon as the thought came out, as Ruth was already climbing up. Leon was passing up more peanuts, and I could hear Margarite helping him. Leon probably tried to get Ruth and Claudia to pass the peanuts up, but they wanted a "more perfect" adventure.

****

The rain came down with what seemed like a thunderous vengeance. The presence of this rain was more prolific than I had seen for some time, and it was not relenting. If this rain had been playing a character in a play, it had all the features of making sure it was going to get its stage time in, since the sun was always present. The sound alone made images in my mind like someone tap-dancing wildly on our roof.

Looking out of the window made for a distorted view. Everything that was once clear looked like it was melting, but staying in shape at the same time. Additionally, it felt like the

"Talladega Sky" was going to fall in, plummeting on top of all the images.

I couldn't imagine what it would have been like had the peanut shocks been outside. They would have been at risk of molding if they couldn't dry out quickly enough. After a little while, the rain slowed down, giving me a chance to run to the barn to start pulling the peanuts off the plants.

This wasn't a bad job at all. It was a matter of getting to the loft and filling the burlap bags with the peanuts. This was the final process to "sack them up." The burlap bag was a rough and sturdy material that allowed circulation around the peanuts.

As I pulled the peanuts off, I thought of what I read about President Theodore Roosevelt in class. The word "hunter" stood out to me, and I stopped right there. I really didn't think of presidents ever hunting, so an instant fascination was injected into me right then. I guess I thought they were always doing work in the White House and making decisions from there. I continued to pull off the peanuts, and I could hear the tap dancing again. Before I knew it, I had six large bags of peanuts. The rain was waning, but not before I found myself falling asleep. When I woke up, I ran to the house, and what once looked like melting pictures upon a canvas was bathing in fresh sunshine. The grass was wet and still had bubbles on the blades.

When I walked into the house, I found Mama making butter. She was pouring the butter into wooden butter molds that had several different flower designs. Mama had help from Bertha, who was assisting her by pouring butter into molds also.

"I got peanuts. I got peanuts!!! I shouted.

"I knew that's where you were," Mama said with joy.

She knew I was probably on one of my adventures, but with it raining, she knew I was not out in the fields.

"I was sacking up some peanuts and fell asleep."

I had come in at just the right time. It was a moment where the kitchen was a center of goodies being prepared. Additionally, it was also a good time for the sisters to make a batch of their peanut brittle candy.

I usually liked the desserts and foods made in our house, but peanut brittle was not one of them. It had nothing to do with how my sisters made it, for I just believed I was not designed to be a peanut brittle fan. Nevertheless, I enjoyed that my sisters got a lot of joy from making it together.

"Mama, can I have a hoecake?"

"Sure, Junior," Mama said.

"Mama, what do you know about Theodore Roosevelt?" I asked.

CHAPTER 14 – THEODORE ROOSEVELT

I figured if I was going to research a president, it was going to have to be one that I could get some information on. With the encyclopedias being so old, I wasn't going to get anything on Franklin Roosevelt or Harry Truman. The encyclopedias we had didn't even have these presidents in them yet. I thought I would be better trying my luck with the other Roosevelt, Theodore. I looked around, guessing what other people were going to choose.

Miss Slater was certainly no stranger to the methods of good teaching. She arranged us in groups; that way, a few of us would be able to look at the encyclopedias. Some would be working on arithmetic assignments while others would work on science assignments. This wasn't a bad idea at all. She spun the classroom into a carousel that gave us a block of time to work in one area, have us shift to another, and then move to the next.

I looked across the room, and it seemed that this process was working as well as a sewing machine. I knew this was favorable to Charles. He was all teeth. I don't know how Miss Slater thought of all this, but we liked it. Had everybody been at the encyclopedias at the same time, we wouldn't have gotten a chance to at least explore all our options. She did alert us that we needed to have about three presidents in mind, just in case someone was using the encyclopedia we required at the time, but she didn't think that was going to be a problem.

I had decided. I would research Theodore Roosevelt. I got the encyclopedia with "R." Miss Slater explained to us how these books were set up in alphabetical order, giving information about people, places, and things. When I looked through the pages about President Theodore Roosevelt, something stood out, and I knew this was going to be the president I would research.

I started at the beginning and saw President Roosevelt was known for his quote, "Speak softly and carry a big stick." I let my finger glide me to the next sentences, and I let the words carry me into a world where I felt I had traveled to in minutes. When I read he was a sickly child, I immediately saw myself. I was carried back to all the days I was sick with a scrotal hernia, where I was basically debilitated for days at a time. Those days were sad when I couldn't go out to run or play or do anything as others could do. My sister, Margarite, would be my eyes and ears, and capture the sounds and things of nature when I couldn't go outside.

Since Roosevelt had asthma, I wondered if he couldn't play outside or if he couldn't get involved in activities because of it. However, his father had him exercise more to help with his condition. I assume this was probably why he liked the outdoors so much.

"He was way, way, before my time," Mama said. She laughed with a burst of sinister laughter that told me she was trying not to let me know where she was in terms of her age. She attempted to be far from his term so that I wouldn't figure it out. I thought I would try to nudge it out of her anyway.

"Were you a little girl when he was president?" I asked, hoping she would answer quickly.

"I told you he was way, way before my time." But I do remember my mother talking about how he always said, "Speak softly and carry a big stick!"

We both said "big stick" at the same time.

"How do you know that, Junior?"

"Miss Slater is having us research a president, and I chose Roosevelt. I read that he was known for that saying."

"Why did you choose him?" she said with a curiousness, but not with any objection.

"I saw that he was sick as a child with asthma, and he liked to hunt. But the first word I saw was "hunter" in the encyclopedia, and I wanted to know more right then."

"Well, you know a little bit about him already, I see," Mama said. "You know my mother also told me that he went hunting one day and ..."

Mama suddenly stopped.

"Mama ... and what?" I asked, waiting.

"NO!!!" Mama said, and stopped.

"What is it?" I said.

"NO! I can't tell you," she said.

"Why not, Mama?" I said.

"No, it won't be a good idea," she said.

"Yes, it will," I pleaded.

"No, I'm going to let you find this out for yourself," she said.

"But ..." I said as Mama interrupted.

"It will be better when you find out, and then you can tell me what it is, and I will let you know if you are right," she said.

"Okay," I said reluctantly.

How was I going to wait over the weekend to find out about Roosevelt? I felt like I was going to burst wide open. Mama said, "hunting," so that was a clue. Could I ask someone? Did someone in my family know? Maybe I could ask everyone I saw to see what they knew about Roosevelt, but there was one thing I was going to have to do. I would have to be sure to let everybody I know that it was Theodore – not Franklin Roosevelt – who was our President just a few years ago, that I wanted to know about. If not, I was going to get the wrong information.

****

"Leon, what do you know about President Theodore Roosevelt?"

"What I remember about him was that he said, "Speak softly and carry a big stick."

"Stick," I said at the same time.

"Oh, you know about that," Leon said.

"What else do you know?"

"I don't know ... I wonder whether he was kin to Franklin Roosevelt," Leon said.

I wondered who I could ask next. I didn't have any books around that were going to tell me about President Roosevelt. Now Mama said "hunting," so it's got to be about that.

"Leon, what about hunting? The encyclopedia said he was an outdoorsman, so it's something about hunting."

"Junior, I really don't know anything about him when it comes to hunting," he said, readjusting his cap.

"Okay," I said. I made my way down to Ruth and Claudia.

"Ruth, what do you know about President Roosevelt?"

"Now, which one are you talking about?" She fired back like a cannon.

"Theodore!" I responded.

"Theodore," she repeated, touching her face with her index finger. "Umm...I always remember that phrase 'Speak softly and carry a big stick."

We said, '...carry a big stick' together.

"Everybody knows about that, BIG STICK!!!" I said.

"What about you, Claudia, what do you know about him?"

"Same thing, the main thing I knew about him was 'Speak softly and carry a big stick.' But also, I knew he was from New York. Oh, how I dream of going to New York one day," Claudia said.

I let her dream of the big city last for a moment longer before asking her more questions. There were stars in her eyes. Maybe she would be able to get something from those memories that I could use.

"Oh, he was the Governor of New York!"

"Well, did he hunt there?" I asked, thinking I was getting closer to my answers.

"I bet he did," Claudia said.

"Now here's something else I remember, when that other President was killed, Roosevelt became the new president.

"That's right," Ruth said. "I also remember Roosevelt being sick as a boy."

They continued to talk, exchanging facts back and forth. I stayed around listening for a little while. Claudia was back to dreaming about New York, and she wondered how he liked growing up there. She started comparing how she thought he would have liked and disliked Alabama, as she felt the two states had to be like night and day.

"Do you also know anything about Roosevelt hunting?" I finally had to cut in.

"All we know is that he enjoyed the outside." They both replied, finishing each other's sentence, as they would commonly do.

They returned to the conversation about Roosevelt and everything they knew about him except hunting. I left, and they were still talking. I decided I should go elsewhere for this "hunting" mystery that Mama had ignited within me.

I walked over to Kyser's house, and it was about a two-mile walk. I could hear frogs croaking along the way, and I guess they were responding in their own way to all the rain we just had. It was a wet walk and, in some places, a few puddles.

When I got to Kyser's house, he was outside playing with marbles on the porch by himself. I always kept a few in my pocket, and today I had a few mixed in with the peanuts I had pulled off the plants in the barn.

"Hey, Junior," Kyser said.

"Hey Kyser, what have you been doing today."

"Not much with all this rain. What have you been doing today?"

"I've been pulling peanuts and sacking them up in the barn," I said, showing him the ones in my pocket.

"I would have come over and done that with you," Kyser said with eagerness.

"Well, come on over next week. I have a lot more to do," I said. Hey, I got a question for you. "What do you know about Theodore Roosevelt?"

"Speak softly and carry a big stick!"

"Everybody knows about that big stick!" I said

"I don't know much else right now," Kyser said.

I heard Kyser's door open. The creaky sound didn't disappoint. Something about the sound of doors opening told a story about each house. The way the door's frame and the door opened and closed was a greeting of its own. Some sounds were loud, and some scraped as they were opening. I was one who should know with all the moving we had done. I had heard the sound of four doors, and if I were blindfolded, I would know each one if a thousand doors were opened and closed. However, Kyser's door had a comforting sound, and it was always welcoming.

Uncle Ernest came outside, and I crossed my fingers, hoping that maybe he knew something about Roosevelt.

"Hi, Uncle Ernest!"

"How are you, Junior? What have you been up to today?"

"I was in the barn, pulling the peanuts off the plants and putting them in sacks."

"Good, Good. Kyser could have gone over there and helped you," Uncle Ernest replied.

"He told me that he would have come," I said. "Can he come next week?"

"Sure, he can," Uncle Ernest said.

"Uncle Ernest, may I ask you something?"

"Of course, Junior."

"What do you know about Theodore Roosevelt?" I asked, hiding my exhaustion from repeating the question.

"Well, I know he loved hunting like me."

I nearly jumped out of my skin. I rubbed my hands together with a grin on my face, hoping I was getting closer to the answer.

"Who's that coming up?" Uncle Ernest asked.

I saw a whole carload of men coming up.

"Is that who I think it is?" Uncle Ernest said.

My heart began to sink. I was now going to be further away from my answer. Should I still ask? Could I navigate this question into the conversation with all these men?

I was willing to give it a try. But first, I had to listen and find out who everyone was.

"Ernest, we haven't seen you in a long time," said the first man.

"John, it is good to see you," Uncle Ernest said with a hearty laugh and a hug. Men two through four all did the same thing, and it was a reunion with hugs and pats on the back.

I waited. I waited more. The conversations were about what they were doing the last time they had seen each other – the jobs they had, and their cars, and where they lived now. It seems that time was passing slowly, and I wasn't sure if I was ever going to get the answer to my question.

Kyser shot his marble off the porch and jumped down after it.

"This is my boy, Kyser," Uncle Ernest said.

All the men shook his hand.

"...and this is my nephew, William. We call him Junior."

The ceremony of handshaking started again.

Kyser and I stood there, and the men asked us how old we were and also asked us what we enjoyed doing.

Maybe that was my chance. Perhaps this was the time to go after my answer, but I didn't exactly feel right about it.

"What's your favorite subject in school?" one of the men said.

This was it. I was not going to let this opportunity go by. I was jumping in ... no ... diving in, with both feet, swimming fiercely to get my answer. Since I hadn't asked the question to Uncle Ernest, he couldn't be offended that I opened it up to all the men. My mind was working fast and spinning as if I could see my own thoughts on a blackboard.

"We are researching presidents," I notice that I didn't say a subject. I had to get it out there.

"... Ah, in History"... I hurried to say.

"So, you like History?" one man said.

I really did like science and math most, but I wasn't going to tell them that when I needed this answer.

"Yes, sir. I'm asking everyone what they know about Theodore Roosevelt?"

"He wouldn't shoot that bear," Another man said.

Uncle Ernest chimed in, "He sure wouldn't."

"What's this all about?" I asked, hoping I wasn't overstepping my place.

Another man said, "He was on a bear hunting trip, and everybody had shot a bear but him, and somebody tied one up for him, but he couldn't shoot it. That's what my daddy said. Said he felt sorry for the bear. Didn't think it was right."

I listened intently as my eyes widened. This must have been what Mama was talking about. I thought I was going to have to hear about that stick, but I would have listened, just as long as it got me to this point.

"That's how the Teddy Bear started. Since he wouldn't shoot the bear, some people started making bears and named them after him – Teddy for Theodore," another man said.

This circle of men seemed to know this story without any talk of the stick.

"Umph, I sure wish some of my people thought of that," Uncle Ernest said. "Now all the children want teddy bears. Can you imagine how much money has been made selling teddy bears?"

"Did this happen in New York?" I rushed the question in between the conversation.

"No, that happened not far from here in Mississippi." A man said, who hadn't said a word the entire time.

"He was this close to Alabama?" I asked.

The same man chuckled, "He was the president, he could go anywhere he wanted."

Well, I had a lot of information that I needed to remember. In Mississippi ... on a bear hunting trip hunting ... President Roosevelt hadn't hunted one ... someone tied a bear up for him ... he saw the bear... didn't shoot the bear ... people made and named a teddy bear after him.

I said my 'goodbyes' and 'thank yous,' and walked back home well before it got dark. I was saying all the information in my head that I heard, but I could tell it wasn't going to stay there. I stopped where I was and recreated everything I had heard.

Where I was standing, I could see an area where the whole scene could have taken place. There were a lot of trees, but a lot of open spaces where a bear could be tied. Just as I had heard nature while I was walking to Kyser's house earlier, I could hear the frogs croaking, but not as many as before. However, the crickets were beginning to organize their tunes, making a musical backdrop to my recreation.

Since Theodore Roosevelt wore glasses, as I saw him in the encyclopedia, I pictured him standing with his gun. He was carefully examining it, making sure it was ready to fire. Then, I could hear someone calling him, saying, "Over here, over here," in a deep southern Mississippi accent where the word "here" sounded like it was two-syllables. The man who tied the bear would be repeating the phrase, waving his hands wildly, leading the president to the bear. Excitement would be in the air, the same kind when Kyser and I would be hunting, ready to take down the hunted.

But the air became still. President Roosevelt must have seen something wrong with this picture. He must have seen a helpless animal with fear in his eyes. I let that scene stay in my head, and now I could see the facts I had heard and not just in a list I was repeating over and over in my head. It was making more sense. Now I could see why President Roosevelt couldn't shoot this animal. It was already captured for him. It wasn't the same as if he hunted the animal. There was not enough time to look into the bear's eyes when one has to decided to kill.

He couldn't do it. I understood. Not only did I understand this recreation, I appreciated the reason behind the research. We could learn from what once happened. Even though President Roosevelt's hunting trip had taken place over forty years ago, I had now gone there in my mind and was there at the same time.

I don't know how long I had been standing at the edge of the field but the sun had gone down. I could hear Mama calling me, "Junior," with a long-extended call on the first syllable. It wasn't a call of worry, but a call that it was time to come on home.

I started running, leaving the scene. I couldn't wait to tell Mama what I had found out.

When I got to the house, I had to catch my breath. I stood on the porch and huffed and huffed until my breathing had at least returned to where I could talk a little bit.

"President Roosevelt wouldn't shoot a bear, and some people made a teddy bear because he didn't. Teddy was the name given to the bears after the name Theodore," I said in a mouthful, at record speed, and didn't slow down until I said it all.

"That's it!" Mama said.

"Why didn't you want to tell me?" I said.

"I wanted you to find out on your own. What I didn't know is that you would find out today. I thought it was going to take a few days. Actually, I thought you were going to find out when you read more books at school. How did you find out?"

"I went over to Kyser's house," I said.

"So, he knew already?" Mama said.

"He didn't know, but I got ready to ask Uncle Ernest, and some old friends of his came up, and all of them told me," I said.

"Well, here's what I do know. You will always remember the Teddy Bear story since you found out on your own. Had I told you, you wouldn't have remembered it."

I silently had to admit that Mama was right. Had she told me about President Roosevelt, I would have never recreated that image in the field on the way home. Something about this research experience made me feel like research, and I were going to be lifelong friends.

"Boys and girls, we have a few more minutes before we finish researching all our information," Miss Slater said.

This time we had other books about presidents.

I had gotten everything I needed. Miss Slater wanted us to research five facts and write them down. Just as Uncle Ernest's friends had said, I read about the Teddy Bear in these other books. Claudia was right about President Roosevelt being from New York. I had already read that he liked hunting and was sick as a boy with asthma. So I did have one more fact. He was Governor of New York.

"Who can come right up here now and give their five facts about your president? I don't want you to read your paper, but I want you to tell the class about your president in your own words."

I didn't see any hands up to volunteer, but I did see the edge of the field. All I had to do was to go back there and tell where everybody was standing. I could tell the story right from there. Why not include where the president had traveled from, and how if he was a boy, he might not have been able to be outside since he had asthma.

Suddenly, I heard a round of applause, and I saw a smile on Miss Slater's face. Again, I had to admit to myself, Mama was right – I benefited from doing my own research.

CHAPTER 15 – GIVING MYSELF TO THE LORD

Knots were in my shoelaces. I must have pulled my shoes off too fast without untying them. Eagerness led the way because I wanted to visit the tributary of the Coosa River. The day was clear, and it was matching my desire to explore.

"Son, I want to talk to you," Mama said.

"Yes, Mama," I said.

Mama was cooking rabbit stew, stirring it clockwise and counterclockwise, as she had just added a little flour to thicken the gravy. I was puzzled by her tone. As she wiped her hands on her dishtowel, the stew simmered. Normally, Bertha was around to add seasonings or some helping hand, but she must have gone somewhere else for a moment.

Mama walked me to the table. Her hand touched my shoulder, soothing all my senses. I felt assurance, acceptance, and "all is calm" in that one touch. In that touch was encouragement and invitation, love and compassion, and at that moment, it felt like the sun after the rain, and birds singing in the morning. It was the kind of feeling to always keep and never surrender. I was fighting hard to keep it. I just wanted to bask in this feeling just a little longer, but I was experiencing a feeling that wasn't going to let me stay. I was traveling further from this feeling, and I could do one of two things. Fight it or surrender.

My mind flooded with questions. Former thoughts of moving house to house made me wonder if this was a "We are moving again talk," but why would Mama just tell it to me? I would think we would all be together if this is what she had to say. I kept thinking. Where would we be going if we were moving? What would the lay of the land look like this time?

I absolutely hated this feeling. It was a gritty feeling, similar to a rug being pulled out while standing on it. I could be standing with balance, and everything around is steady and stable. Then, something or someone decides this is not the way it should be. The feet move without warning, the mouth opens, ready to yell. The arms move outward, hoping to catch the fall. The mind spins and turns, looking for reasons why. The hands hit whatever surface below, taking all the pressure – if, they break the fall.

"Junior, Junior," Mama called me.

"Oh ... yes, Mama," I finally answered. "I was just thinking about something."

"What were you thinking about?" she asked.

I didn't want to trouble her, but I didn't want to lie.

"How long do you think we will be here?" I asked.

"That's up to the Lord, son. Many times, we think we got it figured out, but we don't. If He knows the number of hairs on our head, then He also knows the number of days we will be here."

Mama could tell I was concerned.

"I thought we would talk because I want you to start thinking about asking Jesus Christ into your life as your Lord and Savior."

I paused and thought about what she said.

"Now, I'm not pushing you, but I want you to think about it."

I must have given her a perplexed look, a look that told her that I didn't quite understand. Actually, I didn't understand fully. I knew that people were moved by God when we went to church. I saw people shouting and jumping when they felt His presence. There was always a multitude of "Amens" said after scripture from the Bible was read.

A question suddenly entered my mind. Had the people who were currently attending church asked Jesus into their life as their Lord and Savior? Is that what made them respond the way they did in church? What did I have to do? I knew Jesus was God's son, and I knew about the Trinity, but how did you accept him?

"What do I have to do?" I had so many questions, but I decided to go with just one. I decided against asking about what others did or what they have to do, but instead, what I needed to do.

"First, I want you to pray and ask God to forgive your sins," Mama said.

I knew what she meant, and I didn't have questions about this, but I obviously still had a perplexed look on my face.

"You will know when God hears you," she said slowly, almost whispering.

The food on the stove had gone from simmering to a boil. The steam made a sound that caused both of us to look in its direction. Mama got up quickly and stirred the stew.

"That looks good. That's just how I want it," Mama said, stirring one last time. I came over and looked before Mama put the pot lid down. The rabbit looked tender and full of flavor, for this was one of Mama's specialties.

She put her hand back on my shoulder, and all the good feelings surrounded me once again. I could keep all these feelings without interruption, and I didn't have to share them with the fear that we were moving. Her hand was like the warm melted butter she poured into the wooden butter molds, and at that moment, I could feel all that she ever wanted for me to become.

****

The weight of Mama's conversation hung heavily on my mind, just as the warm touch of her hand was on my shoulder. I sat on the porch, thinking. I wasn't sure what sins I had to pray for, or those I had even committed, but I did know that praying to God was the right thing to do. It had long been evident to me that prayer was necessary. It was as essential to us as people, as rain and sunshine were to a crop. Once Mama said, she prayed to God about our family, asking God to help us make it through. She was praying for our well-being, our safety, our health, and all the things mothers pray for, and I remembered what she said happened next. She mentioned she saw a snow-white dove land on her bed, giving her peace beyond all understanding. In almost a testimonial manner, I heard her declare that everything was going to be alright, and all of her fears were no longer present. She likened this to the dove that landed on Christ's shoulder after his baptism, and then the voice of God said, "This is my Son, whom I am well pleased."

This testimonial was like an imprint in my mind, a scene I couldn't easily forget, even in the short years I had lived. Indeed Mama had lived it longer, but I certainly could vouch for our struggling years. I had lived through the drinking that my father did, and the money he spent on things that were not to the benefit of his family. I had seen all of us miss days of meals due to his priority of drinking over food, clothing, and shoes, as my father seemed to be unbothered by this choice. Then, there was the instability of a home, the moving from place to place that was always haunting. I was concerned that this instability was going to be often, so much that as soon as I settled into the land of one place, I would be ripped out that place and move again.

As I thought about it all, I had to sum it all up. If Mama was not worried or fearful during our hard times, what was it that I had to be afraid of? I was amazed that Mama had believed for our family all along. Therefore, if it was my turn to believe, I now knew I could do it before I even said, "Our Father which art in Heaven."

What I began to recognize was that prayer was Mama's communication with God. This communication with God was quite different than any other form of communication I had ever experienced. People usually talked to people face-to-face or over the telephone. However, this communication was between a person and a God no one could see.

I decided to walk outside, and I could smell the earth. My nostrils seemed to be consumed with the fresh dirt. Suddenly, I could hear planes flying over my head, and their distant sound made me wonder how a plane could actually fly. I could see the airplanes dance across the sky. The white streaks that trail behind them made me feel the plane was leaving its autograph on the sky for all to see. I felt suspended between the earth and the sky, and all the wonder in between that God made. There it was ... earth for me to walk upon, and a sky for me to look toward. God, the earth, and the sky were a trilogy that appealed to my senses. Just to hear the planes calmed my being, summoning me to relaxation, and piqued my investigative mind all at the same time. The sound alone made me wonder how a plane could manage to stay in the sky.

No one but God could make all of this happen. I walked further, letting God's wonders take me on a stroll. Usually, I knew where I wanted to go. I originally wanted to take a walk to the tributary of the Coosa River, but I was led another way. Normally, I could hear birds and see some insects from afar, but my walk seemed to be guided. I saw a tree from a distance, and out of the millions of times I had seen it, this time, it seemed unfamiliar.

The branches looked like arms that were ready to invite those who wanted to come. The leaves were like fingers that pointed all that came near to safe directions. Why was I seeing this today?

A gentle breeze came by as I was standing under the black walnut tree. I looked down and noticed the walnuts on the ground. I picked one up and examined it closely. There was something about these walnuts I hadn't seen before. There was so much protection around the meat that it had a slightly "bitter-first" taste, and then sweet. First, there was a shell, then a green outer husk that was like green tar paper used to insulate old barns. When I was looking at the tree, the walnuts hung in clusters like a family of people. They looked heavy and dense, but at the same time decorative. Miss Slater had been teaching symbolism, and I guessed what I saw. I was guessing that this was how families really were – heavy and dense – some family members had too much of something that was undesirable or appeared undesirable. Yet, they were still created for a reason and designed to be a representative of something great for the cause of mankind.

Why would God go through so much trouble protecting a walnut? It wasn't alive, and it wasn't human? What was so important about black walnuts? Why did they need so much protection? As I was in mid-thought, one of the walnuts dropped on the ground. It wasn't a loud sound, but a thump. It wasn't a helpless walnut, but it had arrived at its destination. The more I looked at it, I saw it was a warrior – a protected walnut who knew where he was going. At once, I remembered something. Something about the word "falling." I repeated the phrase *falling...falling...falling...* Then I knew it. I heard it in a church benediction – "Now unto Him, that is able to keep you from falling..." Something connected within me. I knew Mama was right. God had kept us and allowed us to make it through our most challenging times. God, who made the walnuts, knew these walnuts had to leave the branches to prepare for their next stage. Therefore, as they fall, they will have protection.

If God was concerned about a walnut, He must have even more concern for us. I began to pray as Mama asked me. I kneeled and formed phrases that seemed to fall in place. Before I asked God to forgive my sins, I felt a leading to thank Him for everything first. I thanked God for the family I had and how we managed to come through our nutritional challenges. I thanked God for allowing us to live and recognize where we were and how God didn't leave us there but brought us to a place where we could see the differences.

Mama's dove experience had to be reassuring, for this black walnut tree reassured me and made everything come together. Just as people would often say the stars were lining up, Mama's faith, her testimony, and this walnut tree set my faith in order.

I continued to pray, still in the mode of Thanksgiving. I was thankful to God for sharing my brother James with us for the twenty years he was with us. The more I prayed, the better I felt. It was an unbelievable connection that I was having with God. I was sure I was going to hear from Him, and as it turned out, I was hearing from me. I was hearing what I was saying, what I had not been saying, and what I would forever be saying. Thanking, God was freeing. It was the acknowledgment of His work and what he had done for my family and me.

Oh, how I was glad that Mama had talked to me about accepting Christ. That talk led me to a place that let me see things on my own terms, but through the lens of God's journey at the same time. The day I prayed under the walnut tree, I continued so far out on a journey of Thanksgiving that I forgot to ask God to forgive my sins.

CHAPTER 16 – OUR PRESIDENTIAL PROJECTS

I had to admit that when I went back to school, I felt as though I was gliding through the hallways of Talladega County Training School. I saw Charles in the hall, and he told me it was his day to present his President. It was my preference to stay in the mystery, for I wanted to be excited to hear who he chose.

"I didn't know Theodore Roosevelt was a hunter," Charles said.

"Yeah, I didn't either until I did the research," I said.

"Well, when I looked up..."

"No...don't tell me!" I interrupted. Let me be surprised.

"Okay...do you want some clues?" Charles said in his friendly way.

I trailed off and saw my whole first-grade year flash in front of me. The roars I heard seemed to all come back at the same time. "Bill, Bill...Bill!" Charles yelled.

"Yes..." I had forgotten where we were in the conversation.

"My president is from..."

"No! ... I want to guess and be surprised," I said.

"I thought you wanted clues," Charles said.

I trailed off again. The sight of Maude Barnett passing by made me think of how she made me wear that musty black dress. I had to admit I was angry, and maybe a little sad, that I had experienced something like that.

"Bill, do you want any clues?" Charles asked again.

"I'm going to wait and be surprised," I said as close to normal, without letting Charles know I was swept up in a storm of memories. I was reliving the first grade, at the sight of Miss Barnett, while talking to him at the same time.

I took my seat and quickly started thanking God for the classroom I was in, and the nurturing by the brilliant Miss Slater. Most of the anger left, but I could tell that enough had stayed. It felt like something was in my throat, and it needed to get out, but I couldn't clear it. All the coughs and "umpums" wouldn't make it leave. It was also like a tie too tight that needed to be loosened.

I was glad I could pray and could do it without anyone hearing me. Communication with God this way was absolutely great. I could pray without saying anything out loud.

Things were more apparent now. Before, I really didn't know what sins I had to ask God to forgive me for, but I knew now. However, I knew why I needed to pray, and additionally, I knew what area I needed prayer.

"Miss Slater, if it would be okay with you, I would like to present my president in the form of a mystery. I would like to tell the facts, and the class will have to guess what president I researched," Charles said.

"That will be fine, Charles. I think that will be an exciting way to present. That way, the students will really have to listen to what you are saying," Miss Slater anxiously agreed.

Charles had a big smile and was ready to start. One girl raised her hand to ask Miss Slater a question.

"Can we take notes...can we write down some things that he is saying?"

Miss Slater replied, "You all are all full of great ideas today. This should be exciting!"

"Now, did everyone hear the question? It was about taking notes. While your classmate is presenting, you can take notes on the facts he gives about his president," Miss Slater stated. "This is a great way to learn information about the other presidents that you didn't research."

All the students grabbed paper and pencil and were ready to listen. We all felt we were in some time machine going back to the past. Surprisingly, we all looked as if we were happy to go to a place long before our time.

"Okay, Charles, you can begin!" Miss Slater alerted Charles.

Charles began with a booming voice. It wasn't so loud that we couldn't follow. Actually, it was the kind of booming voice that was just right to keep us alert and interested. I heard words like "Old Tippecanoe" and "Battle of the Thames." I didn't hear anything that rang a bell yet.

Charles was midstream in his presentation, and I still didn't know what president he had. This really was a mystery that I was beginning to wish I hadn't taken on. I wondered if I hadn't told him that I wanted it to be a mystery to me, whether he would have presented like that. Maybe I should have let him tell me who he chose. I guess that would have given me an unfair advantage.

Nevertheless, as I listened further, it did make it more interesting. I had to get real honest with myself. What if I didn't know who this president was when he finished? Was I going to be disappointed that I didn't know? I decided not to be hard on myself. If I didn't know who he was, this was going to be a time that I could learn.

"This president only stayed in office for just thirty-one days." I thought about this. Only thirty-one days. Who would assume the office of the president just to stay thirty-one days?

'He..." I almost blurted my thoughts out. *He was killed, wasn't he,* I almost said, but realized that wouldn't have been what Miss Slater wanted us to do. Nor would she want us to raise our hands during someone's presentation. She would like us to ask any questions at the end, and I could understand why.

Only Charles would decide to ask to do a presentation like this to make a president sound so interesting. My mind became hinged on the thirty-one days; I had to force myself to listen to the end. I was glad we could take notes, so I had a focal point to keep me on track. I had a few notes on my paper. He was born on February 9, 1773; he was the ninth president. His nickname was Old Tippecanoe, and his father signed the Declaration of Independence. He gave a long speech in the cold, with no hat or coat. His bad cold turned into pneumonia, and he died.

Charles was wrapping up, and I still didn't know who this president was. Well, there was one thing I could say about Charles' presentation – it was interesting.

We all applauded, and we were thoroughly entertained. We didn't know who he was talking about, but we did know that we enjoyed it.

"Do we have anyone who has any questions for Charles?" Miss Slater asked.

"So who was this president?" someone asked.

Miss Slater jumped in and wouldn't allow Charles to answer.

"Charles, don't answer," Miss Slater said in haste, but not in a mean tone.

"Boys and girls, I have an idea, let's see if we can research this answer in groups and see what we come up with," Miss Slater said.

I thought that was a great idea.

"When you find the answer, put it on a piece of paper and place it in this jar," Miss Slater continued.

I looked at my notes. This couldn't be that hard. All I had to do was find presidents who were born in the 1700s and narrow it down from there.

While some were working on arithmetic, each group who was researching Charles' president rotated every fifteen minutes.

I saw smiles. I saw perplexed looks on faces. Some didn't have notes written, so that made it harder for them to start. One person remembered a fact or two, while others thought they heard a date.

Our turn had not come up yet. I thought I better get back to my arithmetic and strategize about the research when we were called up. Charles had to feel good that he had made a change to the routine of our class. No one had presented as he had. Those of us who had already presented started with the name of the president. Afterward came all the facts about their life.

It was our turn, and we huddled together like football players in a circle. I had my notes, and some of the other people had some too.

"He was the ninth president. We ought to start there," someone whispered.

"Yeah, we could start there," another voice said.

"We can't use the encyclopedia, because we don't know the name," someone said.

"We can look up presidents in the encyclopedia, and then they can give us a list," a different voice added.

"Let's do that," said a voice that had spoken before.

I didn't say anything; I listened. I went to get the "P" encyclopedia, and I turned to the presidents, and there was a list.

"There it is!" A voice that had not spoken before shouted.

All of us looked around at the same time, thinking we were too loud, but Miss Slater didn't mind. She realized that we were in the moment of learning, and that was what she really cared about.

"Okay, boys and girls, time is up, and we are going to reveal the answers," Miss Slater said.

I rubbed my hands together with excitement. I knew we got it right. I saw another girl across the room smiling, so that made me think that she and her group had the correct answer also.

"Charles. since it was your presentation, I'm going to have you draw the names out of the jar, and you can tell us which one is right."

We were Team Four. Miss Slater gave us all team numbers on a paper, and we just had to write our answer on the back of it.

Charles, being his upbeat self, took center stage with his smile and approached the jar. You could hear the spines straightening up, as they were excited to see if they had the answer correct. Charles' magnetic personality also had students eager to turn toward him and hear everything and anything he had to say.

Charles put his hand in the jar and pulled out the first paper. It was Team Two's answer.

"Charles, don't say the answer out loud, just say whether it is correct. Is that the correct answer?" Miss Slater asked

"Yes, it is!!!!!" Charles responded.

Team Two roared like a lion and clapped fiercely. They were smiling ear to ear.

"Are you ready for the next team, Charles?" Miss Slater asked.

"Yes, ma'am," Charles said.

"Here's Team Five, and their answer is also correct."

The cheers were pouring in, and they were jumping up and down.

Miss Slater was happy also. She could see that students understood the importance of research.

"Miss Slater, I have another correct one," Charles said, as he switched the order of delivery.

Instead of Charles calling the team's number first, he revealed whether the answer was right and then the team's number. He was going to have fun with it.

"It's Team Four!"

I yelled, jumped, and clapped. I saw all the people on our Team jumping around like a party was going on.

Just when we thought Miss Slater was going to make us silence our celebration, she joined in. I guess with three teams getting the answer correct; it was worth her jumping up and down also.

"If these last two answers are correct, everyone is going to have an extra fifteen minutes of recess," Miss Slater said.

Another roar came over the class. I saw people crossing their fingers and putting their hands together in the form of praying hands. This was my time to go to the communication that I knew best. As new as I was to this communication with God, I thought to thank Him first. I thanked Him for allowing us to get the answers right, and I also thanked Him for letting the other teams get the answer right. Then, I chose to ask God to let us have a little more recess, even if the answers were wrong. The answers were not going to change in the jar, no matter how hard I prayed, but I could pray that God would touch Miss Slater's heart to give us more recess.

Charles still had a smile on his face, and he pulled out the next slip of paper. His face was still and expressionless. The class was silent, and the tension that could be felt throughout the room.

"It's correct!" Charles said, changing his face to a smile.

"You fooled us!" a voice said.

Charles didn't say a word but smiled slyly. He had gotten us.

There was one slip of paper to go. I decided that whatever happens was going to be okay.

"Charles, it's your last one! Let's see if everyone got the correct president's name," Miss Slater said.

Charles reached his hand into the jar. It felt like minutes turned into hours. He unfolded the paper, and Charles was expressionless again. His brow furrowed this time, and I saw him swallow.

"Come on, Charles! You can't fool us again," a student said.

"Alright, Charles, give us the report!" Miss Slater said spiritedly.

Charles didn't move. He didn't say anything.

"Come on, Charles!" a voice said.

I had never seen Charles this still. If he was fooling us, he was doing it. He was keeping us on the edge of our seat, waiting in anticipation.

"Charles, don't keep us waiting," Miss Slater spoke softly. "We are all anxious to get the report."

"Miss Slater," Charles said and paused.

Charles wouldn't say anything out loud, but he whispered something to Miss Slater.

"Class, we had four teams who got the answer correct. I want to tell you that I am proud of all five teams because I know that all the teams learned something and learned about the process of research. I have come to a decision. Because Charles made a great presentation, which made everyone listen, take notes, and do further research, I'm going to let him and a friend of his choice have fifteen minutes of extra recess. As for the other students, I am giving you ten minutes of extra recess."

The class roared with excitement, and everyone was happy.

Charles looked at me across the room and signaled to me that I was the friend he had chosen. I knew I couldn't change the answers that were already written in the jar no matter how hard I prayed, but who knew that I would still get fifteen extra minutes of recess, even though all answers were not correct from the class? Who knew Miss Slater let Charles choose a friend? Who knew it would be me? No one but God.

****

"Charles, you sure made the class fun!" I said as we were running to the playground.

"When you said you wanted it to be a mystery, and you didn't want to know the president, I thought, 'I'm going to let my president be a mystery to everybody.' I didn't know if Miss Slater would let me do it, but I thought I would try," Charles said.

"Well, we all were glad you did. Thanks for picking me to come to recess."

"I should be thanking you. That word, "mystery," stayed in my head," Charles responded.

"I thought all the teams were going to get the name of your president right," I said.

Charles had that same look on his face and when he furrowed his brow while pulling the last paper from the jar.

"I didn't want to tell the bad news. Everybody's dream of having more recess was going to be dashed," Charles said.

"Charles, I prayed before you pulled out the last paper."

"That all the answers be correct...right?"

"No...I would have prayed that earlier before we all started to write our answers if I had known we were going to have more recess if we got all the answers right."

"How did you pray? Whatever you did must have got us more recess," Charles said.

"I prayed that God would touch Miss Slater's heart no matter the outcome," I said.

There was the furrowed look on his face again.

"Well, it worked!" Charles said.

I could tell Charles heard me, but he would rather get the "particulars" of prayer later. I understood. We ran around the playground, which seemed like hours. The other kids were just as happy with their extra time. When it was time for them to go in, we still had five minutes. Miss Slater nodded to us and put up her hand, "blinking" her four fingers and thumb. We gestured back, with our thumbs up, letting her know we saw her.

There was another teacher who always went in five minutes after us, so we could use her class as a gauge to get back on time.

CHAPTER 17 – TRYING TO FORGIVE MISS BARNETT

"Lord, thank you for today and our class. It was a class that was exciting. I realize I can call on you wherever I am, and I am thankful."

I found that I was praying out loud. I thought I was going to pray silently, but as I was standing under the tree, where it felt like shade was around me only, there was a calmness, ease that let me pray out loud.

Breezes were swaying, and the leaves on the branches looked like hands were reaching outward toward me. This was such a comforting scene as I was continuing to pray. I felt I was on an island where only God and I were standing. Time appeared to stand still in the midst of my thanksgiving, and it was a feeling that could have lasted eternally.

However, it was time. Time for me to make a transition in my prayers. I knew it was time to ask God to help me with my feelings towards Miss Barnett. The anger that was seething within me in the hallway could not compare to the placidity that was surrounding me. I wanted the breezes to cleanse my memory, and blow all the debris of Miss Barnett's abrasive demeanor away.

Nevertheless, I knew it didn't work quite that way. I was going to have to communicate with God and asked Him to forgive me for having the feelings I had toward her. But even in the midst of placidity, I was suspended between keeping my feelings of anger for Miss Barnett or staying in the breezes of thanksgiving. It was like I was between two very opposite ends. I could ask God to forgive my anger towards Miss Barnett, which felt like it would require me to forget everything Miss Barnett did, as if none of the horrific encounter with her didn't really exist.

I wasn't quite ready to let Miss Barnett off the hook that easily. If asking God to forgive me for being angry at Miss Barnett was going to wipe her slate clean, I wasn't ready to make that deal.

I prayed more, thanking God for the day, and all that he had done, and continued to enjoy the breeze, shade, and the leaves on the branches that were fanning over me.

****

"Junior, where have you been?" Mama said softly and with concern.

"I've been over by the black walnut tree praying, Mama," I responded

"So, you've been asking God to forgive your sins..." Mama said.

I shied away from the question. "I was thanking God for what he did for me today," I said, hoping she wouldn't ask me to explain.

"That's exactly what God's word says. 'Enter His courts with Thanksgiving.'"

I felt a little better. She didn't question me further, she supported my 'Thanksgiving.'

"Well, Junior, I want you to continue to pray, and again. You will know when God hears you." Mama stated.

"I will, Mama."

It was like she knew I had not fully asked God to forgive my sins. At first, I didn't know which ones I had. But when I saw Miss Barnett, I knew. I didn't want to ask Mama right away about this feeling I was suddenly getting about forgiveness, so I thought I would just put my thoughts on something else.

****

I had been to the walnut tree now for thirteen consecutive days. I would go the same time every day a few minutes after school to pray. I was keeping my commitment to Mama to ask God to forgive my sins, and accept Christ as my Savior. Looking around, I could tell the sun would be setting in about an hour, and dusk would cover the land.

Time was drawing near, but it really wasn't a race against time. I had heard a revival was coming to our church, and I wanted everything to be in order. Being in this service would be my outward confession that I wanted Christ to be my Savior.

Revival for some churches was a big tent meeting with people coming from all over the country to hear visiting ministers preach the Gospel. It was not that kind of revival. However, there was going to be a visiting minister. Something about an out-of-town preacher made people feel they were hearing a new version of the Gospel, some version that made them want to be revived within themselves. I didn't hear Mama say these words, but I could hear the people talking about a "Rev. So and So," who was going to bring the house down, and make everybody jump and shout, and take off running around the church.

What Mama told me was to be prepared. Pray for forgiveness, accept Christ, and when the revival comes, you give the preacher your hand, for you would have already given God your heart.

I had been keeping these steps in my minds daily as I returned to the black walnut tree. The forgiveness step was attempting to wrestle within me. I had always heard "forgive and forget," but how could forgetting be possible? This equation to add forgetting to forgiveness made for a fascinating combination, and I did not know how to arrive to such a sum. How was I ever going to forget the awful things that Miss Barnett had done? How? I knew forgiveness meant to stop feeling anger toward someone, but how could one turn the faucet of anger off toward someone who did such horrific things? I had lived through the abuse of Maude Barnett for a year and a half, and I had the memories to prove it: Daily beating with switches from day one, sitting in corners, wearing dunce caps, and musty dresses. My hands were blue on the inside from the beatings, welts were on my legs from switches, and my eyes were swollen from crying.

Although I am no longer in her class, the sight of her causes an eruption within me like a volcano. How am I to stop this hot lava from moving forward, spewing into only God knows where? This scene actually hung in my mind after I had these thoughts. I had seen volcanos in books at school, and I knew about the eruption of the lava, ashes, and gas being dangerous to those surrounding it. Was I dangerous?

Was I dangerous to myself and others? Could this volcanic liquid fall out somehow and surround me, and keep me from what I needed, and me from it? I just didn't know. If I let go of the anger, it would be as though Miss Barnett did nothing wrong. She didn't deserve any favors. She didn't deserve to be set apart from what she had done. Did she didn't deserve to be released from her wrong doings?

I had experienced enough with Miss Barnett to be scarred for life and to never work to my full potential. I had heard Mama talking about how she wanted all of her children to work to their full potential, but when I was with Miss Barnett, I couldn't add, couldn't read, and couldn't color. There I was, a little dark-skinned boy afraid to learn. Afraid to attempt anything. Everything I did was wrong. I did nothing right in her sight, and to her, I was simply wrong.

I began to wonder how I even loved school at this point. Being so deep into a dark abyss of pain, how Miss Slater and Miss Gibbs got me out was nothing short of a miracle. They were angels. Yet, after receiving the brutal beatings from Miss Barnett, I would have thought I needed a legion of angels. After that ordeal, I would have guessed that I would have needed angels visibly standing around me so I could see them at all times, ensuring my safety, physically and mentally. I would also need some fluttering of their wings around me, giving me constant assurance of their presence while giving me peace of mind.

There was that breeze again that always met me here at this black walnut tree. I could count on it like knowing that the sky would be up, and the earth would be underneath me. I began to furrow my eyebrow like Charles when he was perplexed. Just as I was thinking about angel's wings, the breezes blew in a manner that seemed deliberate, like they were on some assignment from God.

I had to pause my thoughts about Maude Barnett for a moment, because these breezes put me at ease just like Miss Slater and Miss Gibbs did. I closed my eyes and let breezes surround me. There was a peacefulness that wrapped around me, like a cocoon. I, at this moment, felt nothing could disturb this bliss of peacefulness, unless I invited it.

Unless I invited It ... Unless I invited it ... Unless I invited it. I held onto this thought. Is this why I was so peaceful in all the fields where we lived, and all the creeks, and natural bridges? Is this why I was so peaceful hearing the birds, frogs, and seeing the fluttering butterflies. Did I not invite the thoughts of Maude Barnett when I travelled to see God's creations? Is this what was happening? Was this the key to help my anger pass? Had God arranged these moments of peace all along?

The questions were mounting in my head, and not necessarily in any particular order. Was God around all the time? Was He around when I had this ordeal with Miss Barnett? Could this be why I would be able to learn later on, even though I was educational stunted in her class? If these breezes could put me at ease in this moment, as I paused from thinking about Miss Barnett, would God continue to let me experience the features of His creations and move me beyond anger?

Maybe I was onto something here. No, God had to have given me these thoughts. I reviewed it in my head. If I had to pause from thinking about Miss Barnett to fully experience the breeze, I could enter into a place of peace.

"God, will you continue to allow me to be in the midst of your creations, to teach me and to help me remove the anger of Miss Maude Barnett? Will you help me to not invite the thoughts of her, but to concentrate on the beauty of your formations?" I prayed this out loud and listened. I let the breeze continue its play of touch and go, only to return again. Then I heard a walnut fall. It had a thud with a slight roll. I guess it was time to descend from the branch to the ground. I picked it up, and like the others I had examined, they were all different in their own way, only this time I got a chance to see this one fall and land, taking its intended journey.

CHAPTER 18 – THE MOURNER'S BENCH

The piano seemed to be playing a tune of its own. If I hadn't known any better, I would say the piano got the spirit. The choir sang differently from on a Sunday, and the people who were normally quiet had a tap in their feet and clap in their hand.

The songs were in a rhythmic pace. The kind of pace that made the people feel the shouts and echoes of heaven. It was a thunderous sound that filled the soul and the people rejoiced. The songs seem to go on for a solid hour, yet it was probably shorter. The voices and clapping stimulated the mind and body, not only immediately, but hours later.

"Can I get an Amen?" the preacher asked.

I didn't know whether it was just one "Amen" he wanted, but if he did, he got many more. He got hundreds of them and they kept coming. He got a few "Thank you, Jesus," and "Lord, you been good to me" phrases mixed in also.

Kyser and I were kneeling at the mourner's bench. Aunt Lillie Mae wanted him to come to revival too. We had been there since the beginning of the service, and actually it was our fourth night of the five-day revival. I couldn't imagine why it was called a mourner's bench. Why would anybody be mourning? I guess I could be at least thankful the bench was on the inside. Mama told me when she was a child, and was on her journey to accepting Christ, there was an actual log behind the church in the woods. The new aspiring converts would go down there and sit, while older people prayed over you. With all the copperheads in Alabama, this had to be a scary feeling that clung to the mind. Surely, those praying were secure with being in the woods, believing that their faith would far exceed the appearance of any snakes, but some of children must have been haunted within their imaginations.

Kyser and I had been at the Mourner's Bench, and we were waiting on the spirit. It was totally different for me and Kyser to be in such a close proximity of each other and not talk or at least whisper. This, however, was not the time for us to talk or communicate, even with gestures. The church deacons were praying over us, as we were praying as well. I had to admit all the sermons had been stirring, and if anyone had not desired to walk in God's way, these sermons would have convinced them.

I wondered what all the other children at the mourner's bench were thinking. Did they ask to go to mourner's bench during this revival or had their parents encouraged them to go as Mama encouraged me. It crossed my mind as to what kind of preparation they did before they came to revival. Kyser was the only one I knew who was coming, but we didn't talk about anything that referred to it. We didn't talk or ask any questions, and maybe that was the way it was supposed to be.

I was glad that I had gone to the black walnut tree. Each day, I felt God's Spirit around me. However, it wouldn't be until the last few days that the scales of anger fell away. When I focused on God with thanksgiving, it was like a snake shedding his skin. Just my reflections of this made me go back into a session of thanking God for all he had done at the mourner's bench at this moment, and how he had shared His creations with me. I thought of Grandpa Robert's land and saw scenes of all the places we had lived, along with the ecological advantages God had allowed me.

The choir sang another song, this time it was a slower-paced song, not one where the tempo was fast. I continued thanking God, and I thought I was even saying it out loud. I had been used to praying out loud at the walnut tree, unashamed, and not worrying about how it sounded.

In the midst of the singing and shouting, I was within a peaceful place. It was a place that was just like the preacher painted referring to the scriptures, as the peace of God surpasses all understanding. My being was mirroring this. It was as if I was in an abyss – totally opposite of the most terrible, horrific day one could have. My focus was no longer the dreadful things that had happened to me – not the lack, the licks, or the lingering questions that would sometimes haunt me. I felt an elevation ... more like a levitation ... where I was carried beyond myself. I felt like I was miles, no, more like an eternity away from my normal thoughts. Actually, I could not reach any thoughts of turmoil within my mind. I was just suspended between time and space, and between flesh and spirit. There was no above or below, no front or back, no side-to-side, just a suspension, where I was hinged upon peace … peace surpassing, moving by, going around, and never coming in contact with my understanding. If I could have seen my understanding, and touched it with my hands, peace would have fully engulfed it.

During my suspended journey, I was free, and nothing could enter my mind and nothing could pollute it. Then suddenly, without warning, I felt a sudden release, where there was something pouring out within me, or maybe it was something pouring upon me.

Tears fell like rain coming down. I was not crying an open cry, but the sign of tears made me feel this was a cry. There was no sadness, no loss, nothing that I could explain that would make this act a cry, but instead, it felt like a fountain within me. I couldn't stop them, for the tears came without my consent. I couldn't control them, I couldn't stop them. They just kept coming.

Mama left the choir stand and brought me tissues. She returned. But as soon as she returned, more tears fell, and she made another trip. This whole process repeated over and over, and it seemed like Mama must have made a hundred trips, yet this was no burden to her. She fully understood the magnitude of this journey, and this is why she wanted me to experience it.

I don't know how long this journey lasted, but I started hearing people say, "I think he's got it!" and "Praise the Lord." I felt a breeze. Someone was fanning me. I got up and moved slowly around. My balance wasn't as strong as I knew it, but someone was taking a hold of my arm steadying me.

The whole church was rejoicing and clapping incessantly. There were more thunderous sounds ringing out now than when the choir sang.

****

Friday night revival held a special place in my heart. I was able to sit in a pew and was no longer required to kneel at the Mourner's Bench. Mama had explained to me overnight why the word "mourning" was a part of the bench. It was because those kneeling are mourning about their sin, and seeking God to show them how to live, as He desires. Before she had explained it to me, by the time I got up after my dizzying state, I could pretty much put together why it was called "mourning."

I was glad that a new life had emerged from within me, and I was glad that I had traded in my anger for God's focus for me. I looked at life differently now that I was seeing it through His eyes and not my own.

I almost glided when I walked through Talladega County Training School. This was nothing magical but indeed spiritual.

I remembered the scripture: "And be not conformed to this world: but be ye transformed by the renewing of your mind, that ye may prove what is that good, and acceptable, and the perfect will of God."

My mind had definitely been renewed. Mama, nevertheless, reminded me that this was no one-time activity. This was an ongoing activity, where I had to continue a constant relationship with Christ. She also told me I would not have to go to the Mourner's Bench again, but I would have to continue to pray to the Lord without ceasing.

A tune suddenly came into my head. This wasn't a song featured in the revival, but it was a song that somehow visited me in my mind.

"Oh, when the saints go marching in, oh when the saints go marching in, oh, I want to be in that number, when the saint go marching in."

Each word made me attentive to the overall meaning. I guess this was preparing me, as I listened to all the songs as a new convert – it was not the tempo or a thunderous sound that I was focused upon now. It was the words and the passion that they accompanied each song. Everyone I saw singing from choir to congregation wanted "Jesus to come by Here," or they "did not want Jesus to pass them by," when they sang songs like "Pass Me Not Oh Gentle Savior."

I looked at those who remained at the Mourner's Bench, and I saw something that I would have never seen, had I not been there myself. I knew what it was like now to be on "both sides" of the bench. While at the Mourner's Bench, I didn't know or understand everything about it when I first knelt, but now that I had experienced it, I knew that as someone on the "congregation side," I should be praying for those who were there.

I was not sure whether those still at the bench were worried about getting up or whether they were worried about having a particular experience. My goal was to pray that all would seek the power of God and allow Him to move them within Him as He wished. What I did not know was how all of them prepared before they came to the mourner's bench, but nothing could change that now. God was in control now and could meet them where they were, and I felt all I needed to do was pray.

A beautiful song began, and the words just seemed to be parallel to my prayer.

I want Jesus to walk with me
I want Jesus to walk with me
All along my pilgrim journey
I want Jesus to walk with me...

My own experience had indeed been a journey, and I prayed that those at the mourner's bench would see themselves also on a journey. This would be a walk, taking them from where they currently are to the place to where God would want them to be.

My cousin Kyser had gotten up shortly after I did, but I could hardly focus outside my own experience. When we got up, the deaconess and mothers of the church took us away to a nearby pew and were fanning us, where it seemed many people were surrounding us. There were five now left at the mourner's bench.

I continued to listen to the words of the song and prayed at the same time. I thought about Mama and wondered how I would have accepted Christ if she had not talked to me. Would I have done it on my own, would I have been encouraged by someone else, and would it have been years later? There was no absolute answer, but I had to be thankful for my mother.

Not too long afterwards, I saw two people get up from the mourner's bench. The wobbly knees underneath the body were present. They needed to be stabilized with the help of the Mothers or Deaconess of the church. The thunderous reception was in full effect. I clapped and rejoiced as well. It was an exhilarating feeling to experience and see those that had this experience. It had to be a time to rejoice, when two more people get a chance to meet God in a time and space, where no one human could possibly interrupt or intercede.

"These are two more for God's kingdom," the preacher said.

"Unless you change and become like little children, you will never enter the kingdom of heaven," the preacher continued. These children have been seeking God and met Him at this time. Some of you older folk out there, there is room for you too. You do not have to be a child to accept Christ, for that is not what we are talking about. You must become childlike as you obey, as you listen, and as you honor God, as you are with your own mother and father."

Right in the midst of his address, another thunderous roar came. Another person was coming up, but not wobbly, and no dizzying effect.

"Another one for the kingdom," said the preacher.

Well, there was one more to go.

"Church, let's continue to pray. We have one more seeking," the preacher said.

He began to pray, and the people answered him outwardly with many "Yes Lord's" and "Hallelujah's." There was swaying in the congregation, a movement that went side-to-side, where people were waving their hands, as the preacher was praying.

The choir sang. This time it was a slow hymn – more of a meditation. Everyone could tell the congregation in the church was praying for the last one at the mourner's bench.

****

Mama could tell that I had something on my mind.

"Junior, I know you have a question," Mama said inquisitively.

"Well, I do," I said reluctantly.

"You want to know why the last person didn't get up from the Mourner's Bench," she said. "Remember when I told you about accepting Christ?"

"Yes, Ma'am."

"Well, I told you I wasn't trying to rush you, but I wanted you to be ready by praying to ask God to forgive your sins."

"So, he didn't do that?" I asked.

"I'm not saying that. I am, however, saying that he may have needed more time," Mama said.

I was beginning to understand.

"Will he be able to go to the Mourner's Bench again?" I said.

"Yes, he will, and we will continue to pray for him to seek God, as God will direct his path."

This conversation was different from the conversation I had the night before. We spoke briefly about my Mourner's Bench experience. It was a quiet conversation, one of acknowledgment. It was not congratulatory or one of fanfare. Mama was welcoming me to a new life. I was now going to have a Comforter. She was happy that I was saved and would have protection from the adversary because I now had a relationship with Christ. Mama was proud that her son had put on "the whole armor of God."

It was late, but sleep was far from my mind. When Mama and I finished talking, I began to prepare for bed. I could hear my father's footsteps from a distance. It was not the thud sounds of the time everyone had harvested my first peanut crop. There he walked like a man with stone legs, stiff in disbelief that we had done such a task. This time his walking was lighter, where it seems his joints were more flexible.

The sheets on the bed were softer than usual. Maybe my senses were sharper. Therefore, I had never noticed them before. I reflected on the week of revival, and if I didn't know any better, I could still hear the songs that were sung. It was like some internal thermostat was inserted within me, and I could recall the songs from Monday through Friday in order.

I found myself humming the songs, where the humming turned into singing. I was not loud, although I was singing out loud, I was mindful that it was after midnight, and everyone was trying to rest.

For some reason, I was without the memory of going to church five days in a row. This was indeed an important feature. My mind kept playing the service over and over. I had already heard the songs, but now it was taking me through the sermons. I just chose to let them playback to me as I listened intently. My father was still up, and I could hear the chair move as he pushed it back under the table. Perhaps he heard all the sermons of the week in his head as well.

As my mind was still "playing" all the sermons, and I was on day four, Thursday. I could not only hear the service. I could see myself kneeling, and praying. It was at this point I could see the tears that Mama had wiped and wiped and wiped. My senses had alerted me of something, as these tears were falling. The tears were cool as they were streaming down. It was like they had come from a spring that was always refreshing to the visitor. The tears that I had came from Miss Barnett's beatings were so hot they burned my face. Even the tears from Mama's spankings felt different upon my face. They were not exactly hot, but were warm, yet admonishing.

When I compared all three kinds of tears, there was something I could see that was revealing in the tears at the mourner's bench. They were tears, which were cooling and cleansing. They stayed on my face and did not seem to move quickly. They held on to my skin as if to fan outwardly across my face and not run downward. There was a purpose within these tears.

I found myself getting sleepy, but I wanted to explore the thoughts of these tears more. I could not have imagined this process. Only God could bring these thoughts to my mind, and I felt a need to explore them further.

We were all standing at the creek, some of us looking down and some of us looking forward. I had a giddy feeling, but still respectful thoughts, as we were lining up. It wasn't the solemn feeling, I thought I would feel, but one of joy. All the paintings I had ever seen of baptisms seemed so quiet that the only sound one could hear was the water surrounding the person when they were immersed, right before the minister would say, "In the name of the Father, the Son, and the Holy Ghost." Yet, it wasn't the quiet setting I assumed.

I was in the last stage of my conversion. What I had long recognized, this was not the last and the only stage. There was more: I had to live a holy life and not a life of going through the motions.

I couldn't remember having this much uniformity with anyone or any group. We were all standing in white robes, each waiting for our moment of baptism. But long before that would come, we had a mini-service. There was no sermon or preacher, but some songs and addresses.

The older members sang like it was an audition, and it seemed like a celebration that they were happy to see us baptized.

I wanted to look around, but I didn't want to be disrespectful. I didn't want to be noticeable looking around, but I was sure that some cottonmouths were out there. If I knew Alabama as I thought, there were some lurking below. However, I was positive that God, who I had prayed to so earnestly, would keep them at bay. I believed God had already ordained that the cottonmouths couldn't swim to where we were, and if so, they were out of their appointed jurisdiction. It made me think of the story of the frogs in Egypt and how they couldn't come any further than the distance God wanted them.

The songs had moved to a kind of hum. This was not birds humming or bee's buzzing. This was a tune that I had only heard Black folk do. It was a wordless moan and almost a groan. It was a culmination of "Amens," "The Lord's Sho Been Good to Me," and "Can't Nobody Do Me Like Jesus," within their souls, and it was an earnest cry out and praise to God. They wanted Him to know they were singing to Him.

I saw some of the converts in line with me getting restless. There was an anxiousness in the air, and some were ready to get in the water. I didn't know what to expect about being baptized. Mama had told me that a girl who was baptized with her came up shouting. I had to admit that God had blessed me richly at the mourner's bench, and I was open to experience whatever He wanted me to have.

I took a quick look around, not meaning to fall out of the uniformity of the group who was looking straight ahead. Looking into the faces of those who were around us, I was humbled. Not all were family members. Not all were members of the church. Some were from surrounding churches who came in to support our step in the direction of Christianity. I felt his decision was not just about me, or even Mama, who got all of this started, but it was about the community – all who were going to depend on us to carry out what God had started for mankind.

"Young people, you have decided to follow God, and if you follow Him wherever you go, He will lead," the preacher said. Lots of "Amens" followed, along with other confirming phrases.

"This is your outward expression and confession of your faith in Christ. You have turned from an old life of sin to a new life in Christ. We welcome you to this new life."

The preacher and his helper signaled for the first candidate. The first person moved toward them. They whispered words to him, and with their hands on both his arms, they dipped him backwards with a quick immersion. There was no reaction other than the boy spit out a little water and wiped his eyes. I thought the crowd was going to applaud, but we could tell they held it back. There was a feeling of happiness and rejoicing that hung in the air.

The same procedure happened with each candidate, and then it was my turn. Both men took each of my arms. Their grip was firm, and I was ready for my immersion. I looked to see what was in front of me to see the last vision before my baptism. I didn't want to turn and look back, so I relied on my memory, where I saw the faces of the people who were there supporting us. I virtually felt their "support" holding my arms as well, and I relaxed my weight.

My last look was my reflection upon the water. I saw myself as I was, and I wanted to remember this memory. I could see my white robe, the preacher, and his helper. My reflection moved in the water, rippling back and forth. I could have looked at my reflection for a long time, seeing my old self before my new upcoming self.

"William, we baptize you in the name of the Father, Son, and Holy Ghost," and I held my breath as the men fully immersed me.

The water came all around me, and an enclosing feeling rushed over me for just a moment. It was quick, but the water wrapped around me as if to saturate my body, and then released me. When I came up, everything looked exactly the same, and I'm not sure if I thought it was going to be different. However, there was one thing that I knew. This baptism was a symbolic washing away of my sins, whether everything around me was the same. Yet, what was most important was what would be different, and this difference would be how I would allow God to lead me, and I would not lean into my own understanding. I was now armed with the vision of Christ as a new creature, and I turned around, looked at Mama, and smiled.

CHAPTER 19 – MR. ARMSTRONG

A few years had gone by, and things in my life were finally progressing. Nevertheless, some things were at a standstill. Taking a long look around Alabama, I didn't see where I would be getting to a place where I could progress in my life in the full manner in which I would like to. I was now in tenth grade, and I wanted to be able to know what kind of life I was going to lead.

The day I pulled off my white baptismal robe at the creek, I did put on the whole armor of God. That didn't mean I had become perfect and was ready to ascend to heaven by any means. What I meant was outfitted from my head to my toe with everything God desired to give every member of His flock. I was wearing the "sandals of peace" because things that once troubled me were no longer haunting me as they once were. I remember the mention of moving to another house made me feel as if rugs were pulled from under me. At the beginning of any conversations that began with, "I need to talk to you," made my heart sink. I would fall into the wonders of "why's" and "what's going to happen now?"

It turned out that we moved not only once, but twice since I was in fifth grade. First to the Gamble Place, and then our current residence, the Tom Jackson Place. It didn't make a difference whether I knew the particulars as to why we were moving. I just chalked it up to my father's decision not to pay the rent, or he couldn't pay the rent. Although my father's decision to go back to church helped him see his family in a different light, I did, however, feel he should have seen this all along. He finally fed and clothed us properly, which made me believe that instead of a conversion, he had an epiphany. It was still very much evident that some of his former irrationalities were still present.

Many of my middle school years had been filled with absenteeism in certain seasons. Papa would ask me to plow, and I didn't have most of it done by the time the bus came in the mornings, even starting as early as six. Even though I missed some classes, activities, and even some tests, my teachers would allow me to make up work and take tests that I missed. These were teachers that had seen my efforts and knew I was driven to get my school work done.

After plowing in the field in the morning, my walking did not stop there. I would walk approximately eight miles to school, and be wringing wet with sweat as I arrived. The walk would take me over utility lines, where gas ran underground. I would be in the midst of lots of weeds in the spring, with grass growing wild. I recognized I was the only child my father had home, with the exception of a niece and a nephew who lived with us, so maybe that is why I was tasked to do these duties. Although, I was hoping for my father to see the benefit of me having an education, where tending the farm would have been more of his responsibility, at least during my school hours.

Taking a deeper look into this picture of my life, I somewhat felt like this was all it was ever going to total. No matter how I added it up, this was it for me. I could add a perspective, I could subtract a perspective, and I could even “carry” some other ones. However, my father was only going to see me as a farmhand. I had to admit, no one loved plants, farming, and God’s total environment as much as I did. I had examined the differences between poisonous and non-poisonous plants, inspecting lots of thorns and bristles. It was also thrilling to me when I planted my peanut crops, tending to them from planting to harvesting. I felt a sense of responsibility and hope, as I could see my hands producing. There was a comfort in understanding how the sowing and reaping process worked. As it related to my life, I had gone over it again and again, “I wanted to add greater opportunities into my life so that I could become someone great.”

I had come to some thoughts of my own and asked Papa for over two years if I could join the military. His responses were like blistering blows, the kind you hold your stomach and cough deeply and uninterruptedly in an attempt to recover your balance. Had he been standing in just one teaspoon of dust when I proposed my question, he would have kicked up that same amount of dust into a storm that would have covered the entire city of Talladega.

"Hell no, you not going to no military. You need to stay in school. I got work around here for you to do." His booming voice surrounded me, submerging me deeper into my ambitions.

I chose not to respond. No reply was needed. He was trying to get me to change my mind, and not even the force of his words was going to get me to do that. This was often a tactic of his that he practiced on some of my siblings, where they would become so intimidated, they would take leave of their initial thoughts. Subsequently, this was not going to happen to me. I was just going to bide my time and add more preparation to my plans.

Grumbling on ever further, my father said, "There are fields to be tended to. We got to get this work done before winter. All these fields got to be plowed. Ain't no need of going to the military, when you can work and make a living here."

This was precisely why I wanted to leave. My father was forever going to see me as some farmhand, someone who was always needed on the farm. I had to make some decisions, and I had to ask myself: When am I going to pursue any of my talents and interests beyond Talladega if I don't leave? Am I ever going to know more about the plants God has shown me? When will I be able to explore more about those plants that are poisonous or non-poisonous?

Although my father's words were forceful and were intended to be a blow, I postured myself in a resilient position, and I didn't let it bother me. I knew the day was coming when I would enlist, even if I had to enlist at a time when I no longer needed his permission.

****

Charles and Kyser had finally met, and we were one fun trio just as I had always predicted. Kyser came to Talladega Training School in the ninth grade, and we were always looking forward to meeting at school. It couldn't get any better when we found out we were all in the same class. Now, we were together again in the tenth grade.

I always imagined us hunting together, and doing some farming together, like planting peanuts and harvesting peanuts. It wouldn't have mattered to me if we just walked around for hours in the fields and meadows, just laughing and talking. Between all of our humor, we could walk and talk about anything, and that alone would be the entertainment.

When Kyser and Charles met, there was no warming up period. They simply clicked. Charles was his jovial and adaptable self, and Kyser had his down-to-earth and accommodating personality.

"Well, this year is going to be a good year," Charles said optimistically, as we were walking into school. We had a few minutes to spare before it was time to go inside for class. "Just two more years and we will be out of here. Out of Talladega County Training School. It's doesn't look like I've been at this school going on seven years."

"This is my second year, and it's not too bad. I actually like this school," Kyser chimed in.

"Bill, you've been here every year from the beginning, haven't you?" Charles said.

"Yes, I've been here since first grade," I responded.

I was proud of myself. I didn't dwell or even speak about the first grade and all

the chaos.

"Just two more years. I can't wait!!!!" Charles said with a booming voice.

"I can't imagine what that will feel like, being finished with high school," Kyser said.

I was thinking, but I couldn't share in their enthusiasm. My dream of leaving Talladega was so far in the forefront of my mind that I could have left right there on the spot. I would have said proper good-byes and let everyone know I cared for them and thank them for all they did for me, but I would have taken a fast exit.

"I've been asking my dad if I could go to the military," I said.

"I'm sure he will be okay with it," Charles said. "He will have two years to prepare for you to leave.

I gathered from Charles' response that he didn't understand what I meant.

"I've been asking my dad to sign for me to go before I graduate. I was hoping to have been gone by now."

"Wait a minute. You mean you want to leave before high school is over?" Charles questioned, with that furrowed brow that always shows when he's really perplexed.

"What is your Mama saying?" Kyser added before I could answer Charles.

"Well, Papa was really mad and told me there was work to be done on the farm," I said, abbreviating what he really said. "Mama really hasn't said anything."

They both had looks of despair on their faces. I could tell they didn't understand why I would want to go to the military.

"When I look around in Talladega, I have to ask myself, what is here for me? Where will my life go? I've been thinking about these questions often, and I have thought about them for the last couple of years now.

"Do you think you would have more answers within two years?" Charles asked as Kyser agreed.

"I just don't think there is going to be anything that will be different. I have lived in seven different places since the first grade, and I want to be able to be in a position where I know there will be stability. As long as I stay in Talladega, I will always be plowing fields or working in a factory at best, and I don't believe this is going to give me what I think my life needs. I also know there is no money for me to go to college. If I had the money to go to college, I wouldn't think of leaving."

Charles and Kyser had looks on their faces that revealed they were beginning to understand.

"Well, when you put it like that, I can see where you are coming from," Charles said.

"I'm still thinking about what my Aunt Grace might think, but I do understand what you mean," Kyser added.

The school bell rang, and we all ceremoniously walked inside.

****

"William, I want to talk to you," Mr. Armstrong said.

I didn't wonder or worry about what it concerned. Mr. Armstrong was the kind of teacher that everyone should have in their lifetime. He was not only a teacher but a listener, a friend, if anyone could process the meaning of a friend. He was able to see students and know their good and bad characteristics, but not hold it against them. If anything, he was there to smooth it all out – to spackle in the places that may have had rough patches.

When he said he wanted to talk to me, I knew I wasn't in trouble, and if I were, he wouldn't present it as trouble. It would be a gentle correction or a life lesson that would challenge anyone to do better. When I said, "Yes, sir," responding to his request to talk to me, I didn't know then, it would be one of the most important conversations of my life.

CHAPTER 20 – NEW FARMERS OF AMERICA CONVENTION

"I want you to make a presentation at the New Farmers of America Convention. It will be in Tuskegee, Alabama, on the campus of the Tuskegee Institute. I will give you the topic soon, and we will have months to prepare."

I swallowed. I had to catch my breath, quickly, silently, for I didn't want it to be evident that I was caught off guard. Mr. Armstrong was asking me to attend a convention, go to Tuskegee, and give a speech. The three kept going in and out of my head, and I didn't know how I was chosen. "Tuskegee," "Speech," "Convention," this time, the words were moving around in a different order in my head.

"William!" Mr. Armstrong said.

I quickly composed myself. I didn't want Mr. Armstrong to feel I was not composed as I was listening.

He was the type of teacher who was not just any teacher but an academician. He did everything with precision, and every rhyme had a reason. Yet, he didn't do it with arrogance, or teach with the stance, "I got mine, and you got yours to get." He was reachable, not in a place where students felt they could never live up to his expectation. He taught with a sense of community, where every decision he made was going to have a rippling effect. It was not only to reach the student he was teaching but those all around.

"Yes, sir," I said.

Mr. Armstrong chuckled, "I chose you because I know you are going to do a great job. The New Farmers of America Convention is a great place to see what project students across Alabama are doing. The work you and the other students here at school should be showcased as well, and I think you are one of the students who should do it," Mr. Armstrong said emphatically.

I didn't need to be sold. If Mr. Armstrong wanted the class to meet at a local hog pen, make observations, and write up our findings, I was there. I trusted that whatever he wanted us to do it had great significance.

I don't even remember saying the word "yes." I suppose I did. But surely, I gestured it, if only in the gleam of my eyes.

****

The bell rang, and it was time for lunch. Kids were in the hallway, making their way to the cafeteria. I couldn't tell whether kids were hungry or if they were glad to have a break from classes to see their friends.

I was walking along, where my feet felt they were moving to a tune in my head. It was no known tune that had been penned, just a happy tune in my head that Mr. Armstrong's good news had given me.

"William, you look like you won a million dollars!" Charles said.

Charles' voice somewhat shocked me ... I suppose back to reality.

"I ... I ..."

"What are you trying to say?" Charles jumped in.

"I'm going to Tuskegee!" I said.

"When?"

"It will be a while."

"This doesn't have anything to do with going in the military, does it?"

"No, this is for school ..."

"College?" Charles raced in without letting me finish.

"No ... this school."

"What?" Charles said.

"Mr. Armstrong asked me to go to Tuskegee Institute to make a presentation at the New Farmers Convention."

"Oh yeah. He picked the right one. Are you going to talk about your peanuts? Remember when you planted your first peanut crop. I remember asking you, 'how do you keep the mule from walking on the plants?' and we laughed...."

Charles had trailed off into his memory of my crops and kept talking. I could tell that was his way of letting me know he was excited for me as well. As much detail as he remembered, I thought he would be an asset to the process of any agricultural project.

"Well, congratulations, William! See, you are getting a chance to leave Talladega!"

I knew what he was getting at. If I left Talladega if only for a little while, I might not want to leave school and go to the military. I knew he meant well, but I had a lot of thinking to do, and my life could not be left to chance.

"Thanks, Charles."

Before we knew it, lunch was over, and it was time to go back to class.

****

I had to admit, it did feel like a million dollars to be recognized by a teacher for academic achievement, and that teacher actually wanted me to compete in a speech contest. I couldn't shake it and nor did I want to, for if I could have kept this feeling and bottled it up for years as a keepsake, I would have just been able to revisit it at any time.

I had many of my teachers at Talladega to thank for preparing me with the confidence to sit down and delve into a project with the belief I could bring it to completion and be quality work. After leaving fifth grade with Miss Slater, my sixth-grade teacher, Ms. Drake, kept the academic wheels turning in mind. It was a continuation of Miss Gibbs. This felt like a five-year educational plan from second to sixth grade, which was designed for my learning style with three teachers, where the lessons linked and synced. They were appropriately paced and continued right where the other left off each year. I knew this was not by the school's design, but I was a firm believer that it was by God's design that school moved for me this way. He knew my struggles, strengths, situations, and this was His way of anointing my path.

Now in the tenth grade, I had the same teachers from the seventh grade, but a different teacher for each subject: Miss Hopkins for English, Mr. Phillips for Math, Ms. New for Science, and Mr. Rossa for Social Studies. Mr. Rossa left to teach another grade, and Mr. Cokely replaced him in my eighth-grade year. This was by the school's design that teachers would follow the students in each grade. However, I still was a firm believer that God had orchestrated this model also. Students benefited immensely because the teachers knew the strengths and challenges of each student, knew where they left off each year, and how to catch them up.

When it came to Mr. Armstrong, I had him in the ninth grade, so this was my second year with him in Agricultural Economics. This was the type of class that boys took, as the girls took Home Economics. The first year we had learned about animal husbandry, raising cows, chickens, hogs, farming, and more. This second year was geared toward applying what we learned. We had small projects in the first year, but this year we were going to put into practice what we had learned. Many students had become members of the New Farmers of America Organization, where we were going to plant, observe, harvest, raise animals, and determine what would be the best farming practices.

It was great to have an organization like the New Farmers of America. This was an organization created to accommodate Black students in the south who had farming interests. Future Farmers of America was the organization that was created for White students with farming interests. However, Black students were not allowed to join this organization. Hence, in 1935, the New Farmers of America created their organization where Black students could join, participate in activities, and compete in contests and other leadership activities. Three men were responsible for this organization: Dr. H. O Sargent, George Washington Owens, and J.R. Thomas.

I was glad to be a part of this organization. Since farming was what I had seen all my life, it was great to take a class under Mr. Armstrong that introduced students who lived in farming communities to understand more innovative aspects of farming. Many farmers had done things by trial and error or based their farming decision on knowledge passed down to them. With Mr. Armstrong's leadership, students were introduced to and furthered their knowledge of agricultural practices.

****

I looked over the football field, and it was without me. The guys on the team were running and practicing, blocking, and intercepting. I was upset that I couldn't be there. Papa made sure I was not at practice. I had an appointment to pick cotton, and he made that clear. This statement was precisely one of the reasons that strengthened my decision to leave Talladega. It was not only picking cotton but all the other work Papa wanted me to always do. I didn't object to working. I pretty much had established that I had a good work ethic. However, it was the fact that he didn't seem to make school a priority for me or any of his children. It wasn't all that long ago that food, clothes, and shelter weren't the top priorities. I guess since he raised those areas higher on his priority list, the school could stay where it was, where it had always been. Seemingly at the bottom.

I got on the bus begrudgingly. I knew my fate as soon as I got home. The whole ride home, I reminisce about playing sports as if I perhaps could play professionally.

When it came to playing sports, I believed I was good at them: track, baseball, and football. Yet, there was never any practice time that my father allotted me. As fast as I was on track, I couldn't make it to practice, and the same thing was true for the other sports. Once, when I was able to compete at a track meet when the baton was passed to me, I shot out so fast, I was able to pass my competitor, who was actually thirty yards ahead of me.

I grabbed the sack, flung it over my shoulder, and headed for the field. Just as always, the hot "Talladega Sun" was out front and center, and right there to meet me. I rubbed the sweat from my eyes, as it was coming down before I even started on the first row.

I almost went down the "Why Blvd," wondering "Why couldn't I be out on the football field? Why couldn't I practice?" but I stopped. A breeze passed me by, reminding me of the walnut tree I stood under years ago when I was in a conundrum of thoughts. A "conundrum," a new word Miss Hopkins had added to our vocabulary list. I had written down the meaning: A confusing and difficult problem or question. That was surely a word that I could place in many areas of my life growing up. When tested, I was going to get that one right, and I would be able to use it correctly and write a sentence if needed.

I bent over to approach the cotton plant. I carefully pulled the cotton off the boll. If not too careful, it would prick my fingers, and blood would trickle on the cotton. Blood in the cotton was not a good thing. It was hard enough to get a pound. It definitely was not good practice to have to discard cotton that had blood on it. Every bit of it was needed to make the pounds.

I made a point of judging the distance just right before I pulled the cotton off the boll. I didn't want to leave cotton in the burr, which was called cow licking, and that was leaving money on the plant. Looking carefully, I took the cotton from inside the bolls. As a child, I would see Mama pull the cotton off the bolls, and she could pick hundreds of pounds a day.

Picking cotton was not for the faint of heart. This was hard work, requiring attention to detail, and usually, the surrounding heat made it seem like a person riding on your back.

After going many rows, I stood and decided to look at the whole field and survey the land with my eyes. I scanned and looked from side-to-side, and I remembered the view. No, this was not going to be the vision I was going to see for the rest of my life. I decided with everything within my being that this was going to be the very last year of this.

****

"Okay, boys, we are going to get the wheels turning today. Let's design a farm with forty animals, fifteen acres, and three types of crops of your choice. I will want to know what kind of animals, what kinds of crops, and how these fifteen acres will be used for the benefit of this farm."

I had ideas that were turning rapidly in my head. I had lived on seven farms, and I had a preview in my mind of how each of those farms was laid out, and how I would lay out my own. I never thought of owning a farm before and making one my own, but this was an exciting challenge.

I first thought of Grandpa's land. There was a large space to run and roam, and a big barn to house all the things that were harvested. This was a great place to start, and then add things around it. Additionally, I did like the tributary of the Coosa River that was at the Carl Leonard Place. The spring was nearby and could give water, whether it was for drinking, washing clothes, or watering animals if it was needed.

Many ideas were spouting forth like a fountain. I wrote down the things that I liked most about each place we lived, and thought of what might be best when I sketched my farm.

I wouldn't say I was disadvantaged when it came to not having livestock. We didn't have cows, pigs, goats, and chickens, etc. We had one cow or one mule at the time. What I didn't realize was this: Just like the "city boys" were going to have to research and imagine animals on a farm, so was I. However, this was not going to be that difficult. It seems like I was going to need that tributary for the animals that were going to need water.

****

MAMA'S RESPONSE

"Son, this is great news. You will be going to Tuskegee in April with Mr. Armstrong?" Mama asked.

"Yes, Ma'am," I replied.

"Tell me what it is you will be doing?" Mama asked with excitement.

"I don't know all the details yet, but Mr. Armstrong wants me to make a speech at the New Farmers of America Convention."

"Well, you are no stranger to the stage. I remember when you were in the *Womanless Wedding,* and you were so excited. That's when you got your first stage experience and truly thrived."

"Yes, I remember. I was so glad that Miss Gibbs helped me," I said.

"You and Bertha were on the stage together, saying your poems," Mama said enthusiastically.

I smiled and remembered all the good things that Talladega County Training School had contributed to my educational growth. There's no doubt that I would have never been considered for making a speech had it not been for Miss Gibbs and Miss Slater catching me at a young age. They built my confidence and relieved me of my fears about public speaking.

"Junior, we want to make sure to prepare ahead of time to get you ready for Tuskegee. I'll start getting the suitcase ready for you to pack your clothes as the time gets closer," Mama said.

If it was anything I knew, I could count on Mama to make sure things ran smoothly for me.

PAPA'S RESPONSE

"So, you are going to Tuskegee," Papa said, as we were at the barn putting the cotton inside.

I really didn't know whether he was making a statement or asking me.

"Yes, Si...."

Before I could get the "r" on the end of "Sir," he continued, "So you are going to be gone for a week."

I knew what was on his mind. His farmhand was going to be absent. What was he going to do without the benefit of my labor?

Closely I observed his demeanor. He actually furrowed his eyebrow the way I used to see Charles' brow when he was perplexed.

"Un-huh," Papa said.

I had heard this before when he realized everybody had gotten the peanuts in when he was gone five years ago. When he made those two-syllable sounds, there was something that turned over in his mind. I was almost positive that he wanted to object, but he wasn't. He couldn't bring himself to do it. He had kept me from football, kept me from baseball, kept me from track, but this time was different.

Furthermore, Papa dare not go up against Mr. Armstrong. He met him last year when I was in the ninth grade. Mr. Armstrong traveled to his students' homes in our community and the surrounding communities to see the projects the boys had done.

Papa let me raise a little bull that our cow had. We were assigned to raise an animal or grow a small crop. I fed it, watered it, brushed his coat, and cared for it. I kept charts and notes on how much he ate and where he grazed. Mr. Armstrong told us that he would be coming by to see how everyone's project was going, and that's when Mr. Armstrong met Papa.

The day Papa met him, I could tell that Papa respected him right away. Papa shook his hand, and he and Mr. Armstrong started a conversation. Even though they were talking, Mr. Armstrong fully engaged my father in the conversation, yet he was still fully observant of my project and all our other agricultural developments. I saw him put his hand on my father's shoulder, confirming a point perhaps, or maybe admiring something my father said. Before Mr. Armstrong left, he put his hand on my shoulder also, and said, "Great job, William," and checked off some squares on his clipboard. For the remainder of the day, I had a smile that was almost permanently affixed to my face. It was practically waiting for me in the morning.

"Going to Tuskegee," he repeated. He must have been trying to get the thought of me going to Tuskegee to sink in. Then came an "Umph." I knew he had reached an internal wrestle inside. A conflict where he was at war with himself: wanting me to work in the field, or having to explain to Mr. Armstrong I couldn't go. He wanted nothing more than to say a flat out, "No," or maybe the same "Hell No" that sprang forth so quickly out of his mouth when I had asked about going to the military two years ago. But this time he couldn't. There was no way he was going to go up against Mr. Armstrong. Deep inside, he respected him as a man and as an educator, and the thought of having to explain to him why I couldn't go was going to be a contradiction that I felt he didn't want to present to Mr. Armstrong.

Mama had obviously told Papa because I just didn't choose to say anything to him. It wasn't that I thought Mama would soften the blow; I just didn't feel he was going to respond with a positive emotion anyway. If anything, telling him I was going to Tuskegee was going to make him acknowledge that he was going to have to put more time on the farm for one full week.

I heard the same thuds I heard when he walked through the house at The Carl Leonard Place, after the peanut harvesting, where his legs were clay. His legs spoke the volume that he didn't. This whole day mirrored that one.

No benediction ended this conversation. It was just a dialogue that fizzled out like bubbles disappearing on a soda.

I left the barn, ready to haul the next load of cotton to the barn.

CHAPTER 21 – THE PROJECT

I saw Charles and Kyser from a distance, and I couldn't wait to talk to them.

"Hey, Charles and Kyser!" I said, ready to go into my question.

"I already know what you are going to ask," Charles said.

"I know too," Kyser jumped in.

"Well, since you do, let me have your answers," I volleyed.

"I'm going to have chickens and hogs on my farm because I want to eat a lot of fried chicken and a lot of ribs!" Charles said without any shame.

"I want the same thing, but I want it to have a lot of pork," Kyser replied.

I chuckled, and before we knew it, we were laughing for what seemed like an hour.

****

"Do you remember what we were working on last year when I asked you, 'How's your project coming along?'" I asked Charles.

"Yeah, I remember, I asked my mother about getting some bitties," Charles said.

"What did she say?" I wondered, thinking she probably had a few reservations about this project.

"She said it was alright as long as I did all the work. She said she did enough with chicken's herself as a child, and she was finished," Charles said.

"Now, thinking of last year, we chose animals or crops."

"I know you didn't even have to think up anything to do. You had a whole lot to do where you lived. You could have picked anything," Charles replied.

"Yeah, but I did something different from what I normally would do and solely focused on an animal," I said.

I thought about the cow that my father made Ruth burn up. I quickly moved on from that thought.

"I was glad I raised that little bull," I said.

"Yeah, you talked about him, and how he was growing," Charles said.

"I didn't get a chance to raise Will. We got him when he was about twenty years old. Of course, I fed and watered him, and I certainly have plowed enough with him, if I had the chance to go back in time, I would like to know what it would be like to have raised him from the beginning," I said.

"Now that we have to create this farm with twenty acres, forty animals, and four different crops, I can see how last year's project makes sense to prepare us for this project. After seeing how much land was needed for the bull, I might not need forty of them, but a combination of animals and crops," I continued.

"You're right, Bill. Those chickens blew up from fitting in my hand to becoming really big. Then, they wanted to strut all over the place. Why didn't you tell me I would need to put up a fence or keep them in a coop?"

"I thought I told you how chickens are..."

"I must have heard you, but had a totally different perception about chickens. They want to roam everywhere."

"...Or they stay in a coop," I added.

"Judging by the way that the chickens were, I can see how to put the 20 acres of land to good use."

"Remember, that means barns for storage, crops, and where the livestock is going to eat, sleep, and graze," I said.

"We didn't have a budget with this, did we? Is there an amount we can spend on all this. I mean, not including the house and farm equipment? Those items would already be there," Charles wondered.

"I don't remember him saying that."

This time I furrowed my brow. This would be a totally different deal if Mr. Armstrong added that to the task.

We both let the air circulate around us for a moment, and a still quietness took over. I took a deep breath, and so did Charles.

"Why don't we ask Mr. Armstrong? That will help us with our approach," I suggested.

"That's adding more on. I figured he just wanted to know what we would have on a farm and see where it all would be placed and write up why we chose those crops?" Charles said emphatically.

I had always known Charles to like change and didn't mind going into any area to start a new venture, but he was distant on this project. Something didn't exactly feel right about the way Charles was acting.

"Charles, he may want us to stay within a certain dollar amount to see if we could run and create a farm on that amount. Take $200. We could buy seeds, and animals like chicks, pigs, depending on how much we can buy."

"Well ... I guess ..."

"Charles, we'll just ask."

"William, I don't want ...

"Charles ... I don't think he would just want us to create a picture of a farm ..."

Before I could finish, he jumped in.

"I know, but I think he wants a drawing or a model, and a written paper on why we created the farm with these animals and crops, and how they work together," Charles said.

"Now I see how that probably is what he wants," I said slowly, yet still thinking.

"So, are you going to ask him about a budget?" Charles said, trying to confirm that I wouldn't.

"I tell you what, when we get to class, let's listen carefully and see what he might want," I replied.

"Even if you do, I can see your point. If we were farmers, we really would need to know our expenditures."

"Now, you are thinking like a farmer, Charles."

"Don't get too excited yet, I'm not joining the club," Charles said.

"I got some Galaxy overalls for you," and in good Charles fashion, he laughed, and then I laughed, and it was time for our first class of the day.

Feet were scuffling and moving quickly. Paper and pencil were placed on desks, all while the wind was shuffling in the process. Hurried students were walking quickly in the hallway, heading to their destination, and a book or two fell trying to get to class on time. None of the students wanted to get to Mr. Armstrong's class late. Mr. Armstrong had standards, and it was expected that students arrive to class just like they were going to a job. Mr. Armstrong stressed the importance of arriving on time, and "doing your very best in all that you do," as he always stated. He emphasized that we were members of the New Farmers of America, and we should represent the organization, whether in class or in the community. Every young man joined the New Farmers of America at ninth grade in Talladega County Training School, and it was a real honor to be a part of this association.

"Good morning, boys," Mr. Armstrong said in a deep voice. His clothes were neat, pressed, and matching, always parallel to his demeanor.

"Good morning," we responded like we were in church doing a responsive reading in the back of a hymnal. That's the kind of uniformity he commanded, not a sloppy "Good morning" that lingered on and on as if students were sarcastic.

"I want to talk about your projects. I know you have to create a farm with twenty acres, crops, and livestock, and I want to know how that is going."

Charles looked at me. I knew he wanted to know if I was going to bring up a budget.

"So, Mr. Armstrong, do we draw our farm and place everything on it, like the crops and animals?" a student asked earnestly.

"Yes, I do want you to have a model of some kind. It depends on what kind of supplies you have. Some of you can draw it on a 22 x 34 piece of paper and indicate where everything is. Then, some of you can make a 3-D model, where you may have clay figures of the animals, and add things as you like."

"So that's all we have to do?" one student said, hoping that was all.

"No, there is much more to the project."

I could hear some hesitation in the air, but it certainly wasn't a loud objection. No one would disrespect Mr. Armstrong in this way.

"I am looking for how you would utilize twenty acres with livestock and crops, according to your interests. Also, I'm looking for how much it will cost you to run your farm for one month."

Charles and I looked straight at each other, knowing exactly what the other one was thinking. We widened our eyes for emphasis, for we knew there was no need for the budget question. It was basically self-explanatory. But I needed further clarity.

I put my hand up and looked at Charles, and I could tell he had green lights in his eyes for me to ask whatever I wanted. He, too, wanted clarity.

Mr. Armstrong, "What would be the type of things you would be looking for when it comes to cost?" I asked.

"William, I've visited your farm, and you had a bull you raised. You had to feed him, how much was that? Did you all buy the feed? If so, how much? You all have a mule that plows and needs food also. How much was his food? How much were the seeds when you planted your crop?

"Yeah, William, you had a peanut crop way back in the fifth grade, and you told me your father let you buy some seeds," Charles inserted.

Mr. Armstrong didn't get upset that he just said it without raising his hand. He was glad to see Charles' enthusiasm and glad that he was able to recognize that a crop didn't just come up voluntarily, as some boys never had any experience seeing one. Mr. Armstrong was glad that Charles had at least experienced the understanding of raising a crop, if by no other way, but vicariously.

The other students in the class were beginning to nod. They were beginning to see what Mr. Armstrong was trying to get us to learn in the project. I wasn't exactly right about a budget attached to begin a farm in the project, but I wasn't exactly wrong. I thought he would probably want us to find out how much it cost to set up a farm. As it turned out, Mr. Armstrong wanted the operational cost for a month, which was going to require us to research and prove how much it was going to cost to keep a twenty-acre farm, with four different crops afloat.

I was eager to see this project through, for it made me wonder how my father made calculations as he farmed. What did he put into an equation from the Thornton Place to the present? Actually, I had to wonder if he really made any calculations, or did he just work day by day, and letting whatever happen, happen.

****

"Look at the direction this project is going!" Charles said.

"I know. It wasn't exactly what I thought, but it did have money involved. I had a feeling we were going to have to calculate something," I responded.

"Well, you had a huge part of it right," Charles said. "The good thing is, we get a realistic view of how to run a farm, and how much things cost."

"Yeah, you are right. We can see our expenditures and then see what we would profit later," I said. I quickly wondered whether my father ever had a starting point with how much things cost and what he spent. I pulled my mind away from the thought, knowing that I already somewhat knew the answer.

"Mr. Armstrong is going to make some farmers out of us after all," Charles said like the jovial Charles I knew. He had finally arrived at a restfulness in the project, and I was glad. I think because he had not experienced a farm first-hand, he was a little apprehensive, but he seemed like his old familiar self.

****

There was something about being in Mr. Armstrong's class that really was the center of my studies. It was as if his class was the sun, and the earth rotated around it. Just as it takes 365 and a quarter of a day to rotate fully around, it felt like the same rotation when it came to Vocational Agriculture. Mr. Armstrong enveloped all of us the entire year during our ninth-grade year, and it continued as our tenth-grade year was progressing.

As my focus was aligned, all the other classes fell into place. What I really could see was how all the other subjects were utilized as we worked on Mr. Armstrong's projects. This project was a practical lesson that was requiring our background knowledge from math, science, history, and English.

The mathematical focus was obvious, but we were going to execute the other core subjects in our project. If I knew Mr. Armstrong, the write up was going to need to be very detailed, including the history of farming practices, and how weather plays a part in producing certain crops.

****

"Kyser, where have you been?" I asked. "We haven't seen you at lunch or in the morning?"

"I was talking with ..."

"I know, what's her name," I teased him.

Kyser had a girlfriend, and he was splitting his time with me and Charles and her. Charles and I understood, but we still joked him incessantly about it.

"So, what animals are you going to have on the farm, Kyser?" Charles asked.

"I'm going to have a few chickens, some cows, and some pigs," Kyser responded.

"We're just glad you can focus ... on your studies," Charles said.

We all had a round of laughter again. Kyser didn't get mad; he actually joined in.

CHAPTER 22 – FESTIVE TIME OF YEAR

The lights were festive, and the auditorium had turned into a Halloween Haven. We didn't have the live bats, but it was someone's idea to have live owls. This was a school tradition; who started it? I don't know, but a selection of boys would go in the woods and catch the owls and have them sit on a ledge in the auditorium as they let out a succession of hoots. It was our annual Halloween Dance, and it was something the entire school looked forward to attending.

The song *Still a Fool* by Muddy Waters was playing, and even though it was a Halloween Dance, the music didn't match the theme, just the decoration. Halloween Dance didn't mean we were going to be spooky and turn into goblins or mummies. We were going to dance at Halloween time.

Across the room, teachers were standing at their designated areas, but they weren't confined to them. That's what was so great about the teachers at Talladega County Training School's dances. They were there as chaperones, but they were also festive in their nature.

"There's Charles," I said to Kyser. He and I had ridden together in his father's truck.

"He's dressed up," Kyser said. "I guess he could leave here and wear the same clothes to church."

We didn't see Charles dressed up often because we didn't really see him on the weekends. We mainly saw him at school.

"He sure is," I agreed.

The girls were dressed in Sunday dresses, and some had party dresses with shiny material, I was guessing silk, and some dresses were made of chiffon. I knew that because I had heard mama and the girls talking about it.

"Hey, hey," Charles said as he made his entrance. Up close, he seemed even dressier. It was evident that he took his time. The shirt was pressed, shoes were shined, and he had on a tie with a tie pin.

"Charles, you went all out for this dance," I said.

"You sure did!" Kyser followed.

"What's a dance without us looking sharp. You guys look great as well," Charles said with a booming voice.

I had to admit, I did. I pressed my slacks and had a crease that was at its sharpest. My shirt was crisp with extra starch, and I had a tie that was my "special occasion tie."

The song *Rockin' and Rollin'*, by Lil Son Jackson, started playing, and the floor started filling with students. It was a fast-paced song that had everybody popping and snapping their fingers in concert with the beat. Charles found a girl to dance with, I asked a girl, and she said yes, so we were off to the floor, moving the way the beat told us. We were shaking our shoulders, moving our torsos from side-to-side, and moving our heads all in some choreography of our own. The song went on for what seemed like an hour, and the dancing was fun and uplifting. When I spun around on the dance floor, I saw Kyser still standing. He was just looking, tapping his feet occasionally, and drinking punch. I didn't know whether he had asked someone, and they said no, or he just didn't ask.

Finally, the song went off, and everybody left the dance floor and moved to groups of conversations that must have enlightened them at the time. I saw people who I had never seen talking during the school year, not during lunch or in the halls. Maybe this was just a relaxed setting for everyone to be who they really were, and people just took a chance talking to everyone. For the next half hour, people were either dancing, talking, or eating. Yet, it didn't seem Kyser was ready to do that, and then I asked.

"Kyser, who are you going to ask to dance?" I asked, not wanting to be intrusive, but I wondered if he had asked earlier.

"No, I hadn't asked anyone," he said as he took a sip of his punch.

He had been to the refreshment table, where, it too, was festively decorated. Maybe he was just enjoying the punch, which was made of orange sherbet ice cream and ginger ale.

As soon as he answered, a teacher snatched him and chimed in, "He sure hasn't asked anyone," and she took him to the dance floor and started dancing. The look on Kyser's face was priceless, but it got him to the floor. This is what the teachers would do if they saw you being a wallflower. They wanted all the students to participate and make memories that they would be able to look back on forever. Kyser's face had finally evened out, and he looked as if he was having fun. As for Charles, he had been over the floor millions of times.

Now that Kyser was having fun, I was going for a few more spins myself. I think the owls had fun because they hooted throughout the evening. The teachers were right to want us to have lots of fun. We were going to remember this dance for decades to come!

****

Before we knew it, Thanksgiving was upon us, and we were all preparing for the holidays. Our school was putting up all the fall decorations, and teachers were changing bulletin boards from the summer. Things were changing at home also, as we were preparing for our own holiday time. I was counting on Mama to have her "cuisines" front and center. Turkey wasn't going to be on the menu, but Mama knew how to make anything we had to be ready for guests, even for a president to dine.

I was truly counting on the hoecakes and the rabbit stew Mama would make. Her gravy should have been jarred and marketed. It would have been a great addition to any dish with rice or potatoes. As for our Thanksgiving dinner, there would be rutabagas, sweet potatoes, and some type of green vegetables making their appearance, along with some other dishes from our garden.

Now that all the kids were out of the house except me, our family gathering would be smaller. It had been a while since many of my sisters had left and gotten married. Leon had also left a few years back. However, my nephew Thomas and niece Janet were with us, and they were more like a brother and sister. Thomas was Velma's son, and Janet was Ruth's daughter. The two of them gave the home a new beginning for Mama and Papa. I believe what they may not have seen or thought of the first time as parents; they were able to share with Thomas and Janet the second time around as grandparents. Since I was also there, I was able to benefit from these new parenting styles. It was evident my parents were trying to redo some of the things they may have done earlier but in a better fashion.

****

"Kyser, you got all your stuff ready?" I asked.

"Yeah, I got it," Kyser responded.

"Let's see what we can get today. I'll get the dogs," I said.

"We always have fun hunting, and I can't wait to get here," Kyser said.

The weather was perfect. We had on light jackets, and that was just enough. Sometimes, it would be colder, and we would have on heavy coats, and then it would warm up till we would be sweating underneath. But not today. Kyser and I probably covered about five miles alone, and through the woods. Sometimes we even forgot to target anything. We hadn't talked in such a long time, and we were just glad to be walking around, catching up.

"Junior, are you still thinking about going into the military?" Kyser asked.

I could tell he still had the idea that I would change my mind.

"Kyser ..." I took a long pause and looked over the woods. I saw a rabbit, but I decided to let that one get by and not aim at it.

"Kyser ..." I repeated. I didn't have to search for words. I just wanted to let him know it wasn't a fly by night decision. "I have worked and worked on the farms we have lived on, and I don't see how anything is going to be different. I have plowed from the time I was about eight-years-old, and I am glad that I was able to do it and glad to be a help. But Kyser, I don't see anything for my future here."

"But ..." Kyser started to say something, and I was saying something at the same time.

"This may sound like I'm saying the same thing over and over, but Papa only expects me to work on the farm."

"Have you talked to him?"

"About going in the military?"

"No ... I mean ... other options such as working outside the farm."

"He can only see my time tied to the farm as a farmhand. Look at the practices I missed. I couldn't play baseball, football, or track. Yeah, I play a few games, and then thank goodness the coaches understood that I had to work, but what if I was able to play at all the games? Maybe I could at least be considered for a scholarship to a college."

Kyser didn't want to respond in a way that was disrespectful to my father. I knew he wanted to say something, and I also knew he understood. However, the Kyser I knew didn't want anybody bothering me or disturbing anything that I set forth, so I knew he had an opinion about the matter. When anybody our age bothered me, he was right there to let it be known that he was there to put an end to it. Yet, Kyser was silent at first.

"Junior, well, can you wait until we graduate?"

"I don't see how that is going to help anything. I will just prolong my discontent. There will be nothing considerably different. I mean nothing. It will be like living the same two years over again, and I will be looking forward to nothing."

"But ..." We seemed to have started speaking at the same time again.

"This has been a long and arduous process. We have lived in seven different places. Moving and moving and moving. It wasn't until after our baptism; I could finally feel at peace. When we were at the Mourner's Bench, I found resting within the presence of God. That's when I knew I wasn't fearful anymore."

"I didn't know you felt that," Kyser said with astonishment.

"Yes, and that's why I know my going to the military is a way for God to guide me to the next stage in my journey."

Kyser smiled. I could tell he felt relieved and somewhat sad at the same time, but he knew that this must have been something I had thought about thoroughly.

"Look at that rabbit," Kyser said.

"You better aim now," I said quickly.

The gun went off, but the rabbit kept going, and the dogs went right behind it. Talking so intensely, focusing on the target wasn't really the priority. Since we didn't have to be back to the house anytime soon, we could make a full day of talking, aiming and shooting, and having a good time.

****

Kyser and I repeated the same hunting schedule on Thanksgiving Day, and we were glad to have a school break. Kyser, Charles, and I had been working hard on our Farm Projects, and we were getting rides to town to get prices for feed, seeds, and tools. Mr. Armstrong had us keep a daily schedule inclusive of people who may harvest our crops if we had to hire people to help if there was no family.

"Junior, look at that squirrel," Kyser said. We jumped up and moved into a hunter's stance.

"I think I can get him," I said.

The squirrel jumped and went up the tree, but I stayed on him. I took the gun and pointed toward the tree. I got a good targeting point and aimed. The squirrel fell.

"Junior, you got him. But I have never seen anybody shoot a squirrel and split it in half."

I had never seen it either, and we were somewhat mesmerized.

"That's got to be a one in a million shot," Kyser said.

"I sure didn't know he was going to split like that.

I picked up the squirrel, and Kyser and I continued to search and hunt.

"I'm about ready to eat," Kyser said.

"Yeah, me too. I can't wait for some of Mama's rabbit gravy."

"I think I had some once upon a time, and it was out of this world. My mama cooks rabbit with gravy sometimes too."

"I think they must have seen their mother fix it. With them being sisters, I imagined they cooked together, and got a lot of recipes from their Mama that we eat right now," I said.

"I sure can't wait to have some of those dishes when we eat today. I've worked up a big appetite just out here hunting," Kyser replied.

"Well, we can head back now. I think we got what we came for – a few swamp rabbits and a few fox squirrels," I said.

"Off to dinner," Kyser pointed like he was some captain ready to sail his ship.

We gathered the dogs and head to the Thanksgiving tables.

****

When we arrived home, the dogs were wagging their tails, as if to say, we've done a good job, and actually, they had. As I looked in their eyes, I could tell they wanted some dinner too, because they could smell it. We could smell it ourselves, way before we got to the porch.

I said goodbye to Kyser and pulled off all my clothing. I was a little damp underneath, but not to the point where I would catch a cold. Kicking off my shoes would have to do instead of untying them; that's how eager I was to get to dinner. Upon entering the kitchen, I saw Janet in the role of Bertha. She was helping Mama with the food and setting it on the table as Mama passed it to her. I imagined how wonderful it would be if Bertha and all my sisters and Leon were home. The stories would be endless about how we were worked in the field, saw witches in the barn, and so many rutabagas that sprouted from one season to the next.

"You all get ready and wash up," Mama said. Thomas had been to the house getting wood and getting water, doing chores that set the day in motion. He reminded me of myself, where he learned to plow and do the duties I did at his age.

We headed to wash up and get ready for our Thanksgiving meal. Papa wasn't there yet, but I didn't think he wasn't going to be gone that long. When it came to putting his feet under the table, he was definitely going to be there, and most of the time that I remembered, he took the biggest and best of the foods, even when the children had little.

Janet finished setting dishes on the table with Mama, and just as I had predicted, Papa came riding up with somebody he knew. He was walking without the stone legs and stepping spryly and light. His mood was quite chipper. I didn't know what had enhanced his mood, but maybe it was Thanksgiving.

"Grace, is the food ready?"

"Yes, William, it is. By the time you wash your hands, we'll be ready to sit down."

"I thought all I would have to do is sit down when I came in."

Mama didn't say a word in response to his words.

"Children, come gather around the table," Mama said, not too loud, but loud enough for us to hear. She was too much of a lady to yell. However, sometimes I wished she would. Today would have been a great day to begin. I suppose she quickly gathered the children around the table to avoid responding to the insult she just received.

This soured my mood for a second. He knew Mama was cooking all the food and doing her best to make Thanksgiving memorable. I immediately went back to the time Old Man Jim Houston, Mama's father, insulted her years back with his statement, "...See what this nigger got my daughter living in." I sighed out loud but quickly cleared my throat to cover the sigh. I didn't want Mama or Papa to think I was sighing in response to what had been said.

I just didn't like it when I thought Mama was getting the short end of the stick when she had sacrificed so much. She had ten children, worked in and outside the house on the farm, took care of her father, Old Man Jim, and dinner was still on time.

I cleared my throat again, but this time before I chose to sigh.

"Let's bow our heads," my father said. I wanted to clear my throat again, but I didn't.

"Good Lord, let us be true and thankful for what we are about to receive. Let it be for the nourishment of our bodies, and strengthen us. Thank you, Lord, for the hands that prepared this food. Amen."

I could have cleared my throat one last time, but I didn't. In my mind, I didn't want to be disrespectful, even though no one but me would have known what I was doing. My interest was not to mock my father's prayer but to just sigh or clear my throat against how I thought his remark was unfair to Mama and the time she had put in the meal.

We all said, "Amen," and Mama looked radiant as if no adverse comments had been made. She continued being the Lady of Grace she was, just like her name, as she passed Papa the sweet potatoes.

My mood lightened when I saw Mama's rabbit stew and gravy. This immediately took my mind off my father's comments. When I tasted it, it was just like I thought: Smooth and velvety, with seasonings that all blended together in harmony. The consistency was perfect, not watery and not too thick. Just as I always thought, it should be jarred, marketed, and sold to those who would love to have gravy on potatoes, or rice, or any other dish of their choice.

****

Before we could blink our eyes, the New Year had come in. It brought winds and chills and temperatures, almost welcoming, a far contrast from the summer heat. The ground was frozen solid. If anyone used a hoe attempting to weed, they would just be scraping the top, barely getting any dirt to move.

I looked around and how I wished for snow. In Alabama, we rarely saw it, like a stranger that would seldom come around. I had experienced it only twice, for that's how many times the snow had come in my short lifetime.

My sisters had a real knack for capitalizing on what we had, whether it was little or much. When the snow came, they made snow cream just like they made peanut brittle, where they all took roles like on an assembly line. Someone was gathering the snow from a clean area or catching it in something as it was falling. Someone was getting the sugar and bowls ready for mixing, and someone made vanilla flavor, milk, salt, and sugar ready.

I watched as my sisters dipped, poured, and stirred. The vanilla flavoring made brown streaks that went through everything white, like mama's rabbit gravy on potatoes or rice. Instead of staying on top, it was stirred in, and slowly the brown faded, as the once white became cream before our eyes.

What was interesting about my sisters making snow cream was that their collaboration was as interesting as their outcome. It was always good to see them work together. It was like some symphony written with the perfect melody. When the project was finished, it was an excellent treat. They would even sit the snow cream outside to make it even colder and frostier. When it was time to eat it, I could hardly wait. My spoon handle would be cold, and my tongue would also be cold and refreshed.

It would be over soon, the falling snow and the snow cream, and I didn't know which one I would miss most. It was important to appreciate the sight and savor the taste of the snow because it would be a mighty long time before we saw snow again in Alabama.

As I was looking around the yard today, it would be a long time before I would see snow, but the closest thing I could see to snow was the falling temperatures that felt like snow was coming and was on its way, but there was no precipitation planning to make the cool weather's accompaniment.

I guess I would have to wait a few more years to see snow in Alabama.

CHAPTER 23 – BACK TO SCHOOL

"Okay, boys, how are we coming along with our farms?" Mr. Armstrong asked.

"I'm having trouble," one boy said.

"What seems to be the trouble?" Mr. Armstrong said attentively.

"I don't know exactly what type of animals to put on my farm that will benefit the crops, and how the crops will be a benefit to them," the boy continued.

"Before I answer that, let's see if I can get someone from the class to help this young man with this problem," Mr. Armstrong said, looking around the room.

Mr. Armstrong looked around the room, up and down, trying to find the candidate he knew who could help this young man. I didn't divert my eyes. I looked right at him, but he didn't call me.

At first, I didn't quite understand why he didn't call on me, but then it came to me. He had an idea, and I knew he was thinking about our farm when he had visited me. I showed him what we were farming, so I knew why he didn't call on me. He wanted to see where the other students were in their understanding of Balanced Farming.

"If we have our row crops in the fall, then we will need to have cover crops in the winter to replenish the soil and keep it from soil erosion," a boy said before Mr. Armstrong could call on him.

Mr. Armstrong usually disliked students being out of order, or even speaking out without getting called on, but when it came to helping out a fellow classmate, he didn't mind. That's when the class had a living room feel, where everyone could join in, if respectfully, without raising hands.

"Young man, you are right. Balanced farming is what every farm needs to be effective."

"And, if you have animals, you need crops that can be food for them," another boy said.

Mr. Armstrong had a glow on his face. I could tell when he was satisfied with the way his students were learning.

"That's exactly right; you want your farms to work as an interlocking system, working together – animals and crops. You want the animals to be able to rely on the crops if need be, and you want the soil to be enriched by the different crops planted, so it will have the proper nutrients," Mr. Armstrong summarized.

"Take out your paperwork on your farms and see if you have crops where the soil and your animals will benefit," Mr. Armstrong requested. During this time, students could review their farm choices and see if there were any changes they should make. Mr. Armstrong was available for any questions and suggestions.

When I looked around the room, there was not one student without his work, that's the kind of impact Mr. Armstrong made. Not one student would disrespect him or themselves by not coming to class prepared.

Students worked quietly and raised their hands when they had a question or needed clarity from Mr. Armstrong. This session went on for the rest of the period, where we had about thirty-five minutes. Not one student was idle. Everyone used their time wisely, working fervently on their farms.

"William, I want to see you after class," Mr. Armstrong said as he walked by, going to a student with his hand up.

"Yes, sir," I said.

It was almost time for class to end.

"We have five minutes, so let's start winding up. If there are any questions or comments, you are free to ask or state them now." Mr. Armstrong was walking to the front of the class.

"When is all of this due?" Charles asked.

"All of this will be due before Spring Break. This will give you time to continue to research your budgets, revise your crops, add or subtract the number of livestock, and write your reports to share your findings."

I could tell Charles breathed a sigh of relief. As a matter of fact, everyone did, and it wasn't because anyone was behind. Everyone wanted to be thorough and accurate with their work because they could see the benefit of the assignment.

As I approached Mr. Armstrong's desk, he was looking for something in a folder.

"William, I want to give you the schedule for the conference at Tuskegee. Between now and Spring Break, which is the week we will be there, is going to fly by. You are going to deliver your speech on "The Benefits of Balanced Farming," just the kind of information we spoke about today. I want you to be able to define it, give examples of it, talk about different farms where it has worked, and the importance of it when one is even considering running a farm.

"Yes, sir," I said as I began to take notes on what he said.

"I want you to start preparing your speech, and we will start practicing your delivery with a few teachers. Miss New, Miss Gibbs, and Miss Slater will be excellent choices, and they are all willing to help you with your speech.

I looked at the itinerary of what would happen that week, and it began all too real that I really was going to Tuskegee. Not just Tuskegee the city, but Tuskegee the Institute, where Booker T. Washington was president. I took the paper and carefully placed it into my notebook.

"William, don't worry, because you are going to do well. I know you are knowledgeable about the benefits of balanced farming, and I have heard you recite poems now for many years."

"I'll start preparing tonight," I said.

"Here's a pass to class, because I've kept you a little while."

"Thank you, Mr. Armstrong."

"No problem, William. Have a good day!"

****

"What did Mr. Armstrong want to talk to you about, William?" Charles asked.

"He wanted to give me the itinerary for the Tuskegee trip. It's during the whole week of Spring Break."

"That's got to be a great school, and you will get to see it and be on the campus for a week," Charles responded.

"Yeah ... one whole week," I said.

"Well, you don't seem too excited. I thought you were going to be over the moon."

"Yeah, I am. By all means, I am excited. But right now, my mind is on the speech that I have to present. My speech is going to be about the benefits of balanced farming. I have a head full of ideas, and I have to bring them to the paper. I got to find a way to hook the audience and make them listen to the end.

"But this is the New Farmers of America's Conference. Everybody ought to be listening and interested," Charles said.

'Yeah ... this is about farming, and here's hoping everybody might find it exciting," I said.

"Do you remember when I presented my research on President William Henry Harrison?" Charles said.

"I sure do. We got a chance to have extra recess, and we ran and ran."

"Well, I got the idea to start with a question of guessing first from you when you said you wanted to guess who I had," Charles said.

"Yeah ... that's right," I said.

"Maybe you could try something like that when you begin?"

"That's an idea, Charles. I could start with examples of what's not balanced farming, and then finally present what is balanced farming. Umm ... I should kick that idea around and see where it goes."

"See ... and it may or may not work, but you sure look like it's getting your ideas to settle now and line up better. Don't you think?" Charles said.

"You are right! I do see some order now," I said.

"And look, you don't have to do it that way ... Mr. Armstrong may have a way he wants you to start."

"He told me to go to Miss New, Miss Gibbs, and Miss Slater to help me with tips for my speech."

"Well, you are in good hands then," Charles said.

"But you have helped a lot. The order of thoughts is much better in my head, and at least I can land. I was floating around with my thoughts."

"I was beginning to think you didn't want to go."

"No, I definitely want to go on this trip. I haven't even been to Tuskegee before."

"Me, either."

"But you have been further away, like St. Louis."

"Yeah ... I see."

"I'm planning to travel far one day."

"Don't tell me you are thinking about going into the military again," Charles said, maybe quicker than he intended.

"Charles, I never left that idea, and the idea never left me."

"I know. I didn't mean to shoot it out like a bullet. I'll just miss the idea of us being in school together."

"Yeah," I said as I took a deep breath and looked around.

"Charles, sometimes, we have to make decisions that are going to be the best for us in the long run, and I cannot see life getting any better for me in the long run."

The bell rang, and it was time for us to go to our next class. It was Biology, and while there, I could ask Miss New if she had any time to hear my speech as soon as I finished it.

****

"If a farmer has ten-row crops in the summer and no cover crops in the fall, is this balanced farming? Will his soil erode, or will it replenish?"

I practiced that entrance and wondered how it would go over. Looking out of the window, I could see Will. He was eating those crunchy, mouthfuls of grass that he so enjoyed. These were the times that I was so jealous of when it seemed that Papa took our lunch dimes down the road for good times.

"Good evening, New Future Farmers of America, I hold these truths to be self-evident," I snickered. I was not going to say that. I was just kidding around, kicking around the line of Thomas Jefferson.

"New Future Farmers of America, we are together today for a common purpose. Farming." Okay, maybe that was too preacher-like.

I decided to stop and give it a rest. I could always think of the opening later, getting to the meat of the process was best, and making a list of everything I knew about balanced farming would get the ball rolling.

"Junior, you working hard on something?"

"Yes, Mama. I'm trying to work on my speech that I have to present at Tuskegee Institute."

"What is it about?" Mama said.

"It's about the benefit of balanced farming," I answered.

"Mr. Armstrong picked the right person for the job. If he didn't think you could do it, he wouldn't have chosen you." Mama said confidently.

"I ... I ..."

Before I could finish, Mama proceeded.

"I don't know if that was a hesitation, or you want to be modest and not agree, but Junior, not many boys were plowing and planting crops at your age. I would venture to say that you know just as much about farming as the men who farm around here. Not only have you seen it done, but you have also had hands-on experience, doing it as well."

It wasn't every day I heard Mama using words like "modest" and "venture," but Mama had an excellent vocabulary. She would give us spelling tests and words to remember. When we had rainy days, she would hold spelling contests, and we loved them.

Mama was right. I had plowed and planted several crops with and without Papa. I knew the benefit of balanced farming by the time I was around twelve. However, I didn't know what it was called, but I could see then how necessary it was to farm with the future of the soil and animals in mind.

"Mama, you just gave me a great idea. I think I could write this speech in a testimonial way, as well as being informative."

Now I was using words I hadn't heard myself use. Miss Hopkins, my English teacher, was teaching us about the different kinds of writing. It was beginning to become clear now why we needed to know the different types. I wasn't going to be persuading the audience about the benefits of balanced farming; I was going to be informing them – sing some of my experiences would be the testimonial part.

"Junior, I have no doubt, not even one iota of doubt, that your speech will be outstanding," Mama said with enthusiasm.

It was getting dark, and I thought I should give Will some supper. I didn't usually wait this late, but I was thinking hard and long on my speech.

As soon as I got to Will, he looked happy to see me. I gave him a hand full of sugar, along with his usual food of oats and grain.

I looked around and pretended to be on stage. "Good morning, New Farmers of America. It is great to be able to speak to you today about the benefits of balanced farming."

I repeated multiple openings, and Will listened and ate intermittently. I was satisfied practicing, and Will turned his head to me each time I put an inflection in my voice. I extended my hands, laughed, and pretended I was in front of a big audience until the sun completely set.

****

I stretched my arms upward toward the ceiling and yawned. Before I knew it, it was time to get up. I could hear Mama calling, "Thomas," with a long accent on the "Thom" part, as she was trying to get me up for school. Next, it was "Jan-et" as if two separate names. It was time for her to get up and get ready for school next.

I already knew what I was going to wear. It wasn't like I had a variety, but I always kept what I had accessible and very neat. I quickly got ready and asked Thomas if I could help him with anything to make the morning move smoothly.

"You all get ready for breakfast," Mama said.

I could smell eggs, fatback meat, and my all-time favorite, hoecakes. This put a pep in my step, and I moved quicker. I gathered my things and grabbed the beginnings of my speech, packed it into my bookbag, and went to the table.

"Good morning, Junior."

"Good morning, Mama."

She looked at me like no time had passed since our conversation about my speech. The gleam in her eyes told me she still believed in me as much as she did yesterday about my speech.

Janet and Thomas joined shortly after I sat down. They were eager to have some hoecakes as well.

"The bus will be here in about twenty minutes," Mama said.

Mama was no last-minute person. She wanted to make sure we were all ready and had enough time for breakfast.

"Thomas, I want you to say grace," Mama said.

"Junior usually says grace when Papa is already gone," Thomas said.

"But I want you to say it this time," Mama said softly, not overpowering. He understood and knew not to refuse again. Mama was not going to blow up or begin yelling at him, but he had enough respect for Mama to not make her ask again.

"God is great. God is good..."

This was a very familiar prayer, and I knew Mama was going to have him graduate from this prayer very soon. Mama wouldn't criticize you, but she would let you know when it was time to move from a standard grace to one you could create yourself.

We ate quickly, and then we were standing outside waiting for the bus. When it arrived, there were faces that looked glad to be going to school, and some that looked like they weren't so happy to go. I quickly assumed they probably wanted more sleep, where some probably had to do morning chores. I knew all too well about this one.

Since we had a little distance to go before we got to school, I decided to continue on with my speech. The ride was going to be about twenty minutes, and I was going to use my time wisely. If there was anything that Mr. Armstrong drove home, it was using your time wisely. He would quote Ben Franklin, "Lost time is never found again." I found that he was right.

Some students were looking at me, wondering what I was doing. There were different kinds of kids who rode our bus. The ride for them was just that a ride where they thought they could "ride" others. I thought of the boy who kept thumping my head and wouldn't stop. I retaliated, and I was suspended. That changed, however, when Papa went to school. That was the one time that Papa came out to the school in my defense. Everyone was trying to tell the bus driver and the principal it wasn't me who started it, but I suppose they had their own way of screening the situation.

‘Crops must keep their soil rich in nutrients and keep their soil from erosion,’ I wrote down when a big thump came and somewhat distorted my writing. It was okay, however. I was able to erase it and begin again.

“When adding cover crops in the fall, this is one way to keep the soil from eroding,” I added.

I took a moment and tapped my pencil on the side of my head. I was in deep thought as I looked out the window for a moment, then I thought this was an excellent time to add examples. This was the perfect time to let the New Farmers of America hear the variety of crops that could be used to keep the soil from eroding.

We weren’t far out now. The ride seemed bumpier than usual, and maybe that was because I was deeper in concentration than usual.

****

We could see the school in our view, and everyone on the bus was readying themselves to get off. Children were putting on scarves, and those that had pulled off hats put them on. As for me, I put my papers and pencils back into my book bag and zipped it up, so I would be ready to go.

When the bus turned into the school, it leaned over much more noticeably than usual. All the kids said, “Wooaah.” It sounded like devastation was about to happen.

We had been in one bus accident that resulted in Claudia hurting her hand, and Papa wanted to find the bus driver and have a few “words” with him.

Soon the bus steadied. I heard all the kids exhaling behind me, but we were alright.

“Look like y’all bus was about to turn over,” Charles said.

“We were okay, but I could tell some people were scared,” I replied.

“You should have seen the faces when everybody got off. They looked white as a ghost. I think you are a shade lighter,” Charles joked.

“Nah ... I was just writing more to my speech, and putting my papers and pencil in my bookbag when the bus turned into the school.”

The bell rang, and we headed to Miss Hopkins' English class.

Miss Hopkins was waiting by the door. I could smell her perfume. It seemed like almost every Talladega County Training School female teacher had a fragrant smell and a pleasant disposition to match. After passing by her, the perfume lingered, and it was evident that this was not *Evening in Paris.* This fragrance became forever tainted in my mind since Miss Barnett wore it, and it bore the memory of her.

"Good morning, boys and girls, or maybe I should say, ladies and gentlemen. I've known you all for four years now, and I still remember you as seventh graders. We have grown together as a class, and now we must put all of our skills together to write an expository essay."

This was right up my alley. I was already working on my Tuskegee speech. I would just have to find a topic where I could inform someone about something. There were millions of topics that I could choose.

I wondered what I could possibly write about. I thought about football, baseball, and track. Maybe I would write about the rules, the uniforms, the 'how-to score.' I was in the midst of making a list when Miss Hopkins called on me.

"William, I know you are working on your speech for the New Farmers of America. Mr. Armstrong told me all about it. We are planning to help you every step of the way. Therefore, you don't have to assume another topic. We want you to have ample time putting this together."

"We know how hard you work on the farm and how you have plowed mornings and didn't get to school until noon. On top of that, you had to walk to school. Mr. Armstrong has already told us he chose you and two other young men to go to Tuskegee with him to represent our school," Miss Hopkins said.

I didn't know what to say. I was shocked and genuinely thankful for such compassion that I did not see coming. My teachers had always been so supportive, but I wouldn't have thought I would be allowed to use one assignment for both classes.

"Mrs. Hopkins, I really appreciate this! I've been working on my speech, and I want to be able to add all the right details and illustrations to make the speech effective," I said.

"William, I've known you a few years now, and I have not seen you half do anything. As your English teacher, I will guide you in the right area. It will be all your work, of course, but we will help you to reach your optimal best."

I was astonished to hear such news. Now my focus could be directly aligned with my speech. I owed it to Talladega County Training School to do my best. Giving it my all was what I was going to do.

As we all had class time to work on our expository essays, I was gifted with time to just focus on the speech. I saw students outlining and making notes for their essays. Some were making lists for a variety of topics.

I poured over my subject, adding examples, details, and illustrations. Comparisons and contrasting would be great also. Everyone could relate to things even better when they could see similarities and differences.

Just like I tapped the pencil on the side of my head on the bus, I tapped it on the desk lightly. Other ideas began flooding in, and I had to capture each one.

I realized Mr. Armstrong was right when he asked me to get Miss Gibbs, Miss Slater, and Miss New to help. No matter how much useful information I might obtain and write down, I was going to have to convince the audience and make them believe they would hear information they would one day need.

****

"You lucky duck," Charles said.

"Trust me; I'm working. Just because I don't have to choose a topic, I will be working on competing against the other students across the state. Plus, I have to present mine at the conference," I said.

"I know, William. I was just kidding. Actually, I think that was a great move Miss Hopkins made by letting you do that. I think I'm going to write about "How to Sell Anything."

"Really?" I said.

"How long have you been thinking about that?"

"Well, I always wondered how people sell things. How they can take them to town and stand on the street and sell them," Charles said earnestly

Something about the way he said it made me think he was really interested in this subject. I suppose that was the way all students should feel when they are excited about what they are writing.

"I see people selling cakes and pies and other things, and I wonder what's their secret."

"Well, it sounds like you have thought about this a lot," I said.

"I just sometimes wonder how I would make it if I had to sell anything," Charles said.

"I know one thing ..."

"What's that?" Charles asked.

"You definitely got the personality for it."

"I do?"

"Yeah, you do!" I said.

"You could have sold William Henry Harrison dolls on the day in Miss Slater's class after you talked about him. And maybe you could have sold the entire collection of Presidential Dolls. I think the students would have brought the one they researched and probably brought the one their best friend researched," I added.

"I didn't know the kids enjoyed that so much. You talk about me presenting about William Henry Harrison often, so I guess it made kids remember it."

"You did, Charles," I said with encouragement.

"Well, I guess I have my first paragraph."

"What will that be about?"

"What you just said, personality."

"That's right," I agreed. "It takes personality to be able to sell things that people want and don't want."

"Here's what I'm going to do. I'm going to interview some of the people I see selling stuff and ask them how they got started."

Now Charles was right. He was on to something. Asking people about what they did and how they did it wasn't a bad idea. Maybe that is what I needed to be doing also.

"Charles, now that's what I think I need to do. I'm going to see if I can talk to farmers about their way of farming."

"Well, it looks like we are bound for our "A's," Charles said.

"Yeah, I didn't realize our essays have so much in common. Well, I don't know how much personality you need in farming, but we do have many products, and it sure is a process."

"Well, hold on now. We may just have our essays outlined here. There is personality...I can use that," Charles said.

"I know what you are going to say next, "product," I said.

"Yeah, that's right, and then we have to inform our audience on the ...

"Process," we yelled at the same time.

We high-fived and hollered and jumped up and down like our name was pulled out of a raffle box. That conversation was one we had no idea was going to move our writing forward.

"Miss Hopkins might want to use this in class. Two people working on their writing and sharing ideas," Charles said.

"We'll have to at least tell her about our meeting," I said.

"I think you are right," Charles agreed.

It was time for us to go to our next class, and as we were walking, there was none other than Kyser and his girlfriend. Charles and I didn't say a word to him, but teased him with our eyeballs, making silly faces, where he knew we weren't mad, just being our hilarious selves.

CHAPTER 24 – KIMBERLY-CLARK

My old friend was slowly coming back, and the temperatures were rising beyond fifty degrees. It wasn't the late eighty and ninety degrees that usually enveloped me, but it was just enough to let me know that "he" was on his way. The chill in the air was being replaced by "his" rays of sunshine, where the ground had puddles of ice in the morning; it was just a little water and pebbles of dew on the blades of grass. One thing about Alabama, when it was hot, it was hot, and when it was cold, it was cold. Thusly, the in-between temperatures were truly welcoming.

I was glad it was Saturday. School had been challenging. We were now in the time of school, where the teachers were looking for us to do culminating activities, where we were showing what we knew in each class. These projects were thoughtful, meaningful, and were realistic in their nature. We all knew we were better for it, whether we wanted to admit it or not. Nonetheless, we were all ready for some fun. The break in the weather gave us warmer temperatures and gave us just the kind of break we could use.

Kyser and I got out our old hunting things, and we were ready to head to the woods. Before we could get there, a truck pulled up that we didn't recognize. We looked cautiously at the truck, along with the driver and the passengers. They got out, and I wondered if they were there to see Papa, and had I allowed it, a million reasons would have readily come to my mind.

"Good morning," one the men said.

"Good morning," Kyser and I said in unison.

"I'm looking for a few good workers who are willing to work."

Kyser and I looked at each other and wondered what kind of work they wanted us to do. It wasn't like looking at each other was going to give us an answer, but I guess it was a habit that people did to see the reaction of the other.

Surely, we would like extra money, and I'm positive we could see how we would use the money. We didn't have large amounts of money, but no matter the amount, we weren't going to be outlandish about it; we could use more.

I knew my needs, and I knew them all too well. The basics were essential to me. Good slacks, good shirts, and good shoes were things that I would need to be presentable when the time came when I would need them. The first thing that came to mind was what I might need for Tuskegee, which wasn't as far away as it once was.

I didn't know if Kyser was going to answer or whether I should jump in, but after a pause, I answered.

"We're good workers." I thought I would begin there, and they would reveal about the kind of work.

"Well then, you all would be great at setting out trees," said one of the men. Kyser and I looked at each other again.

"Is this with Kimberly-Clark?" Kyser asked.

"Yes, young man, it is. How did you know?" the man responded.

"I've heard some boys at school mention it," Kyser said.

"Well, here's what we can do. Talk to your parents about it, and we can stop back by here, Monday evening. If you want to work, we can start you next Saturday, and we can pick you up by 6:30 am and drive you to the site."

"Well, thank you so much, sir," Kyser said.

"Thank you, sir," I followed.

The man and the crewmen backed out and drove down the road. I assumed they were going all over Talladega to find help setting out the trees. For some reason, I thought the other men were going to be introduced to us, or maybe they were going to tell us their experiences, but no one introduced them. Perhaps, in their own way, they were just there to show the different ages of men that were eligible to work, and that was some unspoken way of telling us. There were some boys our age and some older.

"So, you know some boys that have done this type of work, Kyser?" I asked.

"Yeah, they said it was alright work. They get to work on the weekends, and it's just a half-day job."

"So, you think we ought to do it?" I said.

"Yeah, I think we ought to. You think Uncle Will and Aunt Grace are going to be okay with it?" Kyser asked.

"I think they will, especially with it being half-day. How about Aunt Lillie Mae and Uncle Ernest? You think they are going to be fine with it too?"

"I believe so," Kyser answered.

We gathered our hunting things and walked toward the woods. I could tell we were going to have our usual fun day of talking, and with this new work development, we would be talking for hours.

****

Just as I thought, Kyser and I had a fantastic time hunting, and the laughter was refreshing. I could still hear the laughter clearly, even after Sunday's church service.

Sunday evening found me working on my speech. I could see the sundogs in the sky, and the top of the trees looked like a painting in a landscape. There was the sweet aroma of honeysuckles in the air. This time it was not mixed with the burning embers of the cow that made for a sickening smell when Papa made Ruth burn it after its demise. I immediately rerouted my thinking and turned my attention back to yesterday and today.

Along with the setting of this day, I didn't want it to leave without making a placid backdrop for me to put varnishing touches on my speech for Tuskegee. I had exactly twenty-eight days before I was set to go. A lot of thoughts were crossing into my head because for the next four Saturdays, Kyser and I were going to set out trees for Kimberly-Clark Paper Company. There was a certain excitement about it that made me feel this was going to be a memorable adventure. It would be the first time I would plant something in the ground for someone other than Papa or myself.

I wondered if there would be some kind of training. Maybe we would be trained by the guys that got out of the truck but didn't speak. Did we need special clothes? Did we need to have uniforms? Would they supply them? Was there a fee?

The questions were flooding in, but I decided that I would just let the questions shoot out like a comet and let them land wherever.

I was beginning to hear a headful of ideas about my speech, and I did the same thing. I just took out a pencil and a tablet and recorded what I heard in my mind.

There was no need trying to wrangle these thoughts in, for I thought it to be better just to let my mind process some information. I had to focus and not think about who I thought would like the speech or wouldn't like the speech. When it is all said and done, Mr. Armstrong would be approving the copy, and I could just focus on the delivery from there.

Some of the men I spoke to within the community couldn't talk about "balanced farming," for they were not familiar with the term. It was evident that some were putting into practice what Mr. Armstrong had been teaching them. Mr. Armstrong had not been teaching just the students at Talladega County Training School. He had set up farming classes to train local men about farming, extending what they knew already. Many only knew what they had seen and what had been passed down to them. Mr. Armstrong furthered their knowledge, and it allowed them to maximize their profits. These classes were usually at night or on some Saturdays, and Mr. Armstrong would teach about soil, soil erosion, fertilizers, crop selection, crop rotation, animal husbandry, and more.

My head was filling up again, as I could see Mr. Armstrong riding in his well-kept black sedan moving through the farms. He visited many farms, either looking at student projects or looking at the adult farmers' crops. When his car came up, you couldn't hear a sound. The engine ran smoothly as he had just changed the oil before he left his last destination, where the little noise it did have resembled a sewing machine.

The shine on his car preceded the dust trails that blew behind him ever so majestically. It was as if the dust knew to move out of the way because he was coming. That was just how things looked around Mr. Armstrong; regal and rational because that was how he always presented himself.

Well, if I was going to follow his ever so continuous example, I was guessing I better add a few touches to my speech. I got a glimpse of Will from the window and thought when I add these lines; I'm going to run out there and try them out on him. Although he wouldn't give any feedback, I knew he would tilt his head and listen intently, just like he knew what content should be included.

However, I knew one thing. Will knew for sure if anyone knew anything about pulling a plow under the "Talladega Sky" with temperatures ranging from 100 degrees on down. I had to add something else he knew too: Will knew how to stay by my side until the very end.

****

"William, this is excellent. I know this is a winner. You have explained your point well. It is engaging, and I would further say that this is a teaching process. You have put the steps in place for young farmers and old alike to see how the process of farming is really done. You have thoroughly explained the benefits of balanced farming."

As Mr. Armstrong told me these words, I was elated. I don't know if the sun could have out-beamed me. I'm not sure if the moon could have out-shined me. I don't even know if all the stars could have out-twinkled me. What I did know was that I was beaming with joy, and if my feet were on the ground, I couldn't feel it.

This conversation felt like I was listening and speaking at the same time. It was also a rewind and a fast forward all at the same time. I traveled back to the first day I stepped into Talladega County Training School, and I saw the tears. I traveled forward to the good years, and here I was in the present.

Mr. Armstrong shook my hand with a gracious grip, one that extended admiration and confirmation that I had crossed a line, somewhat of a finish line. This was not a finish line indicating that I had reached all I needed to reach, but it was a crossing line, showing I had moved to a new level in academic achievement.

"Now go and let Miss Gibbs, Miss Slater, and Miss New listen to your speech, and they can help you with your delivery. They are excellent in advising you when to pause, add inflections, and emphasize points where you want the audience to zero in."

"Yes, sir," I said. "And thank you, Mr. Armstrong."

I honestly wasn't sure if I had said thank you after he had given me many wonderful comments about my speech. Mr. Armstrong patted me on my back.

"We have just a few days now, William. Here's a checklist of the things you need for the week we are there."

"Yes, sir." It seemed like that's all I could say. I was still in deep thought.

"... and William?"

"Yes, sir." There I go again.

"I am so proud of you and all you have become."

I was going to change up now.

"Thank you, Mr. Armstrong, and I sure appreciate the opportunity to be a part of the New Farmers of America Conference, and thank you for choosing me to go."

"William, I've seen you from the time you were in Miss Gibbs class, and then Miss Slater. I saw you in plays, and I saw you recite a lot of poems all through the years. I knew you had the goods to get the job done."

"Thank you again, Mr. Armstrong."

The bell rang, and I turned to walk out of the class. I was looking in front of me, very aware of everything going on. I could see the desks, chairs, and hallway, but as far as me walking, I still couldn't feel the ground.

Charles and Kyser waved me over to our usual table in the cafeteria, but it seemed like I was getting there in slow motion. I looked at the students in the cafeteria and wondered if the number of students would be the same size as the size I was going to deliver my speech to at Tuskegee. I figured the crowd would be larger, and for a moment, I imagined the lunchroom about three times the size. I would need to practice projecting my voice and practice looking throughout the audience.

"William ... William," Charles called.

"Junior, Junior," Kyser said.

I finally heard them calling.

"What were you looking around for?" Charles said.

"I was just sizing up the crowd. I was pretending this was the size of the crowd that I would deliver my speech to," I said.

"If the crowd is the size of Alabama, everybody in the crowd is going to listen, because you got something to say, even if they never saw a farm in their life," Charles said, while later taking a swallow of his milk.

****

My face received the wind like a dog who panted and couldn't wait for the wind to keep coming. The only difference, I didn't have my tongue out or the ears to flop backward. The wind was going by, and Kyser and I were riding on the back of a truck bed on our way to plant trees for Kimberly-Clark Paper Company. We were picked up early Saturday morning around 6 am, and we didn't quite know what to expect in terms of orientation, but if it was one thing we knew, it was planting.

We saw houses pass by us, even though we were actually passing them by. The lines of clothes passed quickly, along with sheets that blew wildly in the wind.

It wasn't a cold day, and it wasn't a hot day. The day was about 59 degrees and relatively pleasant. Finally, the truck slowed down, and the tires began to have the sound of a "burrrrrrr," as we had reached our destination.

I looked around as I got off the truck, and everywhere I directed my sight was a sea of land. I didn't believe I had ever seen so much land all in one place, uninterrupted. The land I had seen usually had a house or a barn on it. Additionally, ditches would be in the middle to divide the pieces of property, where water would drain off.

However, the land here had rows and markings that seemed endless that were ready for millions of trees to be deposited. Yet, I assume that this large area was what made the land such an asset to Kimberly-Clark.

When it came to land and planting, Kyser and I had a lot of experience. Uncle Ernest, Kyser's father, had acres of land, so Kyser was no stranger to knowing how to plant anything in the ground. With all the peanuts I planted in the ground, I believed I could handle a tree. The only thing was, this kind of planting would be different – long, straight, and continual.

"Boys, I need all of you to come over here," the head man said. He was the driver and the man that approached Kyser and me at the house.

There were five other boys besides Kyser and me, who were in the truck bed. We didn't do a lot of talking, nor did we make a lot of eye contact. Number one, we were so excited to ride in the truck bed and view the scenery, and two, we wouldn't have been able to hear each other over the motor of the truck when it was at full speed.

We surrounded the head man as we moved quickly toward him. I could tell these boys had a good work ethic. They didn't lag behind or murmur, and we were going his direction before he stated he wanted us to come.

"Okays boys, listen here, we are paying you all for half a day's work, and that's what we want. Work. We don't want to see you half working or lollygagging around. We got trees to put in the ground, and that's what we are going to do."

I looked around to see if anybody had irritated looks on their faces, but they didn't. Evidently, Kyser and I were the new ones to the crew. I believed these boys were students too, although I didn't know them, who needed the extra money for a number of things. If they were seniors, they could sure use the money for prom, class rings, graduation, or some for future endeavors. If they were juniors and sophomores, they could use the money for the same things, just minus graduation.

I knew I would spend my money on necessities. It would be correct to say everything, but Tuskegee was on the top of the list. Things like a dress shirt, pants, tie, toiletries, etc. were things I could use. Mr. Armstrong had already given me a checklist with the items we should bring and those that were optional. Working this job on Saturdays would help get some of the things I needed.

Before Mr. Armstrong gave me the list, I had already "inventoried" what I had. I had slacks that I kept in pristine condition, along with shirts that were always washed, ironed, starched. I had good Sunday shoes and a good belt. However,

I could use a few more things since I was going to be there for a week.

"Okay, boys, we are going to use this right here, and put the plant right in it, and put it in the ground. Now it might be hard at first, but everybody gets the hang of it," the head man said.

I cut my eye over to Kyser, and he had a look of sheer confidence. Some of the other boys had a look ranging between clarity and confusion. Maybe these boys hadn't planted plants in the ground before, but Kyser and I had this in the bag.

"Now boys, this here is a dibble. I'm going to demonstrate how you put this in the ground," the head man said in a slow southern drawl.

Maybe we had become immune to our own accents, but it seemed he had an extended pause between his words.

Kyser and I smiled at this. We knew how to do this. I couldn't help but think that Charles would love the idea of doing this work.

"Now look, I'ma show it to you again," the head man said. This time he seemed a little annoyed and less patient. Some of the other boys weren't quite getting the hang of it.

"Wait a minute, wait a minute ..." Kyser and I looked at each other again. We didn't know what was coming. He was looking over in our direction.

"You see how these boys are doing it? I want you to look at them. They are doing it right!" Kyser and I were relieved. We thought he was getting ready to say something totally different. The head man said "them" and "right" like they were two-syllable words.

The other boys examined our techniques with their eyes. We demonstrated by slowing our dig with the dibble, so they could see how to insert the tool, apply pressure to get it in the ground, and then put the tree seedling down, close the earth around it, and pull the dibble out.

"Dere you go, dere you go, boys," the head man shouted.

He was actually saying there, but with a hard accent that turned the "th" to a "d" sound.

The boys looked a little longer, and then they were on their way. I could see the head man looking and shaking his head in agreement.

"Them two yonder got it down pat," the headman said while adjusting his cap.

We kept going and had a rhythm that made the job enjoyable. It was redundant, and we did the same thing over and over, but Kyser and I were no strangers to that. We had planted so many things in gardens and crops over the years; we could do it blindfolded.

The other boys looked like they were finally finding their own rhythm. Some of them started singing. Kyser and I didn't try that. We didn't know if that was permitted, but we listened. I was waiting for the head man to say something, but he never did.

The boys were singing some bluesy tune that seemed to have no end. They were singing one song and would go right into another one. Some songs even had a spiritual sound, and I would be willing to believe that some of the songs were made up right there on the spot. I had to admit; it did make the time pass by quickly. Another thing that was moving just as fast as time was the sweat. We had begun wiping it, as it came down profusely. Occasionally our eyes burned, and we had nothing but our sleeves to wipe it away.

We looked over what we had done as the time had passed, and we had done a few rows collectively. As large as the land was, it didn't look like we had even put a dent in it. However, little by little, tree seedlings were making their way across the land.

I could feel my stomach begin to growl.

"Boy, I'm beginning to get hungry," Kyser said.

"Yeah, my stomach is beginning to talk to me, letting me know just how hungry it is," I said.

"Looking at where the sun is, it looks like it's around 12:00 noon," I said hopefully.

"Well, the boss man said we have just a half-day, and I'm glad of that, cause I'm ready to eat," Kyser said emphatically.

Just as he said it, the head man blew a whistle. It was the signal to head back to the truck. I was more than ready, and so were the other boys. We all were holding our dibbles in different positions, walking back toward the truck, ready for the wind to refresh us.

****

The truck turned into our lane, delivering us to the house, and Kyser got out where I lived. He had already told Aunt Lillie Mae that he was going to be dropped off with me.

"Boys, this is your pay for today!" the head man said.

"Thank you, sir," Kyser, and I said in unison. Our eyes widened with zeal. It was some cash that we earned, and we were happy that we could make it.

"Can we count on you boys for next week?"

"Yes, sir!" we said again in unison.

The fact that he wanted us next week told us that we had done a good job. Unsure if he would ever come right out and tell us, he did have the other boys look at our method when we started. At the same time, he didn't look like he was the pat-on-the-back type.

Kyser and I could have acted out the kid's rhyme Miss Mary Mack. We could have jumped so "high, high, high, and touched the sky, sky, sky." We felt a sense of accomplishment, as we had made some money on our own.

"What are you going to buy with your money," Kyser asked.

"I got to get some things to go to Tuskegee," I replied. "I'm sure there are kids from all over Alabama there, and I want to look the best I can since I'm in the speaking contest."

"Yeah, I understand," Kyser replied.

"So how about you? You going to buy something for your girlfriend?" I said, with an emphasis on *girlfriend*, while I blinked my eyes femininely to tease him.

"I knew you were going to say that!" Kyser said as he laughed at the end.

"Yeah, you know, Charles and I don't ever see you much around school since 'she' came into the picture."

"Now you know that isn't true, I see you all at lunch," Kyser said.

"Yeah, I'm just kidding you. So, are you going to buy her something?" I added quickly.

"I'll think about it," Kyser said slowly.

We got to the porch, and Papa was standing there. "Well, how are you boys doing after a hard day's work. Well, half day's work," Papa said.

"It was good, Uncle Will. We got the hang of it rather quickly. The headman wanted the other boys to see our work."

"That's good. So, they probably want y'all back again."

"Yes, they do," Kyser said.

I saw a gleam in Papa's eye that I didn't quite understand. I didn't quite feel he was proud of us, but there was something I couldn't put my finger on.

"Uncle Ernest is here!" I said, somewhat surprised and sad because that meant Kyser had to leave.

"Hey, Uncle Ernest. How are you feeling today?"

"Doing fine. The question is, how are you boys doing?" Uncle Ernest said as he emphasized, *you boys.*

"We had a good day, Papa," Kyser said.

"We sure did," I chimed in.

"The head man thought we were doing a good job, so good that he wanted all the other boys to see how we were planting the seedlings," Kyser said. "We were handling those dibbles great since we used them every day."

"Bill, how are you doing," Uncle Ernest said to Papa.

"I'm doing fine, Ernest. Look like we got ourselves some working men here."

"Yeah, I know. Kyser was so excited about going to set out those trees."

Papa had a look of delight on his face, and again, I couldn't quite understand it.

****

"So how much did you draw?" Papa said.

Uncle Ernest and Kyser probably hadn't been gone a full thirty seconds when Papa formed his question. I felt a knot suddenly appear in my stomach. It was clear. Like a camera bringing a picture into focus, I now understood that gleam in Papa's eye. It was abruptly clear why he had such delight across his face.

I swallowed and looked at the ground for a second, and I told him what I made.

"I need to hold..."

Before he quoted an amount, I gave him half of what I made.

I knew exactly where that money was going. Papa was headed straight to a store and exchange every bit of the money I gave him for a liquid that he was going to pour straight down his throat. He may have gone back to church five years ago, got a job, and became more responsible about feeding us and seeing that our bare necessities were met; however, he still kept alcohol flowing abundantly toward his direction.

I couldn't believe it, but then again, I could. Whenever Mama cooked, he would get the biggest and best of whatever it was, without any consideration of whether the food would be distributed to all of us. For years, he sat down at the end of the row, looked at our progress while we all worked. I had actually been shaken down by William L. Groce, Sr. And for what? He knew I was going to Tuskegee to compete in the New Farmers of America's Speech Contest and participate in judging livestock and other special contests. I wanted to save up some money to have the proper clothing and supplies I needed. This was my motivating factor in getting the job in the first place. Papa wasn't going to go out of his way to get them for me. Yet, all he could think about was wetting his throat with some liquor.

I really wasn't as hungry as I thought I was going to be when I arrived home. I took a walk over to my friend Will. I looked at him as he was enjoying those crunchy, mouthfuls of grass that he always made look so delicious.

I decided there was no need to let this moment with my father fester. This was a pattern that I had seen over the years. I was not going to continue to join my father any longer by thought. Why not take in the environment and let it speak to me? While I looked around, I could see the planes that were moving through the clouds, reminding me of the ones my sister, Margarite, would tell me about and narrate their journey when I couldn't go outside because I was sick. I absorbed everything about this moment. The memory was a welcomed distraction. Actually, I didn't want a good memory like this one to let my mind package it into a distraction. It was a welcomed "life lane" that I could cross right over into and keep the journey of my life going.

I decided there was no time like the present to practice my speech. Will turned his head and moved his ears like he usually did when he was discerning something. I practiced once, and once more from my memory. I'm sure I didn't have every word in place as I had it written on the paper, but I wasn't trying to memorize it in that fashion but to deliver the points clearly, even if the wording was different.

Will stood there and listened. I must have said that speech about twenty times until my stomach growled with a vengeance. I was so hungry before I left the tree farm, and somehow, I forgot all about eating after "the Shakedown."

I didn't consider myself a selfish son or an inconsiderate teenager. Yes, I wanted some spending money, because luxury of any kind was far and in between. I recognized all that my Papa did, even if it wasn't all it should have been. But what pierced my thoughts, and a little bit of my very being, was how it seemed that he was just taking my money because *he could*. He didn't recognize that I had worked hard or acknowledge the fact that I even had the desire to work for what I wanted and needed. I would have been more than glad to contribute to our household, because at no time did we not need additional money. However, what continuously troubled me, between the time I rehearsed my speech, was that this money was not going to fill our cupboards or help build our future. It was on its way to Howell Cove, the center of his "good times."

CHAPTER 25 – PREPARING FOR TUSKEGEE

"William, that speech was fantastic," Miss New said. All the teachers agreed. Miss Gibbs and Miss Slater were there cheering me on. Their eyes were glowing, and the smiles were bright. They had actually taken the time to see me during lunch to critique my delivery. I knew they were not just pretending. These were teachers that had invested so much in me, and I could tell that they knew it had paid off in that exact moment.

I couldn't feel the floor. It was the same feeling I had when Mr. Armstrong approved my speech. No big head was coming upon me, where I was floating because I thought I was so great. If anything, I felt a mixture of a light-headed feeling of pure elation, mixed with gratefulness that I could be seen in such a light by my former and current teachers.

"We didn't know exactly what you would be doing from the time we met you until now, but I'm sure I speak for everyone, that we knew it would be something like what you are doing now," Miss Gibbs said.

"I agree wholeheartedly," Miss Slater said.

"I do, too," said Miss New.

"You have great diction and inflections in the right places," Miss New said.

"What are you going to wear?" Miss Gibbs asked.

"I was planning to wear dark slacks with a shirt and tie," I responded.

"I think that will be appropriate," Miss Slater interjected.

"We already know you are going to have your shoes shined and shirt pressed," Miss Gibbs said.

"Yes, Ma'am. I'm going to definitely have that done."

"We want to make sure you have a great hair cut that is going to render you sharp and ready," said Miss New.

"I'm sure his father has a barber he takes him to," Miss Slater added.

I didn't say a word about that. Nor did I bother to say what my father did or didn't do. If I were going to the barbershop before I went to Tuskegee, it would be on my own initiative to get there, not because Papa was going to say, "I want you to have a nice haircut before you arrive on campus, because you need to stand out in all areas to be your best."

I hurried up and dragged my mind out of that thought. There was no way I was leaving my thoughts in such a marsh, when three of my best teachers were depositing their time into me, grooming me to be a New Farmer of America speech contest winner.

"William, we've seen you speak before, and we feel confident you will do well. I believe it is the consensus of this panel of teachers that you are going to be groomed well from head to toe," Miss Slater said. "So, I think we ought to ask you a question. How do you feel?"

"I feel pretty good. I practice at home." I didn't tell them I practiced in front of Will. For whatever reason, I thought they would see that as an act too juvenile for me to be a participant. But then again, if any of them had lived on a farm, maybe they would understand.

"Do you practice in the mirror?" Miss Gibbs asked.

"Yes, Ma'am, I have practiced there."

"Continue to do so," Miss New added.

"Yes, Ma'am," I said.

"And William, I also want to say something else. If there is anything you need that we could help you with, please let anyone of us know," Miss New continued.

"That's right," Miss Slater and Miss Gibbs said in unison.

I knew where they were going. Miss New had given me a trumpet to participate in the band. She had identified my need and had freely given it to me. I was grateful to have such teachers, and along with just wanting to do the best for me, I felt the call to do my best for them also.

"Thank you all so much for extending such an offer to me. I really do appreciate it ... and thank you all for seeing me during your lunchtime."

When I turned to leave, I could hear their echoes of admiration about me. It felt absolutely fantastic to be thought of this way. Before I could turn the corner, I just wanted to stand and hear more, so I could remember to play these wonderful votes of confidence in my head when I took the podium at Tuskegee Institute.

****

"Okay, that's it."

Those were the words I heard after I felt the barber's brush sweep briskly across the back of my neck as he brushed all the hair off. The barber took the cape off and spun me around to the mirror.

I'm not sure how long I stared. I looked and looked, and I saw the most handsome version of myself. It had less to do with what I saw, but more with what I heard from the melodious memories from the trio of some of my favorite teachers: Miss. Gibbs, Miss Slater, and Miss Knew. They were right about my haircut, my delivery, and my overall presentation. I was getting the whole "package" ready for Tuskegee.

I gave the barber the money for my haircut, including a tip.

"Thank you, young man," the barber said happily. Not many young men know about tipping.

"You are welcome," I responded.

Somewhere in Mr. Armstrong's class, I had heard him speak about tipping when it came to service-oriented jobs. He was pretty emphatic about it and how important it was to show your appreciation when you receive excellent service.

I walked out with Papa, Uncle Ernest, and Kyser.

"That's a nice-looking haircut," Uncle Ernest said.

"Yeah, it is!" Papa said.

I had a thought that tried to pierce through. It actually made it. It was payday for Kyser and me, and Papa definitely was reaping the benefits of it. With Uncle Ernest bringing us to town, it was like he had hit the lottery twice. He got a ride and some money. Yet, I wasn't going to let the thought of this take me down into the quicksand of despair. I turned my mind back to the melodious place of memories from "The Trio," where my feet didn't touch the ground.

"Uncle Ernest, could I go to the clothing store to get some pants and a few shirts?"

"You got some shirts at home. You might need a pair of pants," Papa said.

"Junior is going to Tuskegee, Bill, and he is going to be there for a whole week." Uncle Ernest said.

"He doesn't need to buy a whole wardrobe of clothes," Papa responded.

"He just wants a few pairs of pants and a few shirts, Bill."

"He doesn't need to be spending up his money on clothes."

"Bill, he gave you some money, 'cause I saw him. Now, what are you going to do with what he gave you?"

Papa was silent. He dropped his head and waved Uncle Ernest off.

They weren't mad. It was the kind of banter that I had been used to hearing men do. They could be truthful with each other about something and not be angry.

Uncle Ernest dropped Kyser and me off at the store, and I looked for some pants and shirts. I went through my head and wondered if I needed a belt, but I thought the belt I had would be okay.

I couldn't go wrong with a black pair of pants and a dark blue pair. The tag said they were made out of gabardine fabric. I liked the look and feel, and it seemed like it would last a long time.

Off to the side, I saw a Khaki pair of pants and thought that would be a good option also. With dark pants, I could rotate them a few days, and perhaps I could wear the Khaki pants once since they would be more noticeable.

I moved on to the shirts. It was to my advantage to be practical. Keeping the dress shirts white as my best option, for I had different ties.

What I was buying wasn't frivolous. It was just things I needed. I couldn't understand why Papa was so wound up about me spending money on necessities, when I know he spent my money on frivolity. I would be gone for a week, not just anywhere or for any cause, but for school, and at a prestigious school, Tuskegee Institute.

I stopped myself. There I was again in the quicksand. I turned my mind back to the melodious memory of the trio, gathered my clothes, and headed to the counter for the sales lady to ring them up.

****

"Junior, this is the suitcase."

Mama handed it to me, and my eyes widened. I had never seen this suitcase before, and I even wondered when anyone had used it. I didn't even remember seeing it when we moved so many times.

"We haven't used it for a long time," Mama said.

"Thank you, Mama. I'll take care of it."

"Now, you all will be gone for a week, right?"

"Yes, Ma'am, from Monday to Friday."

"Well, I'm going to make sure you have five sets of everything," Mama said.

Mama folded everything so neatly and placed it inside the suitcase. She wasn't leaving this task to me even though she knew I could handle it. It was Mama doing it because she was part proud and part contributing to my opportunity.

"Junior, I'm proud of you. I just want you to know that."

"I know you are because you always cheer me on," I said.

"I am really proud of you. All the times you spent in the fields, jumping and running through the land and the meadows as a little boy, it surely prepared you for all the things you do with the fields and farming. I can remember when you had your first peanut crop, and you got everyone involved. Your brother and sisters couldn't wait to help you and harvest the crop."

I smiled and thought I would add this to my memory of the "good" that the teacher trio gave me. I was going to surround myself with all the goodness I could when I got on that stage at Tuskegee – for I assume it was a stage. I figured it would be like our auditorium, just a lot bigger.

For a moment, I thought of what the audience might look like. I didn't see an intimidating crowd, but I did see boys and girls with their teachers, just like we would be with Mr.

Armstrong. I also assumed that all the students were serious and engaged in agriculture.

"Junior, you have gotten the approval of Mr. Armstrong, Miss Gibbs, Miss Slater, and Miss New. They have all given you their tips. Now I want you to go to God and ask Him if you haven't already, what He will have you do."

"Yes, Ma'am," I said attentively and knew that this was what she was going to prescribe for me.

"Man can only do but so much, even when they have done their very best and their all," Mama said. "In your preparation, you may have everything, and when you get in front of the audience, all you will need is peace."

"Yes, Ma'am."

"You may need your stomach calm if you have butterflies come unexpectedly. God can do that," Mama said.

I could tell she was on a roll, and she had more to say that was going to seal this whole conversation with wisdom that could not come from anybody but her. I was more than grateful that I had a mother that could reach into the depths of her soul and pull out what I needed. No one but her personal Savior, Jesus Christ, could give this to her and then have her to pass it along to me.

"You may not need to add anything else to your speech, but I know what you still can add now. You can add acknowledgment. By adding acknowledgment, you are acknowledging God, who has made this possible, and when you do that, the whole thing will be complete."

I didn't say thank you or respond, because I was so lost, no, actually I was found, in the thought of what Mama had said. Then, I heard her say more.

"You know the bible verse in Proverbs, 'In all thy ways acknowledge him, and he shall direct thy paths.'"

Mama remembered that something was on the stove and exited the room.

I couldn't feel the floor again. I was really floating. If for some reason, I was not fully prepared, I was certainly prepared now, even if I had to give my speech in five minutes.

Cool, crisp air met me in the arms of my excitement. I felt a brisk feeling that I could only experience on the morning of an anticipated journey. As I looked up waiting for the bus, the Talladega sky was an indescribable blue. I had never seen the sky this way before, with clouds so clear and so close, it seemed I could almost touch them. It was like cotton candy ready to be bagged for the county fair. The whole view, as far as I could see, was a backdrop for dreams to come true. The sun seemed to be on assignment just for me, delivering rays that would not allow any disappointment, any despair, or any undesirable moments to come in the midst.

I entered the school bus with more than my books, but with a brown suitcase with buckles, revealing many years of departures and arrivals. It had been in the family a number of years, solely used when someone was taking unexpected trips since family vacations were non-existent.

I could see Mr. Armstrong's car as the bus pulled up to the school, a black Chevrolet with four doors, and a motor that hummed to the tune of his regular maintenance. Two other boys were coming from their buses, and we were all ready for our adventure.

"Good morning, boys!" Mr. Armstrong said with a lot of cheer and enthusiasm.

"Good morning, Mr. Armstrong!" We all responded with the same enthusiasm. It was everyone's first time going to the Tuskegee Institute and, for that matter, Tuskegee, Alabama. I could tell in the other boys' demeanor that they were excited too. As tenth graders chose to compete in an Agricultural Contest, we were trying to be sophisticated, but the excitement was too hard to contain. I was so happy that I could have jumped and touched the sky and come back down before they missed me.

"Did you boys get enough sleep last night?" Mr. Armstrong asked with a slight smile on his face, looking like he really knew we didn't, but he was just checking.

I didn't answer at once, for I could hardly sleep. The other boys chimed in with a big, "yes," and I just let their "yes" answer for me.

"Well, if you didn't, hopefully, you'll get some sleep on the way. We want to be ready for our competition in a few hours. I know I'm taking three of Talladega County Training School's best."

His words felt like a rested hand on my shoulder, a pat on the back, and applause all at the same time, which seemed like we had done well before we even started.

As for sleeping on the way, I'm sure none of us were going to do that. We weren't going to miss one bit of this trip, even if sleep pressed down harshly upon us.

"Let's put your bags in the back," Mr. Armstrong said as he motioned for us to walk around the car. We all went to the back of Mr. Armstrong's sedan and waited for his orders to show us how we should place the luggage in the trunk. Even though we were big enough to put them in ourselves, he kindly took our bags and placed them inside. He put the trunk down, slapped his hands together, letting what little dust that was on his hands fall off, as he looked toward Talladega County Training School for a brief moment, as if to say, "we are coming back with the gold."

"Are you guys ready?" Mr. Armstrong asked.

We all said, "Yes, sir," in unison.

"Now you won't be back for a week – a school week – but you knew that already. We won't be back until Friday. You boys aren't going to be homesick, are you?"

I did not think of this before, but I wondered who was going to cover Mr. Armstrong's classes while he was gone for a week. How that managed to come in my mind and penetrate through my excitement, I did not know, but it was in my head. I even thought of Will.

"No, sir!" we all said again in unison. I doubted if any of us were going to be homesick. Returning to a mule and a plow, with the hot "Talladega Sun," wasn't going to be missed. However, as for a mule like Will, returning to my friend would always be something I couldn't wait to do.

****

I sat in the front seat at Mr. Armstrong's command, a seat that afforded me the opportunity to study the man I was beside. I was able to see the road ahead and look to the right of me through the window to see Talladega to Tuskegee, Alabama, as a motion picture film.

I began to wonder what made him so dedicated to his teaching, students, and community. His dedication alone was a fixture in Talladega County Training School. Mr. Armstrong's classes covered everything from woodworking to livestock inspection, everything that young men needed to have a sustainable foundation.

The old black Chevrolet was running as smooth as a Singer sewing machine. When Mr. Armstrong turned the car out of the parking lot, I could now settle in, for I knew it was really happening. We were headed toward Tuskegee, on Highway 21 to Sylacauga and Highway 280 to Auburn. I could hear the gravel popping under the tires as he turned the sedan, and the sound was like a song to the tune of my desire. This was going to be my first trip to Tuskegee Institute, and I could hardly conceal my composure.

As soon as Mr. Armstrong's car got on the two-lane highway, I stuck my hand out of the window, and I was catching the wind the way children do, in the palm of my hand. Sometimes I grabbed it, and sometimes I let the wind just dance between my fingers. Although I was beyond childhood, but still a teenager, I still found playing with the wind a fun thing to do.

Everything seemed to have a tune and was in sync with my excitement. Even the hum of the motor gave the sound ofa relaxing accompaniment. I believed the hum was a testament to how Mr. Armstrong always kept his cars up and made sure they were in top condition.

I got a chance to further study Mr. Armstrong, a man who was about 6'2", yet he wasn't a big man. He was medium size, with light brown skin, and a receding hairline, but was far from having a receding personality. He was the type of man that had the ability to look into your soul and had the type of personality that you couldn't lie to him, for he would be looking right through you. He was engaging outside the classroom and was equally as nurturing as he was inside. He was immediately accommodating and offered us food. I had not been with many adults, where they allowed the food to be self-served. On our way to Tuskegee, if you got hungry, you got yourself a sandwich, a piece of fried chicken, or a piece of potato pie. Mr. Armstrong had announced early on that the food is back there, where "back there" meant in a cooler on the backseat floor and some in the trunk.

As I think about Mr. Armstrong's teaching style, there was a similarity in this self-service style. He made knowledge of agriculture, livestock, canning, woodwork, and meat, cutting a readily available menu of learning. Just as he had offered us the food in the car, he didn't mind how much of the learning you took away, and as a result, we gained lifelong learning skills. He encouraged us to learn; he stimulated us to learn and asked questions that stimulated our minds.

****

Excitement had a way of slicing into my hunger, and I can't remember when I ate my first bite of food. I looked out the window, watching the "movie" of this trip, and I could see many fields where men were plowing with mules and getting the fields ready for planting. The next scene seemed to be segments of a repeat – a line of clothes, ranging from the linens to unmentionables, smoke from a chimney, and a dog somewhere in the yard.

The ride was about two and a half hours long, but it seemed like time stood still, as much as it was moving. This suspension between space and time held for me what I never knew was coming. Somehow, I felt I would be traveling this road again and again, toward the life God intended for me. It was a feeling very similar to my Mourner's Bench experience. All while I was in the car, I still felt I was somewhere in the future.

We didn't stop; it was a non-stop trip. Mr. Armstrong was the savvy type to gas up ahead of time, check oil, and things like tire pressure. However, it wasn't just his savviness that prompted him to do these things. He remembered that race relations at the time didn't always lend itself to "service for all" at a service station.

When we arrived, Mr. Armstrong led us around the campus for a tour. Although I had no camera, the images became burned indelibly in my mind, extending to my future. My eyes surveyed this place that Booker T. Washington had poured his soul's ambition into, a mold from which only God could have formed and given him.

Washington was a mere 25 years of age when he founded Tuskegee Institute in 1881. It was hard to believe that the campus had only begun with two buildings, but now in 1956, there were over fifty buildings.

There were buildings and features, unlike what I had seen in my sixteen years. There were statues, the European landscape, and art that was similar to what I had seen only in books and magazines. I could see the moment where history and reality met, a surreal experience, where I could hear the pages turning from what I had learned in the textbooks, all while you are standing inside the story and walking upon the hallowed ground at the same time.

From 1881 to his death in 1915, Washington transformed fields to fascinations, dedications to dreams, unkempt comments about the negro race to uplifting commentary, where all Blacks could turn from wherever they were and look forward. In his thirty-four years at Tuskegee, students were given education with a side of culture, that no doubt, many had not seen. Upon entering Tuskegee, students would now be able to think beyond the world they once knew and be ready to fully immerse themselves into a world that would help formulate our thinking.

Mr. Armstrong led us to our quarters, and on our way there, my eyes scanned every inch of Tuskegee's campus.

"Boy's, are you glad that you are here?" Mr. Armstrong said.

"Yes, sir!" we all said at the same time. Something about us being in unison made the answer richer. It wasn't like we planned it that way. I guess it was more like a classroom response when students answer the teacher.

"Okay. That's what I like to hear," Mr. Armstrong said. "Now I want you all to hurry up and unpack, so we can all meet for lunch. We are going to eat in the dining hall. I don't know what they are having, but I believe it's going to be good."

"Can we get a menu of what we will be having for the rest of the week?" one of the boys said.

"Yes, I'm sure they have it posted in the cafeteria, or you can get it from the cafeteria manager."

We went to our quarters; we all had separate ones. I guess that was a good thing. It gave us enough independence to see what it was like to be away from home. I didn't get the impression that the other two boys had been away from home for a whole week, just like me.

I thought I would take advantage of the time before we had before heading to the dining hall to unpack my clothes carefully. If Mama had helped me pack so carefully, I wasn't going to just jostle my clothes around and put them anywhere. I was going to keep them neat and place them in a "ready to go state," when it was time for us to go to our first activity as New Farmers of America.

****

The dining hall was like stepping in the largest eating place I had ever been in. It was far larger than the lunchroom at Talladega County Training School, and of course, it would be, since this was a college.

When it was time for us to eat, my eyes widened. The food choices were absolutely wonderful. There were plenty of vegetables, mashed potatoes with gravy, and chicken as the main course, and chocolate cake for dessert. But long before I saw the food, I saw all the students that just arrived from all over the state. These were all boys who had the same agenda since we were all members of the New Farmers of America Organization and appeared to be agriculturally inclined.

I had to admit that as I ate, I did size up the competition. I listened to the voices to see if they were deep, rich, and with a baritone sound. It was all somewhat in fun because there was no way to determine who was going to give a speech.

Putting my attention back to my plate, I ate some chicken that was cooked to perfection. It seemed as if I could taste every spice they used. This was no insult to Mama's food. Her food was always good and seasoned well. For a moment, I wondered what she was doing. Was she taking care of her father, Old Man Jim Houston, or was she back home getting supper ready for Papa, Janet, and Thomas?

"How are you boys enjoying the food?" Mr. Armstrong asked.

"Good." There we were again, all in unison. However, I still thought I wanted to add more.

"The chicken reminds me of Mama's."

That's all I said. I somewhat thought the other boys wanted to add something, so I didn't want to hog the response. It was all silence, just some chewing. Not any smacking that I could see; their mouths were too full.

Mr. Armstrong chuckled. "Everyone usually compares their food to their Mama's cooking."

"Boys, now I want to tell you something."

You could almost hear our spines straighten up all at once. I think Mr. Armstrong could see the tension in our faces.

"Relax, boys; it's nothing bad. I just want to tell you that all the food you are eating is grown right here on the farms of this Institute."

Our eyes widened as he told us. There seemed to be so much food needed for every day, three times a day. How could they have so many crops and raise so much livestock to last throughout the whole year?"

"This college is self-sufficient, meaning all the food that is served comes from their own farm," Mr. Armstrong continued to clarify.

"So do they know what they are going to serve each day and how much is needed?" one of the boys asked.

"Yes, they do. They have farmers, nutritionists, dieticians, and cafeteria managers, along with teams of people who know how to effectively plan all this out."

I believe knowing that information made our food taste better. Maybe it was because we had a better appreciation for it.

We still have a little food left, and we slowed down to savor the rest of it. That gave me time, unsure of the other boys, to look around and see more New Farmers. Some of the boys were dressed in slacks, and some wore khakis. I had my khakis on. I secretly wondered what kind of home many of these boys had come from. Seeing so many different styles of clothing and different levels of how worn and how new some of the material appeared just simply caught my eye. I remembered how tattered my clothing was in the beginning years of school. How I had wished Papa cared, and not let us appear in public like we were thrown away. It would have been one thing if tattered was the absolute best thing we could have possibly had. But it wasn't. We had those clothes out of negligence, and that was all there was to it. If we could have worn the bottles Papa drank from, we would have been well-dressed.

I transplanted my mind back to the present and ate my last morsels of food.

****

"William, I see you love ice cream," Mr. Armstrong said jovially.

"Oh, yes, sir!" That ice cream tastes like none I had ever had. It just seemed to have the right amount of sugar and cream, which had a perfect blend."

"So, I take it that everybody had a great lunch?" Mr. Armstrong asked.

"We did," we all said. Not so much in unison, but this time our answers were staggered a little bit. I was thinking that one of the boys was going to expand on his answer, but he didn't.

"Well, alright, boys, we are going to take a walk around and look at the campus."

Our eyes were fixed on every building. They all seemed like something out of a magazine, and each building looked like it was ready to tell a story of its own.

"When were these buildings built and who did it?" one of the boys asked.

"If I were you boys, I would jot down the names of these buildings and look up the history of each one. That way, you will remember more about them than me just telling you. That's how real learning takes place. Oh, by the way, that would be really impressive to Miss New, because she attended this school."

"She did! ... What! ... When?" we all said differently.

"Not too long ago," Mr. Armstrong said with a smile as if to not give away Miss New's age.

Miss New was young, a little younger than Miss Gibbs and Miss Slater. We couldn't tell how much, but we all had heard that in the "Talladega Talk" as people gossip around. What we didn't hear was anything that wasn't parallel to these ladies teaching standards and procedures because they were simply great.

"Well, boys, I'm going to let you stroll around the great Tuskegee Institute by yourselves. May your walk around inspire your curiosity for learning," Mr. Armstrong said, as he waved and went on toward a new direction.

The boys and I set out at a steady pace, and it seemed without discussion, we agreed to just walk over the campus without deciding which way to go.

The walk was still filled with wonder, and the cameras in our heads were like reel-to-reel loading it all in.

Seemingly, without notice, there were two men in front of us. I stared closer, and it looked like the men had been waiting for me. I was instantly gripped within the folds of my mind's captivity, as the men were part of the statue.

I couldn't move, and I was temporarily immobilized for a moment. The other two boys were looking at me and questioning why tears were rolling down from my eyes, profusely.

I could hear them saying, "William, William, William," like an echo swirling my mind, only I couldn't answer. I could hear more of these muffled chimes, but my senses were directed in another place.

I had only remembered tears falling so freely when I accepted Christ at a revival when I was about thirteen. The overall joy I felt was quite similar, and these tears that were coming were just as steady. This time, however, unlike at the revival, I didn't have my mother to bring me tissues after tissues. I quickly arrived at an understanding that this, too, was a revival, an awakening that was social as well as educational. It was a baptism, by all cleansing means, that made me see beyond my visible sight. Thoughts I should be thinking... words I should be hearing... work I should be doing... the educational journey I should be taking.

"Do you think we should go get Mr. Armstrong?" one of the boys said.

"I don't know, let's just wait," the other one said.

They continued to look at me, and then they looked at each other, sometimes shaking their heads when they didn't understand what was happening.

I was looking with a conscientious eye and a receiving heart at the anointed work of Charles Keck, who had so beautifully captured Booker T. Washington and a slave. At every curve that was chiseled, Keck had so eloquently defined these two men in front of me. There was Booker T. Washington, captured in the midst of his yesterdays and his tomorrows, lifting the veil from a slave. Here was Booker T. Washington's life's work within a statue, and what he wanted to portray to every Negro. To see him lift this veil from a slave spoke more than volumes. It spoke to my very soul, and I could tell it would reverberate in my mind for decades. For me, this was a baptism without immersion, but baptism by revelation.

Here was this slave that did not have the privilege to even go to school or see the inside of a classroom. He was not allowed to read or write or be seen with a book. But Booker T. Washington is presenting him to the world in sculpture with words printed: "He lifted the veil of ignorance from his people and pointed the way to progress through education and industry." A recognition of myself was all too real. I had an overwhelming feeling that took me to a mountaintop experience to see the goals and standards that I wanted to set for myself.

This veil was a thin cloth, and Booker T. Washington no longer wanted it over this slave. No more shielding... No more hiding... No more distorting... This veil did not belong over the slave in the statue anymore. Booker T. Washington knew the slave needed to see the world by educational and industrial terms and not those defined by his course of slavery.

I immediately recognized that I was that slave, and I, like him, needed to see the world with new terms. I wanted to be pointed toward the way of progress through education and industry, for there were things I had not seen, and I had a desire to know more and become more.

The vision of this statue activated feelings within me that came up like volcanic eruptions - more like eruptions of declarations. I would return to Tuskegee one day as a student studying at the institution that Booker T. Washington had headed and lifted so many veils for each student that attended. Studying would be my first priority, and I would get everything that Booker T. Washington wanted to give the slave in the statue, and to all Negroes he wanted to see uplifted. This was a promise I made to myself before I could rise, and my knees straightened, and before my tears could dry.

CHAPTER 26 – THE ADVENTURE BEGINS

After walking around Tuskegee's campus, we slept well in our quarters, like babies who entered the world without any cares or worries. I was in Dorothy Hall, the guest hall, and the other boys and Mr. Armstrong had different sleeping quarters. They were in the Emeries, which were dormitories where students were housed. I wouldn't dare say it was the luck of the draw that I was placed in Dorothy Hall, because I had long learned that whatever happened was because God had arranged it for me. I felt good to have been in the guest house.

I felt refreshed as I got up, stretching, touching my toes, and twisting my torso. Looking in the mirror, I washed my face, brushed my teeth, and combed my hair. Getting my clothes together was not going to be a big decision: just overalls and a shirt.

I was ready to begin the day. For a second, I wondered how home must have been different without me there. Thomas and Janet were probably doing quite a bit of chores, and Mama was washing and cooking for both her home and her father's, Old Man Jim's home. I wished that Mama would simply say "no" to the demands of her father. Actually, I thought she was being overworked to have to wash and cook for both places. Without complaint, Mama obliged, and never did I remember her doing anything differently.

I couldn't entertain the thought much longer and reach for my clothes for the day. Today was not going to be a dress with pants and sport coat day. It was a day of judging livestock and getting right in the midst of the farm. The clothes I had were the most tattered ones I had, but a good clean, respectable set of overalls that farmers would have if they went to town to pick up farming supplies.

I looked at the time and made sure everything in my area was neat before we met Mr. Armstrong for breakfast. I gathered my bookbag and made sure I had my key.

As I approached the outside, Mr. Armstrong was right there where he said he would be. The other two boys were walking toward us, and we arrived at the same point, as if on cue.

"Good morning, boys. How did everybody sleep last night?" The other two boys said "good," but I said "great," and they looked at each other like they were glad to hear it since they were so perplexed the night before at Booker T. Washington's statue.

Breakfast was in the dining hall where we had dinner, and it seemed to go in slow motion, but that was because it was moving against the speed of my eagerness. As good as it was, I was interested in our agenda for the New Farmers of America Activities. I was revved up like a motor ready to take off, in spite of the orange juice that was in front of me that we never drank home. I did take a moment to enjoy every swallow, yet I had my mind ready to see everything the New Farmers of America could offer us.

After leaving breakfast, we set our course for the day. Mr. Armstrong led us to our destination, as we had a strong pace. It almost seemed like we were in lock-step.

As we moved to the Agricultural Section of Tuskegee, not even manure or mud could kill my spirits. I saw boys fanning the stench of excrement away and making faces, but this was agriculture, and these were animals. Surely, they could put up with this for a little while.

"Let's get you guys some clipboards," Mr. Armstrong said. I could tell he was ready for business, and he couldn't wait until we were ready to start.

I saw some of the same boys that were in the dining hall, and I wondered who was going to actually present their speeches. I was unsure how it was decided who would actually start where, because coming from all over the state, a few schools at the time had to view and judge the livestock.

Mr. Armstrong passed us the clipboards, and I looked carefully at the information. He gave us pencils, too, as we would have to make marks and comments about the livestock.

****

"Okay, boys, execute all the things you know. Remember to look at all details of the livestock and make the determinations according to everything you have studied," Mr. Armstrong said.

My mind dodged around to the boys I saw and who would probably be giving a speech. It wasn't like I was going to have a leg up on the competition just looking, but I was curious. I guess it was something about knowing who they were that was going to quench my curiosity. But I had to think for a second that none of this was going to help, not a bit. Only Mama's advice to acknowledge God was going to help me be who I needed to be when I made my presentation. I was determined to use the spiritual formula. In all thy ways + Acknowledging God = A Directed Path.

I was not going to worry about who I thought was speaking anymore. I had to remember that I came with confidence. Therefore I was going to carry the confidence and leave with confidence – no matter the outcome.

Parading in front of us were the Hereford cows. These cows were not average cows. These were huge cows like none I had ever seen in Talladega. Yes, I had seen them in books and brochures, but not on the average farm. These were purebred cows that had been introduced to only the best grains and care in the state. Tuskegee had some top livestock in its Agriculture Department and to see them in person was impressive.

I looked at the first one, and I saw two brown ears and a white face. That showed the markings of a cow that could be registered. If even one ear had too much white, that was going to be a cow that was going to be prepared to be culled – fed for food. However, the registered one was going to be ideal for breeding. I looked on my chart on my clipboard, and this was a cow that was definitely receiving the mark of an A. On our charts, the animals could receive A, B, C, or D, according to their physical characteristics as we judged them.

Looking around, I didn't see nearly the people I saw in the dining hall. All of the boys would not have been able to successfully be in the area where the animals were to judge them. In many ways, I felt like an Agricultural Extension

Officer that reported information to farmers and companies. This was actually something that was very interesting to me.

As I walked around to see the other animals, this was a wonderful experience that I thought Charles and Kyser would have probably enjoyed. They would have marveled at the animals and the people we were meeting across the state of Alabama. With Charles being a stranger to no one, he would have probably held card games in the evenings.

I caught a glimpse of the other boys that rode down with me, and Mr. Armstrong way off in a far corner. I knew he couldn't interact with us as we were judging, but I surely couldn't wait to hear what he was thinking. Surely when we had dinner, if we were going to eat together, we could talk about the livestock we had just seen.

As I moved on to the other cows, I saw Guernsey, Jersey, and Holstein cows. My eyes widened. I knew this was a barn, but the word barn seemed to be too insignificant for these animals. These animals looked like they could walk right through a barn. The hair on these cows looked as if it were groomed, and we were not judging that. We were to make a determination of whether these animals would be registered as breeders or whether they would be culled. To an untrained eye, even those that were marked to be culled were great looking animals. However, there were standards that had to be kept for the livestock to be at its best for breeding.

We had more cows to see, and I was far from being tired of this adventure. I was a little hungry, but I could push that away for a little while longer to be able to see cows in the way that God had designed them while at their very best.

****

"That was some adventure!" I said with lots of enthusiasm.

"William, you looked like you were enjoying every minute judging those animals," Mr. Armstrong said, as we were in line at the dining hall.

"I sure did. Those animals were so well maintained. Those that I graded to be culled still had a beauty that was evident."

"Yes, they were great looking animals," Mr. Armstrong agreed.

"What did you boys enjoy about the judging today?" Mr. Armstrong asked the other two boys of Talladega.

One of the boys looked at the other one as if to defer to him to answer first. Honestly, I didn't remember seeing them at judging once we all were moving around and writing on our clipboards.

"We were amazed. Since we hadn't really seen a lot of livestock on a farm, this was a big deal," one of the boys said.

The other one agreed but remained somewhat silent. These guys were in my classes, but for whatever reason, I had never really known a lot about them. They had academic qualities about them. Their work was neat, and they answered questions with detail, but other than that, I really didn't know them well. I didn't think Charles and Kyser knew them that well either because I never heard them mention or refer to them. However, they had to be good guys if Mr. Armstrong chose them because he was definitely choosing those who were the best representatives for the school.

"Thanks for having dinner with us, Mr. Armstrong," the other boy said.

"You are very welcome. I just want to check in and see how you all felt about the judging, because tomorrow we are going to see some other animals, and it will be just like today. We can't see all of them at once with roughly one-hundred and fifty students filing in and out!"

"So tomorrow, we will do the same thing with different animals?" one of the boys asked.

"Yes, but please note. They could be cows, but different breeds of cows. Trust me; if you enjoyed it today, you will like it just as much tomorrow."

I felt like a child getting ready to shoot marbles, when they rub their hands together, in hopes of getting ready to win the big "cat-eye" marble or one that was mostly coveted by the players. Tomorrow couldn't come fast enough for me.

Dinner was excellent as usual, and I had my mind on the ice cream. I had not only seconds but thirds and fourths. It was something about the milk and sweet taste that ran together and swirled into a bursting delight.

"Boys, tomorrow I'm going to have dinner with some of my colleagues that brought students also, and that will give you some independence. By now, you know how to get around the campus and where to meet."

"Yes, sir," we all said.

"Now tonight, I want you to get a good night's sleep, but before you go to bed, I want you to write about today's activities in a journal, and make a point to writing down what you saw, what you did, and include what you expect the next day to be like."

"Journal?" one of the boys said.

"Yes, journal," Mr. Armstrong began to clarify. "This can be a section in a tablet that you already have, and I want you to write down what you did today. This was the first activity that required you to give the animals a grade of A, B, C, D."

"So, we are writing this down to share with other students?" the other boy asked.

"That's exactly what I had in mind," Mr. Armstrong continued.

"Sometimes, we as teachers can tell all that we know about things that happen in the agricultural world, be it at a convention, conference, or contest. But, when students get a chance to tell their experiences, they tend to become even more interested in the subject and interworkings of agriculture."

"When did you become interested in agriculture, Mr. Armstrong?" I asked before I had a chance to change my mind.

Mr. Armstrong gave me a perplexed looked that I couldn't' figure out at the moment. Maybe he didn't think students were interested in knowing why he was so passionate about agriculture and teaching it to others. When he began to answer, I could tell he was glad to explain.

****

"William, I don't get asked that question very often, not by students. I guess they just think I just appeared here, and it just happened. But I grew up on a farm, and I saw the in's and out of farm life, and it was not an easy road, not by far."

"What do you mean when you say not easy?" one of the boys asked.

"It was hands-on, and that is expected. It involved lots of hours, and the weather isn't always predictable. Spring is nice when it comes to farming, but not every crop grows during that time, nor is it harvested during that time," Mr. Armstrong replied.

"But, there was always something about it that I liked. I could see that what you put into the farm was what you got out of it. The formula was foolproof. When you plant your crops and nurture the plants, you get a great harvest. And you all know that when you nurture, that means watering, fertilizing, removing grass and weeds, or whatever hinders the crop from growing."

"Wow! It sounds like you love farming," one of the boys said.

"Actually, I do. That's why I go out into the community and help farmers make the best of their crops and livestock. I didn't forget that. The animals have to be attended to and nurtured as well. A lot of times, what hinders a farm from being at its top-notch point is what the farmer might not know," Mr. Armstrong extended passionately.

"So, do you find that many farmers are in need of lots of knowledge to better their farm?" I asked.

"Many are doing the right things, but just need to be more efficient. Most farmers are doing what they saw their parents do, and there is nothing wrong with that, but there are some tips and techniques that they can use to save on expenses and make more of a profit at the end."

We all saw Mr. Armstrong's passion and could see why he gave two-hundred percent when he did something.

"So, was the farm you grew up on an efficient one?" one of the boys asked. I wouldn't have wanted to ask that question. I knew Mr. Armstrong wouldn't mind, but I thought of it as one that was requiring him to tell more than maybe he wanted to.

"Well, like most farms, we ran them according to what we knew. Then, when we had more knowledge about how to plant according to the animals we had, the food we needed, and what we needed, we were better at farming," Mr. Armstrong revealed.

"What also really helped was reflecting on how things worked the year before, and what could work even better."

"Don't you have different things from year to year?" the other boy said.

"Yes, indeed, but you still think about things like when to start planting, and when to get the seeds. Also, if you are going to have more or less livestock."

For a moment, we all ate in silence, pondering what we had just heard. We knew Mr. Armstrong was always sincere, but we got a chance to really see the drive behind his passion for agriculture.

I got up and got one more helping of ice cream, and I thought that would do it for me. I saw the other boys go back for something, but I didn't exactly know what they were getting. On my way back, I saw Mr. Armstrong sitting at the table with a look on his face, not exactly staring into the crowd or looking into a space of nothingness, but it was a look that one could have read as satisfied. I wanted to believe he felt he had chosen three students who were earnest and passionate about agriculture as he was. If they weren't before we came, I think he felt that based on what we were seeing, and what we just heard him explain, had cultivated our minds properly about farming. It was as if the look also said, "My work is done!"

"Boys, I'll see you bright and early, and don't forget to journal."

We all went our separate ways, and I began to think about my presentation. It was still days away, not too much, but I was determined to keep that look that Mr. Armstrong had on his face a permanent one.

****

Tomorrow came fast, just like I wanted it, and today was here. I got my breakfast in the dining hall and ate a variety of things that were offered. The eggs were deliciously scrambled; they got the center of attention once I put them on my plate. I got toast, bacon, and preserves. I didn't wait for the other boys; I decided to execute my independence and just get to the dining hall to eat, take in the scenery, and reflect.

I saw Mr. Armstrong from a distance, and he waved, I waved back. He was sitting down with some other teachers that had brought students to the conference. That was quite understandable; I'm sure he wanted to exchange their experiences and techniques about farming.

"Good morning," the other two boys said as they came up.

I hadn't seen them come in, but I had to admit, I was looking around at the décor in the dining hall and dividing my attention with my eggs.

"Good morning," I responded."

"You must have gotten up really early," one of the boys said.

"Yes, I did. I couldn't wait until today."

"Yeah, I couldn't wait either. The judging was really something that all the students at school would love to participate in."

"I think so, too. I even believe some of the girls would like to be a part of this program," the other boy joined in.

"I think you have a point," I added. "I do have sisters that would do a great job if this were open to girls. My sisters have done a lot of hard farm work, and they definitely could do this examination of animals."

I thought of Ruth and how my father made her burn the cow. I would have much rather seen her do something productive like learning and judging them than to be burning them.

"I'm sure one day girls will be able to be in the New Farmers of America organization," the other boy said.

"Yeah, I think so," I said, and we all agreed.

"Wonder what's happening at school?" one of the boys said.

"The normal stuff," the other boy said.

"I'm sure they are wondering what we are doing," I said.

We all laughed and finished our breakfast, and made our way to the "Ag" side of the campus.

By the time we got there, we all had our clipboards and pencils, and we were ready to get started. We saw Mr. Armstrong come in and we were already prepared. We had a little while before we were to begin, and there was an excitement in my being. I thought of thinking about my speech, but I was not going to think about that now. I decided to pray and ask God to guide all our minds, not only Talladega Boys, but the entire group, while asking Him to recall all things to our remembrances. Our answers on the scorecards were going to judge on how well we worded them and how detailed our rationale was about the livestock.

"Amen," I said part quietly and somewhat openly. The two boys were looking directly at me, but I suppose after seeing me at the statue the first night with all my emotions, it wouldn't have surprised them if I prayed out loud.

I didn't know if we were going to see only cows, or pigs, or chickens, but I was excited just the same.

It was time to begin, and we were escorted to our areas.

My eyes were widened when I saw these cows. These cows were blacker than any of the nights I had lived in Talladega put together. Their coats were shiny and looked smoother than any feathers on a raven. It was easy to look all at once and be overwhelmed by their color, and see all the black at once. But, looking at the Angus required closer examination.

When I saw the first one that required intense examination, there were brown and white spots. This alone was enough to recommend that animals be culled.

Time passed by so quickly because we were so involved. It was a long day, but it surely wasn't anything but cultivation to a young farmer's mind.

CHAPTER 27 - THE SPEECH

This was the mornings of all mornings. It was finally here. I thought I would stop where I was and pray. I knelt and talked to God the way Mama had always taught me. This was something I did every morning before, during, and after Tuskegee, but this time, I had requests, along with thanksgiving, and acknowledgment of all God had done for me. Today I needed Him to command me to do all the things that he designed me to do. I was going to pray that God's will would be done.

The clothes that Uncle Ernest had taken me to town to get were on the bed. I arranged them, along with the socks, belt, and shoes. I knew from the beginning out of the clothes I bought, what I wanted to wear.

I showered and made sure I had everything in order. Brushing my hair made me think of Miss Gibbs, Miss Slater, and Miss New, who suggested I get a sharp haircut. I stared at myself and saw a winner, whether I presented one word or not. Everything Mama had taught me led me to know that I was made in God's own image, and He was a winner.

I straightened my tie and took one last look in the mirror. There would be more time in the afternoon for judging livestock after the speech contest, so I gathered clothes for that and carried them in my bag.

The eggs didn't excite me this morning, but I got them just for nourishment. Actually, none of the food did, but I was more than grateful that it was available. The truth was that my mind was on the day at hand, and I was ready to start.

I didn't wait for the boys. I left and went to the conference area, where everyone was going to meet. We were not going to meet where the livestock was but in a conference area.

I wanted to be there to size up the area and know the distance to project my voice. It was my belief that God was going to direct my path, but I needed to do my part in the preparation.

When I went in, there were people there setting up.

"Good morning," came from somewhere, but I couldn't see. I responded with a confident "Good morning." It was a man who was setting up, making sure everything was ready.

"How are you, young man?" the gentleman said.

"I'm doing well," I said.

"Where are you from?" he asked

"I'm from Talladega."

"Oh yeah, I know some people in Talladega."

I wondered which ones but didn't ask.

"Could I help you with anything, sir," I asked.

"I'm just finishing up, but thank you anyway."

"Is this your first time at the New Farmers of America Conference?" he asked.

"Yes, sir," I replied.

"What have you enjoyed most here?" this gentleman asked.

"I have enjoyed seeing the livestock and judging them."

"Well, you must really do well in your agriculture classes and see the purpose in it," he said.

"I have a great teacher, Mr. Armstrong, and he prepared us so well, it seems like everything is just like he taught it and described it."

"That's great! I've asked many boys, and I think all have enjoyed the conference, but many have said they enjoyed a lot of things outside the conference, like the food, and the campus."

"I understand. The food has been great," I said.

"Well, you are in for a treat today. There will be singing and speaking presentations that will be excellent."

I almost said I was going to be one of the speakers, but I changed my mind. I thought I would just let this gentleman be surprised.

****

The conference area was beginning to fill up with students. Boys I had seen all week were easily recognized now. Some I knew because they were extremely tall, or they resembled someone in my family.

Mr. Armstrong and the boys had not arrived, but I knew they were coming soon. I decided to meet some of the boys that I hadn't met before and ask them where they attended school. Some of the cities I hadn't heard of before, but it's hard to know every city in a state and every little town. I decided to do what the gentleman asked me when I first came to the conference room. I asked them what they had enjoyed most about our visit to Tuskegee, and sure enough, many boys named things that didn't, at first, relate to the conference. After listening to them, I had to understand that many didn't grow up on a farm; I made sure to ask that. Many hadn't traveled long distances before, for I hadn't either, and I think there were so many other things to be excited about outside the conference. However, after talking to them further, they enjoyed the study of agriculture, and they loved the sight of the animals they had seen."

"William, you sure are on the ball," I heard coming from a distance.

"Good morning, Mr. Armstrong."

"Good morning, William. It looks like you know your way around this place."

"Yes, sir, I wanted to be here extra early and get a feel for my audience," I said, feeling he would understand.

He patted me on the back.

"You got the right idea, and you are going to be great today," Mr. Armstrong said.

I saw the boys coming.

"Good morning," we all said at the same time.

"Let's get to where we are going to be sitting," Mr. Armstrong said.

We went to our area and sat down.

"Thank you," I said, as some young men passed our programs to us.

I looked inside, and I saw the order of the program, and then I saw where the speeches were going to be delivered. I felt energy run up and down my spine.

In the front, a man stood and called the program to order.

"Good morning New Farmers of America."

If I had been blindfolded, I would have thought it was Mr. Armstrong. The voice resembled him, even the way the gentleman paused between his words.

"I know I'm speaking to the best and the brightness in the state of Alabama."

Everyone clapped wildly and enjoyed the greeting, along with the vote of confidence.

"We are going to get started with the Invocation," the gentleman said.

We all bowed our heads and listened to the words. I let every word speak to me, and I was thankful yet again for my mother, making sure I knew Christ as my personal Savior. By doing so, the words were no stranger to me, but instead, a light unto my pathway.

"Amen," everyone said collectively.

"Today, we are going to hear speeches from young men across the state of Alabama on a variety of subjects about Agriculture and Farming, but before we do, we are going to hear a group of young men bring us some joy in song."

The crowd began clapping profusely. I didn't know whether everybody else knew the boys singing, and perhaps I didn't, or whether the students in attendance were glad to experience a different plan in the program. I didn't know there was going to be singing, but when these boys started, I couldn't do anything but stare with my mouth opened in awe.

****

The music was like none I had ever heard live. I had heard singing in church that was good, but these boys seemed like natural performers. There were twins in the group, and one of them had a solo part. He captured the audience on the first note, and he held every listener in the room captive.

Soon, everyone's feet were patting the floor as if to keep time with the singer. Some of the boys had begun to clap their hands. It wasn't like there were any rules that commanded them to do it differently. Tuskegee was indeed a dignified campus, but one thing I could tell right off the bat, they were not, as I heard in church many times, "Ashamed of the Gospel." This was just my assessment, but if we couldn't be Future Farmers of America with the White students, we could be with God in our organization, New Farmers of America, and remember the God that had kept us.

This young man had a voice that was beyond extraordinary. He was ready for the "big times" voice. Had he chosen to sing professionally on this "self-same" day, he could have. He was also an identical twin, so one could only imagine the combined talent from the two of them.

I believe the audience was far removed from any agricultural thoughts. It was more like church. But that was what was good about; it brought us back to our roots, as we acknowledged the God to whom we belonged.

The group sang two more selections, and if the audience was feeling anything like I was and what I was perceiving, they could have sung all day, and no one would have said anything differently. With all the speeches we were to deliver, we would have been willing to deliver them later in the night. However, the time had come for the program to change and take shape into what we were there to do.

The gentlemen who I had titled the "MC of the Program" in my head, was back in front.

"Was this not a fine group of singers?" the man said.

I could not have agreed more if I had been paid to agree. These guys were phenomenal. We all clapped wildly again and again. It seemed that the crowd went on responding with an hour of applause. Everyone was revved up.

"Let us begin to start our speeches for the day," The master of ceremonies said. The crowd was clapping, and I wasn't sure it wasn't still from the singing.

"Each school has a representative who will speak about their given topic, and we cannot wait to hear these young men give their speeches. We know they have been working hard because the young men have been working for a few months gathering their information."

The MC was right about that. I had researched, gathered information, written, rewritten, edited, and did everything I could to make sure my speech was all that it should be.

"We are not going to go in any alphabetical order by school or name. We don't want to cause any worries along the way. When you hear your name and school, please proceed to the podium."

After the MC said that, I listened for the first name and school. Since I didn't hear William L. Groce, Jr., I couldn't honestly say I focused on the name or school. I just took a deep breath and prepared myself to listen to this speech.

A young man with dark pants, a white shirt, and dark tie walked up. He was clean-cut and sharp, just like my teachers suggested for me. I had to admit, they were right. The look was just what was needed. He walked up with great posture and great confidence, and he stood behind the podium.

I waited for his opening words. It seems like it was minutes before he began. I could hardly wait to see how he was going to begin. Was he going to open with a question? Was he going to open with a quote? Was he going to present a situation where the audience participated? He finally began, and his opening was definitely worth the wait.

****

I saw a vision of self-assurance. Check, I had that. I saw knowledge of the subject matter. Check, I had that. I saw someone commanding the audience. Check, I had that. I was not looking for anything to dislike about this speaker, for I was actually looking at what he had with admiration. I was not out to critique him against who I was, yet, I did want to make sure I had what I saw in him and the other speakers. If the judges and audience were used to these features, why give them less?

This guy was giving it his all. It was a packed speech of farming and techniques that he made seem practical. Whether a person had been farming for years or just beginning, they would have been glad to try his techniques. His speech was about the techniques of winter farming. As much as Papa was stuck in his methods of doing things, I believe he would have been ready to convert.

It was evident that the schools in Alabama did not send any unprepared students. These boys were sharp. Just like I had been coached and advised, so had they. And to be honest, that's exactly how it should have been. I was glad to know that there were black educators who wanted their students to do well. We already didn't have the best resources. Some black schools had buildings that were just holding on. However, we really were fortunate at Talladega Training County School to have a good building, a cannery that Mr. Armstrong ran and produced wonderful beef stew from, a good sports program, and many good teachers. However, some of the books were handed over from white schools, but we made it work to our best.

A rousing applause came. This young man was very deserving of it. His speech was clear, precise, and easy to follow. Check, Check, and Check. I had all those things. It was a matter of me bringing them to the podium when my time came.

Each time a name was called, I "stretched" my ear to listen for my name. Other students were called, and I had nothing but the same critique for the rest of them. I could only imagine where these boys would be in twenty years. They would be doing what they enjoyed because they loved learning and would be diligent in their interests.

Then I heard it. I heard my name, William L. Groce, Jr. It had finally come. I moved the muscles in my body, and all of them were alerted to get to the podium. I called the name of my Lord, and before asking Him anything, I chose to thank Him for the opportunity. I had already asked Him for success and victory in my delivery, so I decided with every step, I would give thanks.

I vividly remembered what a prayer of thanksgiving yielded when I would go to the tree to pray, just like when I was preparing for the mourner's bench. I told God just how grateful I was, in spite of how I may be feeling or previously have felt. I gave thanks for the mere fact that He created me, and I had a future he especially designed.

I was going to thank God for all He had done for me. Yes, I had experienced lack, but I was still going to thank Him. I began to thank God for His existence, for without Him, I couldn't imagine where any of us would be.

I was just a few steps from the podium, and the walk wasn't just any walk. The thanks just seemed to roll from my heart. How grateful I was that we could pray silently, and no one could hear it. That was one of the benefits of knowing a God like mine. We could thank, pray, and praise Him whenever we wanted to, even if we were told we couldn't.

I took my last step and gave God one last thanks, and this was for allowing me to be right here at Tuskegee.

The previous speakers had many different openings. Some were questions, some were statements, and others were quotes from famous people, but I was going to begin with a scenario. After all the time I had prepared, I thought this would be best months ago. I had heard my share of speeches through the years with many styles of openings, but I wanted the audience to first activate their imagination.

****

I took my last step to the podium, and I felt like I was on home plate, ready to deliver a home run. I positioned myself toward the audience with enthusiasm and eagerness to speak. Surveying the audience, I could see faces of anticipation. I had heard that some speakers never choose to look directly into the faces of an audience as they spoke, but I decided that I didn't want to miss the moment of seeing what the faces looked like in the audience of the New Farmers of America.

It was evident that we were all students who had earned our spots to come to this conference, and everybody was very sharp. Every speaker had great passion, and I knew I would speak with the same command that they had. In fact, I was so confident about this group of young men that I felt every speaker behind me would speak with the same passion and fervor.

As I was about to start, this venture felt less like a competition and more like I was in the midst of a camaraderie of stellar students – all with great agricultural messages.

The time had come for me to begin.

"Imagine you have inherited a one-hundred-acre farm with twenty cows, forty chickens, and twenty pigs. Barns are already a part of the package, and so are the fences. But once you are settled into this new farm, what could be done to make this farm the best? Do you plant the same kind of crops on all the available planting acres, or do you plant a variety of crops? Do you plant crops to feed the livestock? Do you turn the livestock out across all or most of the land? Do you plant crops with the proper timing to keep the soil from eroding?"

"I'm sure none of the answers would be alike. Actually, many answers would be different. Yet, as different as our answers may be, our answers must include the benefit of balanced farming for our farms to be most productive."

As I was speaking, I saw my peanut crop. I could see Will, who was with me at every step, and surely the Talladega sun was present, who wouldn't consider missing a plowing, planting, or picking session.

I kept speaking, and I saw heads nodding and smiles throughout the crowd.

I begin to see the fields and farms of some of the places I had lived. First, I saw the Thornton place with Mama's tomatoes. I could see her standing in the garden after school as the bus dropped me off. Mama always had a garden, and even though she had not formally learned the benefit of balanced farming as Mr. Armstrong had taught us, she was pretty sharp when it came to keeping the soil rich by planting different things after we would harvest the vegetables.

My mind somehow became a dual activator inside my head, speaking words from my speech and chauffeuring me through the fields of my life.

"After you harvest a crop, it's important to plant other crops behind that crop to prevent soil erosion."

Next, I could see Grandpa Robert's Place. The rows were long, and the sweet potatoes were numerous. The barn was filled with them in cool temperatures to bring the sweetness of them to an optimal point.

I kept talking, and I was making stops mentally to various fields, but I couldn't help but circle back to my peanut crop. That experience was truly farming as I saw it from start to finish. There were so many steps. I truly experienced planting, weeding, and harvesting that crop. However, at the same time, it brought all my family together in the field. Agriculturally speaking, I knew that planting crops, rotating crops, and making sure the soil was rich was so important, along with planting crops that supplied food for the livestock. But I saw my family in the field all at once, with the exception of my father, and saw something that was very balanced that day, for everyone had believed in my crop. By the time I saw this last scene, I had said the last words of my speech. I heard thunderous applause.

I could see Mr. Armstrong, where I had not seen him before. Maybe he was standing in the place where he was the whole time, but I didn't see him earlier. Maybe I was in one of the fields I had traveled back to. It was as if his clapping was in slow motion. His smile was gleaming, and if I had been deaf, I would have known just by what I saw that he was proud of the job I had done.

CHAPTER 28 - REAPING THE REWARDS

Friday had finally come. Not that I was glad and wishing it was the last day of the conference; I had a feeling in my stomach that was mixed with excitement and unpredictability. I was glad that this last day was going to reveal our agricultural work, which was going to be great to see.

"Boys, this is our last day here," Mr. Armstrong said. "I just want to tell you that you boys did excellent work. This was a wonderful week, and you all represented Talladega well."

"Thank you," we all said.

"Do we have to do anything at this last event?" one of the boys asked.

"It's purely an awards celebration," Mr. Armstrong replied. "You will all get to see how you placed in the competitions, both judging livestock and making speeches."

"I can't wait to see our results," the other boy said.

"Well, I can tell you this, no matter what the scores say, you boys are winners. I took the best three, and we made a major contribution, as did the other students that came. The New Farmers of America has had one of its best conferences today," Mr. Armstrong expressed.

We finished our breakfast and walked to the conference area. While we walked, I took a good look around. This was the last time I would be here. This was one of the best weeks of my life, and I had gotten here because God saw fit for me to see a part of the world I had never seen. Even though it was just a few hours away from Talladega, I hadn't seen Tuskegee or Tuskegee Institute before. I couldn't help but think, what if I had not been redirected in my school work? What if there had been no Miss Gibbs? What if there had been no Miss Slater? What if there had been no Miss New? I was not thinking about them helping me to prepare for my speech; I was thinking about what if they hadn't been in place to redirect my learning and further develop it in my high school years?

Things looked like they were in slow motion for a few seconds. Maybe I chose to slow everything down in my view to be thankful, for I just wanted to take it all in. I wanted to hear and see the equation that was surrounding me. God plus the teachers he ordained to help me equaled me being here on the campus of Tuskegee Institute.

I had walked around for so many days in my life, wondering why so many things had happened in my family, from my father's absence. Even though he was physically present, he was absent in things where he should have participated, like providing our basic needs, shelter, food, and education. Somehow, he must have been under an "influence" that was not just drinking with his buddies, but something we probably would never know.

We had arrived at the conference room and were ready to take our seats.

****

"Good morning, New Farmers of America," the MC from yesterday announced.

"Good morning," everyone responded.

When I heard the words "Talladega County Training School" and "second place," it was as if water were in my ears and temporarily drowned out my hearing. We had come in second place for the entire state, with combining scores in judging livestock and the speaking contest; I was all but frozen.

"Boys, that's us," Mr. Armstrong said. I heard him, but I stood still.

"William, that's us," he had to nudge me on my shoulder.

"Oh," I said, and then the air seemed to shoot up through my lungs and out of my mouth, and my feet moved. If I could have run and jumped around, I would have, but I regained my composure, as I had heard teachers express to students when they were out of line.

"We actually placed second place out of the whole state," I repeated to myself.

When we reached the stage, the MC announced us, "These young men are from Talladega County Training School, from Talladega, Alabama, and their teacher, Mr. Daniel Armstrong.

"Sir," he said to Mr. Armstrong, "These young men have done some fine work. Their scoring was some of the best we have seen. The rationales they wrote to support the grade about the livestock were very detailed, and showed that they knew every breed of livestock to determine which ones would be certified."

The crowd cut in with applause in between the words. We were so happy; we couldn't keep it inside. All of our smiles combined could have lit up the whole city of Tuskegee. We were given our trophy and certificates and a path that showed us that we had the power to achieve by the route of using the minds that God gave us.

The audience applauded again as we were leaving the stage area to return to our seats. Just as I had thanked God before I spoke my first word in front of that same crowd, I was thanking him in every step back to my seat.

I knew God was real, and no matter where I was going to eventually go, He was going with me. I thought of the statue I had encountered just days ago, "Lifting the Veil of Ignorance," and I thought of my promise of coming back to this college one day. I didn't know how, and I didn't know when, but I did know it was going to happen.

I saw and applauded as other schools won, and we in the audience were equally as happy for them. I held this thought in my mind, just like the certificates we won, and I didn't want to forget it. We were happy for each other. We saw each other's strength, and in turn, it made us recognize our own.

I was off into my reflection when I heard the MC say, "Now we are going to announce the winners in the speaking contest."

Mr. Armstrong shot me an encouraging look. It was like his look was saying, "Get ready!"

I was satisfied with whatever the outcome would be, for I had seen young men from all over the state who were a dedicated group that took agriculture seriously. We all were here, not by chance, but because we were chosen on our merit. This conference showed us many aspects of agricultural life, and additionally, I left feeling a great sense of community and brotherhood.

I smiled at Mr. Armstrong and brought my hands from my lap, clasping them together.

"And now for our first-place winner in the northern region of Alabama, William L. Groce, Jr., of Talladega County Training School or Talladega, Alabama."

I was frozen again, but eventually thawed, and hugged Mr. Armstrong before I went up to get my award.

****

The hum of Mr. Armstrong's car didn't disappoint. It was the same hum that bought us to Tuskegee, where I was able to see new horizons that I had never seen before. I took one long-lasting look at Tuskegee Institute and said silently, "I'll be back."

Mr. Armstrong helped to place our bags in the trunk, and soon afterward, we were headed back toward Talladega. I was in the front seat, reminiscing about all of the week's events. I didn't watch the "movie" that I saw coming to Tuskegee, where I looked at all the houses, farms, mules, and lines of clothes. This time, I saw scenes from the campus of the Tuskegee Institute and the New Farmers of America convention.

I didn't know if these scenes would ever leave my mind, for the images were indelible. I believed I would welcome them for a lifetime. My goal now was only to add more images that would be equally as enlightening. It was a must that I go nowhere but up from here. If I had to write the credits to this wonderful movie, God's name was going to be first, for He was the author and the finisher, because, without Him, none of these wonderful scenes would have happened in my life.

Then, I would put Mr. Daniel Armstrong as Teacher and Encourager. Additionally, I would add my mother, who was not just my mother, but a caregiver, prayer giver, and support giver. No title would be too good for her.

I would have the teachers at Talladega Training School who contributed to my educational growth, but I would have to include Miss Gibbs, Miss Slater, and Miss New, as my "preparatory teachers," who especially helped to prepare me for my speech contest.

Then there was Uncle Ernest, who drove me to town to get my new clothes, and I would have to thank Kyser and Charles for their continued friendship and support.

As hard as I tried, I wanted to remember some contribution, any contribution, my father made when it came to my trip to Tuskegee, but I couldn't think of one. Of course, he was my father, and I loved him, in spite of his irrationality that was present more than it was absent, I had developed an aptitude for agriculture because of him. Because I *had* to work since Papa was often gone off with his buddies, this edhonestly help with my interest in agriculture. However, I had to admit; when I asked him to let me plant my first peanut crop, he bought me the peanuts. It was the first crop that I tended to from start to finish, giving me a full knowledge of what it was like to be responsible for preparing, planting, and harvesting a crop. I thought this was worthy for me to credit him.

Then, there were my sisters and brother that helped to harvest the crop, and each would have their names included with titles that included synonyms of the word *supporter*. The scene of them all in the field at once was a scene I would always remember.

Now, I couldn't forget Will. He had listened to my words. I had practiced my speech many afternoons as he listened. Although non-communicative with words, I could feel his support.

This mental "movie" production of my life, as I saw it, was going to be the beginning of what I was going to do with my life. There was no holding me back now!

"Boy's, now when we get back to school, Monday after next, after Spring Break this week, we are going to be on stage, and you all will be recognized for your fine work at the New Farmers of America Conference."

I was okay with that. If I could present in front of all the strangers at the conference, I wouldn't be frightened of the school community. That was just going to be another segment in the movie.

I was sure this was going to be one of the best Spring Breaks I had. I might not be going anywhere outside of Talladega, but it was where I had been that totally counted. The time I had in Tuskegee would last well after Spring Break was over. My memories would be all that I needed, and I was going to be happier than ever.

It seemed that we got to Talladega faster than we got to Tuskegee, but I'm sure I was on the inside of my mind with my "movie." Mr. Armstrong offered us drinks and crackers that he had in the car. I didn't eat anything. If I was hungry, I didn't notice it. I was too involved in my thoughts, and I was grateful for every moment of this experience.

Mr. Armstrong's sedan turned into our yard. I could hear the same popping sound on the gravel that the tires made when we left the school. This was now the signature sound that I put in my "movie" at the beginning and end. As we got nearer to the house, I could see Janet and Thomas playing in the yard. They came running, and I ran to meet them. All the sophistication that I had in my "movie mind" went right out the window. I jumped up and down when I saw them, and let out greetings with high pitch shrieks, as I could hear my echo.

I couldn't wait to see everybody and tell them about my journey. I knew everybody would love hearing about it, but it was really Mama whom I could not wait to tell all about it.

****

Usually, any school break wouldn't be long enough, but this Spring Break seems to creep by. I wasn't in a hurry for the break to go faster, but I was eager to get back to school to see Charles and all the well-wishers of Talladega County Training School. I had a full mental list: the teachers and students who wished us well before we left. When we returned, it would be time for them to see that their faith in us was not in vain, but sewn in a fruitful soil, where we delivered what we knew and with all the confidence God, the father, allowed us to have.

I stepped on the bus, and the sound I could always count on, where the brakes would squeal coming to a halt, welcomed me back to the place where I was so familiar.

I strolled to the back of the bus and took a seat. It was the same route of steps I had taken now for ten years. Flashes of the statue "Lifting the Veil of Ignorance" ran across the screen of my mind. A question proceeded to enter my mind. How many steps would it take me to get back to the statue? Now, I knew that wouldn't be the best measurement to use? I had a little fun just thinking about it. But I did wonder how many years would it take for me to return to Tuskegee's Campus as I promised myself. I wasn't promising myself to go back as a guest or speaker again at a convention; I wanted to go as a student. My best measurements couldn't be in steps, but perhaps I would look at years. How many years would it be before I was a student there? Could I go in two years? I just couldn't see it happening in two years. I believe it could be if the money was there, but where was there ever any money?

In the midst of my thoughts, the bus had arrived at our daily destination. I saw Charles and Kyser, and I couldn't get off the bus fast enough. Of course, I had seen Kyser over Spring Break, and I had relived all my adventures by telling him about Tuskegee, but I hadn't seen Charles.

"William, how are you!" Charles said.

"Good," I said as we hugged and patted each other on the back within the hug."

"I heard you did good things down at Tuskegee!"

"How did you hear about that so soon?" I asked.

"Even if I didn't hear a word, I know you did well," Charles said emphatically.

The bell had rung, and all our homeroom classes met first thing in the auditorium. As we began our day, we started with devotion and a song. But on this day, an addendum was added, and the principal, Mr. Franklin, introduced Mr. Armstrong, me, and the two boys to the school. With proudness in his voice, he announced that we had represented the school well at the New Farmers of America Agricultural Competition at Tuskegee Institute. The school welcomed us with thunderous applause and a "ticker-tape" like welcome, and they were excited to hear our presentations.

When I got ready to deliver my speech, I remembered my classroom experiences from first grade to the present. I was a boy who once stuttered, and with help from teachers and participation in plays, I overcame this impediment.

As I began my speech, I surmised some nods, some smiles, and some surprised looks, because many students and teachers didn't know of my inadequacies or perhaps my potential. I shot a look over at Mr. Armstrong, and it was evident he was proud of me. I was one of the fruits from his labor, and so were the other two boys. As far as I could see, I saw a sea of smiles.

After we finished, it was time to return to our first class. I stepped down from the stage, and each step seemed to mark my time at Talladega County Training School. I could hear the echoes from the wood beneath my feet like a tune delivering the soundtrack to my years. I saw former teachers and current teachers congratulating me, and the melody in my head that was an exultant, upbeat tune. But suddenly, what was a tune of glory was becoming a little offbeat and somewhat discordant. I tried to keep in step and I continued walking, hearing cheers and applauses, but the tune became severely offbeat.

I saw former teachers, current teachers, and other teachers I had never had congratulating me, but then there was one teacher coming toward me as if she were destined to come to me at that moment and time. My mind was beginning to be mixed with shock and the memory of this woman's pedagogical practices.

"I want to congratulate you on how well you did," she said with a voice of what sounded liked sincerity. I attempted to keep the melody in rhythm, but the memory of her placed upon me discordant overtones in my victory song. Nevertheless, I had to keep it together, and although shocked, surprised, and appalled, I said, "thank you," and let the flow of the crowd carry me quickly into my next destination to my first-period class.

When I got to my seat in the class, I wondered was this her way of saying the things she couldn't say. Was this congratulatory package formed with an apology at the same time? I had to wonder, did she reminisce during my speech and see the little boy that she had never sown joyfulness into, but instead the little boy who she tore the very fabric of his feelings and state of being? Now that a decade had passed, what was going through her mind? Was she now the victim of her own discriminative practices, wishing she had done more?

I was now far from just the dark-skinned boy that was in her class. I was a brother to the sisters she loved better than me because of their hue. Her congratulations to me were no doubt hinged on some aching form of regret that was like a fountain coming up without her ability to control it. Perhaps there, in the moment of my speech, there was a mirror where she could see herself while reflecting her that people are people, no matter who or what they looked like. Also, maybe she saw the mind as a valuable entity that God created, and with the right influence, investment, and interest, it is worth being a part of a student no matter how he looks. But now it was too late. She had sealed her fate as an investor, it was already determined how she would be remembered, and there was nothing now but to say the words, "You did a good job," the last effort to place a hand on my life, perhaps removing some of the layers of yesterday. A little sorrow, a little sincerity, and a little sympathy came through from her that day, but I remembered each day all too well before her compliment of my speech.

It wasn't going to be that day or even a decade later that I would forgive her, but for the moment, I could respond with a "thank you" for her recognizing that I could do something outstanding. This woman was the first, the beginning, to my educational journey. This "thank you" came from the very first teacher I ever had.

As I continued through the crowd, if every 'thank you' was a piece of confetti, we would have had mounds to clean up. Our school was extremely proud of us, and it was just the beginning of experiencing achievement as I would eventually know it.

Mr. Armstrong was so proud; he had a particular glow to his complexion that morning, you could see pride all over his face. But there was something I had been keeping from him, and I had been thinking about it for the last two years. I thought of leaving school and had I done so; I would have missed this experience.

****

The same pats I had gotten on the back from Charles when I hadn't seen him for two weeks, he was again giving them to me in less than two hours. This time he was giving them because he knew exactly what I had said at the Oratorical Contest in Tuskegee.

"I knew you were great there!" Charles said.

"Thanks, Charles," I managed to get out as the people were coming around me in droves.

The 'thank yo's' from the crowd were in loud verbal forms, while some mouthed to us silently from a distance. After Charles' hug, Miss Gibbs, Miss Slater, and Miss New came to me like a tornado making a path to a destination. They were making their way over to me. All I could hear were a bunch of "Williams," and I felt more and more hugs, whereas, at one time, I thought my feet were no longer touching the ground.

Kyser squeezed within all the people around me and gave me a hug as well.

"Kyser, I want to thank you and Uncle Ernest for me just being there. I appreciate how Uncle Ernest took me to town and convinced Papa to let me do some shopping for clothes, so I would be in presentable clothes."

"You know Papa didn't mind," Kyser responded. "He was so glad to help you."

There was a continuation of "I knew you could do it," "We are so proud of you," and "Thank you for representing us so well."

I had decided that this could be the beginning, or it could be the end of a feeling of accomplishment. If I stay in Talladega, the end. If I leave, the beginning. I couldn't let it be the end. I wanted more. Everything that had transpired at the New Farmers Convention up to this point told me I had to go further. If I slowed down everything that was happening, it was like a celebration where everyone cheers all at the same time. Hands are clapping, mouths open with cheers of joys, eyes widening with excitement. It was all anyone would want if the celebration was about them, but I knew, right in the midst of this celebration, that the time had come for me to make good on the decision that had been sitting within me.

CHAPTER 29 – MY MILITARY DECISION

The next weeks of school moved quickly, and Spring was on its way out. The birds were still chirping happily, but the sun seemed like it was bursting open to beam with its most prominent rays and hottest of temperatures. The "Talladega Sun" always took its job seriously.

I had become more unwavering about going to the military, and Charles and Kyser were becoming more inclined to the idea themselves, wanting to know more as well.

"Okay, we are going to go today!" Charles said, referring to the Military Recruiter's Office.

Charles had gotten another classmate of ours, John Elston, to come along as well, joining Kyser and me. We had known John for a long time and had a lot of classes over the years. He had a humorous personality, somewhat like Charles, yet slightly more reserved. Yet, I had no idea he was interested in the military, but I suppose he wanted to hear the options the military had to offer.

The four of us put our heads together like fraternity boys who make pacts in the darkness of a chilly night. It was nothing for frat boys to run through graveyards or open fields to complete missions that would help them cross over. It was as if we were sitting in front of gravestones, reading unfamiliar names, wondering how they died, especially those who died young. Ironically, that's what we were trying not to do, die young – dying in Talladega at the hands of a dead-end life, a place we were all trying to escape. Charles, John Elston, Kyser, and I were ready to put a plan into action, placing our names on the line.

It was our lunch hour at school, and we didn't have much time to go to the Recruiter's office and hear what they were offering.

I was on my way to the back seat of Charles' car. I didn't practice getting into the front seat of anybody's car unless I was invited.

"Come on to the front, William," Charles said, looking around for the others to come. I was honored to be invited there.

"Why do you *really* want to go, William?" Charles asked. "You seem more serious about this than all of us. I don't know about the other boys," he said quickly before the others arrived at the car.

"I am. I just know there isn't anything here in Talladega but the fields, factories, and the pulpwood waiting for us."

The other boys were here, and we didn't have much time to talk further. They jumped in the back, and we were off.

I took a good look at Talladega on my way to the Armed Forces office. I saw the people who were doing their daily duties, moving steadily, rapidly, yet I knew they were standing still. No matter how much they were working trying to get ahead, they were not going to go forward or ever catch up unless something was going to change.

The military had been on our minds for a while, and especially mine. I had been thinking about this for over two years now. I was a serious candidate, with one hand already raised to the military and the other on the Bible.

Yet, like everything that God ordains, it comes with a divine timeline. Just like God created light on the day, one of creation and not people first, there was an order that God wanted my military experience to be listed in to be to my advantage.

Looking back, had I gone two years earlier, there would have been no Mr. Armstrong, no Tuskegee Ride, no Booker T. Statue, and no Oratorical Contest.

Just like God magnetically holds the rings around Saturn, God certainly wanted to empower me with the agricultural, oratorical, and academic rings before I entered the military.

The boys and I had all come to the realization that Alabama had nothing else to give us. There were only long rows of crops, scorching summer temperatures, and futures that were ambivalent. We were tired of being behind mules, seeing the world in an unprofitable slow motion that was sending us fast into nowhere. I had goals. I had made myself an ultimate promise at Booker T. Washington's statue. But how was I to get there from Talladega, Alabama? How was I to get to Tuskegee Institute? I had been thinking about this, and I was two years in on the thought of joining the military and two months thinking about Booker T. Washington's statue. It was time I had to do it. I had to leave Talladega.

I thought of teachers like Miss Gibbs, Miss Slater, Mr. Rossa, Mr. Armstrong, Miss New, and all of their efforts. They had long invested so much in me. It was their time, kindness, and encouragement, along with the way they centered me in the midst of my educational development that made me feel this was going to be heartbreaking for them. Nothing would please them more than for me to walk across the stage for graduation in two years, but I sincerely believed on the inside that they would understand my reason to quit school and go further. Although the words "Quit school and go further" didn't sound promising, I had to plot my course, believing this was the way to the beginning I wanted.

The four of us now had about forty-five minutes left in our lunch break. Charles, John, Kyser, and I got out of the car, and we were in front of an 1800's courthouse building with sidewalks and steps that would chauffer visitors' thoughts back toward the pre-antebellum period. The recruiting office was next to it, and we walked inside, not exactly knowing what to expect. However, it was evident that the recruiters wanted to fill their quota. Like any other recruiting office, we saw lots of literature about military missions, troops, airplanes, and uniforms, which intrigued me even more.

When we went to sit down, the wooden chairs moved across the hardwood floors and echoed with a sound that seems like official business was already in progress for someone, somewhere, and whatever you were there for would be handled soon.

"How can we help you all today?" the recruiter asked.

I detected from his firm handshake, his rigid exterior form, and his facial expression that some would be intimidated by him. However, I had seen this posture in so many military men.

"What do you want to do?" he said in a direct but palatable way.

"I'm interested in going into the Air force. I want to be able to ..."

Before I could finish, he began to give me a litany of perks that the military could offer me. I couldn't say I knew what all of them were about, but I heard a few things that caught my ear.

"You know you will be able to play baseball, and you would be able to travel on a team," the recruiter said.

I was already interested before I arrived at the office, but this clinched the deal.

The other boys went to different branches of the military to inquire, but none of them came out with serious interest. I, on the other hand, was sold. I would be returning to take the written test.

****

It was time for me to get things done outside, and I thought I would first feed Will. My heart sank as I opened the barn. He could no longer stand. I went over to him, and I had to accept it was just his time. He must have been about twenty-years-old when Papa brought him, so he was definitely mid-thirties now. Will had been with me during everything in my life. He was there on my first day of school when the times weren't so good. We were co-workers, a pair, a twosome, which made the work easier in the "Talladega Sun." He was there when I was so hungry, and as I saw him chew the grass on the land, I was so jealous. I didn't have an envious, jealous bone toward Will, but the mere fact that the crunchy, big mouthfuls of grass he was eating was not even what I had.

He was there when I practiced my speech for the New Farmers of America Convention, and even though he couldn't respond verbally, his mere presence was the emotional comfort that engulfed me. I believe had he been able to speak; he would have been honest. He would have told me my strengths, my challenges, and any additions that were needed. Most of all, he would have been kind and objective.

****

Will passed through the night. It must have been a few hours before I reached him, long enough for the dogs to start consuming parts of his flesh. Kyser helped me take him to the edge of the field, where we placed him. Just as he had in life, he was giving of himself to others – this time to other animals. I didn't consider this inhumane, but the best thing to do. I wasn't going to burn him as Papa had ordered Ruth to do with the cow we had. However, I thought the best thing to do was to prepare him to be food for scavengers of the environment. I stood there reflective, peaceful, and sad, yet glad I had experienced the opportunity to have spent so many years with Will. I did not say good-bye to Will, but a heartfelt silent salute to a friend, as the scene became blurred with my tears.

Through the night, I tossed and turned, remembering the days with Will. Sometimes I think animals have a feeling that separation is coming. He must have sensed I wanted to leave Talladega and go in the military.

My mind was a continuous volley between Will and the written military test, like a ball going back and forth between two tennis players. I decided to pray and ask God to comfort me and give me strength for the outcomes that were going to take place. My mind eased, yet it felt like I could feel every thread on the sheets as I lay waiting to fall asleep.

****

Before I knew it, the time had come for me to go to the recruiter's office. I got up and did all the chores that I needed to do.

"Junior," Kyser called.

"Yes, I'm right here," I said.

"So, you're ready to take your written test today?" Kyser said.

"I sure am."

"What is it going to be on?"

"I don't know exactly. I think they probably want to know what I know in different subjects. The recruiter didn't exactly say. Probably want to know what I might be good in, and how I might react to different situations."

"Do you need to take anything? Like your own pencils and papers," Kyser asked.

"I think they have everything, but it won't hurt me to take my pencil and pen," I said.

Kyser and I went out the door, and we were off to the Recruiter's Office. He told me he was willing to give me a ride when the time came for me to take the test. Kyser started the car, and it had made a rousing response, like an obedient child, anxiously awaiting a reward.

The motor was running steady and sounded like it was ready to run like this for fifty years.

"Kyser, this is a good running car," I said deliberately.

"Yes, it is. Papa carried me around, and we looked at different cars. I knew I couldn't get a brand new one, but Papa helped me to get one that was good and dependable," Kyser said.

It seemed I couldn't get there fast enough. I would be closer to my future, and I saw it with a capital "F." I had seen "F's before, but this time it meant my future I was going "Full Steam Ahead." I rubbed my hands together, wondering what would be on the test. I thought of all the strategies my wonderful teachers at Talladega County Training School had given me, and I put them into one big, accessible manual in my head. I was going to read the question – one time carefully – and I was going to read it again, assuring myself of what the question was really asking. Then, I would select answers that seemed the most accurate. How could I go wrong? This was a battery of questions that could be about anything, and I could have covered and learned this information anywhere from any grades. I was determined to do my best, and I would let God do the rest.

We arrived at the building, and it stood just as it did when I went the first time. My first official conversation about the Air Force with a recruiter had been here, and now my aptitude score would be there also.

The chairs made that familiar sound again, moving against the wood floor, like a slight jarring that seemingly echoed one's fate. The sound had a melancholy sound, where bad news followed. I approached the desk and told one of the recruiters I was here to take the written test.

"You can have a seat until we call you," he said with a twang that extended longer than the usual Alabama drawl. Perhaps he was from another southern state or maybe a neighboring southern state. I walked toward the seat but detoured to a section of brochures. I looked at the other branches of the military, yet I was certain I had chosen the best one for me. I took the Air Force brochure to read it again; only this time, I imagined myself in the pictures.

Before I could take my seat, I heard my name.

"William Gro.."? The man was on his way to say my name with a slight question in the end, but I interrupted before he could complete the question.

"Yes, sir," I said.

The gentleman looked puzzled. I wondered whether my assertive, "yes, sir" made him wonder if I was imitating the military. I quickly realized that the Black men of all ages in Alabama said "yes, sir" to white men, but it was a "yes, sir" with timidity, drawn-out within the multiple syllables, but the words were supposed to basically bow down.

I was looking at him directly in the eye, and maybe that puzzled him also. We locked into a quick gaze as I awaited his directions. It also dawned on me that many Black men didn't look white men directly in the eye, either, which was a once upon a time big no-no.

"Come on back," the recruiter said. I followed and began asking God to guide me. The recruiter's heels were in a rhythm that matched with the words in my prayer. "I will lift my eyes into the hills whence cometh my help ..."

"You have one hour," he said with an authoritative, but polite tone.

I continued my moments of meditations as his heels clicked, still keeping in time with my thoughts to God. "My help cometh from the Lord, which made Heaven and Earth.

I prayed to ask God to strengthen any skills I needed to pass the test and asked Him to bring what I needed back to my remembrance.

I saw the first question, and I read it carefully as I had been taught. I processed the information into an equation. Surely whatever the question was asking had to be equal to an answer. Perhaps that sounded simple, but it worked for me. I applied that method with some good common knowledge as well. I thought about somebody selling pies at $1.50, and they had twelve to sell. Do they want all the money from the pies sold or half of it? Would I want it all? Yes. If I had to draw or make a graph, I did. I added, subtracted, multiplied, and divided. If they wanted sequence, logic, or estimation, I gave it to them. My future, the one with the capital "F," depended on it.

When I finished, I handed my test to the Recruiter, and I could hear his heels again. This time it was in sync with the joy and thanks to God I felt, because I believed that my help arrived, and I was closer to my future.

I saw the Recruiter score the test. He obviously had a key. I looked at his face until I chose not to see him grimacing any further. At the time, I didn't understand, so I looked away and let the joy continue to surround me.

"William Groce," the recruiter said.

We went down that road of assertive "yes sirs and looked in the eye again."

"You passed..."

I was ready to say "thank you or something," but before I could, the recruiter had continued his sentence.

"... So we are going to now schedule you for your physical."

I refused to let the joy go away. It felt good, but a sudden dreadfulness attempted to encamp around me.

By that time, the recruiter was walking around again, and I knew that was my cue to "look to the hills whence cometh my help," when I heard his heels.

"I'm scheduling you next Saturday, and prepare to go to Basic Training right afterward. As soon as you pass the physical, you are immediately shipped out."

I listened to the words, and his words didn't say "if." I realized he had acquired confidence from me passing the written test, and additionally, perhaps the reason for his grimace. His contorted face was evidence of surprise that I had many answers correct.

"You will go to Montgomery, Alabama, to take your physical."

Our “Yes sir-look in the eye routine” took place for the last time and ended with a firm handshake. On my way to exiting the office, I could hear his heels head back to his desk, and my eyes “looked to the hills,” realizing my help and giving thanks.

****

In the meantime, I thought of the physical exam. I had a scrotal hernia from the time I was very young.

It was not in my nature to panic, but I wondered. What if that was detected? What if this hernia is a deciding factor for my new life? What if this is not my way out of Talladega? What will I do instead?

I chose not to focus a long time on this hernia thought. It had already consumed more of my thoughts than I needed it to. Just as I looked around, I saw the tin whistle that Velma had given me at Christmas, which had given me so much joy. I held it for a moment and blew it. I heard a tune that had a fluid tone that went beyond the normal range I had heard as a child.

This sound was so symbolic of where I was now. I was a man now, who had so much to give the world, and like the sound of the whistle, it was up to me to use all my strength and give my life the start it deserved.

CHAPTER 30 – TELLING THE FAMILY

When dusk fell, Papa and Mama were on the porch. I couldn't think of a better time than now to tell them that I had passed my written test, and the only thing now was the physical exam.

Papa was pulling off his boots, and Mama had come in from planting some beans in her garden.

She was wiping her hand on her dress, brushing off the excess dirt before she entered the house.

"I've decided to go into the military."

I waited for the unexpected, actually the expected, or anything else that could be expressed. I continued into what test I had taken and what would happen next.

Then, I heard words that I didn't expect.

"If Uncle Sam wants you, you must be a man," my father said when I told him and Mama together, I was now closer to going in the Air Force. Papa was surprisingly without many words, unlike what he had said two years ago. However, I knew Mama didn't mind me going and didn't have any objections. She knew I was old enough to make this kind of decision.

I saw my old baseball in the corner of the porch and thought of my opportunity to play ball in the Air Force. The thought of the recruiter telling me there was a semi-pro baseball team in Hawaii filled my mind. Just that information alone gave me dreams that lasted for days. I was good at baseball, and I knew I had a great chance as anyone to play in that league.

The conversation trailed off, and I could tell that all hearts and minds were clear.

All I had to do now was pass the physical, and I would be an Airman in the Air Force.

****

The music was playing, and everyone was swaying to the sounds that were carrying them away in the night. Many of the top Rhythm and Blues songs of 1955 and 1956 were making an entrance of their own. I saw the students dancing like it was the last Prom they would attend, and I guess that was true for many of them because it was true for me. Most were seniors, and even though I was a sophomore, it was going to be my last dance at Talladega County Training School.

I looked around the room, and it wasn't the music, the attire, or the decorations that were within my focus. It was in everyone's future. Although the teachers and students on the Prom Committee had done an outstanding job producing a magical evening, I looked at all the students and wondered where everyone would eventually be five years from now and if we would ever meet in the same place again. I wondered what our futures would hold and if we would ever meet again.

Along with this thought, I had something right on the end of my nose that would enter my mind intermittently. I had been plowing the fields earlier in the day, and a bee stung me on my nose. It initially had an annoying feeling, yet I found that Noxzema was the only thing that would help. Its cool menthol helped the burning sensation, but also it dulled the shine that made the sting more obvious. Why this sting had to present this day was not anything I could answer, but it didn't interrupt the exciting evening of the Prom.

I looked carefully around the room as if it were my final glance. I saw Charles and Kyser, my friends, classmates from grade one, and teachers that had made contributions to me in ways I would not have imagined. This night would forever hold a picturesque memory of Talladega County Training School in my mind.

As days passed by, moving toward the summer, the end of the school year closed silently. I didn't broadcast my decision to make this my last year in attendance at Talladega County Training School. I didn't do anything out of the ordinary, like hug my teachers like it would be the last time I would see them. I would return and see them again.

****

I thought I heard a whippoorwill as I sat fishing with my father on the Coosa River, my favorite spot to fish. The water was making a soothing sound of its own, creating a babbling background to the thoughts that were swimming around in my head like the fish that were inside the river. If anyone had told me that my father and I would be fishing a day before I left for Montgomery, I would have told them they couldn't be further from the truth. They could have told me a thousand times, and I would have rejected each thought at the time – the rejection more powerful than the last. However, it was my father himself who told me that he wanted to go fishing with me before I left.

I had never seen my father fish with a pole before, but on this day, he did. I was used to seeing him with a trotline or a net, but I think he used a pole today for unity, solidarity, for he had a desire for harmony. I truly believe he wanted to identify with me today – to do some things I did, or to perhaps be who I was, even if it was just for a day. Maybe he saw that I was taking a huge step, something he might have wanted to do, but I couldn't be certain. It couldn't have been the military, because he had done that, but it was hard to believe he had served. He was unstructured, undisciplined, unattached to a reality that included his family. His being was juxtaposed to what I thought anyone would be who had even been in the military for a minute. I had always thought that the military made men get up, go, be neat, straight, have a "get up, and go attitude." Nevertheless, William L. Groce, Sr. had a walk that was tuned to something that I couldn't understand.

I couldn't ignore the questions inside my head. Questions that I had asked from the age of six. Who is my father, and what makes him who he is?

I had to admit, Papa taking off work to spend the day with me totally threw me for a loop. I cast my line, and I threw it in, waiting for a nibble.

My father began to cast his pole, and suddenly I thought about a cottonmouth snake with a silk piece of cloth. Papa somehow thought that if you had a silk cloth just right, you could catch him by the teeth. I wasn't very old when I heard that, about seven, and I thought to myself, that's a good way to get bitten.

"So where ... what ... do you think you will be doing in the Air Force?" Papa asked.

I could tell my father wasn't exactly sure which question he wanted to ask first. I guess he was reminiscing about his days in the military. He had been in the military for a year and a half. How he was able to come home every weekend and see Mama was truly a mystery. He was AWOL and seemingly without concern of being caught. I would have loved to have known what made him become such a risk-taker. He left his base every week and was never seen leaving or returning. Was this why he was so carefree with our lives? Was it that he was never held accountable from the military, thusly making it okay to live life gambling?

We fished the entire day. The only day I can remember not catching anything. I think if there was anything that I caught that day, it was my father trying to make amends. This was a redemptive moment, and probably the closest way he could let me know he was sorry for the "cracks" he allowed to happen in our family's life. He wasn't an "I'm sorry" kind of man, for him to choose to take off work and fish with me the day before I left for Montgomery told me he had experienced a reflective moment or maybe many of them. I figured he had probably experienced a season of wishing that some things had been different, but at least wanted to spend time with me, and "spackle" in some of the cracks.

CHAPTER 31 – MILITARY LIFE BEGINS

I sat in the bus station and saw two worlds carefully and hatefully designed. There were two separate entrances for the only kind of human beings God made – the kind He made in His own image. Seemingly, a certain population from that very human being pool thought the people with black skin were inferior, and those with white skin were superior. As a result, turmoil rose and made many appearances throughout the centuries, and has continued throughout time.

Somehow, the feeling in this bus station was like another snake decided to slither about and was deliberately hanging from a tree, talking to whoever would listen. Finally, the snake finds someone who will listen. Someone who will converse. Someone who had just heard God inspire the words:

"There is neither Jew nor Greek; there is neither bond nor free, there is neither male nor female: for ye are all one in Christ Jesus."

Then, the snake responds with, "Did God tell you that *all* are one in Christ Jesus?"

And the one who listened said, "Yes, actually He did."

"You know," he slyly chuckles, "This means ... the ones – *who are worthy* – are one in Christ," the snake responds.

"But God says all are one," the listener volleys intently.

"Think about it," the snake says with a contemplative delivery. "All cannot be one in Christ, for he is pure, and those that are not pure cannot be in Him," the snake adds, with all intentions to be convincing.

The listener furrows his brow, and from there, rethinks his original position. The lie is now deposited, rained upon with more acrimonious thoughts. The lie is on its way to germination, spreading roots, and creating a cornucopia of vile produce.

I continued looking around this bus station, and all the human beings I saw in this bus station had one head, two eyes, two ears, one nose, and one mouth. Upon further inspection, they had two arms, two legs, and one torso. Yet, they could not go through the same door. The determining factor? The largest organ of the human body. Skin. How could this continue to be justified throughout the ages?

I had seen some similarities of this before when I was a member of the New Farmers of America. White students were Future Farmers of America, and Black students could not join. We weren't even allowed to put our seeds, raise our livestock, and propose our farming management in and on the same soil. Soil that God created. Although I was appreciative of the creation of the New Farmers of America, which gave me the platform to learn, study, and present my farming methods, I always wondered whether we were seen by the Future Farmers of America as second, aliens, or "new" to the farming scene behind them.

"Bus to Montgomery boarding." I was awakened out of my thoughts. I took my bag and walked through my designated side, and boarded the bus. As I took my seat, I could see the faces of the passengers, and for a second, I attempted to guess why some were leaving Talladega. Maybe some were going to visit family, maybe some had official business, and perhaps some were leaving with no intent to permanently reside, like me, in Talladega again.

****

When the bus pulled off, I could feel the wheels on the bus underneath me, not like the school bus I had been used to riding all my life. This was different. It was my first time on this kind of bus. I had been used to the springy ride and the screeching halt. It was my daily affirmation going and my benediction before ending my school day.

For years, the school bus had taken me back and forth to learn everything from shapes, colors, numbers, and the alphabet. Somewhere on those rides, it also took me to see shapes of my desire, the color of my ambitions, the number of my chances to succeed, and the alphabet to form the language of my courage – to seek what I was going to need to survive beyond Talladega.

The ride to Montgomery was eighty-seven miles, and I had about an hour and forty-five minutes to think, dream, and wonder. My future was the first thing on my mind, and then my physical exam.

I took a nod and woke up when we were in Montgomery. I was looking for my bag after the baggage area was opened on the side of the bus, and I took it and went to my destination.

When I got to the inside of the physical exam room, I didn't see anything that resembled segregation. There were no two doors of entry and no separate waiting rooms. Obviously, the snake of segregation didn't calculate that the cost to build or deliberately set up a facility with two of everything, and putting up additional signage, meant an additional expense. As for the military, they were not practicing this method. I saw men of all persuasions in lines, and they were ready to go through what some would perceive as an obstacle course. Uncle Sam wanted his men to maintain a physical acumen, where they would be ready for whatever came.

"William Gross?"

"Yes, Sir ..."

I didn't see the same eye contact when I took the written test with the former Recruiter in Talladega. This was like a processing center for potential airmen, and the climate was part sterile and mechanical. Examiners' faces were faced toward clipboards, and ink pens were in hands.

"Please sit up here," The examiner said.

Everyone was already down to their shorts. I suppose this made the transition to each person faster and easier.

"Please open your mouth."

A tongue depressor was on my tongue, and I could taste the wood that almost made me gag. I surmised he was looking for swollen glands or cavities. Perhaps he was looking for something totally different. Then, there was the cold stethoscope that met my chest, and I would have jumped, but I thought it better to keep my composure. The examiner moved it to my back and said, "Give me a deep breath." I obliged and inhaled enough air to expand two sets of lungs.

Before I knew it, a light was in my eyes, piercing my clarity. The examiner put a check on the clipboard and scribbled something. Then a tug on my ear told me the exam was moving to my ears. I heard a faint sigh, but the usual check and scribble took place.

There were more areas where I had to bend and touch in the process of this exam, along with other performance tasks, to determine my strength.

When I received the news I passed, I was thankful to God, who I had accessed by a look to the hills on the written test and the same route of access on the physical exam. The childhood days of my hernia didn't show anywhere in the existence of this exam.

"William Gross?"

"Yes, Sir?"

Passing meant I was not returning to Talladega. Passing meant I was on my way to the Air Force. *Where?* I could imagine. I could play semi-pro baseball in Hawaii. Go to places I have never been to. Learn to do things I could only dream about before, and where that was, I didn't know, but I couldn't wait to find out.

"Listen up!" a strong voice said.

"Be ready be to catch the train to San Antonio, Texas, tomorrow morning."

I met some of the guys, and we decided to get a soft drink and a hamburger. I could tell they were city boys from there accents, but there was no way I could tell they would be loud on the streets of Montgomery.

This was no place or time to draw attention to yourself if the largest organ of your body was black. Little did I know that Montgomery was in the volcanic eruption of the Civil Rights Movement, and in the hotbed of segregation; I had no idea that a woman named Rosa Parks had caused such an upset in Montgomery when she didn't give up her seat to a white man. She was arrested, and this caught the attention of Black people. A young minister, Martin Luther King Jr., arranged a boycott, where blacks wouldn't ride the buses. They hadn't ridden the buses since Dec. 1, 1955.

Here I was, with these loud city boys, talking no doubt in a loud celebratory time, but Montgomery was not celebrating.

These boys were probably like me, didn't know what had happened in Montgomery, and the celebration becoming airmen needed to stay within us.

"You niggers better get off this street. If you don't, I'm going to put you in jail," a policeman verbally hurled at us.

We immediately ceased all communication, and just minutes later, we saw the same policemen, so busy looking and focusing on Black men, that he ran into the back of a black man's car.

The police ran out of his car and pulled the black man out of his. There was no asking for a license, no request for registration either. What we saw next was like a scene out of a movie.

We could hear the man yell, but there was no director saying, "cut." The blood we saw ooze from this man's head was no prop. This raised baton was not a soft stick, and the sounds we heard were not made by Foley Artists, who enhanced sounds for the movies. This man's head was beaten with a baton, along with a principle that he couldn't be one of those who were one with Christ. His life did not calculate to the total sum of worthiness, as expressed by "the snake," so only a baton to the head would be fitting for him.

We saw the man slide down the side of the car, like rain sliding down a windowpane.

We didn't stay around to see if he ordered him to move his car or get up quickly, but what I did know; we would be in San Antonio tomorrow.

It was approximately 750 miles to basic training. The sun was going down, and I could smell the blossoms of honeysuckles in the air. No matter how sweet they smell, it would not be able to cover the racial scenes I had just encountered in Montgomery. These were permanent scenes that had been created, and I would be able to recall them for a number of decades. They were etched in my mind with some kind of indelible ink, serving my memory with twisted excerpts that initially served my thoughts little to no purpose. The thoughts were more like distractions. But later, what the memories did do, as haunting as they were, forced me to stay in good company. They appointed me to stay out of the line of fire that wreaked havoc on Blacks, as I would always continue to elevate myself to better surroundings whenever possible. There was no need to ask for trouble, but there was always a need to present well, whether it was able to be seen, detected, or appreciated. I thought it best that my best was going to be on display if nobody could see it but me.

****

The train pulled out with a quick, but a slow drag, and I could hear the engine puffing in quarter notes like a song, but with a momentum that was building quickly, the ride was smoothing out, where it had once been a chugging effort.

I looked around and saw recruits that sounded like they were from a variety of geographic areas. I was now very sensitive to any accent I heard. I found nothing wrong with city boys, but I would be careful to be around those who were not loud or boisterous, and unfamiliar with the likes of racially divided cities. I did not intend to draw attention where I didn't need it, as I had experienced in Montgomery.

"Hey man," a recruit said to me.

"How are you? I'm William."

"Now, I know you are a southern boy. I feel the hospitality in that welcome alone. I can almost taste the buttered biscuits with preserves on the side."

This recruit had a personality that immediately filled the train car we were in.

"Yeah, I'm from Talladega."

"Talladega," he took it right from my mouth almost before I could get it out.

"I know some people from there; you know some Mitchell's?"

"I believe I do," I responded, connecting just as quickly to his statement.

"Now, where are you from," I asked, surmising that it was somewhere as big as his personality. He definitely wasn't a southerner. There were no signs of a drawl, and he was clearer in his speech than most blacks I had encountered. I also looked at him and noticed he had a close cut hair cut on the side and more than normal on the top that looked like it had come from a highly-skilled barber. He wouldn't have that haircut too long. Uncle Sam was going to mow that down like grass on a lawn. His hair was a reddish-brown that complimented the yellow skin mixed with a few freckles in his face.

"Where do you think I'm from?" he said.

"Well, unlike me, I don't hear the grits, eggs, or bacon on the plate, so I would say you are somewhere from the Midwest."

"Talladega, you right on the money. I'm from Missouri."

I thought *Missouri* would be a good name for him in my head.

"William?" he had switched back to my name, "Do you know any Williams from Talladega?"

We must have kept the name questions up for probably an hour and a half. Although *Missouri* was a city guy too, he was very conscious of who he was and where he was. It was evident he had a family that intended for him to go places in life and be deliberate about his decisions. He could make a conversation about anything, and it felt engaging. Looking back, I could see him being the talk show type, preacher, or politician. We progressed in our conversation from family members to food, and hobbies to sports, and before we knew it, we were way down the road toward our destination. I don't know who went to sleep first, but the conversations, card games, and unapologetic laughter once were, silence came and fell upon the train as the night carried forward.

We were only about two-thirds into our trip, and daylight had not quite arrived. Everybody was either wiping their mouths as they moved their heads over or stretched their arms out in what seemed like some unconscious trance. By some means, they still remembered they were sleeping in an unknown place and within limited space with a stranger next to them.

I was up a long time before the sun came up. Even though I had no alarm clock, internally, I knew I wouldn't sleep but so long. I wanted to see San Antonio in its full splendor. I had seen it in pictures, and I wanted to compare and contrast what I had seen.

I wasn't disappointed, but I wasn't certain what I was seeing. My vantage point was not as clear as I needed it to be, but I could see the Texas horizon. Between the blueness in the sky and a yellow burst of the sunrise, I couldn't tell which was more spectacular. It was clear that both the sky and the sun were doing their job to the fullest, and together it was a stunning display.

"William, how long you been up?"

"Oh, I say about an hour," I responded. "Just seeing the early scenes of Texas."

"You are used to getting up with the chickens," he said, accompanied by a hearty laugh and a slap on his knee. *Missouri* knew who he was, and he didn't care if anyone knew it. Those that weren't up were surely on their way now. The thunderous laughter rivaled any of the peripheral sounds on the train.

I couldn't help but chuckle myself, as I had been used to hearing this phrase as soon as people find out you are from "the country."

I tried to mask the sound, however, but *Missouri* could clearly see my intentions.

"You might as well laugh just as hard. These knuckleheads need to get up now anyway. It's good practice for them, 'cause my uncle said we gonna be getting up early anyway."

"I'd rather wait until then," another recruit said.

Missouri didn't care about what the recruit said and went right back into our conversation, but not before he said to the recruit, "You gonna thank me tomorrow. My uncle said, expect an in your face wake up call."

That recruit responded with a request that he could tell his uncle, but *Missouri* responded with a "you'll be going back home just as fast as you came."

I was almost expecting a showdown, but I soon knew that wasn't *Missouri's* style. He didn't need to beat a dead horse. He was fine just stating his point, not beating anybody with it.

Before long, we were pulling up to the base. I was looking at the architectural design, and if I could have seen far into the eight weeks I was going to be here, I would have a look at that too.

When the train finally came to a halt, we stood up and steadied ourselves, progressing toward the middle of the train. We could barely call it an aisle, that was an overstatement, but we managed to make it accommodate all of us. We stepped outside the train, and there to meet us was the drill instructor, who lived up to the name from start to finish.

We were waved over to stand in a line and to fall in place.

"Put out you' cigarettes; you're in the Air Force now! You ain't no jigglebugs."

His voice had a haunting ring in every word he said as if smoke and onions could be a normal accompaniment to every word. His voice was loud enough to cause paralysis to the moving and cause fear to the focused.

"Git' into formation!!!!" All I could hear was the short 'I' he said. I couldn't hear any 'e' all.

If anyone had told me that we would be in a drill upon arrival, I would not have believed them. I cut my eyes toward *Missouri,* and he looked like one of those kids that no matter where he was, he was going to be happy because that was the way he wanted it. Besides, he had listened closely to his uncle, who had given him the run of the mill lessons about the military.

We "hut-ted—one-two-three-four" and more "one-two-three-fours" for what seemed like two hours. I couldn't complain about the weather, for it was early in the morning, and I didn't think the burning sun of San Antonio was ready to present itself fully, since it was still early summer. *Missouri* looked like he was in his true element of glory, only as he could define. He was happy and looked like a recruit from an assembly line if one could be made. I found the drill natural, not stilted, but just a part of the military. I knew from the moment I started, as I put one foot in front of the other, and made what seemed like about-faces and quick corner turns, this was going to be the beginning of my life as I knew it. Everything I did from here was going to add steps to my journey that would go somewhere beyond my certainty.

****

This was going to be home for eight weeks, and being here a few hours made me feel that I could make it – no matter what came my way. We were taken to the barracks where we would be staying, and what we saw next was some good made-for-T.V. military demonstration. I saw beds made up and torn up, loud voices that would command attention, when we needed to be in the barracks, and when we needed to get up.

"You see what we are doing here?"

"Yes, sir!" We all said with haste and without hesitation.

Our eyes were forward, and we didn't dare miss a moment of this exercise. If a muscle moved, it was because it moved involuntarily and not because we flinched.

We didn't know if we were going to be called any moment to be the one to demonstrate what we had been taught.

As the hours passed, we were doing more marching and drills. I looked around without moving a muscle out of formation; I saw recruits coming in just as I had only hours earlier. I didn't bother to even speculate in my mind what I thought would be the fate of them because I needed nothing but positive outcomes to happen to me. Yet, I saw some who looked like they were struggling to stay on the right foot, while thunderous voices followed them until they were using the correct foot.

"Alright, keep marching. Keep going straight ahead until I tell you to stop," our drill instructor shouted.

If there was someone who hadn't heard voices beyond a whisper, they were in for one rude awakening. Direct shouting was what came, like a wind from the north that could dry the water up in any crop. Only these voices had the opposite effect. They could bring the water out of men.

"Alright, you are getting ready to go to church. I'm assuming y'all been to church. If you ain't, you will today," the drill instructor said. If he had been any louder, it looked like a button would have popped off his shirt, while a vein in his forehead would eject some blood, shooting straight forth ahead.

"You all are going to the evening service. Didn't want to take you to the greenhorns in the morning service."

I figured that was some Drill Instructor talk, letting us know we needed to be drilled and march, and know a little something first. I suppose they didn't want us resting as soon as we got off the train, sitting in a church house, where we hadn't got our "Drill Instructor Indoctrination." They wanted to get some time in to let us know where we were and put a good fear in us. It was their way of doing things, and we were not to confuse them.

We were not even one-hundred yards from the church when along with the yelling, was a popping sound. The sound was persistent, and it went right along with the marching. When I saw what was making the noise, I began to laugh. This was no ordinary laughter that I had been used to doing. I laughed like I had been given permission, as I surely had not. As I continued, so did the rest of the recruits. The marching had slowed down, stopped, and come to a circle of laughter, where even the Drill Instructor began joining the laughter.

One of the recruits had on a pair of white loafers, and he still had on civilian clothes. We, too, had our civilian clothes, but these white loafers made him look like he was on some summer vacation by the beach. As we were marching, this recruit marched into some fresh asphalt, and his loafers were making a noise, where every time he would come up from the asphalt, his shoe would make a popping sound.

I don't know how long the laughter lasted, but we all were in this fit of laughter. Then, the Drill Instructor asked me a question.

"Have you finished laughing?" he asked me.

"Yes ...Yes, sir," I said, and the humorous moment shifted back to the basic training atmosphere.

****

It was hard to believe I had been to Lackland Airforce Base just a little under twenty-four hours. It was just day one week into the eight weeks of Boot Camp. If I had to give it a score, I would give it a 10 out of 10 before seeing the rest of the weeks. I figured if I could laugh at something extraordinarily funny on the first day, without being put in a hole or assigned a million push-ups, while a Drill Instructor was laughing at the same time and at the exact same thing, life here was going to be pretty good.

We heard our fair share of briefing and policy on this first day. This was a steady stream of "what to do's" and "what not to do's," as it was definitely necessary for the safety of the recruits, the base, and for the security of everyone to follow proper procedures as it would relate to all military undertakings.

It almost felt like an about-face to leave the policy and procedure briefings and then go to move to march to church.

This first experience in a church in San Antonio was quite different from the church I was used to attending. I did recognize the Bible, the scriptures, and God, but the order of the service was different. It was supposed to be because everything couldn't be the same, nor should it be. I certainly didn't join the Air Force for things to be the same with me as they were in Alabama.

I continued to listen for the mentions of Christ to validate that this was God, the father of Christ. Then, I would know if this was the God I knew.

I heard the sounds of *...On Solid Rock I Stand, all other ground is sinking sand.* I knew this hymn *My Hope is Built on Nothing Less* all too well. However, the rhythm was slightly different, but that didn't matter, just as long as I could absorb the message.

I was glad we went to church last. It gave me lots to think about and even more to look forward to during this time here. Because I had known the value of the church, it was not unrealistic to be there. Looking at some of the recruits' faces, it was obvious that they wished they were someone else because they hadn't had the introduction to the most common message: God is Able. Yet, I was glad that Mama had introduced me. My prayers were that everyone would have an introduction to God, where they would never believe they were in a strange land without God.

Right here in San Antonio, Texas, was a strange land, but I knew the God that surrounded me.

"Git in line," I heard that familiar sound again. We fell in together more smoothly and naturally today than before. We marched to the administration building, and inside was a sea of desk and office supplies that accounted for every purpose and every person.

"At ease, boys," I heard when we got ready to progress further inside.

"Go over here." 'He-re' sounded like two syllables. Now I had heard it like this in Alabama, but this was a little different. There was an "ah" on the end of "here," that sound like "he-ah.'"

Even though I knew I was officially in the Air Force when I filled out the paperwork, there was an overwhelming sense that felt like this was a life assignment. Finally, my life was being assigned to something that would have the potential to take me forward.

"What's your name?" the man at the desk asked.

"William L. Groce, Jr."

When I was issued my items, I saw a mistake. My name was spelled G-R-O-S-S instead of "Groce," as I had always spelled it.

The man told me I could see someone about it, but this was what he was issuing.

He gave me my I.D. Number and my dog tags. I felt an electrical-like shock when he gave them to me. I knew I hadn't been shocked, but more so charged, charged to take my life and make it all it could possibly be, starting here.

I could hear the same conversations happening with the other recruits, as there were multiple stations receiving them.

We were moved to the next area to pick up our clothing. I chose to assume there would be no more popping noises because we were saying good-bye to our civilian attire: Shirts, pants, shoes, and all.

"Here you are!" the man said. It was loud and abrupt. Not so much impolite, but more like the act of processing, a routine that must have made things efficient, as recruits were retrieving their clothing and moving ahead. I had fatigues, a dress uniform, shoes, and a duffle bag. I could hear the sound of the shoes echoing as they were placed on the counter.

"Thank y...!" I tried to say, but before I could get to the "you," "next" was shouted with a long drawl that told me my time was up.

After all the recruits were issued their clothing, we went to finance, where we issued our first military pay. It was $31.00, but as soon as we got it, it was time to go to the Exchange and get all the toiletries. We bought things like shaving cream, razors, toothpaste, etc., and when we finished, we had $1.00 left.

I had one dollar left, and that dollar already had its destination.

"Listen up!" We were all ears, like dogs listening to unfamiliar sounds. "You are now going to get your hair cut," one of the men said that was taking us station to station.

We walked from the exchange to the base Barber Shop, and I could hear the hums of clippers as soon as we went in, along with footsteps going out.

When it was my turn to sit in the chair, I put my hand up to my ear, instructing the barber which way I wanted my hair cut. I heard a buzzing sound with the clippers going straight down the middle of my head. I didn't even get a chance to open my mouth, but it was open now with a gasp. With a few more of the same cutting strokes, all my hair was on the floor. Looking around the room, it was evident that other recruits were equally shocked by the style of haircuts, as well as the rate of speed they were serviced.

I guess there was a bright side to the haircut. As hot as it was in San Antonio, my head would be a little cooler. There was no doubt I had been used to the "Talladega Sun," but something about this "San Antonio Sun" just about required some kind of beginner's program.

CHAPTER 32 – BASIC TRAINING

"How can I help you?" a man asked. I was in the clerical office of records at the base.

"I see my name is spelled wrong on the things I've been issued. It's G-r-o-c-e, but it is spelled here as G-r-o-s-s," I stated.

"We have your birth certificate, and the information we have is G-r-o-s-s on it." He stated.

"Well, how can I change this?" I questioned.

"Unless you are famous with a rich family name, I would leave it just like it is."

In less than ten minutes, I had a whole new last name that I didn't know anything about. I was going to be different from Papa after all, but I didn't see it happening this way.

Two days had come and gone, and I really couldn't find anything to complain about at the time. I believed the hard farm work that I had done as a child had helped me with endurance. The drills were seemingly constant, and I somewhat felt it to be natural. Maybe it was the pacing I had done with Will in so many fields that made this feel ordinary.

There was no getting by without medical evaluations and preventive measures in the military. On day three, we went to the infirmary. As it would be, it was sterile in every way: Tongue depressors in glass jars, cotton balls also in jars, and bandages were boxed standing at attention.

We, however, didn't have use for any of these items. It was immunizations that we needed. The closer we got there, we could hear curtains opening and closing, accompanied by the word "next" in that Southern drawl again.

Well, this was it. I would be next. I didn't remember getting a lot of shots, but I didn't remember getting them as I got them this day. Both my arms were out, and I felt the needles were piercing, not one, but both at the same time. For a minute, I didn't know if I was going to be able to lift my arm to salute. I didn't want to let the others see the twinge I had within me, but I wasn't sure if that twinge was going to give way to my upper arms, feeling like I couldn't move them.

I was now beginning to feel a stiffness in my arms that made them heavy for just a moment, but I kept on with the day as if nothing had happened.

****

"We are leaving the main base going to Bivouac!" the Drill Instructor said.

"Bivouac!" I heard the word again, and then I repeated it in my head. We were told earlier what it was, but if they hadn't, I would have thought it was someplace a person goes for not so good behavior.

"Git your equipment and git on the bus," the drill instructor said.

We formed into a single file, and all you could hear were boots patting the ground. Even though we were not marching, I could have sworn there was a pattern going to the bus as the recruits were loading. There was a step-step-step-thud configuration that kept repeating as the bus was filling up with recruits.

"You are going to be outside, and this ain't no walk in the park. This ain't no sitting down eating cake, and this ain't no soda pop. This is war!" the Drill Instructor said. The way he said "war" sounded like he said three syllables.

We were riding for about thirty minutes, but it was still considered on the base, but very different. When we arrived, it was a place of clear land, where intense training obstacles were set up.

When we got out, we set up and heard our instructions. We hit the ground running, and there was no such thing as grass growing under our feet or anywhere else. Before we knew it, we were face down in the mud, crawling under barbed wire with live ammunition over our heads. The mud was unpredictable. I anticipated resistance, but nothing like what I experienced. I crawled through the mud with my elbow sinking over and over again, yet I had to pull the weight of myself up, elbow by elbow, and keep going. The mud seemed to be thick and pasty, but at the same time, slimy, and it had no mercy on the recruits.

"Pop, pop, pop" was the sound I continued to hear, we were too low for the live ammo to hit us, yet it was motivation to stay low and keep going.

We got a brief chance to get water from our canteen and eat some of our C-rations. Some complained about the taste of the C-rations, but I thought it was rather tasty.

As we geared up for the next day, I found that what the Drill Instructor said was true. This was not like sitting down eating cake.

I wasn't sure if snot was coming out of my nose or if my eyeballs had turned to liquid when I took my face mask off. My senses felt like they were betraying me all at once. My sense of smell had heightened, as the odor of gas went directly to my brain, while my sense of sight was fading. Everything I saw looked like I was peering through opaque lenses. My tongue was bitter, where I was tasting of some acidic substance, more like poison. If I was hearing or touching anything, it was the sound of some crazed abyss of men gagging, touching their mouths and stomachs, trying to recover some sense of normalcy after going through the gas chamber. When I heard the words, "Pull off your gas mask now," my imagination could have never prepared me for this kind of ordeal. It was not a time to reminisce, as much as I had done so. Just as my senses seem to go on a voyage of their own, so did my memory. Seemingly, pain and discomfort came forward, front and center, with a rattling thunder during these moments.

When I felt my face after leaving the gas chamber, I could feel the skin in little rolls under my index finger and the two fingers beside it. My skin was coming off around my face, and I had a blustery feeling that stung, which was almost parallel to the heat that was outside.

The stinging in my face was short-lived, maybe because it was time to go to the next training activity. I couldn't help but think the Drill Instructor was right, that this was no piece of cake, but if anyone had any character in them, they were going to build it, muscle by muscle, morsel by morsel, and thought by thought.

My face was the object of brutal receptions. If the mud didn't get to my face, as it stuck and hardened in the crawl where it seemed like an eternity, the fumes from the gas chamber and the removal of the mask took its toll. Little did I know there was more.

"Git ready. This is the Parachute Training. Gear up and git your parachute pack on your back."

The high towers looked like they extended to heaven that I had to climb. There were two of them, and when it was time to jump, the cable would extend from one tower to the other. I was harnessed in with a cord, hooks, and rings, but this was almost a panicking moment. A question began to fill my mind. What if the rings and hooks snapped, and I would not make it across? My head was full of doubt, while I could see the other recruits taking their turn.

Air was beginning to swell up in my chest like something had pumped it inside. I almost lost my train of thought, switching from a thought of falling to trying to survive the "mission." I attempted to talk to myself back and forth, telling myself, "You can do it ... you can do it," but the pendulum kept swinging back and forth in my mind. My head, full of "What ifs?" continuously circulated and circulated.

I tried to look for a pattern in the other recruits to would tell me how to posture myself when they took off. Did they take off with the right leg? Did they lead with the left? Did they bend their legs or do something that caused them to leave the towers?

I faced it the best I could, but I didn't have many things in life happen where I felt this kind of opposition. This was the kind of endeavor that was strictly physical, and I had not faced a challenge where I felt I could die if something went wrong.

I didn't know if I was sweating with fear, but I was in a state of paralysis.

"Jump, Gross!"

I didn't move; I stood still. I could feel my knees knocking.

"Jump, Gross; I said Jump."

I felt the saliva hit my face, accompanying the second command. That alone felt like a straight pin. I knew all too well what straight pins felt like, as I had seen Mama with plenty of them when she made my sisters' dresses and got a few in my hand.

A chill rain down my spine, and I thought I felt sweat follow. The anticipation of this parachute training might have been the most challenging thus far in Basic Training.

My face hit the wind after two hands shoved me in the back. The wind began to feel freeing, unwinding me from my original fear. I was gliding across from the first tower to the second, where all of my anticipatory distress dissipated, and I was in a place of sheer joy.

It was so fun to glide through the wind; I wanted to go again; however, I was not granted the privilege. I would never know what it was like to go willingly, but I would always remember how to approach challenging things, knowing anticipation was probably worse than the actuality of the task.

****

"You cheated your way through!" one of the recruits said to me.

We all laughed heartily, throwing our heads back with a playfulness we all understood.

"You know I had my tooth pulled."

"No, you didn't," he said impishly.

"I couldn't help if I had to get my tooth pulled out!" I responded. I knew he wasn't mean-spirited, but joking.

"You should have been there," he said.

A bunch of "Yeah's" surrounded me like bees surrounding flowers.

"I tell you what; it was a little frightening," he said with sudden seriousness.

"Oh yeah," I said.

"Yeah, man. Anytime something is burning, you think the fire is gonna git on you."

He pronounced the word get with the same sound of 'git' that the Drill Instructors used.

"I guess I missed a real obstacle," I said.

"Anytime JP-4 fuel is used to set a fire; you can best believe there will be a huge fire. I am glad to know how to get out of an airplane if we had to."

Even though running through a plane was vital for anybody to do as a safety precaution, I still wasn't too sure I would have wanted to do it.

"Were any of the guys slowing down before they got to the plane?" I said, wondering if it was like the Parachute Training, where they would push you to make sure you got through.

"Everybody was told in advance there would be big trouble if they caused anybody to stop. They told us we had on enough gear, a steel helmet to protect us with an anti-flammable lining. This lining was an insert under the steel."

The guy continued talking without a break, and I let him. It was better for him to do the talking. I had a swollen mouth that was in recovery and full of antibiotics. I wasn't bored listening but actually intrigued that he was able to recall the details. There was one thing that I believed, many of the recruits were going to remember Bivouac till their end date was on the other side of their birthdate, separated by a hyphen.

Bivouac was as much mentally taxing as it was physically. Everyone needed a strong mind to make your body move and to keep going. There was dirt in the mouth, sweat in the eyes, and gas in every orifice of the face. As for some recruits – and me – we got hands in our back if we didn't jump off from the towers, but nothing prepared me for the Guard Duty during Bivouac.

I rinsed my mouth as instructed by the to be sure to stave off infection. When I came up and looked into the mirror, I looked directly into my eyes, and I thought about the first cougar I ever saw going to Guard Duty. I couldn't believe I saw this type of animal. This was a cougar in the wild of San Antonio, Texas. What if this cougar had been close enough to lock eyes with me? I was thankful to God that this cougar had his destination, and I had mine. I saw him running just as fast as I was, going to my duty station.

Guard duty was not a strenuous duty. It was mainly observation. Nevertheless, to observe a cougar for the first time heightened my awareness for anything that could possibly be within my view.

****

"Attention!" the Drill Instructor yelled. The word sounded like it stretched across the entire barracks. As the word penetrated down to my bones, I was sure bed frames heard it as well.

We stood up quickly and with our bodies stiff, looking straight ahead and arms to the side. The atmosphere was filled with the weight of tension. It was time for a locker inspection, and everything was expected to be in its place.

As the Lieutenant walked through, we could hear his heels touch the floor. Each time he put his heel down, it sounded like there was an echo that boomed after each step. I saw lockers open. I saw the Lieutenant's eyes stare in each locker. When the inspections passed, his face didn't show contentment. It was stony and unreadable.

This ceremonial inspection went on, and all you could hear was the hinges on the lockers, and I even thought I heard the air move a little, and I think it did.

"Is that hair in this toothbrush?" The question echoed with a bounce around the barracks. I had a feeling this was a rhetorical question. Reflecting, I remembered Miss New teaching us the different kinds of questions in English. I saw the recruit attempt to answer, and before his lips could open, I heard a roar that made me change my posture from board stiff to limber and gelatinous in my core.

"What have you been doing, brushing your behind with this toothbrush?" the Lieutenant asked.

I began to feel my stomach move as I laughed out loud with a hearty sound. I didn't have time to be concerned if I was going to be in trouble for laughing. My laughter just began, almost involuntary.

During my laughter, I heard something I wasn't expecting. Laughter was trickling out of the Drill Instructor, and then the Lieutenant. To believe they were going to be laughing was most unpredictable. The inspection was officially stopped, and everybody was laughing like they were at a summer picnic, where all the relatives were sharing the memories of the good ole' days. The rips and roars of this laughter seemed to go on for what felt like hours, but after we wiped tears that we laughed out, it was time to return to "attention."

When the Lieutenant got to my locker, I looked closely at his eyes, and again I couldn't read his face to determine whether he was pleased when he saw a good locker or not. Everything was good because he checked the name and wrote some notes, and kept going to the next recruit. Even though I had always been a neat person, the military wanted precision, accuracy, and uniformity. I believed they were right to want this because, in time of war and combat, every person needed to be working as a unit to make sure everyone brings consistency to the mission.

I heard the last locker open, and this time it was again unfavorable, but not as humorous. I listened to see what this recruit had done, and it was something that he left out that should have been inside. I somewhat trailed off when listening at the same time. God had truly smiled on me. First, I had everything in order in the locker to pass the inspection. Second, to be able to laugh and not be punished with all sorts of imagined reprimands was more than I could have processed. Surely, I would have thought that this time would have been the time – but two laughing outbursts! The white popping shoes and the toothbrush? I supposed God wanted the Drill Instructor and the Lieutenant to have some compassionate laughter with me. Maybe they needed a point of laughter to revisit their side of humanity. Talking directly to recruits all day probably takes its toll when they are talking and projecting spittle in a recruit's face, accompanied by a loud, boisterous voice. I chose to be thankful and not try to figure it out. God was a just God who knew what we needed, and I was more than glad that he was leading me to my destination.

****

To hear the name of the country, Mexico, sounded like it was far away when I was a child in Talladega. I imagined any place outside of the United States would seem far away for any child. The comprehension of the distance of Mexico had now shortened as I was an adult. Now, in San Antonio,

Mexico was a hop, skip, and a jump away. It wasn't a walk away, but it sure was closer than I thought. I imagined that's why the training instructors and the drill instructors all got together and decided to go to Mexico to see a bullfight. I had never seen a bullfight, but I could count on my imagination to tell me all I needed to know — a bull running toward a finely dressed man with some soft black shoes. The clothes are sometimes sparkling, as he holds out a cape that the bull charges toward. The bull is running headfirst, with his head downward, horns running positioned toward the matador. The outcome; the best man or the best bull wins.

I was on Barrack's Guard Duty the night the officers went to see the bullfighting in Mexico. It didn't seem like any different night. I didn't expect to see any cougars as I had in Bivouac, but I was vigilant.

This guard duty had come at a time right after I had been on liberty. This liberty was like I had never known. It reminded me of going to town, getting a soda and some candy, which was a special treat. However, on liberty, I took the "liberty" to have as many sodas as I want. I drank them for all the times I couldn't get them as a child. I drank them just because I enjoyed the sodas so much that it was hard to stop.

While on guard duty, I began to feel quite strange. My stomach felt enlarged with a bubbly sensation. These sodas had me blown up like a bullfrog. Concentrating was beginning to be harder, but I continued my duties. As time went by, I had to go to the restroom more and more and more. These sodas not only had me physically uncomfortable, but I had become so sleepy, I couldn't keep my eyes open.

I had an idea. It couldn't hurt if I left guard duty for a while. It wasn't like anything was happening or going on that required excessive attention. I asked a recruit to cover for me. Quickly, I walked around and found myself the nearest bed. I figured it would be just five minutes, but that five minutes turned to a few hours. By then, the training and drill instructors had returned.

The barrack area was unattended when they arrived, and a training instructor wanted answers.

"Why weren't you out there on duty?"

I confessed. I wasn't about to lie and tell them some story. Honesty had always gotten me where I needed to be, and I wasn't going to change up now.

I had asked another recruit to cover for me. However, he must have left. Perhaps, I had been sleeping longer than I thought. Either way, I wasn't sure how this was going to turn out. I was a one-striper but could be without that one stripe now.

"I'm going to set you so far back in basic training, you will have to re-enlist to get out," this training instructor said.

"Wait a minute," Drill Instructor Taylor said. "This is one of my best recruits. Leave him alone."

I didn't know what would have happened or where I would have gone had Drill Instructor Taylor not come to my rescue. I was glad I had done some good work before this debacle. This act really could have cost me, but I'm so glad God was guiding my destination forward.

I don't know when the sodas fully ran out of me. They seemed to move through me like a bus going cross country until it reached the end. My stomach finally came back down to its original size, and since then, I have always limited my intake of soda on liberty.

****

"Right, left, right, left," I could hear the steps clearly when each recruit put his foot down and picked it back up. It was a song within itself where the sounds of unity, precision, and accuracy could be heard. Some recruits loathed the drills. They were long and strenuous and repetitive. But for whatever reason, I liked them. They were synchronized and patterned, and I loved the cadence that was always within the drills.

It was true that the sun didn't seem friendly, not in San Antonio. Maybe one had to be a native to be able to tolerate this sun. This sun made the sun in Talladega seem mild. Perhaps this is why the other recruits felt like they hated the drills. Granted, Will and I had spent years in the fields under the sun, which did help me tolerate San Antonio's sun better. Also, because I was focused on the call and response part of the drills and the movement, I kept my thoughts in that area. It was like we were moving as one, with no individual effort. That alone was somewhat awe-inspiring when I was closely thinking about it – a group of men all with different thoughts, different bodies, and different attitudes, but now coming together flawlessly.

"We are heading back toward the barracks!" the drill instructor said.

That was music to our ears. Sweat was continuously coming down our backs, for it was already in our eyes, and we couldn't wait to take a shower. However, before we were going to take a shower, we were going to the mess hall. I would take food over a shower because it seemed we had burned a million calories and lost gallons of fluids.

"At ease, boys!" the drill instructor said.

That was even more music to my ears. I could smell the salt on my skin, and I was ready for a bowl of anything. I wiped my face with my hand and removed the sweat from my eyes. As soon as I entered the mess hall, the aroma hit me. I could smell beef. I didn't know what kind of beef it was, but it was in some form that smelled very good. Maybe it was some kind of beef stew. I didn't care; anything after that drill would be okay.

I finally got to the line where it was my turn. I reached for my plate, and it seemed my portion was smaller than the portion served right before me. Maybe it wasn't, maybe my hunger was larger than usual, and I wanted more. I moved ahead without question. Questioning and requesting more wasn't something you did in a mess hall.

I finally got to my seat, and I lifted my fork. It was beef, but the flavor was not as vibrant as the smell. I would have liked some of Mama rabbit gravy with this beef. It would be a collision of two different animals, but her gravy would surely be an additive.

"Why are you looking at it so long for?" a recruit asked me.

"I just imagine my mother's rabbit gravy on top of this beef," I said.

"I'm imagining I'm eating something else," he said. "I can't wait to have me a cheeseburger from back home."

I continued eating my food and wondered what was going on at home. August was a busy farming month. It was time for garden planting and garden harvesting, depending on the vegetables.

Then, something else came to my mind. Talladega County Training School. What would Mr. Armstrong think when he didn't see me return?

****

Eight weeks had gone by, and it seemed like yesterday that I had begun basic training. Lackland Air Force Base had been the first stop off to my destination to a new life, and I had seen things in a new way. These eight weeks had shown me a life far from the one I knew in Talladega. However, I was thankful for the many lessons I had learned there. Actually, many of them I learned by trial and error, and observation – especially when I got the bucket to get the sunfish from the well at six. Then, there were the lessons where I actually learned one-on-one. Many of these were from Mama, where she told me how to prepare my life to meet Christ. Additionally, there were the lessons that I wasn't so interested in learning, and those were at the expense of my discomfort when I was so hungry, tired, mocked, and beaten. The lessons that I learned from these ordeals were never to allow any of these behaviors to be upon my children, grandchildren, and as far as I would be with my lineage.

My boot camp graduation could have been without a ceremony, and I wouldn't have objected. Completing it was a milestone within itself. I thought of Papa's statement, and he was right; I was a man. I was not a man because the military wanted me, as he had stated, I was a man because I wanted more. I wanted ... more. I had now completed Basic Training, and I somehow was going to get to Tuskegee Institute.

I was appreciative of the setting. The sky was so blue; it matched the first day of my excitement on my first day of school. However, this time there would be no crying, no tears. There would be happiness and reflections on why I decided to go into the Air Force.

The gentle breeze blew as we were listening to different officers speak. It seemed like it was just a few days ago that I passed the military reception desk.

"You are no longer recruits. You are full-fledged Airmen now!"

I could see myself getting my duffle bag when I first arrived at basic training. Then, I could see the barbershop. When I made my request to the barber, the clippers came right down the middle, as my hair fell to the ground, like it had a destination. I smiled, and all the reminiscing made me realize how far I had come.

"At the beginning, some of you were green, but now you have more vision than what you thought you were capable of handling."

I concurred.

"Now, if you choose not to use that vision to move forward, you got a problem."

The crowd roared!!!!!!

CHAPTER 33 – HOME FOR A VISIT

I hadn't been in the squeeze of Mama's arms in what seemed like an eternity. I always remembered how I would rub her arms when I was small while sucking my tongue. This would be a moment of true contentment, along with just knowing she was there. The memory of her arms was legendary to me, where, for in an instant, I was in the present and past at the same time. This hug, after so many months, was tight and welcoming, and to see her, was a vision coming true.

"Junior, it is so good to see you!" Mama said in the most melodious tone I had heard. After participating in drills, where the words were forceful and sometimes piercing, her words were like soft rain on a tin-top barn – soothing and comforting.

"It's good to see you too, Mama!" I said.

Mama had some of my favorites cooking. She knew I liked rabbit with gravy, and her way of cooking it was better than I ever had and even better than I remembered it. I could only assume I had been away, hadn't had rabbit stew for a while, and Mama probably made it extra special, was why it tasted so good.

Papa walked in, and his greeting was equally as welcoming. It mirrored our time together before I left, where it was evident that he was really proud of me.

I scraped the plate, making a long scraping sound, trying to get all the gravy up.

"We got some more in the pot," Mama said.

****

I looked in the mirror, and I had to look twice. I don't think I could have looked better. Now that I had finished boot camp and back in Talladega on leave, I was going to visit Talladega County Training School.

It hadn't been that long since I left Talladega, but it seemed like there had been a lot of time that had passed. I recognized it had nothing to do with the days, months, or even time that was between me and the last time I was there; it was what I had seen and what I had experienced. I had seen two divided worlds in bus stations and train stations, where everybody was made of flesh and blood, all with the same desire, waiting in different areas to go to their own travel destinations. I had been in the midst of Montgomery, Alabama, in the height of race relations, where police were mean and threatening to Black men just walking and looking around on the streets. I had met people who were just like me, country boys in basic training with dreams, some obnoxious and some serious, who obviously wanted to go as far as life could take them. I had been to San Antonio, Texas, and was only a few miles from Mexico.

I had seen more in those eight weeks than I would have seen had I stayed in Talladega. I'm not so sure if what I had seen didn't make the grass a little greener and the sky a little bluer. Accordingly, when it came to my friend, the sun, he shined differently. It wasn't that it was hotter, but the rays were teasingly therapeutic, probably because this time, I didn't have to sow, plow, or harvest under it.

I touched my name tag and looked at the letters "GROSS."

I had to admit it; I couldn't wait for my friends to see me in my uniform. It was really happening. I was going back to Talladega County Training School. All my old classmates were going to be there. It wasn't about being a showoff; it was about me being proud of my decision, and I felt accomplished. I thought my friends would be proud of me.

How could it be that I would happen to visit on the day that there was a school dance? My visit was timed perfectly. I could see everyone all in one place, while in a festive mood.

Just as it always was during dances, the room was decorated impeccably, showing the efforts of the students and the teachers.

"William!"

"Charles!"

We hugged like two bears wrestling playfully and finished it off with multiple pats on the back. Other students came up and gave me a hug also. Yet, I couldn't wait to talk back with Charles, but I wouldn't break the rhythm.

"You look great! You really did it!" When we didn't see you at school, we figured you went to the Air Force," Charles said with his big personality that he always had.

"Yes, it was great. I just finished Basic Training," I said

"That uniform looks like it was made for you," Charles said.

"I make sure to keep it in regulation,"

"Listen to that talk. You already got the military sound," Charles replied.

While we were standing there, I got a tap on my shoulder. I could determine who it was, but when I turned around, it was none other than my cousin, Kyser.

We bear hugged too, and it was a celebration in addition to the celebration that was already in progress.

"You look great! You must have just gotten here?" Kyser said.

"I did, just last night, because you know I couldn't be here but so long without seeing you!" I responded.

"The teachers were wondering where you were, and I told them you joined the military," Kyser said.

"And it has been a good experience. I had simply enjoyed everything except when I got ready to do a parachute jump," I said.

"Why didn't you like that?" He questioned.

"I just didn't like the height, and I thought the harness that we were buckled into might release in mid-air."

"Didn't you have to jump out of a plane?" he asked anxiously

"No, but we had to run through a burning plane, but I didn't do it because I had a tooth pulled."

"You mean you were able to get out of it?" Kyser asked.

"Yes, and I was teased plenty about it," I added.

I saw some teachers in the distance. My attention was splitting between the current conversation and seeing my former teachers. Kyser looked around and noticed I was looking beyond him.

"Oh, Junior, I don't know if anyone has told you?" Kyser said, somewhat whispering.

I had no idea what he was talking about.

"Told me what?" I asked. I didn't know whether to think it had anything to do with him, the school, or maybe one of the teachers I happen to see in the distance.

"Junior, Miss Barnett died over the summer," Kyser said with somberness, respect, and an informative tone all into one.

"Junior, Junior!" I could hear my name, but I seemingly couldn't respond.

Wait a minute. How could this be? I just saw her in the auditorium, saying her last words to me, "You did well." It was no more than five months ago that I heard those words, but it felt like just a few days. My history with her was always up close and personal, and even that compliment didn't undo the heinous things she had done to me. Even though the first grade had been a decade ago, the scars, mentally and physically, were still upon me. I had put them in a box and moved them, but just the call of her name would cause all the contents to spill out. The room began to spin. I could still hear Kyser calling me.

"Kyser...When?...What?...When?" I stammered. Not even sure what I wanted to ask first.

"Well, let's go outside for a moment," Kyser offered, obviously knowing I needed to get my balance.

I didn't want to abruptly leave at that moment, so I told him I was okay. In actuality, I was, but at the same time, I wasn't. There was no form of measurement that I could think of that would determine when I would be okay with the memory of Miss Maude Barnett. With all that had happened with her, the knowledge of her death hadn't reached me. All I could think about was what I would not be able to say to her now.

I stood silently, not knowing what to do with these memories. Moments kept going by until I heard my name.

"William!"

I knew this voice, and if ever there were any military restrictions that stated I couldn't be excited in uniform, I had just broken them all today.

"Mr. Armstrong!" I said as my voice leaped to a high pitch.

I was so happy to see him that all the thoughts I had about Miss Barnett immediately melted away.

"So that's where you have been – in the military," Mr. Armstrong said with cheerfulness. I was glad he was cheerful. I, at the same time, had my reservations about what he might have felt when I didn't return to high school this year.

"Yes, I decided to go into the military. I had thought about it for a long time, Mr. Armstrong. I looked at every option, and this one just seemed like the right one," I said passionately.

"I know you did. I knew you didn't just leave high school just to be leaving because you were no longer interested; it was evident that you wanted something that Talladega couldn't offer you at the time."

I was so glad that he understood.

"I, personally, would have liked for you to have stayed the entire time, yet, I understand what your goals are," Mr. Armstrong said.

"Mr. Armstrong, I'm going to make you a promise. I'm going to go to college, and I plan to go to Tuskegee Institute," I declared.

"William, I look forward to the day you will come back and tell me that you graduated."

I shook Mr. Armstrong's hand as he extended his hand to mine. This was like sealing of a deal, yet he agreed with my proclamation. Tuskegee was his alma mater, as this probably made him feel like he had groomed another student to walk onto the path he took, which had to make the deal sweeter.

"Well, tell me about the military," Mr. Armstrong said. "Is it what you expected?"

"It is. I just finished Basic Training in San Antonio, Texas, and even though it was rigorous, I thought it really was fun. I understand the seriousness of it, but I found it was challenging us both physically and mentally, so we can always be prepared for the tomorrows of the unknown."

"William, I don't know anyone who would have said it like that but you. However, remembering your speech at the New Farmer's Convention is really only a prelude to what I believe you will go on to do. You are on your way."

"Thank you, Mr. Armstrong, I just want to tell you I learned so much from you, and I thank you for all that you did for me," I said sincerely.

"I thank you for seeing Agriculture Economics as a class that teaches the foundation principles of what is a benefit for everyone. We all benefit from Agriculture in some shape or form. Everyone might not work in this area, but we all benefit," Mr. Armstrong said passionately.

"You're welcome, Mr. Armstrong."

We shook hands again that turned into a hug. I didn't know when I would see Mr. Armstrong again, but I did know when I would be making my path to Tuskegee. I would be working toward that goal every day. Sharing my goal with Mr. Armstrong was not added pressure; it was like an additional sail that I was putting on "the boat" that was going to make me go faster.

The night was not over. There was a lot of dancing to be done, and Charles was taking advantage of every minute. Kyser was even dancing. I remembered him standing around mostly at dances, but I suppose that just as the new school year had found me in a new dimension of life, Kyser was experiencing a new dimension of life as well. This was the first place around family and friends that I had taken my new name, GROSS, out for a spin.

****

The next chapter of my life was falling right into place. My goodbyes with my family and friends were really just that. The word 'good-bye' didn't set the tone for finality when I left. It felt like it was a rating of the season in my life, which they were all saying, "good" and the blessing of "bye," meaning as you are on your way and until we meet again.

CHAPTER 34 – AIRMAN GROSS, ADMINISTRATION

I was on my way to Blytheville, Arkansas, and like San Antonio, I had not been there before. There was a similarity, however. While in Montgomery, Alabama, I got a baptism into the throes of racism when I saw a white policeman beat up a Black man after he ran into the back of him. Had he been more vigilant, looking at the street and not "treeing" the young Black men walking by, he would have never hit this man from behind. Next thing I saw, the policeman was him pulling the man out of the car.

Now, as I was traveling to Arkansas, I saw no sightings that were similar, but I wondered if they would appear. I remember Mr. Armstrong saying there was a sign in Cullman, Alabama, on the highway that read, "Read Nigger and run, if you can read, run anyway." Had I seen a sign like, I didn't think I would feel a chill in my bones or sweat down my back, because I had somewhat been prepared for it. Montgomery gave me my initiation, and I thought it best to be something that policeman who ran in the back of the car wasn't – vigilant. I also saw the many policemen noticing black men who were loud. As for me, I was never loud and boisterous, just for the sake of being loud. Nor did I practice being in big groups of young men. My father once told me, "I see you don't follow the crowd." I knew what he meant, and he was glad that I didn't, because he knew what kind of trouble this could cause with the injection of racism. However, my brother, Leon, loved being in the midst of groups. Had I been prone to follow "the crowd," I would have curtailed it after what I saw in Montgomery.

As soon as I got to Blytheville Air Force Base, I felt like a jet, preparing to land. I could feel my legs getting ready to come down and grip "life's landing strip." This was my first permanent base assignment, and I was no longer in Basic Training; I was an Airman – ready to "forward march."

When I looked around the base, this was a relatively new base, built just fourteen years ago in 1942. As impressive as the base was aesthetical, it wasn't the buildings that summoned my attention. It was the way the men looked — driven, purposeful, and Ambitious. The men had starched khakis with beautiful crease, that showed they took their time and were concerned about presenting their best. Something made me feel this was beyond regulation, but it was something in their regiment they probably had within them, even before they became Airmen, as it continued to develop. Surely this was not just something these men practiced on the outside; I believed their work and desire to become more was prepared at the core.

I looked at my assignment form, making sure I was going to the right barracks. Finally, I arrived and saw where I would be. It was different from the barracks in Basic Training, as I expected it would. It was roomier, and I could tell we would be given a little more latitude as far as how we could arrange our personal area. It was still neat and uniformed, but I saw pictures.

"Hey, how are you?" I heard from a short distance away behind me.

I turned around, and this man had his hand extended. While reaching and extending mine, he said, "I'm Don Allen."

"I'm William Gross," I returned, listening to his accent. I wondered if I had a noticeable accent. It was always something that I could hear, distinguishing those from the Alabama that I had been used to hearing and been around. I took a guess, trying to figure out where he was from. It did sound like Texas, but I wasn't so well versed in accents that I could tell the city.

"Where you from?" he said with a jolly voice.

"I'm from Talladega."

Before I could say Alabama, he had already said it.

"Talladega, Alabama," he said like he was examining the syllables in hopes of bringing something he knew about the state forward, but nothing came.

"Now, are you from Texas?" I asked.

"How'd you know?" His eyes widened, making his crew cut more profound and his dark skin seem to gleam.

"I just left San Antonio, and you sound somewhat similar to what I heard, " I said.

"Got some people from there. I'm from Waco," he said.

"So how long you been in the Air Force?" he continued.

"I just finished Basic Training."

"Well, I've been in eight years," Don said.

"So, are you planning to stay in for twenty years?" I asked.

"Well, I would like to, but I think I better take it year-by-year," he said. I wondered about how he slowed the words up as if there were some hesitations. What I didn't choose to do was ask him about them. I didn't need to let one person's hesitations come and cloud my pathway.

"Well, listen ... enough of this Air Force talk. We have got to go downtown."

"What's downtown?"

He laughed like he had heard a joke, and I had delivered the ultimate punchline with the right timing.

"You really must be country," he said, still chuckling, holding his stomach one second and flailing his arms the next.

"You mean clubs and nightlife. What else is down there?" I asked, hoping he could report on more than drinking and ladies.

"Oh ... you are serious, aren't you?" Don remarked as he trailed off from the laughter.

"Yeah, what else is down there?" I asked.

"Well ... I guess we will just have to go and see," he said.

After that response, I figured he probably made trips downtown for entertainment.

"We can go this coming weekend," he said with a booming voice, indicating his excitement.

"As I get settled in, I'll see if I can go sometimes," I said, hoping no hesitations were visible.

"Now, you are not trying to back out, are you?" he said as if he was losing money if he didn't recruit me to the nightlife scene.

"I'm sure I'll I will make it," I decided to end the sentence right there – not promising when or how soon. It was important to be cordial, and I didn't choose to tell him what I really felt. I wasn't interested in "downtown" nor did I see him differently if he wanted to be there, but I had a multitude of things on my mind. One of them: What would these two years bring for me in Blytheville, Arkansas.

The conversation trailed off, and the last thing I remembered him saying was,

"Imma' hold you to it!" where the voice was booming again, indicating his excitement.

I could tell Don was a nice guy who made friends easily. He was welcoming, bringing down any walls of apprehension I might have had, in spite of the visions I had seen before the barracks. Mainly, I wondered about the work I would do at this Air Force base.

Unpacking my things went faster than I thought. Perhaps the conversation with Don made it go faster.

****

Morning had come, and I was unbelievably excited. I got up and put my clothes on with the diligence that I saw the men possess when I arrived on the base. However, I did see one Airman who looked like hair was growing from his collar upward. Unsure if he was ever asked to cut it off, or if it was within regulation, this looked unkempt and hideous. After close examination of myself in the mirror, I wanted to be sharp and proud of myself, for I was on my way to work in the Office of Administration for the United States Air Force.

Before I left Basic Training, all recruits took a test to be matched to the area where we would work. For someone who had no electricity until much later in my years and no modern household amenities, I couldn't believe it when I saw the area I would be assigned.

"This will be your area," Major Day told me. Something appeared to be very kind in his voice.

"Yes, sir," I said.

I could tell this was a man who carried the ability to listen and exhibited patience as I asked for clarity.

"You will be responsible for making these daily reports. You will type ..." Major Day stated.

Hearing the words were one thing, believing them was another. I had to push apprehension, angst, and immediate anticipation away. I had not as much as seen a typewriter until today. Continuing to listen, I managed to hear the rest of the words.

It was time to believe that "All things are possible to him that believeth." Then I had a thought. I had responsibilities in the fields where I worked, some Papa showed me, and some I learned by observing. Surely, if I could do the farm work that required operating various mechanisms, I could handle a typewriter. One thing was certain, I hadn't had any formal typing lessons, but I knew my ABC's. No matter where they were, including numbers and symbols, I would memorize their positions.

****

My administrative job was becoming easier each day. I was making reports, filing, and keeping attendance records, all while becoming systematic as I performed all the duties. I found it necessary to spend more than the expected hours, for I had to stay later to make sure I was getting the hang of it all.

"You finally in," Don said.

"Yeah, I want to get all the right procedures down," I said.

"I bet you got 'um down."

I was ready to change out of my work clothes and get into some regular civilian wear.

"Don't get too comfortable; we going downtown," Don said.

I almost grunted out loud, but I had promised I would go.

I could still hear him talking when I got my clothes ready for the evening. He was narrating the nightlife, places we're going, and what we were going to see.

"Well, I'm going to the shower," I said. He was still talking and managed to acknowledge what I said and kept right on describing the scenes. I wondered if we would be talking while I faded into the distance of my own transformation.

While in the shower, I thought of a multitude of things. My mind was a merry-go-round of memories and ideas that kept spinning. I couldn't say my mind was full of satisfaction, yet it was a little more at rest. I was doing something with my life that was making me feel I was gaining traction. I was going forward and getting closer to goals in my life. Perhaps, I thought of my goals more than most people, but it was necessary for me to do so. I saw what life looked like in Talladega, even though I survived the hunger, heat, and harsh conditions. Some of these conditions may have come with economic times and environment, but some of this was from Papa, plain and simple, putting himself first with his buddies. This was probably why I wasn't fascinated with hanging out with a bunch of guys who had no purpose. Although I wasn't planning to let these memories be a haunting image forever, from time-to-time, I couldn't help but relive those times.

The water kept falling upon me, getting progressively warmer and soothing. I let the water rain upon my head as the lather was building. I scratched my head in a back and forth manner, as I used my eight fingers across my scalp, like plows across a field.

The steam was engulfing me, reminding me of the foggy mornings back home; sometimes it would be so foggy, I couldn't see down the row when I was plowing it. I turned the shower nobs to off, and I was ready to see what the big deal was downtown.

CHAPTER 35 – A TRIP DOWNTOWN

"I told you we were going to have a good time," Don said, happy that he had recruited me to see downtown.

I didn't answer immediately, nor did I respond to that question at the moment. It was so much to take in, along with the music from the jukebox.

There was a lot of fast-paced songs where I could hear a lot of trumpets. The inside definitely looked more appealing than the outside. I asked myself, 'Would I have gone inside just because I was walking by?' Probably not. Something about the place had undertones of mischief. It wasn't that I saw anything outright, but I bet if the walls could talk, or even sing or dance, they would reveal a thing or two.

"How long have you been coming here?" I asked Don

"Oh, since I've been stationed here," he said.

I figured as much since he was rallying so much for me to come to this club.

There were people dancing, some smoking, and others talking at their tables.

The song changed, and everyone must have thought this was the one to get up and dance.

Looking around at my table where I was sitting, everybody left to dance, except one girl at the table. I deemed it right to ask her to dance.

A loud sound behind me made me wonder if a big fight was about to take place. I heard a booming slam to the floor. It was the kind of sound a farm tool makes when dropped on a wood surface. It slams down hard, and scratches are sure to be left on the floor. When I turned around, Don was over a man. This stance told me Don had knocked the man down. What could this be about? Did Don know the guy? Did he do something to Don? I was hoping I hadn't come on the wrong night. When I looked closer, the man had a knife in his hand. Everybody was circling around, as the whispers and wonders joined.

The guy finally got up and brushed himself off, and slithered out of the place. The crowd resumed where they were, and everybody who was at our table went back –all but the girl I was dancing with on the dance floor.

Don saw I was looking, "That girl was the reason I knocked him out!"

I was puzzled. It must have been some kind of mix up. "What...what did she do?" I asked, just wondering with no animosity.

"When you were dancing with her..." I heard the words Don was saying. I was examining each one like I imagined a blind person examining braille, but I still didn't understand.

"...her boyfriend had a knife drawn back, ready to stab you with it. That's why I knocked him to the floor," Don said, brushing his clothes off.

Air floated into my mouth until I could taste something acrid and putrid at the same time. I didn't know whether it was the buildup of cigarette smoke, perfume, or cologne in the air. I closed it, and by the time my lips came together, I had some new constitutions already in the making.

"He's just some native thug who thinks he can muscle everybody around," Don said.

"So, you had seen him before?" I asked.

"Oh yeah, I see him here from time to time, and he's always ready for a fight, especially when it comes to his girlfriend."

"Don, I'm sure glad that you were for looking out for me tonight," I said.

"No problem, man ... you would have done the same for me," Don said, while composed as if nothing happened.

The whole club seemed to "go back into place" as nothing happened. As for me, something within me was rearranged.

****

I was happy to be back on base after the ordeal downtown. I pulled off my clothes and prepared for the next day. Sunday had virtually already arrived, so I had planned a day of peacefulness for myself when the day got underway.

If I guessed right, Don was going to have a lot to say, and he did. I, however, had silence on my lips for the rest of the night. I didn't ignore him; I just listened. Some of the conversations were about the highlight of the night, and some were about the next time we go downtown. I was like a dog who put his ear up when he hears something that is stirring around. That's what I did when I heard the words, "next time." I was putting my guard up, and I was bringing my ambitions closer to me.

What would have happened to me if that guy stabbed me? Could I have had an injury that would have affected me for a lifetime, where I would have forever suffered the consequences under the harm done? Could it have been that I had received only a scar? I was thankful that it was neither, and that God had a citadel of angels encamped around me. Even if I had a small scar, it would have been a constant reminder that I was at the wrong place at the wrong time.

****

My journey in the Air Force was moving quicker than I imagined. I was learning new tricks that were helping me to be efficient in making all the reports that I had to make. Generally, I was always organized all my life, whether I was putting all the farm equipment in order in our barns, or whether I was keeping the few clothes I did have in order when I was a growing up. Even with my school books, papers, and pencils, I had a system that helped me keep these things in order. Now in the Air Force, I used what I had known that worked for me, and it was working. However, I listened to how I was briefed, took notes, and followed the guidelines for making reports as efficient as possible. The military had to know what and where each employee was reporting on the base. These attendance reports were necessary documents, and mistakes were not tolerated.

I saw Major Day taking a glimpse at me. When I saw him look at me, I wondered if he would require me to do something different or something in a certain way. I continued my work, as I was, all the while believing everything was okay as it was.

Like any set of records, they had to be checked and rechecked for accuracy. There was more; I typed letters and memos that went to other units with requests, and for someone who had no typing experience, I was pecking away. That was where my real tips were coming in handy. I somewhat memorized, "W-E-R-T-Y." It reminded me of a word, maybe because it had a vowel in the middle, so I knew the E-R was always going to be together. The "U-I-O" were together and right beside "W-E-R-T-Y," and those were all of the vowels but "A" right there, so I was going to come back to that row all the time. The other letters were becoming familiar, but all the other consonants positions on the keyboard were a little harder to remember. Why didn't the typewriter just have keys in alphabetical order anyway?

****

When I pulled the chair out, I could hear the sound echo from the wooden floor. It made a scuffing sound, and if I was blindfolded, I would know the location. The familiarity was welcoming, and I knew I was safe. I knew this library on base was going to be like my second home, and I didn't have to worry about men looking for trouble or those who wanted to prove something. It was just me and the wind that blew from the pages that I turned. I settled in the library for hours, reading about things that were interesting – all subjects. It didn't matter what it was, I was learning things that I didn't have access to in Talladega, and I was enjoying what I read.

I thought I would take a look and find out why the typewriter's keys are not in alphabetical order.

"Where could I find information about typewriters?" I asked the person at the desk.

"Well, what do you want to know?" The question came back to me as quickly as I sent it.

"Why are the keys not in order?" I replied.

"You want to know the history of the typewriter. Let's start in the encyclopedia."

I read what seemed like a hundred names, all leading back to their contribution to the typewriter, whether it was in the United States, Britain, Italy, or Japan. But, I had to applaud the effort of what these men had done. Finally, I was getting to what I was looking for about the typewriter. Here it was. The first commercial typewriter was a model by

Christopher Sholes and Carlos Glidden in 1868. Also, it was the first typewriter with the QWERTY keyboard. There were a lot of other names, dates, and other information about tab key and shift keys. I wasn't trying to pass up or glaze over any information, but I really wanted to know why was the keyword in that order. Truly, I was hoping it wouldn't be an insignificant reason to make people more conscious of what they were typing. Maybe I was somewhat cynical, believing there were those who didn't ever want anything running smoothly for anybody. I quickly denounced that believing the hard work of these men couldn't possibly factor in such a feature.

My eyes continued to go on the journey of QWERTY mystery. Now, I was finally to it. I sank my comprehension into it and saw it as a vivid picture. With the letters being on metal arms, the arms would jam if certain keys were struck at the same time. I could see it. So simply put, certain keys were moved that were used more often to avoid a clash if the typist was typing fast. All of this was making sense to me now.

I was using my index fingers for now. Yet, it was evident that the people who were using these typewriters were using all their fingers, contributing to the speed, and that was what was jamming the metal arms. This information was great to know. I could appreciate the typewriter even more because I knew the blood, sweat, and possibly tears that went into bringing the typewriter to where it is today. I guess the next thing for me would be to learn how to type using all my fingers to properly take full advantage of this machine. I wasn't sure when that would be, but I could see the benefit, if only from a historical standpoint.

****

My desire to learn was something that came naturally to me, but that didn't mean that everything I desired to learn was easy. I always enjoyed learning about new things, yet there were fundamental things I needed to review and accomplish to go forward.

Major Day wanted to speak with me about something.

"Airman Gross," he said.

"Yes, sir," I responded with strong resonance. I always did that, for I thought it was a sign of respect.

"You have taken your skills test, and I want to be the one to report to you that you have made the highest score of all the Airmen who tested," he said.

I almost interrupted after he said "skills test," but I waited. I didn't know what to say. I was spinning a little bit and wondered what that meant.

"You are really knowledgeable, and you work with diligence. I think there are a lot of areas that you could pursue in the Air Force," Major Day continued.

"I ... I," I hesitated slightly, "would like to get my GED and work on my mathematics.

"I think we can help you with all of that," Major Day said.

"You seem to have great aptitude on the skills tests, so the mathematics will come with practice."

He gave me information about the GED, and I took it and looked at it intensively.

"This is not going to be a problem for you," he said.

I was encouraged by his confidence. It was great to have a Major who thought of me this way.

After work, I headed to my favorite spot in the library. I looked at some math materials that I thought would help me begin. I hadn't been that far away from the last math class I took, but even when I took it, I needed more practice. I thought I would start with Algebra, as it related to equations.

I thumbed through the book, and some things were clear, but others were vague. I tried to look at the steps I saw, but something was not computing. There was something that was missing. I told myself that I would get someone to help me with this.

****

"William, where have you been? Let me guess, your favorite place," Don said.

"Yes, you're right," I said.

"I want you done with all that reading, and getting ready go to downtown this weekend," Don said.

"Umph," I sighed.

"William, you will have a great time," he said.

"Don, if I can get my GED studying done, I will consider it."

"William, you know that stuff."

Don meant well. It was even encouraging that he said that. He had a lot of heart, and as I got to know him, he was a spiritual guy who had a lot of faith and exercised it. He could sing with a heavy baritone sound that could put a spin on a Gospel tune. His voice alone could make a person consider becoming a believer.

He was becoming like a big brother to me, and I enjoyed his banter about going downtown. However, that was his form of enjoyment, not so much mine. But, as promised, if I had made enough headway toward studying for my GED, I might consider going.

Don stood there looking like he was hoping I was counting the minutes to Saturday, and hoping I was going to reach my goals. I took a few moments to reflect on my skills test and couldn't believe I made the highest score, and I knew who I wanted to tell first.

****

Settling on my bed, while looking out of the window, I could see that the season was changing, and time was moving forward. I counted the days and miles I had been away, and I actually had some distance between Talladega and me. It wasn't about how far I was physically from my home town; it was all about how far I would go mentally and educationally to reach my fullest potential.

I reached for my pen and my stationery.

Dear Mama,

I hope this letter finds you well. With the heat of the Talladega sun packed away, I know being outside must be much better now. No doubt, you already have ideas for a garden as soon as spring comes. The tomatoes I ate while standing in the garden were my favorites. Sitting here as I write, my senses pick up things back home. I can hear Janet and Thomas running around, as their voices are echoing around the yard, and it is as if I can taste your hoecakes as I write this.

I'm still getting used to Blytheville in this land of Arkansas, even though I've been here for about six months. I think I told you in the letters I wrote before that there's something about the weather here that seems warmer, even when the temperature is lower. Maybe I'm just used to Alabama – seemed no place was colder.

The food here is not bad, but it is not your food – what I wouldn't give to have some of your fried rabbit with gravy. Just the way the gravy goes down, as the flavor hits your tongue, makes it unforgettable.

I'm eager to tell you that I took a Skills Test and I made the highest score out of all the Airmen tested. Knowing I had made the highest score has made me want to learn more and more each day. Just the fact that I was able to do this gives me more hope to take my life further.

I am working on getting my General Equivalency Diploma (GED) because I want to complete this area of my life and then be able to go further in the Air Force. When it comes to Math, I'm looking to have a firmer foundation. What I know is, although beyond the basics, but I want to really know more and have confidence in calculations.

I put the paper down for a few minutes while I got some water. It seems like I drank more water in Talladega and anywhere else I had been but had to force myself to drink at other places. There was no hard science for me to figure this out. I was doing more work and more sweating in those fields of Talladega, and thirst was always nearby.

I managed to finish the letter to Mama, and I went to bed. There were ideas stirring in my head about moving forward concerning learning Math, so I would be in full pursuit of them tomorrow.

****

I was at the typewriter with my usual format, fingers moving at the speed I had mastered, where there would be little to no mistakes. My reports would be finished in record time. As the day passes, I met a gentleman who had all the distinguished trimmings an Airman would have.

It was impressive to see black men in the Air Force who were decorated. It told the story that their work stood for itself, and someone recognized it. Additionally, it gave me something to look forward to, as well as hope.

This man was Lieutenant Alston, and I didn't let the grass grow under my feet about an idea I had, and I was going to follow it through.

****

"Right this way, gentlemen," the waitress said. I managed to get Don to go to a restaurant and not the downtown area this time. This restaurant had some of the etching of the "downtown" life, but it was far less crowded.

"Can I take your orders, or do you need a few moments?" the waitress asked.

We all nodded and decided we needed a few moments. Some other Airmen Don knew joined us. We looked over our menus. I couldn't decide right away.

"What you getting?" a question that the men at the table kept throwing out like cards from a winning hand.

The choices kept colliding and changing like cars in a lane. When one man heard another choice, it seems like he liked what he heard better than his original choice.

Meanwhile, I looked around the restaurant and saw people enjoying their dinner. I wondered if it was their first time to this restaurant, or if they were regulars. Soon, the waitress was back.

"William, I don't know if you know Timothy Kennedy, but he is a friend of mine who I thought would be great to come along with us," Don said.

"How are you? Very nice meeting you."

"Same here," he said.

"Where are you from?" I asked. I couldn't hear the drawl of the south I was so used to hearing. His speech was a little faster, more distinctive, with all the syllables present.

"I'm from Philadelphia."

That matched what I was thinking. I didn't hit it on the bullseye, but I knew he was not from the South.

"Where are you from?" he volleyed back.

"Talladega, Alabama," I said with pride.

I noticed I said the city and state, but he said just the city. Most people had heard of Philadelphia, and it was pretty safe to say people knew where it was. It was one of those known cities that could stand without stating the state of Pennsylvania.

The conversation continued, and we kept on swapping facts about how we got to Arkansas and what we had done before we got here.

The meals came back swiftly. Just as I had thought, everyone had gotten the meal they heard instead of the one they initially chose. I guess when some people hear another choice, it sometimes sounds better than their own. There was a pause of silence, but everyone could hear the clanking from their own knives and forks.

"This is good, huh?" Don said.

Everybody was in agreement and responded in some form of "un-huh," "yeah," and kept lifting their forks.

A few moments passed, and half the food had disappeared from our plates, the conversations came back.

Later, I got up and went to the restroom. This gave me a further "tour" of the restaurant. Looking around, I could see more of the restaurant with a better vantage point than where I was sitting. I wondered how much math went into putting this restaurant together. Since this was an area I had on my mind lately, and teachers throughout school were telling us that Math was used everywhere, it just so happened to enter my mind. I saw the number of tables, then the number of chairs. Now that alone didn't create any interest, but it did create other mathematical interests. Someone had to calculate ahead of time that X number of tables and chairs were needed. My head started seeing other questions. How many feet long was this restaurant? What were the height and width? According to the measurements, did that determine how many tables and chairs, along with what kind and where they were placed in the restaurant?

"Man, where you been?" Don said.

"I was looking around the restaurant and just thinking how everything comes together," I replied.

"William, you sho' can think," Don said. "You can think about things no one else wonders about, and that's one of the things I like about you."

"If we are ready ..." Don said, "We can get out of here and go on further," in a singsong way."

We turned to leave, and in the blink of an eye, two hands were around my neck on my collar.

****

A body hit the floor, and Tim was standing over him.

"What was that all about?" I asked.

The man began to rise, shaking his head.

"You were staring at my girlfriend!" the man shouted.

Before I could even respond, Tim had jumped up and said, "You know that didn't happen. He's been sitting there the whole time talking to us about what it must have been like to calculate the size of this restaurant and determining the size of furniture in it."

"I ... I ... saw him looking over at us," he tried to said.

"Oh, you did, did ya?" Tim said.

I thought I was watching a scene from a picture show.

"You make sure next time before you grab someone in the collar," Don said.

All I could think about – one for downtown, one for on base. I had already expected crazy events that might happen downtown, but I didn't think a restaurant on base would have the same kind of action.

"You alright? Don asked.

"Yeah," I said.

"If Tim hadn't gotten to him, I would have taken care of him," Don said.

I knew that was right. Both Don and Tim were semi-professional boxers. They did not flaunt themselves as fighters around the base. Neither Don nor Tim was out to fight anyone outside the ring. They saw boxing as a respectable sport and had seen it as a blessing for both of them to be able to compete. However, in times of protection, they used the weapon they had, and that was their fists.

"William, do you remember hearing about Emmett Till?" Tim said.

I was puzzled. Who was this?

"I don't know who that is," I said.

"Emmett Till was a boy that was lynched last year in Mississippi."

"What happened?"

"A white woman said he was whistling at her in a store," Tim said.

"No, I never heard about that," I said.

"She was probably looking at you, and her husband saw her looking in your direction, and she hurried up and thought of the idea that you were looking at her," Tim replied.

"When you go to the library, go and read about Emmett Till," Don said.

"Next time we go out, we want to get a seat that sets us in a direction that white women can't be looking at us, and we can't be looking in their direction if at all possible," Don continued.

"Things are very different in the South," Tim said. "Now we see things somewhat like this in Philadelphia when it comes to blacks and whites being separate, but not to the extreme of what I have seen here."

We all left and went back to our barracks, and I had more to think about than I wanted.

****

I was at the library before it opened. Waiting for them to open the doors seemed like hours. Who was this boy, Emmett Till?

I could hear the click of the doors as they were opening.

"Come on in," the circulation clerk said.

They knew me so well because I came there so much. Yet, after that incident at the restaurant, I said 'good morning' and scurried on to the tables. I wouldn't say that Don and Tim put a lot of fear in me, but it did make me cautious. I made eye contact just to say good morning, and make a request when it came to white women.

I started looking for newspaper articles on Emmett Till. I was talking to myself through the process of looking at the newspapers on microfilm. Tim said this was last year, so that was 1955. He later told me it was in the summer, around August. I was looking for Mississippi newspapers from 1955. I kept scrolling and scrolling, and finally, I saw his name.

****

When I saw the picture of Emmett Till in the casket, I couldn't believe what I was seeing. Who could do such a thing to a human being? I read that his Mother wanted his casket open so the world could see what had been done to her son.

A chill ran through me. This happened August 24, 1955, and I didn't know when I was going to ever know about this. I didn't even know about the Montgomery Bus Boycott; I don't know when I would know about this.

Emmett Till was a fourteen-year-old boy who was from Chicago visiting Money, Mississippi. A white woman, Carolyn Bryant, said he had whistled at her and grabbed her hand at a store, also saying he had been with white women. It was a Sunday, and he and his cousins went to the store to buy candy.

My mind went back to the pictures. This was horrible. What I read further was how Carolyn Bryant's husband and half-brother came after Emmett Till at his uncle's house during the night. They took him away to beat him and shoot him in the head, and if that was not enough, they put him in the river, making sure he drowned.

I knew what Alabama was like when it came to racism, yet I could not say I had the intense face-to-face experiences as some had. However, reading about Emmett Till was more than just seeing it on the page. It deeply saturated my soul and made me wonder, could that have been me? Could this happen to a cousin or friend? What if this were Kyser or Charles?

Hours had gone by as I read about things ranging from the struggles to the strength of Negroes. I realized that I needed to get up to speed when it came to what was happening to the Negro community. Additionally, I would strive to be all I could be to add to the community in the most positive way.

CHAPTER 36 – MORE TESTS!!

"Airman Gross, let's take this diagnostic test and see where you are mathematically," Lieutenant Alston said.

"Yes, sir. Do you want me to show the work next to the problem or right under it?" I asked. I remembered how some teachers were sticklers about the work being shown right next to the problem or those that wanted it right under it.

"You can put it right under the problem," he said.

Lieutenant Alston was a sharp man who looked like he was made for the Air Force. He was sharp without even trying. Of course, he did, but there was an effortless presence to him. It was evident that he worked hard, but he made everything he did look like he didn't break a sweat.

I began with number one. It was an equation that had me solve for X. After he talked with me about where I left off in math in high school, he created some problems to see where I was in math. After scanning the page, his diagnosis of me was quite accurate. It was like the porridge Goldilocks had at the bear's house. It was just right. The problems weren't too hard, and they weren't too easy; however, I didn't have to work to solve them.

Math problem number two was a word problem. "Umm..." I said to myself. I drew the problem out, trying to determine what it was asking me. I used scratch paper after scratch paper, but Lieutenant Alston had no problem with it.

Each problem had a different approach that seemed to reveal my knowledge of Math in a different way. I could tell he had listened to me and everything I told him about where I was in Math and where I wanted to be.

I had reached the twentieth problem, and by then, I had added, subtracted, multiplied, and divided. Sweat had begun to trickle down a little, and I was pleased. It didn't matter how I had done. What I was glad I had done was follow my thoughts, step out on faith, and ask Lieutenant Alston to tutor me in Math.

****

"Airman Gross, I have examined your work, and I can see that you are a methodical thinker," Lieutenant Alston said.

"What did I get?" I asked like I was being graded on a test. I had about twenty problems on the test, and I figured like the teachers at Talladega, when we had twenty questions, they were worth five points each. If you missed two, you got a 90.

"I didn't look at it like a grade, Airman Gross. I assess it according to the areas of strength and where we needed to go from here," Lieutenant Alston replied.

I sat quietly and wondered what would happen next. I observed him getting pencils and more paper before he came back to the table.

"Let's start with this first problem we will work on today. I wanted to know if you knew how to solve equations, interpret word problems, and understand general math calculations to know where to start. As I followed your method, I can see how you arrived at your answers, but it is not the correct one. First, I want to review with you the order of operations."

It was all coming back to me. I had worked all the problems from left to right.

I heard my stomach rumble, not from hunger, although I knew a hunger rumble all too well from childhood. I knew I probably that I didn't get much right on Lieutenant Alston's diagnostic test.

"When it comes to math, there's an order that must be used when you approach every problem," Lieutenant Alston stated.

I was getting ready to ask a question waiting for a pause, but he continued. His passion for this order of operations was clearly apparent. He began to pace the floor, walking back and forth with the pencil in one hand while tapping it in another. He looked like he was getting ready to make an opening statement for the defense for a murder trial.

"First, you have to begin with parenthesis. Whatever is inside, you have to solve that first." He wrote a problem on the paper.

"See right here. You must start with what is in the parenthesis, and put the answer under it and bring the other number down."

The problem was four plus three in parenthesis, times six divided by two, minus five times five.

"So I add four plus three in parenthesis and get seven, and multiply by six and get forty-two," I said eagerly.

"The next thing you do is solve any exponents and then multiply in the order of operations in mathematics."

"Exponents?" I questioned.

"You're right; we don't have any in this problem, so we will go straight to multiplication."

I didn't admit at the moment that I didn't even remember exponents, but I kept going focusing on this problem. When the time came, I would tell him what I didn't know because how could I progress pretending.

"So, I would know that would be forty-two," I said.

"Now look closely; you still need to multiply here."

"I go on that side and not continue?" I questioned.

"Yes, it has to be this way, or you will solve the problem incorrectly. So write down forty-two divided by two, minus five times five," Lieutenant Alston said.

I did what Lieutenant Alston said.

"Now, you have to multiply five times five."

Everything in my being wanted to go from left to right. I wrote the number twenty-five.

The problem now had three numbers with division and subtraction.

"Airman Gross, I promise you if you follow the order of operation when it comes to math, you won't go wrong."

Lieutenant Alston must have seen a confused and hesitant look on my face.

"The next order in operation is division," he said.

I divided forty-two by two and got twenty-one. I was down to twenty-one minus twenty-five.

"Now the next operation is addition and then subtraction," he said. "Since there is no addition, you subtract."

"The answer is negative 4?" I said more like a question.

"That's correct!" Lieutenant Alston said with enthusiasm.

"Airman Gross, when it comes to math, you have to follow this order. Often many people approaching mathematics want to go from left to right. But, I promise you, if you follow the order, you will solve every problem correctly."

"I'm going to give you fifty problems I want you to work on until we meet for the next session. Take your time and use the proper order of operations," Lieutenant Alston asserted.

"Yes, sir. Thank you for this session, and I will have this assignment completed."

I exited the session feeling a surge of complexity. I had to undo the habit of attacking math my way. Of course, I could do it, but I wish I had learned this earlier.

****

"How many more problems you got to do, William?" Don said.

"I'm going over them to make sure I have the right order of operations," I said.

"You have been at it for two or more hours now," Don continued, wondering how I could be on a task so long.

"When I had my tutoring session with Lieutenant Alston, I needed to review the order of operations."

"That's that parenthesis first stuff."

"Yeah, that's right."

"Well, I got some of that mixed up, because if you do one before the other, I can tell you now your whole problem will be wrong. You made have added right, subtracted right, divided right, or multiplied right, but your whole problem is going to be wrong."

"I don't know how I missed this in math. It must have been one of those periods where I was plowing before school. Then, it could have been a period of time I was so hungry; I couldn't concentrate. I did what I thought was right – and right was doing math from left to right."

"Well, what are you worrying about all this math for now?" Don said.

"Don, I ..."

"You passed all the entrance tests, and made the highest scores on the skilled test," he inserted.

"I got to ..."

"You are not going to use that math in the Air Force," Don said.

I knew Don was trying to make me feel I was fine within the Air Force as I was, and not without a good mind.

"You're a smart guy; I could tell that from the beginning," Don added with sincerity.

"I want to do and be a lot more," I said.

"Well, I can understand that," Don said with a furrowed brow that revealed he understood. "I've heard you say there was nothing in Talladega for you to build a future on, so I can see what you are talking about."

"First, I want to take the GED."

"Okay, I see where you are going," Don responded in an upbeat tempo. "All young Airmen who haven't finished high school ought to be out here doing the same thing."

I was listening while turning my eye to a problem on the paper.

"Maybe they have a different plan, Don," I said without making a judgment. "See, I know what it is to be hungry, with tattered clothes and people talking about you and your family, and I know to I need to move higher in the Air Force, I need my GED, and I promised my teachers from high school that I would finish and go to college."

"William, you keep going. For a young man, you have ambition as I've never seen. I didn't work on a farm, but my family has its own kind of struggles in Texas. I joined the Air Force too for a better future, and I took up boxing to keep out of trouble."

I listened to Don as he continued about his life in Texas. It was different from Talladega, but one thing was the same, struggles were struggles, and no one wanted to be in them.

Glimpses of the Thornton Place, my first home, came to mind, and I stopped past so many memories. I decided that I could not visit all of them, but the main ones I wanted to see were the ones where the teachers of Talladega County Training School believed in me. I owed it to them to do my best because they worked so hard, and to do my best meant I was forever grateful.

I continued working the problems one-by-one. Each time I practiced, I felt a little more confident that I was going to solve each one correctly. While I folded the finished paper in half, I felt a sense of peace, and somehow, I knew this was the first of many beginnings.

****

I sat at the desk, working on the problems Lieutenant Alston had given me. These were more complicated than the ones I had taken home. Something about these required a lot of scratch paper. I could almost look at the ones I took home and not write out the expressions and arrive at the answer in my head. However, Lieutenant Alston wanted to see my work. This time I had to actually calculate doing some long division.

"Wait a minute, am I seeing this right," I asked myself. "Is this is a mixed number in this problem?" I asked aloud. I had let that slip out as I looked around. Lieutenant Alston was looking to see a few more things that I knew or perhaps needed to learn in this new diagnostic work. I don't think he even knew I had said anything. He was deep into grading the work I had done.

Lieutenant Alston was walking back and forth again. That same walk where he looked like a trial lawyer. His pen was positioned in this hand like he was getting ready to sign the most important document in his life. I could hardly pull away from watching him go over my paper. It was a struggle to get to my work or continue looking to see if I could read his expression and determine how I did on the homework.

"Airman Gross, I can see you progressed pretty well on the problems I gave you. You got eighty-nine percent of them right. The other eleven percent was when there was a division and addition within parentheses. Remember, the division has priority over addition."

"I'm going to have you correct these problems, and then we will go forward. Take the ones that I gave today, and we will have a longer session next time, as we will bring everything together."

"Yes, sir."

"Continue to show your work. In math, it is easy to make careless mistakes. Sometimes the mind sees multiply when you are supposed to add. I saw that a couple of times in your work. That is the importance of working the problem out and bringing the numbers down each time after you have solved part of the problem."

"I'll be sure to do that."

"You are doing well, and before you know it, you will be well on your way to algebraic equations."

I didn't even want him to pronounce that again, and now did I try to remember what kind of equations they were. Whatever it was, I guess I would know them when we worked on them.

"Yes, sir," I said again.

He continued to affirm how well I was doing.

"Thank you, Lieutenant Alston."

"You're welcome, Airman Gross."

CHAPTER 37 - G.E.D.

If anyone had told me that time would move so fast, I would have disputed them. I had been working on learning math correctly, and it had become a focal point for me. I said no to downtown, restaurants on and off base, and things that I could catch up with another time.

The library probably knew my footsteps; I had been there so many times the clerks joked about letting me lock up. As I approached the building, I decided to read the current events first. That was an area that I couldn't explore much in Talladega. We didn't have newspapers, and the school didn't discuss local or national news unless it was something major. I don't remember them making a school announcement about things, but I do remember them announcing that we would say "under God" in the Pledge of Allegiance, where we had not before. I thought that was something Mr. Franklin had gotten permission to add. Later, I found out it had nothing to do with Mr. Franklin at all.

We knew things in the form of History, and old history at that. The books we had didn't include the current President of the United States; that was the reason I did chose Theodore Roosevelt for my project in Miss Slater's class.

I was beginning to make it a habit to read the newspaper when I got to the library. That way, I would know precisely what was going on in the world. This was an election year for the president, and this would be my way of having a front-row seat to what was going on in the world.

****

I read the words and finally unraveled the mystery of what I once thought. It wasn't Mr. Franklin who decided to add the words, 'under God,' to the Pledge of Allegiance; it was President Dwight D. Eisenhower. In his 1954 Flag Day Speech, President Eisenhower reveals why he wanted 'under God' in the Pledge of Allegiance:

"In this way, we are reaffirming the transcendence of religious faith in America's heritage and future; in this way, we shall constantly strengthen those spiritual weapons which forever will be our country's most powerful resource in peace and war."

Thoughts were coming into my head. I would be eligible to vote this time. I was nineteen, and I wanted to be able to cast my vote. President Eisenhower was running for his second term with Richard Nixon as his Vice-President. All the talk in the world was that President Eisenhower had suffered a heart attack and abdominal surgery, and people wondered whether he should run again. Adlai Stevenson, the Governor of Illinois, was the Democratic Convention Nominee.

I decided this was all I would focus on in the library about the presidential election and start researching the information about the GED. As I had been working with Lieutenant Alston with math, the area I knew I needed help in most, I was doing pretty well. In the other areas, I thought I could refresh myself.

"Good day, Airman Gross," the circulation clerk said.

"Good morning," I responded. The clerk had a gleam in her eye, awaiting my request. Somedays, I think they looked forward to seeing me, so they would have to help with research. I didn't see many Airmen coming to the library to read leisurely. I did see some officers who would meet in groups who looked like they were working on some strategic presentation, as they would hover on scrolls of papers. Each would be pointing, and then nodding in agreement. Occasionally, one would look as if he objected, and they all looked his way, and then they would go back to the drawing board.

"I want to have information about the G.E.D. test."

"I can help you with that," the circulation clerk said. "Here is a pamphlet about it."

I opened it and looked at the information. There were dates and times, but I was looking for more.

"Can you show me where I can read about the history of this test?"

"Sure, I can."

The information was quite informative. I thought the G.E.D was created for any student that didn't finish school. Upon further reading, I saw something interesting. The G.E.D. wasn't meant to be a test just for anyone that didn't finish high school. It was created for military men.

I immediately sat up straight in my chair, positioning myself to read more.

Since Congress had lowered the draft age to 18 from 21 in 1942, more young men were being drafted during high school years.

I had no idea that was the reason for the G.E.D. As I kept reading, men who had been serving and fighting in wars couldn't go back to high school to complete their education. So the military had an idea and wondered what could be done to give credit to the men that served if they wanted to go to college.

Never had I heard anyone speak of this. I realized this was only 14 years ago, but I guess if I hadn't known about major current events in the world, I surely wouldn't know about this. This was some fascinating reading, and I would return to it a little later. Right now, I wanted to see if I could find out what kind of questions would be on the test, and exactly how I should prepare for it.

"Airman Gross, are you finding everything you need?"

"I did find the history of the G.E.D. I would like to know if there are sample questions or an outline to tell me what to study for on the test."

"Let me see if I can find the information you are looking for."

****

My normalcy in the Air Force was beginning to take shape in the form of more discipline than I thought I would have. I knew discipline was what everyone in the military was going to experience, but somehow I had become more regimented in my personal growth. The math problems began to strengthen my approach to not just the problems that were on the paper, where it made me keep a steady pace, checking things twice, and still recheck just when you think the problem is finished. It also changed the way I approached things around me.

I firmly believe God's hand was carving this out in my life. Maybe I didn't see his hand with the naked eye, but I sure thought God's hand could shape, even when he didn't touch things. I had come to know that even his allowance of things still counted as shaping. Those two men who wanted to knock me out made me think that I didn't need to be certain places, and there must have been something else God wanted me to do with my time. Surely, fun and recreation were good, and sure I had to eat, but after those incidents, I was just going to focus on getting my G.E.D. The focus brought on a new discipline, and it was carrying me away, like a tidal wave from things that could potentially harm me.

****

The day had come. I was finally taking the G.E.D. It seemed weird I would have my High School Equivalency before my classmates since I had two more years to go in high school. But this was the way I had chosen. There was no doubt I would love to have finished Talladega County Training School with Charles and Kyser, but now I would have a diploma showing I had high school-level academic skills.

I listened to the directions. I didn't do anything that would cause my test to be voided or ungradable. I had thoughts in my mind that something as small as a name on the wrong side could stop the grading process. It probably wasn't that severe, but since I had come this far, I wasn't about to take any chances.

As the test was in front of me, I didn't blink for what seemed like five minutes. I worked with each problem in front of me and kept a good pace.

I occasionally glanced at the clock, but I kept working. These math problems were terribly hard, and they did require steps that called for lots of scratch paper.

All the sessions with Lieutenant Alston, working math problems and reading current events in the library had paid off. Each area strengthened me for the kinds of problems I saw today.

When the test was over, instead of being tired, I felt my energy activate within me. Hope was stirring within me because of this achievement. I could move forward to different jobs in the Air Force that could give me new opportunities.

****

It was four days before Christmas. It was the date of today's paper, and I immediately associated the thought of how happy children would be that Santa was on his way. I thought of the whistle Lillie Mae had brought me, and how she made many of my Christmases most special. But there was something else that caught my attention. The words MONTGOMERY BOYCOTT HAS ENDED virtually jumped off the page.

It was just about five months ago that I had come through Montgomery, and it had all the trimmings of racial tension. To be more accurate, it was more like a soda in a bottle that had been shaken vigorously, and then someone opened the bottle. Little did I know that a Black woman named Rosa Parks had refused to move to the back of the bus. That one act caused Blacks to stop riding the bus from December 5, 1955, to December 21, 1956. That meant walking, riding together, delaying shopping, or whatever it meant to stay off the buses until blacks could be treated equally. From the most obvious looks of it, it seemed like the bus company felt the impact of two Christmas seasons. People who were usually shopping and carrying packages had to be encumbered with walking with them or borrowing to rides to prepare for the season. However, it was becoming apparently clear that it wasn't hurting the black people as bad as it was hurting the Montgomery Bus Company. They felt the monetary loss when their pockets felt pinched, so the bus company started to see things differently – a different seating arrangement, where blacks and white would be mixed together wasn't going to be that bad after all.

I stretched my arms and yawned. My chair made a slight movement causing the sound to echo against the wooden floor. The sound seemingly echoed through the library, but it didn't disturb anyone. The library was virtually a ghost town. Everyone was out shopping or preparing for some festivities.

In a few days, I would be on the bus for Talladega, and I was excited to see how changes for Blacks would be traveling home after the end of the bus boycott.

****

My uniform was creased and pressed and would have passed any inspection if I had gone through one-hundred bases. I was wearing my winter blues, with wool material that would stave the cold off. I swept the brush across my hair and gave it a final sweep before I put it away in my bag. Going home for Christmas made me feel as excited as I was the day I was preparing to go to Tuskegee Institute with Mr. Armstrong to speak at the New Farmers Convention.

My last trip home was filled with the expected and the unexpected, so I prepared to be ready for whatever new events were going to take place during this visit.

The Greyhound bus was surprisingly comfortable. Maybe I was just ready to travel, and if I had been sitting on a cylinder block with some cardboard, I probably would have been content.

I looked around the bus, and this was what was called the Chicken Bone Express. I could hear the foil unwinding from the sandwiches as Blacks traveled with their own food; they couldn't be certain that they would be served. I had 214 miles to go travel, so I brought along a few snacks, but nothing significant. The trip was going to be roughly four and a half hours or even more with stops.

The scene outside the window was a familiar scene. Smoke from the chimneys was one. It seemed like the smoke was not that eager to leave the chimney, knowing it was going to enter the bitter cold, lingering as it would rather stay inside. I smiled, knowing I let my imagination have its way. Now that I was in the military, I looked at things with a different eye – maybe even a more creative one.

Six months out of Talladega was carrying me to areas I would have never known I could go. I had been pushed off a tower down a zip wire during basic training, typing on a typewriter, making daily reports for the personnel office, studying, and taking the G.E.D. In these six months, I had also met people who had made things happen in their lives and could help make differences in mine. Don, Tim, Major Day, and Lieutenant Benny Alston had been cornerstones for me at Blytheville Air Force Base.

Each one of these men had helped me in different capacities. Don and Tim showed me, as a young Airman, the ropes about the social avenues of life. They were also good friends who were willing to listen and talk about things I wanted to discuss even it differed from their opinions.

I saw more scenes as the bus was heading into Mississippi. The view, even from afar, had the overt look of racial divide. "Colored," "Negro," and "White Only" signs were prominently displayed on business establishments.

Seems like I heard more aluminum foil and wax paper unwind on the bus. Blacks were obviously unwelcomed in some places, and there was no guarantee of what or how you could be served food while traveling in the south.

The bus was coming to a stop.

"We gonna stop hear for 'bout twenty-five minutes. Everybody needs to be back by then," the driver said with a hint of impatience. I got the feeling not to mess around.

Upon leaving, I saw passengers putting away some of the food they had, rewrapping carefully and zipping up their bags, tucking them away.

I ventured to the front and stepped down the steps to go out of the bus. The "colored" signs were around, and I found my way to the restroom. I was mindful of the minutes, so I figured I had about twenty-three more. The smell of food from the diner convinced me that I might get some food. Looking in my billfold, I counted my money, seeing what I had there, and looked at the prices. I decided on a cheeseburger. It was only .50 cents.

The line wasn't terribly long, but I knew I didn't have more than approximately nineteen minutes now.

"What do you want to order?"

The words had a bite to them, but it was expected.
"A cheeseburger, ma'am," I said with politeness.
She wrote it down and yelled, "one cheeseburger."
I passed her my money before she asked for it, not wishing to delay time or cause any rift.
She gave me the cheeseburger and two quarters in my mind. I kept my hand extended, waiting for the rest of my change.
As time conscious as I had been, I was equally concerned about my change.
"That's all you gonna git, boy!"
Now, what could I do? Ask for the manager? Call for the police? The bus would have been gone by the time they probably got there, and would they have been on my side of the issue.
I thought of Emmett Till and his exchange with a white woman in a store. There wasn't anything that could be done here at this time. I just turned around, went back to the bus, and had to let the realization sink in that I had just paid $9.50 for a cheeseburger.

****

The arms of Mama wrapped around me, and I was as safe as I was with her in church as a child. The only thing absent was sucking my tongue and me pulling on her arms when I was sitting beside her, as they were my personal thermostat. Her arms seemed to keep me cool in the summer and warm in the winter. I rested my head on her arms many days as I heard the "Amens" from the pulpit. The memory of that $9.50 cheeseburger couldn't even invade this moment and nor would I let it.
"Junior, you look so good."
"Thanks, Mama."
"Come on it and put your things down."
I walked in, and I could hear the familiar creak in the floor, and the sound of the screen door shut quickly behind, as I smelled the wood burning in the stove. The familiarities made for a welcoming reception after traveling through a part

of the southern belt that had a litany of signs that were not welcoming to blacks in the least.

"Did you get my last letter?" Mama asked.

"Was it the one where you told me about the..."

Before I could finish, Janet and Thomas came running in.

"Junior, Junior, you're home!" Thomas and Janet said with harmony.

I jumped up to hug them and give them some things I had picked up for them for Christmas.

Mama didn't pick up her conversation about the letter. She didn't mind Thomas and Janet having fun with me.

"So, what are you doing in the Air Force now?" Janet asked.

"Are you going back to Arkansas?" Thomas asked.

"Why are you wearing your Air Force suit?" Janet asked.

The questions came to me like pellets from a BB gun. I knew they wanted to hear about my life in the military and my time away.

"Were you a long way from here?" Janet wanted to know.

"About three-hundred-fifty-six miles."

"I don't know how far that it is, but it sounds far.

"It's about five and a half hours, but if you stop a couple of times, it can be a lot more."

"Junior, I love this..."

Thomas didn't get a chance to finish.

"Junior, come on over and get something to eat."

I knew Mama had been trying to get to this, but she knew what it was like for Janet and Thomas to want to talk to me.

Being home, not even an hour, seemed to make Mama appear more relaxed. I knew she wondered what I was doing in the military like what kind of training I had, and if I was ever going to be in a war.

I knew the Vietnam War had begun just a little over a year ago, but I hadn't really thought about being selected to go there.

As I expected, Mama had some of her hoecakes, and they had the same good flavor when I snuck over to get to them.

Looking over at the stove, I saw some peanut candy, sweet potatoes, ham, yams, turnips, and more in the oven. Before I could look inside, I heard the footsteps that sound liked like the thuds I remembered when I harvested my peanut crop.

"Papa," I said.

"Junior?" He said like a question.

We embraced as he patted me on the back. He looked at me and my uniform. It appeared to be the eye of approval, and one that was making an assessment.

"The military looks like its treating you right!"

I knew what Papa meant.

"Yes, things are going well. I was assigned to work in the personnel office. I learned to type on a typewriter, and I am I'm making reports.

"In the office, huh," Papa said.

"I've been studying to get my G.E.D. I'll get my score in a few weeks."

"I see," Papa said as he bent his head down.

I moved toward Janet as she was pulling me toward her direction to look at a Christmas scene.

I saw Papa in the distance, and he had a gleam of satisfaction in his eye as he looked at me.

****

The envelope was staring right at me. I took a few breaths and swallowed. Prolonging the news was not going to add to anything but worry. I remember Mama saying, "... my peace I give to you ... not as the world gives it to you." What I was sure about was that I had done my best. My work with Lieutenant Alston was not in vain. Not matter what the score read, I had improved not only in math but as a total student.

I took the envelope and opened the seal with my nail. I moved my hand carefully, as not to cut my finger. Looking at the paper carefully, I didn't read it from top to bottom. Instead, I looked around like a pilot circling to land. Only, I was looking for the word "Pass," if they printed like that.

I hummed and "uh-huhed," and yeah, yeah, yeah, silently, until I saw it. The score was there, and I had passed in all areas.

I balled the paper up in my hand as I leaped into the air. I immediately collected myself and straightened my results out. Eyes of other Airmen were beginning to look at me as furrowed eyebrows were wondering what my "one-man show was all about.

****

"I'm so glad you passed the G.E.D," Don said.

"Thanks, I am too!"

"You did it, William! I saw you put a lot of time into your work."

"Yeah," I said, but he continued before I could go on.

"There were nights when I wanted you to come and hang out with us, but you had to study."

Don kept going.

"I think you've taught Tim and me and some of the other guys that sometimes you got to keep your nose to the 'grindstone.' Even though you are younger than us, you taught us something," Don said.

I remained silent and just looked in amazement. I thought I was helping myself. Little did I know that I was helping someone else.

****

A day didn't go by that I didn't think about my future. Sometimes I wondered if it were a luxury when people already knew where they were going or, for that matter, when they arrived. I didn't see it as a burden to think, but I wondered what I would fill my thoughts with when I completed what I thought were many of my goals.

****

I could feel the firm grip of Lieutenant Alston's hand when I told him I had passed the G.E.D.

"Airman Gross, I knew you could do it. I saw that you were methodical in the first assignment," Lieutenant Alston said passionately.

"I couldn't have done it without your tutoring, and I am so glad that you agreed to help me."

"Airman Gross, I never really asked you much about your background. I thought it best that I didn't know anything and just take a real objective stance."

He paced back and forth as if he was preparing for opening comments in court. I had seen this pacing before. It was the prelude to something that he was about to present.

What did he really want to know? Did he want to know why I had a deficit in math? No, maybe not. Did he want to know how I grew up? I didn't quite know what to present first, and nor did I want to tell him too much – where some areas were simply too dismal. "I plowed many miles in the fields of Talladega, Alabama, and I enjoyed the life nature offered to fuel my curiosities."

"I remember you being from Talladega, but what is it that happened there that caused you to not want to be here?"

I think I knew where he was going.

"I simply wanted a better future and opportunities," I said.

"Airman Gross, I think you have a bright future. You can go to many places within the Air Force, and even outside the Air Force. Keep learning all you can, and I'm willing to help you with anything you need."

"Thank you very much, Lieutenant Alston."

"Airman Gross, get ready to be everything you set your sights on being."

****

CHAPTER 38 – DESEGREGATION

Months had passed, and a wave of race relations swam around Arkansas like sharks around its prey. It was like a pot lid clinking, where hot steam makes it rise, and if unattended, it was going to blow.

Before I had even left Talladega, the United States Supreme Court ruled that separating black and white students was unconstitutional in the landmark case Brown v. Board of Education of Topeka in 1954. However, I didn't know a lot about it then, but faintly remember teachers bringing it up in class.

It was like I was living my life in some three-dimensional zone that was freeing me into a place of renewal. I was catching up on life before the Air Force, learning about life in the present, and keeping myself abreast about what I needed for my future.

In my usual learning hub – the library – I was reading about the National Association for the Advancement of Colored People was going to take full opportunity to make sure that black students have the same education. The NAACP was in full stride to register black students in schools in the south. However, it was Little Rock, Arkansas's schools that decided to let black students attend. Nevertheless, when it came down to it, everybody was not in agreement with the decision. According to what I read, I think this was a pressure cooker about to blow a hole through the roof. If schools agreed in 1955, and now in 1957, black students could be admitted, that gave time for great for opposition to rise at an all-time high. Even though Little Rock was nearly three-hours away, the tension could be felt as if were next door. It wasn't tension that you could feel on the Air Force base, but outside the base, I felt like I might not get my change back.

****

"William, we can't go off the base today," Don said.

"I heard," I said.

"If they don't want us off the base today, they must be expecting something serious," Don continued. "I know it's about the students in the Little Rock."

"Eisenhower has called for the 101st Airborne Division of the Army National Guard to go in and get the job done," I said.

"It must be something that is going to go on over there," Don said.

"I think things are going to be interesting. It makes me think of what it would be if my cousin, Kyser, and friend Charles were trying to integrate into a school and were not wanted there. I can only imagine the hate that would be directed at the three of us. Now add six more students with us, my niece and nephew, Janet and Thomas, and if we turn time back a few years, Claudia, Ruth, Margarite, Eunice, and Bertha, I think we all would be wondering what's going to happen. Are we going to be harmed? Will crowds be waiting?

I thought of Maude Barnett, but I didn't want to feed the memory. I wasn't looking for pity, nor wanting sympathy, so I didn't share with Don.

"There are black students who have had problems within their own community, and I mean within their schools, too," I said

"Oh, I know," Don said. "There were teachers that treated us like they hated us."

I listened. I swallowed. I understood.

"They acted like we should have already known something and told us how we were going to be nothing," Don said.

I knew the tune all too well. I could assume this was not just in Talladega, but Texas.

"So, when those black students get into the white school, I don't know how much better it will be," Don said.

"I think I understand what you mean," I responded.

"The microscope will be new, and the books will be up-to-date, but how many days will those black students walk in and people will probably be outside screaming? Will the teachers even want to teach them?" Don said emphatically. "I ... I don't know, William. Integration might bring the opposite effect, bringing a whole new set of problems. I think I would be in favor of just giving black schools more money for better supplies.

Don did make a point. Talladega County Training School had some good solid programs, and I thought about Mr. Armstrong's Department, the Cannery, and what he did for the school and the community. Yet, for a moment, I did wonder if we, as students, had been integrating with another school, would we have lost our camaraderie, sense of self, and sense of motivation?

"I think I know what the NAACP wants. I understand that we, as blacks, should be able to go wherever white people go and learn in the same environment with all the good supplies, but I just wonder what is going to happen – not only when those nine students in Little Rock go in and get inside, but what will go on inside their minds in the long run."

****

The order to stay on base was not at all a tall order for me. If that is what was requested every day and we could only go to the facilities on base, I probably wouldn't feel as if I missed a lot. Since much of my time after work and on the weekends were in the library, the order to not leave the base really didn't affect me.

As the newspapers were reporting about the "Little Rock Nine," I saw that these weren't just nine black students who were chosen out of a lottery to attend Central High School; these were students that the school board approved due to their academic excellence.

Just reading about this felt tense. I wondered if Mama and Papa would have allowed any one of us to go through this kind of adversity on behalf of a better education.

The Little Rock Nine were Ernest Green, Elizabeth Eckford, Jefferson Thomas, Terrence Roberts, Carlotta Walls LaNier, Minnijean Brown, Gloria Ray Karlmark, Thelma Mothershed, and Melba Pattillo Beals. Like most people from the south, I wondered if my family was related to the students whose last names were Green, Thomas, and Brown. Maybe people from all geographic locations think they might be related to someone if they have a family member with the last name. Being that I was only from the south, I would hear it a million times when the last name matched, "I bet they are some of our people!" and they would say it with the enthusiasm of a firework that burst with colors and such display. Whether I was a distant family member of this student or not, that wasn't what was important. I had to admire that they were doing something that was going to create change. While this change was not going to be a smooth sail, it had begun, and we all were wondering what the results were going to be. I was proud of these students and their parents for letting them take a stand of this magnitude. Yet, the question kept circling in my mind, "Would Mama and Papa let any of us walk through this kind of adversity?"

I couldn't seem to let the idea rest, so it was a perfect time to write home.

Dear Mama,

I hope this letter finds you, Papa, Thomas, and Janet well. I am in my usual place that I find like a second home, and that is the library. I have been able to discover things I never knew before, rediscover, and even uncover, as I take in the current events of the world. It seems like there is unrest everywhere in the south when it comes to blacks and whites. I really wonder why? What is it that the Black man has done that makes him so despised that the world does not want him to be part of it? Yet, it seems he can be a part of it if he is in a servitude role.

Now that I am reading more and more, it is as if Blacks are far from things being fair. When I rode home, I saw so many "Colored Only" or "Black Only" or colored this or colored that signs. Some signs even began with "N" following where to go.

I think of my reasons to join the military, and that was to have a better life beyond Talladega. I knew you understood all along, yet Papa seemed to feel there was work to be done in the fields there. Now that I am here, I do feel things are exceedingly better, but at the time, my hurdle was Talladega. I can only wonder if my next hurdle will be trying to prove I'm as good as any white man?

I suppose I question this matter of Blacks vs. Whites because things here in Arkansas have taken a turn. In Little

Rock, there are nine students attending Central High School, and there are protests from those who do not want Black students entering. Have you all heard about this? Each time I read an article, I think of all of us and wonder if you and Papa would even let us go. This is a question that has jumped in my head and has moved to multiple sides of my head, where I clearly can't come to an answer. I guess I should ask myself the question, "Would you want to go if you had the chance to integrate a school." The answer seems to be one I keep circling and circling. I can add up all the cost of why going to such a school would afford opportunities that Black students wouldn't usually get, and then I can add up the hateful, vile, and disparaging comments that come with the territory. I could only imagine the hurling of insults from teachers, students, and others, and the possible effects on my learning. Would I endure? I believe I would. But, I guess what I would want to know is whether you and Papa would have been willing to send any of us to an integrated school for the opportunity of a better education if you knew it would affect us mentally in some way?

****

Arkansas was in a state of trepidation since the Little Rock Nine had entered Central High School. After an entire year, the state was filled with angst, as the whole world looked on wondering what school was going to be next. "Integration" was a dirty word, and not many wanted any part of it, and as a result, the racial divide appeared to be widening.

Now that I was on my way to the Philippines, I wondered what would happen to the South. Growing up in Alabama, I didn't see so much overt prejudice unfolding in Talladega, yet we knew it was there. The Black and White signs were not prominently displayed, and it wasn't like anything I had seen happening in Arkansas.

My trip back to Talladega right before going to Arkansas made me look at things closely. I reviewed my life, where I had started, where I was, and where I was going. A lot had happened, and I was thankful to God, grateful to Mama, thankful to those who had put time into my life to help me become what God intended for me to be.

Mama and I discussed how she would have left it up to us if we wanted to attend an integrated school, but she would have sent the protection of the Lord with us. I imagined Ruth and Claudia getting spit on entering into the school doors, as it happened to the students in Little Rock Nine. If my imagination had been milk in a glass, by the time I finished thinking about Ruth and Claudia, the glass would have included a frothy milkshake. Those two, my rescuers, would have defended themselves, and probably not needed help from the National Guard. I could imagine two typhoons bringing high winds, swirling toward the offenders. If they have Miss Barnett shaking, I believe they would have protesters rethinking their strategies, especially those that include direct contact of any kind. Out of all my siblings, Ruth and Claudia would have been the two that would have concerned me the most had they been in school during a time of integration. Although they had might, will, and tough exteriors, I would have been concerned for their overall safety.

Also, while home, I was looking to have a little time with Kyser; to rest, relax, and recreate. We would go to town, shop, hunt, and just hear about what was happening at Talladega County Training School. Since I had been sending money home, I knew the money would be a problem if I wanted to have some on leave.

I was sending Mama an allotment of money monthly, $100.00 to be exact, so I was feeling confident this was going to be a good leave before I went to the Philippines. I wanted Mama to be able to have things she needed because she had worked so hard, not only for us but for her father, Old Man Jim, who seemingly disregarded that she had a family to take care of as well. My reservations for him always ran deep, ever since I saw him disrespect my mother when I was a child and in front of company, referring to the condition of our house.

If I knew Mama, she was going to use some of the money for food, for the home, and have some I could use when I got home.

****

My leave was far from what I expected. Some things were different, and some things were the same. My father was still running hard alongside his buddies, and the ceremonial drinking was still going on.

Since I was eager to see Kyser and hear about the graduation, I thought I would ask Mama about the money. What I heard next was not surprising, but at the same time, I had different expectations.

"I gave the money to your Papa," she said.

I felt the room spin, turning faster and faster. I had to remember that she could possibly see what was on my face. A brief conversation was going on in my head, where every statement began with "Why?" "What?" "How?" and "When?" but I wouldn't bring any of it out loud. I loved my mother too much, and nor would I ever disrespect her. It was all too obvious what had happened. She was victim to the same tactics I received when I worked planting trees.

Why didn't Mama think about herself for a change? Papa always thought about himself. When was this going to stop? When was he going to consider his family to be as important as his friends and his habits? I felt like Mama had been looking at me and watching me for thirty minutes, but it couldn't have been that long. I could only hope my face didn't display what I was feeling, and she interpreted it as I was upset with her. If one thousand years was like a day to God, then all I needed was only one second to capture the irrationality my father committed through the years.

We never said any more about it. I just went on with another topic like that was the next intended topic that was going to come up naturally. This was the kind of thing that simply made me feel that leaving Talladega was absolutely the best thing I could have done because some things were going to always remain the same.

****

I could feel the hydraulics when the pilots let the landing gear down in the plane. There was a little bounce in the aircraft, and it made the wheels touch the ground, making for a bit of angst. Then, there was a smooth landing.

This was the first time I had been on a plane, and my destination was outside of the United States. When I stepped outside, I was greeted with a balmy presence that bathed me with hope. Unsure exactly what to expect, I stepped off the plane with assurance. I surmised that this would be another chapter in my life, and this chapter would bring me closer to my destination.

I was a Corporal now and had obtained my G.E.D. The gentle breeze passed my face as if to greet me like a lei that Hawaiians put around the necks of their visitors. I supposed it was God's greeting to me in the Philippines at Clark Air Base.

CHAPTER 39 – THE PHILIPPINES

Clark Air Base was sitting on the Island of Luzon in the Philippines. I wasn't here too long before I was made aware of the snake called a king cobra. These weren't small snakes, but big ones that could be found anywhere. I was completely frozen when I heard about them, but I was cautiously treading the land. When looking out among the natives, it didn't seem that they were as concerned. Maybe they were aware and knew exactly how to maneuver. It seemed natives of any place somehow knew how to exercise the best judgment against nature denizens.

As I managed to check-in and get settled, the first place I wanted to know about was the library. Just like it was home to me in Arkansas, it would be home to me here as well.

****

It was apparent that my first plane flight was not going to be my last. As a matter of fact, I was going to be on a plane often.

"Airman Gross, you will be flying to China."

Wait a minute. Me ... from Talladega ... just left two years ago ... I'll be going to China ... I said to myself. It was like I could see Will and me together plowing, then under the tree where I prayed as a boy, and then standing in the field planting sweet potatoes all separately and at the same time.

China ...China ... China ... I repeated it in my mind. Didn't I just read about this Formosa Crisis in Arkansas? Well, how about that. When I got to Blytheville Air Force Base, I was behind, definitely not current, about Current Events in the world. Now at Clarks Air Base, I was right in the midst of what I had been reading.

While at Blytheville, Dwight D. Eisenhower had won the presidency against Adlai Stevenson. Eisenhower had won all but seven states. Since I was in Arkansas, I remembered that Arkansas was not one of the states that he won.

As I was following the news, I remembered Eisenhower addressing the Formosa Strait Crisis. This Formosa Strait Crisis was a conflict between the People's Republic of China and the Republic of China. Now here I was, right in the midst of the turmoil. I was going to fly out of the Philippines to China. My job was to carry mail to the pilots and mechanics who were on temporary duty there.

I was thankful to be knowledgeable about what was going on in the world. This time I wasn't the same person on the streets of Montgomery, not knowing what all the rage was about between Blacks and Whites when the police officer was inflamed looking to beat black men walking by.

****

The propellers on the plane were loud and somewhat intimidating. This cargo plane had made many trips, and this was my first on it and first to China. This trip made me think about what we learned in school. When children heard China, all kinds of thoughts came forward. We saw China as this faraway place with many dynasties, a Great Wall, and alphabet lettering that had to take ages to create and ages to understand. Now in a political uproar, I wondered what the outcome would be during this Formosa Taiwan Strait Crisis.

This was my first Friday carrying mail over there. I didn't exactly know what to expect, but I didn't fear matters either. I knew that God didn't bring me to this distance, geographically or vocationally, to decide to let me just fall out of the sky or let me get lost in China.

Before the plane took off, I prayed, not just for me, but for all who were on board. I prayed for the Taiwan Strait Crisis so that some resolution would take place.

The takeoff was surprisingly smooth. I heard a sound that reminded me of boys pretending they were driving imaginary cars; the duh-duh-duh-duh sound that smoothed out as we climbed in altitude. We were in mid-air for about three and a half hours. Occasionally, I could feel the highs and lows and the nips and dips, but it was nothing that was frightening.

I eased back into my seat and settled in for the ride. My eyes closed, and I was grateful that things began so smoothly. As much as I was used to reminiscing about things of the past, I kept my thoughts in the present.; thinking about what was ahead and what would be awaiting me in Taiwan.

****

Our work was done, and all of us who flew over decided to eat at a restaurant in Taipei. I wouldn't have known before I had dinner that I would have such an affinity for Chinese food. It wasn't anything I had experienced exactly before, but the main familiars were present. I perceived all food to have the basics: meat, bread, and vegetables, and every culture seasoned and presented each food differently. Mama had rabbit; the Chinese had duck; Mama had biscuits, the Chinese had noodles; Mama had collard greens, the Chinese had bean sprouts. I had no problem with the food and actually found it rather interesting. It made me think about how people prepared food differently. I imagined what different cultures of people would make if they were given a ten-pound bag of flour, two gallons of milk, and a ten-pound stand of lard or vegetable oil.

We retired for the evening, and we were going to be in Taipei for a couple of days.

****

Things were back to normal once I got back to the Philippines from Taiwan. I was back at my office, making daily reports. Since I had done the same thing at Blytheville Air Force Base, it was a smooth transition. I often wondered what other areas I would have been assigned had it not been in the administrative area. Sometimes when I looked at what I had done in Talladega in the fields and all the manual labor that came with farming, it would have been a natural fit to be in a manual area. However, this part of my journey was assigned as much by God as it was the test I took to see which field I would work. I'm sure God wanted to place me in an area to let me know I can succeed where I had not yet been, as He would guide me through it, as He had guided me to it.

Sure enough, it wasn't a hard transition, as I thought in administration.

This morning in the Philippines was like the other balmy days. My clothes were pressed and creased, and I was ready to work. As the mid-morning goes by, I complete the reports and deliver them to the Squadron Commander, Major Eckert.

As I handed them to him, he looked at me with a look I couldn't initially read.

"Get me some coffee," a harsh sounding voice said. It had a sharp pitch that had a needling effect.

I didn't flinch, yet I was surprised. This was very much out of the ordinary for an Airman to do. Something about this request wasn't right. It tore the fabric of normalcy. I was used to a proficiently run office, as I could concentrate on my work and focus on how much more proficiently I could get my job done.

That order he had barked to me told me I would be getting that cup of coffee, and a cup every day. Then, I would probably be expected to do more tasks that had nothing to do with the military administration.

"I'm here to bring you the reports." Attempting to exit the request without saying a direct, "no."

I heard papers stirring and a thump on his desk, and I still didn't flinch. There were more words about some coffee, and finally, I shot back my thoughts as I believed they were fitting.

"I'm here to do these reports, and your wife can get you your coffee."

"Get the hell out of my office," he said.

The way I saw it, hell was already there with him. I, saluted him, made my exit, and went back to my area

I suppose this was my second "devil to the door" experience I had encountered as I was pursuing a life in the real world. I had actually had my first one at Blytheville. However, this experience was closer to the exit door of my duty there. I was given a poor performance evaluation, and had that evaluation not be challenged; it would have stopped my duty to the Philippines. However, where ill intention came, God came too at the intersection of the whole thing. Major Day made this officer rewrite my evaluation to include all I had done.

Maybe that's why I didn't fear saying my thoughts to this Major in the Philippines, for I knew the expectations of my job, and I always read the Uniform Code of Military Justice like it was a novel.

****

My day went on as usual, and the Major cursing at me didn't cause me to miss a beat. As soon as I got off work, I went to the library, my usual safe haven and knowledge hub. I was still captivated by current events. I was interested in what was happening in the U.S., as well as around me.

As I focused on math at Blytheville, I was becoming more in tune with my verbal skills. The more I read, the more I was increasing my vocabulary. I began broadening my reading to the sciences of animals and plants, as I saw so many around me in the Philippines.

****

When I looked out at the Philippines, I was captivated the same way I was growing up from when I saw all the land, barns, and ecological life I was afforded. "Afforded" was the operative word. What I didn't have in basically anything else, I did have in the environment God gave. Now far away from the environment I had known in Talladega, as I was assigned to this one, and by God's blessings, I lacked for nothing.

I turned my eyes to this mecca of science. As I was already interested in plants and animals, the Philippines magnified my interests a thousand times.

Clark Air Base has a mountainous surrounding that, upon looking, gave the feeling of being somewhere in a storybook, yet existing in real life at the same time. How God linked these environmental pieces together for me to see was as fascinating to me as the views I saw. He truly knew who He made within me and what I would enjoy. When I stopped to think of all the things He allowed me to see and appreciate within His creation, I felt I was chosen. I felt truly chosen to see and appreciate what He had made in nature. I didn't know if everyone felt this way or saw what God made as special, but I could truly accept that this was not just a fascination that was passing. This, perhaps, was a passion that would bloom somewhere, and He would let me know exactly where.

While taking a stroll, I could see the Magnolia trees, and they were a beauty alone and with a fragrance that wafted through the air. Their shade had a lengthy span that stretched forth to those who desired cool refreshment.

Upon a closer look, I could see frogs that station on the Magnolia tree. They had found a resting spot and were going to be there for a while. I took a mental picture of these frogs. I looked at the color, size and saw how they moved. They didn't seem to be disturbed as I peered closer, yet I didn't get too close. There was a lot to learn about the plants and animals in the Philippines, and the last thing I wanted was to be bitten, stung, or acquire some health problem that would come from my love of science and nature because I didn't understand what was what in a foreign land.

****

I could hear the sounds of the propeller of the cargo plane again, flying back to Taiwan. I had done this a few times now, and the little uneasiness I might have experienced initially was dying down. It was a good planning time for me where I could clear my head and decide what I wanted to do when I returned to the base.

Because I wanted to know more about the frogs I saw, I was going to the library to learn more about their species. Also, I wanted to expand my understanding of the city and know more about the natives and their descendants.

I was fortunate that this plane ride allowed me to manage my time and create a schedule that I would see and learn lots while in the Philippines.

I took a sip of my coffee, but I would not let the thoughts of the infamous coffee incident with the Major invade my thoughts. I had to admit, some adversities I had encountered did cause me to circle and circle, like a pilot who was trying to get a clear landing. However, at this moment, my life was on a different course. I had seen where God had brought me and deposited me in two years. Why would I let a displeasing encounter stain the opportunities of the present? I was on my way to something great, and I wasn't going to let anything or any thought stop what God was putting into order for me.

****

There was something new to explore and learn every day in the Philippines. I saw some natives with blank stares and some friendly as they saw American men come and go. I often wondered what they were thinking. Did they wonder if the servicemen came with multiple intentions to hurt, harm, or what?

I rendered myself as friendly toward the natives, as I met with many of the elders of Luzon to learn more about the island. They, too, were friendly, passionate about their island, and willing to share about their culture. As I aligned myself with the elders of the community, I learned many things about the island.

I saw the Filipino people daily, who went about their lives and were willing to explain their daily culture as it related to their food, their environment, and their life around Luzon. They told me about the king cobra, frogs, plants, and trees.

When it came to the Negrito people of the Philippine Islands, I saw them occasionally. They were a small-statured people who were quick and stealthy, and an asset to Clark Air Base during the Japanese Occupation in World War Two.

However, this was a very different scene from almost two decades ago when the Japanese invaded the Philippine Islands. The people of the Philippines had experienced similar oppression that Blacks had received in the United States during the Japanese Occupation. These people were starved and murdered under the hands of the Japanese. Many women were forced into sexual slavery. This was not the same experience by any means, but it was oppression. I understood what the Negritos must have suffered under the hands of the Japanese. The Negritos were later known as head hunters who would slip into the barracks and cut every other head off, and no one saw them do it. After the Japanese Occupation, the Negrito people's skills of survival proved to be worthy to the Clark Air Base. They knew how to get on base, and actually, no one could keep them off base. Some of them were legitimately allowed to participate in activities that tested our security alert systems to see how fast the enemy could be detected. They were paid and allowed to shop on base, and given the title of Honorary Bird Colonels.

I awaited the time when I would revisit the elders for more cultural conversations.

****

I was careful to get to know the Philippines a little at a time. I knew about the life of downtown anywhere, and it was always the same – dancing and swaying, drinking and smoking, men talking to women, and men and men talking trying to convince someone about a point. Sometimes, if invited, I would go just for a change of pace.

I heard about a disturbance that took me a little by surprise after the night was over, but this was not unusual.

"Why weren't you home?" a Filipino woman said.

"I was coming here just for a couple of hours?" a fellow Airman I knew said.

"For what?" the woman continued.

I could tell where this was going, and I knew this Airman had made a big mistake. He had decided to live with this woman off base, which was highly discouraged for Airmen to do this.

Not long afterward, a scuffle took place. What happened next was like a scene out of an action movie.

"We need to get back to the base!" I said.

I knew what kind of trouble was going to be waiting for us should the police get involved. There would be a floodgate of questions that would surely render Airman Sims guilty.

This dispute escalated when this woman rushed him and fell down. Like a movie playing in slow motion, the woman fell, hair hitting the ground before she did, but not her head. Her expression was one of surprise, where her eyes widened and mouth opened with a yelp. This woman rose with a vengeance that matched the fall she took. It was evident that she didn't really get hurt, but neither did she know she was going to lose her balance. However, she had something for him, and it was not going to go unserved. She picked up a rock and tossed it toward his face. Had this been a sport where she needed to hit a target directly, she would have made it perfect. The rock landed right in the mouth of Airman Sims and split his lip. Blood from Sims' lip found a route down to his shirt.

I immediately thought we had better get back to the base, and we got a jeep cab and headed back. Had we not left, the police sirens would have been coming, and Sims would have gone to jail.

We had reached the gate, and it felt like we were on home plate after running from third in hopes of scoring for your team. However, we had a problem. The Military Police saw blood when we were at the gate. The Filipino Police were also coming to the gate because Sims' girlfriend had already reported the incident. As a result, Sims was held, and the MP wanted to let me go. After seeing blood on my shoes, we were both taken to the police station on base.

The police on base questioned Sims and his girlfriend. I could only imagine what some of the questions must have been. Their responses were going to be mangled with much haze. Things happened fast, and in rewind, they seemed slower. I knew that the interrogation session was going to be an emotional hot furnace that was going to need barrels of water to put it out.

After Sims and his girlfriend told the base police I was not involved, they let me go and took me to the barracks, but I had to report to the Squadron Executive Officer, Captain Franks, for further questioning.

Captain Franks had an intimidating presence that I'm sure intimidated everyone he encountered. However, his presence was not about to intimidate me. I could tell he had worked on this presence to make sure it was in full effect. I could hear the chalkiness in his voice that if he could have yelled at me without punishment, he would have.

"Did you see Sims hit that woman?" Captain Franks asked as if my answer was going to put some decisions in place that were going to be irreversible. I saw his eyes. He wanted blood, and somebody was going to pay. I thought I saw flecks of fire that were within the pupils of his eyes. There was an eagerness in his presence commanded as he awaited the answer.

"I didn't see anybody hit anybody," I said.

I saw the muscles in his face ball up. It was evident it was not the answer he was looking for, but it was the one I submitted. I saluted him, left the office, and his lack of satisfaction traded places with his intimidation.

There I was, back in the face of Captain Franks. Wasn't I here before? Okay, why am I here again? That intimidating look of his was not going to unscrew any answers from me, because I was not resigning myself to a lid just to be twisted off, spilling the contents of what he wanted to hear. Perhaps he just wanted to hear the answer again. Of course, that wasn't what he wanted to hear. He wanted something more. I had read the Uniform Code of Military Justice, and I was not obligated to say anything. Yes, I saw the girl hit the ground, but I didn't have to answer anything else.

He stood up and moved his chair back. It made a scuffling sound that reminded me of the same sound I heard at the recruiting office in Talladega. The chair's wood grazed against the floor and made a scarring sound that I'm sure Captain Franks wished that he could credit. It would have matched his demeanor, which was probably designed to scar my confidence in how I presented myself.

"I'm going to ask you one more time," Captain Franks said.

I heard more in that statement than the words that were being said. I could hear his Kentucky accent loud, clear, and with his cunning edge.

I let him do his job. I wasn't answering before he asked. He was going to work for it since he wanted to call me back for a second time.

His eyes bulged out further as he put a crease in his forehead.

"Did you see Sims hit that girl?"

I guess he was trying for an Academy Award. He put all he had into that question. He was going for Spencer Tracy's nomination. Between the time that I was at Blytheville Air Force Base and the present, I was privileged to be up on a few things, even beyond just the world news. I read Hollywood news, and to be able to reference it made me feel I was moving forward.

I didn't need to put out any acting skills, but if I did, Harry Belafonte and Sidney Poitier would have been good ones to follow. It seemed like these men were headed for Academy Awards one day.

"I'm going to tell you one more time," I said with a steady pace, while I emphasized the "you." Looking him right in the eye, I didn't quiver, shrink, or flinch. I wanted to see if the wolf was going to come out, or was he going to mask his thinking.

To my surprise, he did neither. He cast his eyes down, and I was dismissed. Something made me feel this was not going to be the last of him. Maybe the last time about this matter, but he was going to be presenting some new issues as fast as he could.

****

It was Friday, and it was time to deliver the mail. Going back to Taiwan was becoming a familiar thing, and each time, it was like I reminisced about new adventures I would like to try. It was the time I could process my to-do list, either mentally or written, and I could organize what the landscape of my life would look like.

I wanted to spend more time with the elder Filipinos around Angeles City, which was near Clark Air Base, and learn more about the plant and animal life to see how it compared to what I had seen in the United States. When I was in Talladega, I didn't ask anyone about much. I listened to what I heard discussed about animals and plants. However, some of that I didn't believe, because I sure didn't think I could use a silk netting and catch a cottonmouth when Papa told me I could grab him by his fangs. That wasn't some of Papa's usual irrationality; I just think he was misinformed on this one.

****

The Air Force had been a progressive place for me, and I was thankful for every moment. Whether it was good, bad, or even interesting, I was still far better than I was moving forward to a future I could establish than where I was before. From childhood to present, I could count on one thing: my life could have good, bad, and interesting moments, but it was up to me only just how long I let each one of them pay a visit before I send them on their way.

****

Grandma Josie was gone. I repeated the sentence in my mind several times, and each time it didn't seem like it was right. I felt it was some news that I had heard wrong, and it was real. I guess this was like all deaths. As soon as you hear about them, you repeat them, hoping somewhere there is a glitch in it, there will be a correction, and everything will be back to normal. This was the one grandparent out of the two that I had left that I held fond memories of in my heart. The last two deaths in our family, over fifteen years ago, made for a deep sadness when my brother James died and then my Grandpa Robert – Papa's son and Father, respectively.

I thought of my mother. Grandma Josie was her mother. I already had hailed her as high as a saint. If I had never known her or even met her, I would generate the same feelings. Her hand in my mother's life alone would determine that for me. It was evident that her indelible markings upon my mother made her who she was. With my mother being a gentle soul, a quiet strength, a voice of reason in the midst of irrationality, and unusual situations, I knew my Grandmother had modeled this and executed this in front of my mother.

I had seen my mother too many times amid illogical settings, ill thoughts, and ill will, and she had the grace of royalty during each occasion. Grandma Josie had delivered her absolute best teachings to my mother, for she was the fruit, and Grandma was the tree.

Scenes began to gather in my mind like clouds that gather when rain is coming. I saw scenes of Grandma playing with me under the covers, as I covered my head. She would ask, “Who’s that little monkey I see?” This was no insult or offense. It was her fun “grandmotherly” way to refer to me as I was monkeying around. I would poke my head in and out, and the game would go on until a kettle would whistle or the regular duties of the morning would call. I was glad I had these reflections. They comforted me and reminded me that the cycle of life has a way of extending itself, even when life actually ends.

With all the memories, I was able to comfort myself and wrap my mind in the pleasantries of green pastures. Even though Grandma Josie’s death took me by surprise, as the twenty-third Psalm described, I was beside still waters, where my soul was restored. I only wondered how Mama was doing. If I knew Mama, she was up at the house washing and cooking, preparing for company. It wasn’t that she was trying to be busy to get through the grief; she was trying to make it comfortable for Old Man Jim, my grandfather. That was who she was – a champion of support for others. I wondered how he was doing, because, even though I didn’t see eye to eye with him, I still wanted comfort for him as well. If ever there was a daughter who could render comfort, it was indeed Mama. Now that Grandma Josie had transitioned, I wondered if he appreciated those that were still on his branch just a little bit more.

****

I could not believe how time and events had moved since I have been in the Philippines. Alaska and Hawaii had become the forty-ninth and fiftieth states of the United States, respectively. This would have happened whether I had still been in Talladega, but I loved that I had access to news on the “front row” when I was in the library.

One thing that had particularly captured my interest in the news was the Mercury Seven. These were seven men who had been selected to be astronauts to man all of NASA's orbital aircrafts. I read fervently about how the astronauts were going to be chosen. Originally, it was going to be open to all qualified applicants, but President Eisenhower averted these efforts. He thought it would be best that every candidate be a test pilot.

Even if I was in college right now, I thought to myself, and I would not qualify. I would not have a bachelor's degree, because I wouldn't be finished yet, and I would need 1500 hours of flight time under my belt, while of course, having a pilot's license.

A pilot. A pilot I repeated. I would not mind actively pursuing this, I thought. All the planes I had seen in my childhood have given me a sort of fascination with planes. Margarite was right. She did always see me looking in the clouds. I had questioned about where the plane was going and where it had come. As children, we all waved as if the plane would stop and give us a ride, and have us back before dinnertime. These pilots were not test pilots, but they were pilots that could get a plane up in the air while holding some type of fascination for them at the same time. Could I have a future as a pilot? I was in the Air Force. Now would be the time to make serious considerations toward that goal if it were to happen. I didn't discount any of my thoughts and dreams. If the ideas came, I figured they went for a visit for a reason. Now that I had my G.E.D., I was looking more into many areas that would lead me to many opportunities.

CHAPTER 40 – MY FEET

Something was not right. I was experiencing pain that was not quite to excruciating, but definitely uncomfortable. Every time I walked, I got a funny feeling as if I was walking on open flesh. I pulled off my sock to examine my foot closer, and there was some skin that was peeling underneath. Perhaps I had not seen this because it was under the bottom. Upon closer examination, it looked as if it was between my toes also.

I got back to the barracks and washed my feet and dried them carefully. They were soothed to some capacity – just enough to get me through the night to sleep.

"Airman Gross, this is just a mild fungus," the base said.

I had experienced such a terrible night; there was no way I could wait another day.

"It feels like a wild fungus," I said.

"If you apply this ointment every day, you are going to be fine," the doctor said.

"Do you have something I can spray that helps with itching, burning, and irritation?" I asked.

"This medicine here will take care of all of that," He insisted.

All I could do was ask. I didn't want to leave any stones unturned. If I could have gotten some spray-on skin, and it would have meshed with mine to speed the healing, I wanted to be able to say I asked for it.

I went back to the barracks to apply the ointment. Since I would be there for a little while, I got a newspaper to read. I figured if I couldn't go to the current events, I might as well bring them with me. What I saw next wouldn't normally get my attention, but maybe because I was a bit discomforted and staying put for a while, it was rather interesting.

****

The ointment that the doctor gave didn't seem to work the way I thought it would. I saw some difference but not the significant change I thought I would. Flying on the plane this particular Friday didn't come with all the pleasantries it normally had. My focus fell on my foot, but I made the best of it. I looked forward to the fine delectable foods I was going to eat, but I kept my thoughts as positive as possible.

I reminisced about the Antarctic Treaty. Science had such an impact that a treaty could be written with countries coming together. There could be scientific investigations, but no military activities. I thought that spoke a lot about how science must have been weighed.

Taking a few steps back to think, I loved science, planes, and agriculture. This Antarctic Treaty was created from those that had deep passions for their interest in science, which birthed the International Geophysical Year. The continent of Antarctica proved to have all the variables that could interest many scientists. If I was in the stage of my own interests with just the things I saw on all the places we lived beginning with the Thornton Place, I could understand why there would be a treaty to preserve what was there.

This spoke volumes about science, research, investigation, and everything that had to do with Earth Science. Antarctica had lots to offer, is that it was so cold, and that made for interesting questions alone. Indeed, some scientists wanted to measure, weigh, and determine this and that against the temperature. Additionally, there had already been several expeditions that were made to Antarctica, some successful and some with difficulty.

I felt a rumble in the air, something I didn't usually feel, but I wasn't frightened. There it was again. Maybe it was a little "air pocket" or some kind of turbulence. I was seemingly okay, but it seemed to have disturbed my foot. Perhaps, I would apply more ointment to it after we landed. I patted my foot a little, hoping a little vibration would make it feel a little better, but it really didn't. Hopefully, this would pass.

****

"Um, well, I don't know," the doctor said.

"I don't see much change. This place on my foot is not healing. It seems like it's not making any change at all," I said.

"Well, I can see it's not what it was," The doctor replied.

"Yet, it feels worse. I can't go back and forth on an airplane like this. What are some other treatments?" I asked, advocating for myself.

He looked closely at the area again and touched it gently. I winced a little, and we locked eyeball to eyeball.

"I want you to see someone who can take a closer look at this, and make an in-depth determination about this."

I took the paperwork to go to another doctor off base. Evidently, this doctor have not seen anything like this before, and he wanted me to see a native doctor who might know what this was.

****

I arrived at the native doctor at the scheduled time. No way was I going to be late. The place on my foot had a burning and hard-to-describe feeling, and I just could not possibly bear much more.

While seated in the waiting room, I examined the décor. It was plain with clean lines. The furniture was squared, not boxy, but very sterile looking. The pictures were of abstract things that you could make out to be whatever you wanted. Maybe that was the intention of the interior designer. Perhaps, while waiting, you could set your mind on a course of enlightenment instead of infirmity.

I kept looking around, and in true fashion of who I was, it was easy for me to see scenes of things I had known. I thought I saw the Easley Place in one location and Will in another. Was this some "Transformative Art?" There was no such art title as that, but I was calling it just what I thought it could be as it related to me.

"William Gross?" the nurse said in a question and a confirmation.

"Yes," I said.

"Come with me, please."

"Good morning, Mr. Gross. Let me take a look at your foot." His English was crisp, although he had an accent. Being from the South myself, I had a tendency to hear the way English was spoken and compared it with those from other parts of the U.S. Now hearing it outside the U.S. in the Philippines made me listen even more intently.

I took my shoe off and showed the doctor the spot on my foot. I tried to interpret his look as he peered closely.

"Um-Um," he said, as he wrote down some notes. He cut his eyes back to my foot and continued writing. He then turned and reached into his cabinet and brought out an ointment.

He applied some to my foot.

Maybe I was expecting an immediate change. Well, I knew nothing could work that fast.

"I want you to apply this ointment every day. I know exactly what this is; it is Jungle Rot."

"How did I get that?"

"Don't worry so much about that. You could have gotten it anywhere. Shower, floors, ground, anywhere. The people from here seem to walk right over it and not have any reaction to it. However, we find that servicemen who come here contract it more. There seems to be some form of immunity to it as it relates to the native people."

"Thank you," I said.

I left with a sense of security that I had been in good hands. It was evident that the doctor knew his craft, and he knew this case of 'jungle rot.' The only thing I could do now is to wait it out.

CHAPTER 41 - CHICAGO

The bright lights of the streets had an interplay with the horns of Chicago. The scene and sounds made anyone walking by look around and feel they were starring in a play scripted just for them. Maybe everyone didn't feel this way; perhaps it was just me. This was the first time I was in the United States in the new decade of the '60s. I had been in the Philippines since 1958. Looking at the streets of Chicago was like looking at some surreal place. I didn't want to look obvious gazing at the signs, looking like a country boy who had not been a mile away from home, but I truly was fascinated by the sites. Signs that had lights were spread out intermittently and retracted showed a different side of America that I had never seen. It was beautiful, delightful, and even charming in its own way.

For a moment, I was far removed from the life I had in the Philippines. I had to readjust to everything I had experienced. What I saw in the Philippines had greatly affected my perspective of the country. Now, I was out of the military, with four years completed. Where was my future going?

In these past four years, I had come through a canal, not a birth canal, because I was not born to the place where my future had moved me to. Yet, I was in a place where I was still growing, and I was going forward, but not exactly sure where. Nevertheless, the beauty of where I was made me feel like God had my life like a fetus in some ways – protected and insulated from what could harm it. I would arrive in His time.

I could hear my heels clicking on the sidewalk, but then I didn't. There was a little gum that stuck to my shoe, and it was the least of my worries. It couldn't drown out the sights I was seeing. It didn't seem like just a few months ago; I had jungle rot on my foot. A native of the Philippines knew exactly what to give me, and in what felt like no time, my foot was back to normal. A little chewing gum could be scraped off, and it didn't require multiple visits to s to get positive results.

I went right back to the sights with a consciousness that my journey in these four years had done wonders for me.

"Junior, you've been walking around, haven't you?" Claudia said.

She always knew what it was that I was doing – my goals and my thought process. I guess that's why she and Ruth looked out for me when they spoke to Ms. Barnett.

"Junior, you weren't out there looking like a tourist, were you?" Eunice said.

I didn't get a chance to answer Claudia's question. It was good to be back in the presence of my sisters.

"Here's some warm biscuits I made," Bertha said.

"I was outside, just looking and thinking about these past four years," I responded, taking the biscuit.

Being all together made me think of the time we were all in the peanut field together, and how everybody pitched in to help.

With everybody gathering over at Eunice's house, this made me feel more than my share of welcome as we gathered to share a meal together.

Questions from my sisters kept coming like a round of bullets; all aimed to focus on how they might play a part in my next chapter of life should it be in Chicago. I continued with another biscuit and let the conversation take crisscross turns back and forth around the table. It seemed I chewed continuously, and I added answers here and there.

Bertha, who didn't like outside work, sure had taken her cooking up a few notches. It wasn't bad in Talladega, but it was certainly tasty now. As every sister had a hand in the dishes that were cooked, each one had a taste of home, as Mama had supervised them. Although she was miles away, I could taste that special something that she taught them in the green beans, collards, chicken, rice, biscuits, and pound cake.

I was glad for this moment, as I was in deep reflection and participation in the conversation at the same time. I could see all that I was grateful for and all that I had become in four years.

****

I was finding my time in Chicago to be moving fast. It was like the time in the womb, and soon I would be making my debut to the world. Rekindling time with my sisters was like a heartwarming experience that I couldn't have planned, and I could get used to being in here for a while. I didn't know if I would be here to the tune of a lifetime, but I was open to the possibilities of opportunities that would get me closer to the future I envisioned for myself.

Months passed by like pages turning fast on a calendar. The days were going by as I applied for jobs, and the promise was strong, but the outcome was nil. "We'll be in contact," "We'll let you know," became words that were stated like an endless song. Sometimes I believed it was real and sometimes I thought it was just another phrase that was thrown around to see how fast I could get out of the office. One thing I knew for sure. God hadn't forgotten me, and I hadn't forgotten Him and the distance He had brought me. Reminiscing and reflecting were something I did a lot of, and I felt I did it constructively. Each time I got that famous, "We'll be in contact," I silently finished their sentence, "If it is the will of the Lord." I became satisfied with that approach because if the potential employer said it, whether it was true or not, I felt the will of the Lord would prevail. This way, it took power away from the employer and took power away from any regressing thoughts that were different from my reflective, productive thoughts. God's will trumpeted all of this, and it would prove to place everything, everyone, and everyplace directly where it needed to be.

"Junior, you at it again?" Bertha asked.

"Yeah, I'm in the Want Ads again. I want to see what's out there for me."

"The right job is waiting for you," she said.

"I believe that. In the meantime, I want to do my part and apply and be prepared. That way, my net is out when the fish come in."

"Junior, you always had and still have a way about you. Mama and Papa could always depend on you."

I looked up from the Want Ads and looked up at her. I paused for a moment.

"They knew you would follow through. They saw that in you when you plowed with Will, gathered the turnips, planted the peanuts, and that's just to name a few," Bertha said.

"Now, I don't know everything you did in the Air Force, but I know what you did in the fields. Many days we wouldn't have much to eat if you hadn't gotten the ball rolling getting some of the crops in."

I got ready to say something, but Bertha continued.

"Whatever it is you are saying in the interviews, I suspect you might say what you've done in the Air Force, but let them know that you were a leader before you left home."

Now, this was inspirational.

"Bertha, I thank you for those words. I will do just what you said. Often we forget about the jobs we first learned to do. They should be acknowledged wherever we go, even if we are applying to be president."

We laughed at the idea of applying to be president. We knew it was an elected position. What I remembered about Bertha was her way of getting out of work outside. She was not a fan of the Talladega sun, but she did enjoy cooking up dishes with Mama.

A few minutes later, I heard a plate make an entrance with a clang on the table. In true Bertha fashion, she had made me a breakfast that resembled the hoecakes Mama made with preserves, eggs, potatoes, and choice of sausage or bacon.

I closed the paper.

"Thank you, Bertha."

"Oh, Junior, you know you are welcome."

"No, thank you for your tribute this morning."

"What tribute, Junior?"

"That was a tribute that you said, and I will remember it. We do often forget that our first jobs are the ones that have given us our first bit of confidence, first skills, and the first kind of leadership."

"Junior, I didn't say all that," Bertha said. "I just told what you really did," she said, smiling.

"You said all of that and more."

****

I began partaking in the wonderful breakfast Bertha had prepared. I knew Bertha for a lot of things, but this particular morning, I didn't think she was going to be so inspirational.

Continuing to "sop" my hoecake with the preserves, I thought about where I would go to apply for a job today.

"Junior, I wonder what James would be doing now," Bertha said, which seemed to come right out of the blue.

"Bertha, I wonder that too. I was five when he passed. I remember him carrying me on his shoulder, and I remember him going to and coming home from work."

"He was indeed a working man who knew how to put one foot in front of the other to get where to needed to go."

I paused for a moment. I thought of what I had seen in the past four years. Although I chose to forego the last two years of high school, I had gained opportunities many had not. Bertha was right in her question, "What would James be doing now?"

With the opportunities I had just gained, I believe nothing would have stopped him, had he wanted to go to the moon.

"He would be somewhere setting examples for all of us, that's for sure," I replied.

Bertha brought her hands together in a thunderous clap.

"That's right!" Bertha said.

I chewed the last piece of bacon on my plate, and the flavor seemed to burst forth more than it did when I started.

"His life showed us so much, and even in death, I just learned something," I said.

"He was just so ..." Bertha's voice trailed off as tears ran into her sentences.

"Any word you say would finish that sentence correctly," I said, knowing she couldn't say more at the moment. Just as James carried me around on his shoulders, I'm still there seeing the world from that height, and thankful I knew him and saw him if only for a short time.

Bertha and I continued to share thoughts about James. We later composed ourselves as we finished our breakfast.

"Junior, do you want anything else?"

"Bertha, I'm fine, and this was a good breakfast."

The phone rang.

"Hold on, Junior, let me get the phone."

"Hey, Ruth," Bertha said.

The conversation went on as I heard Bertha describing the breakfast we just had and the discussion about James. I could tell from their exchange about James that it was a lively dialogue, where the timing was perfect.

"Junior! Ruth wants to speak to you."

I untangled my feet from my chair, pushed it back, and ran to the phone.

Ruth's voice was like the first swallow of coffee; you couldn't wait to drink. Although in Chicago, which was about four hours, and some change away, she felt close and nearby.

"Ruth, how are you doing?"

"I'm doing alright."

The "alright" was like the cream in the coffee that lingered and swirled around.

"Junior, I want you to come up here," Ruth said.

"Well, I'm hoping to find a job here in Chicago," I replied.

"Think about coming here. You can stay with me as long as you want, and you might find Detroit a breath of fresh air."

"Okay, let me think about it," I said.

We talked a while longer about Mama and Papa, the Philippines, and what it would take for me to come to Detroit. It sounded promising, but I wanted to exhaust all my possibilities in Chicago first.

****

The bus was pulling into the Detroit station, and I was looking out the window frantically for Ruth. The ride had been a long and exhausting one, and it seemed that people were concentrating on everything but the ride. The rattling of bags was the worst, but I knew it was the best they could do in such small quarters.

I could smell the fuel from the bus for what seemed like the whole ride, but perhaps it was just a few minutes in the beginning, and it was my memory of it that kept it around longer. If I could have complained, I would have, but then I thought, 'Maybe this is the best bus at the time.' Being in the military for four years had me seeing things a bit differently. I was so used to seeing things run with efficiency and fixed immediately.

We were getting closer to Detroit, and I could hear the brakes come to a halt. The sound was like a sleigh screeching.

"Junior," I looked around, and it was Ruth's voice, and I made a beeline to her and couldn't wait for some rest and comfort after the long bus ride.

****

Being at Ruth's home brought back old times, just as it did when I was in Chicago with my other sisters. I was basking in the feel of home with our reminiscing and her cuisine. It seemed every one of my sisters could cook a dish that had the taste of Mama's flavor. Ruth could make chicken that had a taste of Mama's Rabbit gravy. Although chicken and rabbit were entirely two different types of meat, Ruth was able to prepare it with a similar flavor.

Being here in Detroit gave a feeling of excitement, with the trends of fashion, music, and art were just beginning. Even though I enjoyed the time here, it was moving fast, and I wasn't gaining the ground I wanted. I was not getting to the places I thought I would be.

My time was becoming a little mundane, where I was grateful to be with family, but I was just watching Ruth's son, Gregory, applying for jobs and no promises of employment. I kept a positive outcome; however, while looking for the lessons, I should be learning in the meantime.

I kept getting these repeating thoughts of returning to the military, but I wanted to be sure. I indeed had great experiences, but I wanted to be able to chart my course to get back to Tuskegee one day. With the military, I would have a set number of years that I would have to do, but in the civilian world, I could have more flexibility to move and transfer with a job if needed.

I had to admit this wasn't a comfortable place to be in, but I was going to ask God for a lead. He hadn't shown me wrong yet, but I was going to be prepared when the opportunities came. I was doing all I could to keep my end up; starched shirts, ironed pants, resume, firm handshake, good interviewing skills, and a willingness to get a job done. Whatever direction God was spinning the weathervane of my life, I wanted to honor Him by at least being ready.

I heard Ruth putting her keys in the door, and before I could get to the door, she was inside.

"How were the students today?" I asked Ruth.

"They were all working hard, but I want them to pay attention so they won't make so many careless mistakes," she said.

"In math?" I said with excitement. I remembered my tutoring days at Blytheville with Lieutenant Day, and how he reminded me to be careful with my steps and not make careless mistakes.

It was interesting that Ruth was teaching school. She was intense but not insensitive. I chose to believe she thought of me as she taught students, and how I showed her how my hands were bruised by a monster masquerading as a school teacher, and who deeply hurt me.

I pulled myself out of these thoughts quickly.

"They can be careless with other subjects," she said. "Sometimes they don't start the sentences with capitals or end with periods."

I believed if anybody could remind them of what they needed to do was Ruth. I singlehandedly saw how she handled Maude Barnett. However, I knew she had the right to touch with her students.

"I'm thinking about going over to the Police Department and applying there," I said.

"Really?" Ruth said.

"Yes, I want to be able to be self-sufficient, and I don't know how much longer I'm going to be able to do that."

"You are a great help to me, Ruth said."

"And so are you to me, and I have enjoyed being here with Gregory, but I've got to get my future on track."

"Junior, I'll help you any way I can."

I prepared my clothes and my outlook and got ready to head off to the police department to see if this was the direction God had already planned for me.

****

"Go ahead in the back and fill out the application," the man said with a crisp voice.

I wasn't sure he was with the police department or whether he worked only in personnel capacity. I had my own pens ready, black and blue ink, and was prepared to begin.

There was a feeling I had when I added my military. I was proud to add this experience to the lines. To be able to say I served in the military made me feel I had written the first chapters of my life.

I was at the end of the application, and I imagined what kind of day I would have on the 'force.' It wasn't the sirens or the suspects that concerned me; I just wondered how this would fit in my journey to move ahead.

"Sir, are you finished?" asked the same gentleman who gave the application.

"Yes, I am. Thank you," I replied.

****

"Ladies and Gentlemen, Martha and the Vandellas." All the applauding began, and the claps were so thunderous that the sounds reminded me of firecrackers set off on the 4th of July.

There I was, sitting in the 20 Grand, I don't think I had ever seen so much chiffon in my life. If it wasn't chiffon, it was something soft and flowy. I could imagine my mother making beautiful dresses out of this material, as I remembered the dresses she made for my sisters when they were little.

The musical sounds were so rich and beautiful; I could not believe I saw these groups live. To hear them on the radio was one thing, but seeing them in person was like a moment frozen in time. Some of the songs were the same music I heard at the dances at Talladega County Training School. In addition to Martha and the Vandellas were Smoky Robinson, Mary Wells, and The Temptations.

I thought of Charles and Kyser and how they would have loved to have been sitting right here. It would have been one reunion of friendship, where we would have laughed endlessly, and the night would have gone on till the morning as we filled the time with our stories of the past.

When it was time to go home, I found myself humming a tune from some of the acts.

Arriving to Lillie Mae's, I noticed she was still up.

"How was everything, Junior?" Lillie Mae asked.

"I went to the 20 Grand."

"Who was there?" she said.

"Martha and the Vandellas, Smokey Robinson, Mary Wells, and The Temptations."

"That sounds like a good time you had there!" Lillie Mae responded.

"I did. It made me think of Charles and Kyser."

"Charles?"

"He was my buddy in high school," I said. "He and Kyser were my buddies."

"I know you were buddies with Kyser. Soon as you all would see each other, you all were running around like two chickens with their heads cut off."

Lillie Mae and I laughed and talked into the wee hours of the morning. I think we covered everything from me sliding under the dresser with a hoecake in my hand to the tin whistle she gave me for Christmas.

"Lillie Mae, you made Christmas happy for me," I said with sincerity.

"I was glad to do it because I knew how Papa was going to do things," she said.

"I often think about how he drove my car into a bang-up mess and was mad at me for asking about it."

"I remember that," I said.

"Look, let me get on something else that's happy and fruitful," Lillie Mae said as she changed the subject.

"So, you applied for at the police department?" she asked.

"Yes, I'm going to follow up tomorrow."

Upon going to bed, I did what I usually did best, reflect on what was happening in my life. If I dwelled too long, I found myself making lots of conclusions and predictions that probably weren't even close to where God wanted me. So, instead, I told God, "thank you" for everything He had given me on the journey from Talladega to where I was standing right this minute.

****

"Mr. Gross, take a deep breath." The stethoscope was cold on my chest, and I jumped each time the doctor moved it.

"Easy, this is almost over," the doctor said. "Your heart sounds good, and your breathing sounds steady."

I was called back to the police department and today was my physical. While getting here, I did not stress about it the way I did when I had my military physical. I was sure the scrotal hernia was going to be detected, but it returned to normal. I was sure that if I passed that one, I was surely going to pass this one.

As the exam went on, I did everything that was asked of me. "Stand on the scale for me," the doctor said. He recorded my weight on the paper attached to a clipboard. I stepped down.

"Don't step down. I need to get your height." He got my height and continued recording on the paper. Something in his expression made me wonder as he recorded my height. Perhaps it was just his pen that was scratchy or ran out of ink.

Now it was time for me to run, do sit-ups and push-ups. I needed to get into shape after all the home cooking.

Sweat was dripping in my eyes and burning with a salty sensation. I felt great about the whole process.

After changing and putting my clothes on, I reported to the main office for further details.

"Mr. Gross," a recruiting officer said. "You have passed the physical test."

I smiled inside and out and have already planned what I was going to tell my sisters. I could see them in their congratulatory mode, surrounding me with hugs and hope. Actually, I thought they would be a little scared also, but still happy that I accomplished this goal.

"Mr. Gross, you have passed the physical test."

I wondered why he repeated himself.

"But..."

I felt like quicksand was beginning to take me under. Something about that "but" didn't sound promising.

"We had to be sure, but your physical test was fine."

Why is he continuing to talk about that physical test? I got that.

He cleared his throat. I knew then that God had a different plan. Even if I walked out and never heard the reason, I was still okay. No matter where I went, I was always going to be under the walnut tree, where the wind blew so placidly around me, bringing God's vision closer to me.

I could have said thank you right at that point, and never known the ending, but I was no coward. I had no problem staring the truth in the eye. What did I have to lose? I was crossing more finish lines than ever since I left Talladega. If I had to create a list, I had more to be thankful for than to flounder in the thought of what I was going to hear next.

"You are one-fourth of an inch too short," the recruiting officer said.

I didn't question it; I didn't negotiate it. I simply got up and extended my hand and thanked him for the opportunity.

When I got out of the building, I surveyed the street and looked nostalgically. Detroit was a city that's been a mecca to Blacks in the sixties. Many were able to get on their feet and make a great livelihood that would extend to throughout their lineage. However, it was evident that God's destination for me was in another place. He had not been wrong yet, and I was going to trust Him now.

If that one-quarter of an inch made a guidepost to my future, then God already knew before I was in the womb of my mother.

I didn't let the grass grow under my feet and nor did I let one tear roll down my face. I knew exactly what I had to do.

CHAPTER 42 – ELGIN AIR FORCE BASE

"I'm looking at your history and everything you have done, and I believe we can fit you right back where you left off," the recruiter said.

I was sitting at the Military Recruiting Office. It had crossed my mind before, and I imagined life back in the military. I didn't dislike what I imagined, but I wasn't exactly ready to embrace it. I initially wanted to see if I could make my mark in the civilian world.

Yes, I was back to where I started, but this didn't mean I was back to square one. In reality, the squares were adding up, and each one was really a milestone. Now I was just going to knit my life right back with the thread that pulled it all together for me from the start.

"I can give you the same rank right where you left off."

It sounded like a great deal, and I was okay with it.

As I tried to surmise my year since leaving the Philippines, it was interesting. Being between Chicago and Detroit, I had a chance to rekindle life with my sisters and brothers as an adult. That alone was sentimental and memorable. I had a chance to see the world as a civilian and see how life outside was working for Blacks in America.

Since I couldn't find a job as a civilian, and maybe it would have happened sooner or later, I still had my goals on my mind. Now that I was welcomed back into the military world, I was going to take off. I was going to move faster than the speed of sound if that was possible, and that was what I was going to do. I had places to go.

****

Upon arriving at Eglin Air Force Base, I didn't feel the breeze I felt in the Philippines. This was something a little different by design that I could tell was going to serve me well. The air smelled woodsy, cedar- and oak-like, and it felt like some mystery was ready for me to solve.

After I checked in, I decided to explore the surroundings, and I was on a base with grounds of ten million acres of hunting land. Hunting was something I had done many days in Talladega and with Kyser. I believed he would love this. Oh, the conversations I imagined we could have here. I looked forward to seeing everything I possibly could at Elgin Air Force Base.

Florida was quite different for me, yet, it was a southern state that gave a familiarity. It really was a sunshine state. With all the hunting land, I could tell this would be one of my focuses in addition to fishing. With Florida being on the coastline, that was an option as well.

I was familiar with the daily ins and outs of military life. It was work, the barracks, and of course, 'downtown' if you wanted to be there. However, I wanted to be in the progressive lane of life, and I was going places. Downtown had proven to be a distraction at times and I had seen enough. I figured I would go every blue moon.

Additionally, there was something else I was very familiar with about the Air Force, and it was my job. I had done enough reports that they had become second nature. Not even the year I was not in the military could stop me from the fluency I had gained on the typewriter. I never did use the correct fingering, but I had a system that worked for me.

When I reported for duty the first day, it was everything I imagined. I walked to my area, gathered the items I needed, and began my work.

I knew my job backward and forward, yet I didn't take that lightly, but with gratitude. I wasn't haughty, for I knew it was God who had given me nothing but favor as I was placed in Administration. To go from working on a farm in the sweltering heat in Talladega to an air-conditioned post was almost unbelievable. I had done the same thing on the Blytheville Air Force Base in Arkansas, Clark Air Base in the Philippines, and now here at Eglin Air Force Base. Typing the morning reports and typing the efficiency reports with ratings and promotions were like second nature.

"Good morning, Airman," I heard a voice. It was quite familiar, yet I knew it couldn't be anyone I had even met in Florida before. I looked up, and to my surprise, it was someone I had seen before. This man could have easily been a stand-in for John Wayne. I was just guessing, but it was my thoughts that he had undoubtedly been told many times. He not only looked like John Wayne but sounded like him too. It turns out he was my Commander, Malcolm Frazee, and a great man to work under. He had a lot of character, heart, and leadership, and I could tell that my time here would be gratifying.

****

I felt comfortable, stable like things were balanced. I had the amenities and comfort of a regular job, with the recreation of hunting and fishing, and a new city to explore, but I still had much to get done with my life. I had to remember that, above all, my life was indeed "the central focus." I had my mother to thank for that. She had prepared me for everything from the time I rubbed her "climate-controlled arms" to how she celebrated me fishing with a bucket. She thought if I was crafty enough to catch them, she didn't mind taking time out to cook them. She had worked all day in the fields, going beyond the call of duty, and still, she had time to celebrate me. With that thought, I learned that no matter where I was or whatever was surrounding me, be it bright lights or a dirt road, I, William L. Gross, Jr., was still "the central focus." I was made in God's image, and He wanted me to know it because it was in His word. It was worth repeating as often as needed. I am "the central focus," and the future is mine to have.

****

It wouldn't take months and years for me to get a promotion. I had definitely made the right decision to go back into the Air Force. Since the recruiter said I could get my same rank and base of choice, Eglin sure proved this was my best choice.

After I was promoted, I thought about how I applied for the Army Rangers. I would have gone to Ft. Bragg in Fayetteville, North Carolina.

Something told me, “You don’t want to go down there.” It wasn’t an audible voice, nor was it a voice coming out of the sky. It wasn’t the boogeyman's voice. I knew it was God’s voice, and out of the habit of hearing how others refer to God, referred to God as something, but it was the Holy Spirit. Joining the Army Rangers made me think I would be beckoning Vietnam in my near future. The talk of Vietnam was always present and seemingly looming in the future. I couldn’t determine if Vietnam would ever be in my future, but I surely didn’t want to bring it to me faster than it could come. All I could think about was being at some isolated outpost where the Vietcong would run things and take over if they could.

****

“Could I have a hunter’s license, please?”

“Yes, sir.”

“That will be four dollars.”

I reached into my wallet and got four dollars. These four dollars were going to fill my time with an experience that would be beyond my comprehension. Comparing the experience I had in Alabama to what I was going to see in Florida made that four-dollars worth a million dollars in value.

****

I had finally made my way to what I saw as one of the most placid places I had seen. The scenery of green was all too splendid, and I was in awe every step I took as I walked into the woods. With ten million acres of land for hunting, it was my goal to see all it had to offer. My four dollars was finally going to be put to good use.

I brought lunch with me and met some of the local residents. I got on the boat that was owned by the base. As the boat got out and went further into the water, I could hear the hoot of the owls and the singing of other bird species. The water was still, and the area had all the wonder of what anyone who loved wildlife could want. I put my line in the water, and I could feel a little nibble. I stood up and reeled in the fish. This was the beginning of what would be much fishing, and I enjoyed the experience. Every available chance I had, I planned to return to this "Garden of Eglin," where fishing and wildlife was not only relaxing, it was another exhilarating experience I was allowed to partake of within God's creation.

I had been making several trips to my "other" favorite retreat in between work and hunting. I thought today would be a good day to go and see what was happening in the world and read about things that I would let the library dictate to me. As usual, I love books about the environment, animals, plants, but today I was going to read what perhaps spoke to me.

I opened the paper with my arms out, legs crossed, and head slightly to the side, and my breath was nearly taken away. I could feel a tear in my eyelashes and my lump welling up in my throat. This couldn't be happening again. It was like being at Blytheville Air Force Base again when I was reading about Emmet Till. Now the person that was an activist, who called attention to his death, was dead.

Now I was almost like a child but in an adult's body. I was retreating in the place I loved on every base I had been. I would never say the library was a pastime I had, but since I had been to Eglin, I frequented it weekly. But, today was not a happy day. Headlines were stating that Medgar Evers had been killed. I put my hand to my forehead and moved in my chair, where I couldn't seem to get comfortable no matter how hard I shifted — Medgar Evers, dead at 37.

It was happening all over again. Another Black-American was dead. It was not every day that the United States had Black Mayors, but he had been the first mayor in the state of Mississippi during the post-Reconstruction era.

Now, I didn't know him personally, but he had come from a family who believed in advocacy, activism, and leadership. In the state right next to mine, which had been known for its racially-charged moments, his brother was the first black mayor in the state of Mississippi since post-Reconstruction. Medgar Evers himself was a pretty powerful charismatic individual, and a trailblazer. He was a veteran who had fought in WWII in France and Germany and had been a college graduate at Alcorn A&M College.

It was hard to believe he was just thirty-seven years old. He was the first field secretary for the NAACP. He was getting people registered to vote and trying to find out if there were any issues people were facing in all eighty counties.

Evers couldn't understand why his father's friend had been lynched and went further into the role of trying to get equality for Black people.

Evers's efforts got Black people moving, voting, and thinking about what they must do to get equality. I shut the paper and wondered, what now?

****

It didn't take long for the answer to what was to come. The President of the Local NAACP Chapter came on base and asked all the Black GI's to meet him.

This man had a thunderous voice, and I could see why he was President. He was convicted, compelling, and convincing, and I knew he had the idea of accomplishing something on his mind. We were at the service club, and there were a number of us there. I didn't really know how many Black GIs were on base until I saw all of them in one place. I estimated it to be approximately three hundred of us.

"Medgar Evers was killed, and I want to know how many of you want to participate in a commemorative march for him?"

I looked around the room, and I didn't see anyone who seemed to object. All the hands were up at different stages, and even if some were not up, it was pretty evident that they were all in.

"Yeah, we want to do it." I heard a voice shout out.

"Another one of us is dead," another voice said.

I could tell passion was breaking into the atmosphere, and I very well could understand.

"How many of us are they gonna kill?" another voice yelled out.

The president didn't try to counter the temperament that was brewing in the room. I could tell this was exactly what he expected.

"This is the reason we want to march. We don't want to let the world feel this man's life was taken in vain. If we can let people know he meant something to us, then his legacy will not be allowed to die."

I listened as intently as I could. The raw emotion of the men in the room was pronounced even more. If I didn't hear every word the president said or could repeat it verbatim, I knew exactly what it meant.

****

It was Sunday, and we were in downtown Ft. Walton Beach. What I normally would think would be a calm and peaceful day was far from it. I couldn't hear anything that resembled a hymn or see anything that glowed like it had seen the face of God. This was not a Moses encounter where he had seen the presence of God, and when he came down to the people, he was shining so bright that he had to cover his face. This was not this kind of experience.

"You niggers," "What you niggers think you are doing?" "Bunch of communists." The words echoed and were weighted with hate that could be seen on the faces of the natives of Ft. Walton Beach. If hate had a scent that day, people from the west coast would have been able to get a whiff of it. Yet, those up close would experience this stench where it would linger for years.

I would be lying to say this wasn't scary. We were shoulder-to-shoulder with these people who just did not understand. They just didn't understand. Something had to be off-center in a man's mind to hate someone for the color of their skin.

As scary as it was, I was able to pray that we would be covered and keep going to make it to the end of this commemorative march. After a while, I just saw things that looked like someone slowed down a film and turned off the sound. Mouths with hate-spewing words were opening to maximum capacity with spittle coming out, and fingers pointing.

It seemed the volume slipped back on as I focused on the crowd when I saw what I thought was a man mouthing "Mama." His mouth drug open and flapped back up like he really wanted his comment to cut us like a serrated knife. He repeated it, and I understood real clear that time what he was trying to say; I thought it best not look his way again. We heard the same thing as he and the crowd fashioned a similar comment to "Father." We kept moving. This was June, and it was already hot, but the comments that were added made for an inferno. However, we were not going to burn, and we didn't. We prevailed. When it was all over, our dignity was still intact. Our brother Medgar had lost his life trying to help Blacks achieve equality, and the only thing we had lost was sweat, but we gained perspective to take up where he left off.

****

Eglin had held interesting memories for me. Sitting in my barracks made me reflect on one of the scariest moments I had experienced. I had a towel around my neck, just sitting back, trying to gather my thoughts. Hearing all of that yelling made me want to relive better times. I wanted to never forget what happened because I needed to remember that the world did have people who thought Blacks were not worthy or even existed. What I had to really ask myself was the question of how long would I keep this memory, or would I file it away only to retrieve it to measure it against things when the world changed?

I heard a plane outside. I was swept to a place that had given me joy. I was in the midst of a memory of what I deemed as a wonderful day. It was the first time I had seen a president with the naked eye. His hair appeared to give off a red halo in the distance. The sun hit it and gave a burst of liveliness; it was the same burst of energy that he had given America. Blacks who were disenfranchised felt a resurgence of hope when Kennedy became president. In the homes were plates with pictures on them along with Jesus, Martin Luther King, and Kennedy. Blacks had hope that these men were called to change the state of the nation.

This was the day I saw Kennedy. I had been assigned to Eglin for about nine months now. I was sitting in the viewing stands adjacent to a military rocket range. The Air Force hosted a firepower demonstration for President Kennedy. One of the participating squadrons was from Shaw Air Force Base. A black pilot, Thomas Hennigan, was leading a flight of RF-101 airplanes. Hennigan's plane was to capture pictures of the event.

Occasionally, I would see President Kennedy's hand cup his eyes, as if to get a closer look at the show. Although distant, I could see his affirming smile and a whisper to the people next to him when the pilots were at the climax of events.

For a few moments, I forgot I was in the barracks, and I had briefly moved passed the event of the commemorative march for Medgar Evers. I was right back to the question I asked when I was at the library. What now? What can a black man do?

I was taken back in my thoughts to Mama's words. "Study to show thyself approved unto God." If I could be approved by God by knowing His Word, was this the way for a black man to show himself to be worthy in a world that saw him as nothing? What I was sure of was that I could be approved by God, but no guarantee with a man. I felt when approved by Him; He would do the rest. I picked up my bible, and upon going to a scripture, actually, I didn't know which one, I was just going to turn until I saw a familiar one, a scripture seemed to come forward from Psalms. "I will instruct thee and teach thee in the way which thought shalt go: I will guide thee with mine eye."

****

I don't know when I fell asleep, but when morning came, I had a feeling that I didn't have to worry about my next move, I could go on and be exactly what God had called me to be.

I sat at my desk and thought about my next post in life. As I began to explore my "what's next options," I had been kicking around the idea of having Embassy Attaché duty, Court Reporting, and ROTC duties. I was not fully committed to which one I wanted exactly, but entertaining the thoughts of each of them made me imagine myself in each position.

****

The Talent Show

I was on stage performing "The Creation" by James Weldon Johnson at the Service Club. The words were coming out of my mouth at a steady and rhythmic pace. This poem I was performing was a familiar piece to me and the audience. Being here a few times before, I was able to get a good feel for the audience, but for a moment, I was back at Talladega County Training School with Miss Gibbs and Miss Slater in my speech performing days. The lights were bright, and I could barely see the audience, but I could hear them supporting me when I said something with an intentional inflection or a pause for emphasis. It wasn't like the church support where people get up and wave their hats and jump out of their seats to the next pew, but it was a form of affirmation.

I thought about Medgar Evers, how he stood up for Blacks. Surely his standing up was more significant than my act of recitation. Yet, I was conveying the message of what each poem meant, but Medgar was actually doing this every day in his life. He was conveying what Blacks should become.

I wasn't nervous, but this was a different audience from my days in school. Even though I had been reciting poems now a few times at this Service Club, sometimes each time was different, but this time I thought of Medgar Evers.

"You should compete in the Air Force Talent Show," an Airman said to me after I finished.

Could I actually really compete in such a contest? I thought about it for a moment. I let the idea spin around in my head to compete in the Air Force Talent Show. I got all the information, and I practiced. Even if I didn't go through with it for some reason or another, I would know all the entry rules and preparations that I needed. This competition was going to be in California.

Sitting in my barracks, I leaned back in my chair and imagined myself looking at palms trees and seeing the scenes that I had seen in books and on television when it came to California. People with sunglasses, convertibles, and what looked to be prosperity from end-to-end.

****

As I was leaving for California, I was filled with the same excitement I had when I went to Tuskegee with Mr. Armstrong. I wasn't going to hear his tires drive over the gravel, but when I was in the air, I could hear the jet streams and see below what looked like a big puzzle below, without the jigsaw part.

Upon arrival, I went to my hotel room and practiced my signature piece, "The Creation." I had actually thought about doing another piece, but this one was so well received. Why would I change when this poem had been so good to me? I had even been asked to perform it in Pensacola, Florida, just 45 minutes away at a local Baptist Church.

It was time to go to meet and get all the information about the talent show.

"Everybody, could I have your attention. Stand over here, and we can get started."

A gentleman began calling everybody's name, passing out information packets. When he got to mine, he said, "Gra-os," with a hard G.

"Yes, Sir," I stepped up while extending my hand to receive my package.

"This is your itinerary for your stay here. You will have time to sightsee and meet California."

There was a table of food that seemed like it took a week to prepare. I guess this was how it was done in California. Performing obviously warranted good food. The fruit seemed to go on for miles, and shapes I had never seen before. I didn't take the route to eat like I did when I drank soda in basic training. I ate normally, but stayed within limits, and tried appetizers that were arranged so interestingly.

"Me in California," I repeated to myself. Even though I was there, I took Miss Gibbs, Miss Slater, Mr. Armstrong, and Miss New with me. Had it not been for their nurturing, guidance, and coaching, I would not have been able to even know I could stand in front of an audience and say something that anyone would want to hear and be moved by.

The next morning, I was waking up to muscles that were sore due to all the walking I had done. I had seen Peter Lawford's house, and I had actually seen the comedian Candy Candito, even though I had never heard of him. Days moved quickly, and it was finally the day of the contest. I gathered all my clothing and lay them on the bed. I recited the poem toward the clothing as if the clothing were going to be the judge. Just seeing them was showing me how I was going to look in them, and I could feel my projection and see my appearance blend into a place that brought me motivation.

On the ride to the theater, I prayed that God's will would be done. When I arrived, I remembered the gravity of this contest. If I won, I would have a contract to be in the movies. I rehearsed that in my head a few times. This was not a bad deal for a boy who started with virtually nothing from Talladega. Mama would be so proud. As a matter of fact, everyone would be proud; my friends and my teachers. There was only one thing to do, and that was to give it everything I had and make everyone in the audience see "The Creation" come to life right before their eyes, the moon in one hand and the sun in the other, while the man God created would be on his way.

I listened to the other contestants, and they were extraordinary. Where some would have been intimidated and maybe jealous, I was truly entertained and encouraged, while remembering it was indeed an honor to have come this far in the contest and how God had allowed me to even be in the setting.

"... And next, we have William L. Gross reciting, 'The Creation,' by James Weldon Johnson." The man who was emceeing voice sounded like the typical voice on the radio announcing a Saturday evening show. In seconds I was in front of what seems like the largest stage I had ever stood on with the largest audience I had ever seen.

The air smelled so different in Florida than what I had smelled in California. The balmy air in California smelled of summertime, a mixture of beaches, restaurants, and gasoline from convertible cars.

Coming back to Eglin with a second-place win was quite an accomplishment. Of course, I wanted to be in first place, and I really didn't think my presentation of Weldon Johnson's 'Creation' should have been behind the first-place act. I had nothing against country music. I liked it and admired the storytelling it had in every song, but I had to admit it, I felt I should have won.

If I allowed myself to dwell on it, bitterness would set in, and I immediately asked God to put all of this in perspective.

When it was time for me to return to work, I heard cheers and whistles. They were gathered by my desk and gave me congratulations.

"We haven't even been close or known someone who has gone to the Air Force Talent Show. You represented us well!"

I smiled and was overjoyed. One thing I couldn't do was to let that second-place win upset me. It would undermine everything that God had done, how He allowed me to get to California, and how I prayed that His will would be done.

****

The Telethon

I was looking at the scenes moving out the window. "This is happening?" I asked myself. I continued questioning myself how I got here, but I had God to thank immensely for this offer. I was being chauffeured down to the telethon in Mobile, Alabama. I had heard Papa talk of Mobile, but I didn't imagine myself in Mobile on a Telethon. Many of the scenes reminded me of similar scenes that Mr. Armstrong and I saw on our trip to Tuskegee. Lines of clothing and homes with chimneys and children were running aimlessly outside, filled with all sorts of wonder.

We had actually driven one-hundred-and-five miles from the base. It was actually 60 miles from Pensacola, Florida. How did I get on this Telethon Drive? I had actually asked myself more than once. The Red Cross had actually heard about my performance, and they thought that this would be a wonderful way for me to showcase my talent, saying and reciting "The Creation." They were hoping that as currently a local talent in the Air Force, it would help raise money. It was my true hope that three of my teachers who had helped me so much, Miss Slater, Miss Gibbs, and Miss New, would catch a glimpse of it or at least hear about it.

Before I realized it, we were turning into the television studio. I walked in, and I was shown the waiting room. I went to the bathroom where I put on my clothes and came back to the waiting room for someone to tell me "lights, camera, action" or whatever they were going to say. I just looked around and took it all in. I thought about Will, my beloved friend, and a mule. I remembered how I was behind that mule so much that I remember saying, "If his behind was a T.V. camera, I would definitely be a movie star in Hollywood." I sat there and chuckled because this was a close experience, and as well as the one I just had in California. I was very thankful, very thankful the way my mother taught me that I was here, chosen, for an experience just like this.

"And next ... We have a talented young fellow from Elgin Air Force Base, all the way from Ft. Walton Beach, where his home town is Talladega, Alabama. He's going to recite "The Creation," written by James Weldon Johnson. Give a round of applause for Airman William L. Gross." The introduction was like a voice that introduced two prizefighters who were going to go to blows in the ring.

I heard all the hands clapping and got out there and stood before those that was dialing the phone. People were calling in, and I was hoping that I would have a major impact on many more calls. Standing here was like none other because this time, I didn't know who was looking at me. Yes, there was a small audience in the studio, and I didn't know how far this was seen in the Alabama area. I got that feeling again, right at the moment of introduction, hoping that all my teachers could see me. It probably was possible since Mobile was a distance from Talladega. I didn't wish it because I thought so highly of myself, but I wanted them to know that everything that they had instilled in me, that this was a little bit of that payoff. I was using what they taught me for good causes.

When I began, I got lost in words. I was all over in the creation itself –between the sun and moon and the man God made, as Weldon interpreted it. Unsure of it, I was reciting or just carried away wit the words. But, before I knew it, I heard rousing and thunderous applause, and I took a bow.

I was grateful. I was gracious, and above all, I was thankful to God that I could measure where I was. From that dreadful day of the first day of first grade to where I was right now to when I heard, "We want you to recite ..." I could see the distance I had come on my journey.

I was back at the base, and things were, for lack of a better word, "normal." The people were glad to see me as I had gone on and helped some men have some restored confidence like there was a person in the black community who had stepped out and done something positive. I was glad to have fulfilled that role. Even if it wasn't the way I set out to do it, it was something that was leading me on my path to my journey. Some men stopped by the barracks and wanted to hear first-hand my experience at the studio. We talked and laughed late into the night.

****

The next day was a regular day, getting up and going through the routine of things.

As I was approaching my work building, a fellow Airman said, "Bill, we are going to a club this weekend downtown in Ft. Walton Beach."

"What club?" I asked.

"You know the one in Ft. Walton Beach," he said.

"That club is for White's only."

"That's right," he said.

"Lieutenant Hill is on base now, rounding up interest to integrate the club. He wants to set up a demonstration."

After hearing the details, I decided that I wanted to participate. I took a deeper breath and decided that I had to participate. If I had been as far as Hollywood and gone to Mobile to recite "The Creation," surely, I could loan my support, if just my appearance in numbers to see this through. Plus, these airmen would want my support after they had supported me in all my contests.

"Ok," I said. Yet, I wondered exactly how this would turn out.

We were all gathered on the outside of the club, some people looking and wondering why we were there. I could tell that some wanted to flick their cigarettes directly on us, but they didn't choose to be so overt. When we were all ready and assembled, we walked in unison and sat directly inside the club. If eyes had been daggers, we would have been stabbed a thousand times over, and dead on arrival. We didn't move, but if I put my finger on the inside of my collar and turned my neck, it seemed like things were getting a little tighter, but I didn't let my courage flinch at all. We just sat there, calmly; we wanted peace; we wanted justice. We did not want anything rowdy. The waiters walked around us, continued like we weren't there, and they would not serve us. That went on initially for a few moments until the moments turned to what seemed like hours. Soon thereafter, we saw the police come in the door. Now the police came and did exactly what they were called to do.

"You all got to get up and leave here. You know this club is not for Coloreds," the police said.

"The white Airmen go to our Black clubs," a voice rang out.

"Now who said that?" The police said.

No one actually answered.

"Listen," the policeman said, with a twang in his voice that differed from all that I had heard. "If you know what's best, just go on and leave now, and there won't be any trouble."

Many of us decided to just walk out, complying with the request and leave. However, there were some Airmen who chose to make a little more noise by continuing to stay. When they resisted, they were put in jail and reported to the base commander.

I didn't choose this route of sitting in. Maybe I felt that wasn't for me to do at the time, or I didn't really want to face the unknown at the moment. However, this might have been what it took to shake things up after all.

The Commander didn't take the news lying down; he moved forward and called Ft. Waldon Police Department and City Hall back and had a surprising request. He told them, "If you do not integrate the club, I will not let the G.I.'s go off this base, and I will see that they stay on the base until further notice." The tune of segregation was about to be changed.

After Ft. Walton was virtually brought to its knees, the commander got a call saying, "These guys are welcome to our clubs." They didn't like it. It was new to them. But economically, they couldn't survive without the G.I.'s disposable income, and so they decided that the clubs and other restaurants would be integrated.

Soon airmen were free to go anywhere. It turns out they really weren't interested in going to those clubs. What we wanted was to be able to demonstrate our disapproval of the way the city was treating us. It was true that an airman responded the night we sat in the club. White Airmen could go to Black clubs when they wanted to, but we didn't have the same privilege.

I actually found out that General Daniel "Chappie" James integrated the Officer's Club that was actually on Eglin Air Force Base in the 1940s. He decided to lead his Black compadres to go inside with him, and when he went in, the same thing that happened to us that had happened to him. They wouldn't serve him. In his own way, he let it be known that he worked, defended, served on behalf of his country, and he should have the same opportunities as others in the Officer's club. He felt he had fought in a war just like others, and later, after the dust settled, he and other black officers were able to attend the club.

Well, it was time for me to put my bag on my shoulder, and take a long look over my other one, and wave Eglin a hearty good-bye. One of my choices had come through. I was going to another place on my journey. It was great to know that I got the results back from all three tests I had taken: Court Reporting, Attaché Duty, and ROTC Duty. I had passed them all. Now I was going to be in our Nation's Capital.

CHAPTER 43 – WASHINGTON, D.C., ROTC PROGRAM

Washington, DC. Here I come. But first, it was always a good time to count my blessing, and I thought I would count them along with the places the Air Force had taken me: *1. Texas... 2. Arkansas... 3. Philippines... 4. China... 5. Florida ... and now 6. Washington D.C.* God, I sincerely thank you for ALL the things you have done for me. You were there when I had nothing but hope.

Here I was standing in our Nation's Capital, where I had seen presidents wave. They were riding in a motorcade, and the people were as near as the street, standing, wishing to get a glimpse of them or as far away as seeing them on the television. Here I was in the same city where presidents had negotiated policies back and forth with Congress, and after a weary day, it was the same city where they lay their heads.

There were a lot of thoughts that I wanted to entertain, now that I was here in Washington, D.C. But first, I was in awe of the campus; just seeing the buildings of the academic buildings made me feel a sense of accomplishment even though I had no formal academic training as it would relate to a college degree. It had been a long time since I had been on a college campus, definitely not as big as this one. However, it was the sister campus to Tuskegee. The last time I was on campus was when I wept before the statue of Booker T. Washington, "Unveiling the veil of ignorance."

Then, there was something else that fascinated me. Never had I seen so many faculty and staff members – all in what I perceived as one location. At the moment, I felt a little intimated, but I was glad to be a part of such an institution.

Even though I was in Washington, D.C., Tuskegee Institute was definitely on my mind. Here I was, in a place still longing to get back to that campus as a student. All I could do but wonder, *"When was that time going to be?"*

I had been accepted to Court Reporting School, and Attaché Duty, along with this ROTC assignment. When it came down to choosing which one, I thought that it would be best for me to choose this one, ROTC. It was ultimately the college route for me. I would be able to see exactly how things were done in a college setting, and that would give me the ability to sharpen my skills.

Having access to just the campus alone was going to make a big difference in my mentality, in my walk, in my dedication to make sure I was going to go back to Tuskegee.

"Good morning, William Gross."

"Good morning," I replied with a confidence that seemed to be launched about me, yet I was wondering all the time exactly how matters would be at this new post. Our hands shook, and some of my fears were relieved just at that moment.

"Have a seat," this gentleman said.

"Yes, sir," I noticed myself saying it with authority. I would of anyway, but I felt confident and nervous at the same time.

"Airman Gross, I'm Colonel James A. Herd."

"Yes, sir," I said.

"Welcome to Howard."

"Thank you."

"I hope you had a good trip here from Florida."

"Yes, sir, I did."

"I want to let you know that you have an impeccable record. We have never chosen a man who was single. Actually, we thought that would create more problems in a college setting. With a record like yours, we felt you would do a great job and be of great service to these young men."

"I appreciate it, sir, that you took a chance on me," I replied.

"As the Academic Counselor of the ROTC Program, we are looking for excellence, and we believe that is you. You prepared records in your former duty stations, and you will be doing the same here."

"Yes, sir," I inserted.

I knew this wasn't an interview but an orientation. If I didn't ask any questions, I didn't think it would be seen as if I was unprepared. Yet, I didn't want to take any chances, nor

I did I want to be asked the question, "Do you have any questions for me.

"What is the current retention rate of the ROTC Program?" I did want to know that.

"Let's just say, we want it to be as close to 100% as possible. These young men need a man like you to encourage them and let them know that they are here to succeed academically."

I inserted another, "Yes, sir."

"Assist the young men, and never fraternize with the students on this campus."

"Yes, sir, I understand."

****

Bowling Air Force Base was my new residence, and like other barracks, it wasn't anything I had to get used to. I had been to a few, so I could fit right in. I had been here for a couple of weeks, but without transportation, it was a little arduous to get to Howard University. It wasn't far, yet it wasn't walking distance either.

My job was going well. I had the opportunity to work under two fine Commanders, one who had given me "the right hand of fellowship" of the University, Commander Herds, and there was Commander Dryden.

****

"Young man, thanks for coming in," I said with authority.

The young man sat down. It was evident that he knew why he was summoned to see me. I thought about how this young man was sitting on the other side of my dreams. I was counseling him.

"I called you here because I want to check in with you about your academic progress.

"Yes, sir. I realize I'm not doing as well as I could ..."

"Why is that?" I asked. I asked the question quickly, not to attack him, but to get his answer right then.

"I carry 18 hours, and I think that is a factor," this young man said.

"As I look at your schedule, I see you are carrying more hours than your other semesters. Do you think that could be the only reason?" I said sincerely.

This was a little surreal, I was eager to be where this young man was, yet I was disciplining this young ROTC student about his grades.

"Well, I think I could have better time management. It would help me if I got up a little earlier, and do my assignments immediately, and not wait until the last minute."

I was a student for a moment. This is what I aspire to be doing when I get to Tuskegee. That was my dream, and I wasn't going to forget it.

"As I review your file, I just want to let you know that your grades are important, as I'm sure you know. They will follow you, and they will be a determining factor in what people will think of you before they meet you."

"I want to let you know some other things. As young men are being drafted to go to Vietnam, there are reasons that some young men go and reasons that some men who do not. Not all the reasons are disclosed, and nor do I know how things are always weighed. But, I do want you to know that the quality of your grades can be a determining factor in you being selected for the U.S. draft, that could ultimately land you in Vietnam. So, keep your grades up."

The young man swallowed, as I could see the lump in this throat move. I could tell he heard the words I said and took them to heart.

"I want to check back in with you in two weeks, and we will continue to monitor your progress. It sounds like you know exactly what you need to do. You are not so far off base, but we don't want you to go so far off that it's too late into the semester."

We shook hands, and I was finished with this conference.

The rest of my day was just like this. Some ROTC students were not as forthcoming about their reasons for grades, and some were excuse-ridden. I didn't make assumptions, because that really was not where I wanted to be. But along with my list of promises I had made to myself, I promised to be on top of my studies when I'm ever enrolled in college.

****

"Junior, come on, and let's sit down and eat."

My cousin, Caeser, didn't' have to tell me twice. I had experienced a long day at Howard. Examining records and checking in with students was a process that I was still refining.

Caesar was my good cousin-friend, Kyser's brother.

I was visiting him and was happy to be connected with a family member since I really had no family in Washington, D.C.

I had lived with Caesar for a little while when I first got to Howard, and now, I was visiting, and we were laughing, talking, and shooting the breeze as guys do.

Caesar's brother, Joe, came over and joined the conversation.

"Why don't we go out next weekend, Junior?" he asked.

"Sure. This is your town, and I assume you know more about it than I do," I said.

"You've been here a little while," he said.

"Yeah, I didn't realize the time would move so fast. I like it here, and I was really blessed to get to a place like Washington, D.C. I've been a few places, but I feel like this is a place I can kind of take a breather. I know it's the military, and I'm in the Air Force, but I guess being on a college campus, it doesn't feel as rigid."

"I think I know what you mean. I always felt the military was about making your bed right and lock check."

I let out a big laugh. Caesar and Joe looked at me and wondered why I was laughing.

"You just made me think about an Airman who had a piece of hair in his toothbrush," I said. "The Drill Sergeant wanted to know if he was brushing his behind with his toothbrush."

Caesar joined in. "That had to be funny."

"It was, and I couldn't stop laughing. They had to stop the inspection, and then start after I finished laughing," I said, laughing myself.

"You all were laughing like that?" Caesar said.

"Yes, we were."

"The military wasn't like many people think ... all drill and making up beds and artillery. It is discipline, business, and service. It's much more also, but those words are the ones that describe it most to me."

"Joe, who is this?" I said to him, whispering.

"I thought we would all go out," he said.

"Alright," I said.

He could see that I didn't have a lot of words.

"Junior, but I thought you would be ..."

I didn't let him finish.

"Joe, I'm not upset. I'll go through with this blind date, but I can already tell, I'm not interested," I said cordially.

"Fair enough, I just thought we would double date. This is my girlfriend's good friend," he said.

The night went on as usual, but I had just met a girl named Patricia while I was waiting to meet the blind date. As the evening went by, my mind kept going back to Patricia.

She had come out and spoken to me, and I heard a sense of calm in her voice.

I was back in the scene of the blind date. The music was playing, and the conversation was maintaining a fluency that did not give away the idea that I was not interested. A continuance of restaurant music created a great ambiance. The night ended, and all remained well.

****

I felt the firmness around my hand when Charles Dryden shook it.

"I've heard good things, Airman Gross," Commander Dryden stated.

"Thank you, sir."

"These young men need someone who is going to review their files and meet with them to keep their grades moving in the right direction."

I remembered him welcoming me to the campus, but he wasn't someone I saw on a continuous basis. He was definitely one to be revered. This was a man who was one of the Tuskegee Airmen, and those men had earned everything they had gotten. These men were fixtures in the community of Tuskegee and perfectly pierced the minds and memories of those who they encountered on their missions. Commander Dryden was with the 99th Pursuit Squadron that shot down German planes.

Our conversation was not a long one. We talked about the importance of my work and how the young men must develop the discipline to continue in the ROTC program. It was a very distinguished program, not just a way to finish college, but a place where these young men would one day be Officers in the Air Force after graduation.

****

"Bill, Saturday evening will be great. What time?"

"About 6:00 pm," I said.

Patricia had agreed to a date with me. Something about the way she carried herself made an indelible print on my mind.

After talking to her, I was talking to Joe, telling him my plans with Patricia.

"Junior, I think it's great that you are going out on a date with her."

"I'm glad she decided to go."

"Well, you have a lot to offer. Look at what you have done since you have been in Washington, D.C. You got a great job, and you know where you want to go, so it's not like you are somebody who doesn't know where you are going in life, plus you got a car that you worked hard for."

Joe and I talked for a while until it was time for me to go home. Only, on my way home, I thought of what Joe said. I was glad to be on my way to somewhere. I didn't know exactly when I would arrive, but I was glad to be on the highway.

"Hi, Bill," Patricia said.

"How are you?" I asked.

“I’m doing well.”

We continued our conversation as we walked a little around Washington, D.C., taking in the attractions.

“You grew up in Alabama ...?,” she asked.

I didn’t’ know if that was a question or whether she was confirming what she knew.

“Yes, I did,” I said

I thought of Will. “I used to plow with a mule, and do all sorts of farm work,” I replied.

“So, you know about farm work from start to finish?” Patricia asked.

This time I took this as a question.

“I learned at an early age. I saw what Papa did and his father, and I was plowing at eight-years-old.”

“You knew what to do at the age of eight?” Patricia said.

“I did what I saw, and it worked,” I said, guarded.

There was no way I was going to tell her the underlying reason that I was really out there plowing so young. Papa was off drinking with his buddies, and I was left to plow.

“But, I’m glad to have that experience to see where I’ve come from, and how to help encourage the young men on campus towards a great future,” I said.

“So, that’s what you do at Howard?” Patricia said.

“I’m working in the Air Force ROTC Program as an Academic Counselor. I meet with the young men about their grades and about the importance of their role in the program.

After our long conversation, that soon let us know that we had a lot in common. We decided to go and get a bite to eat.

“So, you are from Madison, Virginia? What did you all do a lot of there?” I asked.

“My mother made sure we got our lessons, and we attended church, and we loved swimming,” she said. “We could even see water moccasins from afar, and we would still be swimming.”

I laughed, for I knew swamps, lakes, and ponds that probably had cottonmouths, but nobody had better get in that water for swimming.

The night went on, and we talked like two old friends that had been exchanging stories matching scene for scene.

****

I put one foot on the floor, and before I put the other one down, the sun was already shining. I was always an early riser, but for a minute, I thought I had slept longer than I intended. If I hadn't known any better, I would have thought it was shining for my soon-to-be bride and me, congratulating us. If there was no calendar that read "January 29, 1966," I still would have known what day it was. Just from the beginning, I could tell it was going to be a day I was going to be remembering forever.

Time had moved quite fast, and yet it almost stood still for me after meeting Patricia. I accomplished a lot. I knew my job well. I decided to take a Chemistry Class, delving into academics to see how it would be, and I thought all the stars were lining up. But I couldn't let the stars take the credit; I knew God was adding wonderful accessories to my life.

Just like I had done, whether for a job or for the military, I found myself getting all my clothes together and putting them out. I didn't want to forget anything and have to circle back, causing any delays. If I knew anything, I knew women wanted their wedding to go off without a hitch, whether it was in a barn or in the Louvre in France.

I thought for a moment what Patricia might be thinking. Was she doing the same thing I was at the time? Was she getting her dress together, replete with jewelry, shoes, or whatever women did on their wedding day?

On my way to the bathroom to wash my face, I touched my toes and came back up with my hand returning to my waist. I repeated the process about ten times and clapped my hands afterward. "Yeah, I'm ready," I said.

I got everything ready and put it in my car, and came back and had a little something to eat. Five o'clock was going to be here before I knew it, and I still had a lot to do.

As the hours passed, clouds began to come in from the west, moving powerfully, and it was a bit perplexing. A day that started out so sunny had turned like a person who had a total change of mind.

The wedding was going to be at Patricia's Aunt's house at 440 Longfellow St. N.W. It was crucial that I arrive at the right time. I had come from a people who believed that it was bad luck to see the bride before the wedding.

My mother and father had wished me warm wishes since they could be there. I was sure my mother was happy, and I could feel her love and presence with me on this day.

I finally arrived, and my windshield wipers were on and moving the soft and silent snow. Now I understood why the clouds were forming, and the sun quickly disappeared, because the snow was on its way.

When I stepped into the house, I was met with decorations, complements of Patricia's aunts from both sides of her parents. It was evident that they had worked hard and loved Patricia to make such a day to be beautiful and complete.

I didn't ask where Patricia was, for I knew she would be arriving at the appropriate time. Patricia's mother, however, was not going to be at the wedding because she was having an operation. I knew Patricia was a little sad about that, but her family was doing everything to make this event a special one, and I could truly say that's what they did.

Guests were arriving, and I could hear the minister when he arrived. Something about ministers when they enter, made for a powerful moment: the voice wasn't booming, but it was robust and distinctive at the same time. He was Rev. McQueen, a Baptist minister at Oak Grove Church.

All of a sudden, I could hear the aunts coming together to let everyone know it was time. I patted my hair on top, shook my fingers as if water was dripping from them, and I straightened my tie. I looked at my shoes, and they were polished just like on any other day, but I did add a little buff.

"Junior," someone called me. I couldn't determine the voice, but I said, "Yes."

"We're ready."

I was on my way to my destination that would unite me to my new life. I was as certain – as I was happy – about the choice for Patricia to be my wife A new beginning in my life was about to start on 440 Longfellow St. N.W. Washington, DC., today, January 29, 1966.

****

Patricia and I. That was a new phrase I was going to have to start saying in my head, as well as with others. When I leave Longfellow St. today, I would be a married man, and Patricia would now be Patricia Gross. When I saw Patricia coming toward me, I paused. She was beautiful, even more than I had remembered. My mind that was usually flooded with ambitious thoughts about my tomorrows was simply paused as I took in the vision of Patricia.

"William, do you take this woman, to be your lawfully wedded wife?" Rev. McQueen asked.

"I do," I said

"Patricia, do you take this man to be your lawfully wedded husband," Rev. McQueen stated.

"I do," Patricia said.

It was quiet in the background, but it was as if our family released their breath because they were so happy that we were getting married.

Then came the "from this day forward, for better, for worse, for richer, for poorer, in sickness and in health to love and to cherish, till death do us part."

We both repeated and agreed, and then we heard the part that everyone was waiting for, "I now pronounce you man and wife."

We heard clapping and cheering, and all our relatives came up to hug us.

Mama and Papa were not there, and Patricia's mother was not there, but the other family members who were there made our wedding day one that we would never forget. The decorations and food were unforgettable.

****

Our lives were now united, and we would spend our first night in our apartment. I didn't know that when I was coming to Washington, D.C. that I would be a husband in the capital.

"Bill, what would you like for breakfast?" Patricia asked.

"Whatever you fix will be fine," I said. I did have a moment where I thought of Mama's Hoecakes, but I didn't want to impose that on Patricia. I wasn't even sure we had all the ingredients to make them.

I knew we had some bacon, eggs, and grits. Actually, we did have ingredients to make Hoecakes because, according to what I remembered from Mama, if you had the basic flour and meal with some grease, eggs, milk, and sugar, you had Hoecakes. However, I thought I would request Hoecakes another time.

It was a smooth transition into marriage. I had not lived with anyone but my family from Talladega, men on the base, and Caesar for a couple of weeks. This was like a family again. I was with someone who was a partner, rooting for me just like Mama. All the things I was once doing for myself, Patricia was doing them for me, like cooking, cleaning, organizing my clothes, and preparing a home. When she was doing these things, I didn't feel like this was her job, but what I did feel was that I had been blessed. God had put someone in my life that I loved and admired to willingly do these things for me. I, in turn, thought that I would forever do the same for her, where she would feel as blessed as I felt.

****

I had left all the comforts of B St., the home my wife and I were making, and going back to work at Howard University on Monday as soon as I returned, which had not been, but a few days, I had a new perspective for me. The responsibility for the young men on campus, and the responsibility for my household with a wife. I did not feel overwhelmed; what I felt was empowered. The charge that I believed God placed on all men to head their households and the wisdom He gives, should they seek it.

The snow was still on the ground, but the city was not crippled. Classes were not canceled, and students were making their way to their destinations in spite of inclement weather.

I, myself, had arrived at my office, and as I looked at the schedule for the day, there was one particular student that I was scheduled to see. He was beginning to become a regular. It was time for reality to set in with this student. His future was going to hang in the balance, and he nor his parents deserved that.

"Young man, we are going to turn you over to the Draft Board."

Now I really didn't want to have to say it so matter-of-factly; however, I didn't believe I was doing him any favors pulling punches. I was hired as an Academic Counselor, and yet there was no change in this case.

"Wait, I can..."

"Explain, I believe that is the word you are going to use," I said.

"Sir, I'm trying my best. It's just all that I have, a full load of classes and football, and I do most of my work after football practice," he stated earnestly. Yet, he had said these same things before.

"I believe you need to rise earlier in the morning, as well as be assigned to a tutor," I suggested.

"But everything is during the same time as ROTC or football practice," he yelped out quickly.

"We are going to make arrangements for tutors that will work around your schedule," I said with all the politeness I could give.

"I want you to write down everything you do during a day and everywhere you go," I said, deliberately direct. I was not angry or charged with authority; I was feeling that charge to responsibility now that I was married.

"You want me to write down when I eat, sir?" this student said.

"Everything you can think of," I said.

The moments went by, and I thought of Patricia. What she was cooking went straight to the front of the line of all my thoughts. I thought of our apartment versus the one I had on Rhode Island Ave., and this one was larger with more amenities. But even if I had once lived in an apartment as large as the Taj Mahal, with every known amenity, what would have been missing would be the vivacity Patricia brought.

"Let's see what you have?" I said, snapping myself back into this counseling session.

"I wrote down everything I could, sir."

"That's what I want. I think I see what changes we can make," I said, believing he could pull through.

"Let's make two set times to study, and two set times to review per day. This doesn't mean review for two hours at a time. Reviewing can be done when you are waiting for a class to start. But your notes are in order to review. You need time management help, and I think we can start with a plan to set a time to get you to help with that. I want to see you back here tomorrow, this same time, and we will set something up for you."

I was beginning to wonder if I am doing this for students; I surely should be able to do this for myself. Many times, I had seen preaching be much easier than practicing. Yet, I was grateful that I was being trained to help students succeed, so when it is my turn, I can get right in line.

****

If anyone had told me that my years in Washington, D.C., were going to bring me hope, stability, and a greater sense of self, I don't know if I would have believed them. I would have believed God was able, but I would have questioned how it all would be executed. This was probably an area in my life that I needed to continue to let grow and let God have the wheel of my journey. Time had a way of moving quickly, yet I somehow had a relationship with it that seemed to allow me to make the best deals with it. I thought it was one of God's gifts to me, as it allowed me to be on the pathway of some interesting routes and some people who guided me along the way. I thought if I used the time wisely and not waste it, I would reap from the benefits that life offered. I didn't know what I would be doing in Argentina or Rhode Island, had I been in one of those areas, but Washington D.C. had given me some treasures.

Just months after I had arrived in D.C., Martin Luther King, Jr. had made his "I Have a Dream Speech" from the Lincoln Memorial, August 28, 1963. This was a time of social unrest and social injustices, and the March on Washington was necessary to address the civil and economic injustices that Blacks were experiencing. I always felt we were so far back "up in the woods" before I left Talladega that I hadn't even heard of King when he organized the Montgomery Bus Boycott in 1955. I first heard of King after I left in 1956, and I could see the racial tension with my own eyes when a policeman was yelling and hitting a Black man after he, the policeman, had hit the back of the Black man's car in Montgomery. With King being in Washington, I thought this would be the opportune time to hear him speak, but there was an order from the Secretary of Defense that no military unit could participate in the March on Washington, whether in or out of uniform.

Now that King was on Howard University's campus, there were no restrictions, and I could attend this event. This time he was at Howard for the Gandhi Memorial Lecture. I heard him speak of the Pathways to Peace and the struggle for racial justice in the United States. He stated, "There can be no peace ultimately without justice, and there can be no justice without peace." He continued, and he spoke about the struggle for racial justice.

I could hear the crowd breathing sighs of agreement, along with head nodding. This wasn't a loud call and response rally; no hand clapping moments after each agreeable statement. Maybe this is how things were on a college campus. I somewhat thought that if this same speech was in a southern church setting, people would have responded differently. Perhaps the college setting sets a tone for a different listening style. I had to remember this was a lecture, so that also may have curtailed some outward responses.

I listened intently. What I didn't know of him when I was in Talladega, I was filling up now, as if I could put it all in a drum and save it. We, as a people and as a nation, had a lot to do. Equality wasn't going to fall out of the sky. It was going to have to be established, requested, and unfortunately demanded. But, as King said, "Non-violence is the most powerful and the most effective instrument that the Negro has in his struggle in the United States of America."

****

I looked directly into his eyes, and I couldn't believe I was shaking hands with a part of History. He wasn't just known in the United States, Martin Luther King, Jr. was known all over the world for his non-violent stance. When I shook his hands, it wasn't an electrical volt or a static shock; I felt a sense of peace and humility, yet a quiet strength that he had obviously established from God within.

As I continued looking at him, I saw a peculiar looking man. Not in the sense of odd or strange, but distinctive in nature with an anointing, only God could give. His eyes looked as if they were crying all the time, where it seemed the presence of tears was crossing his eyes as if there was something he was seeing and continuously painful. Whatever he saw, I desired to be more in tune with the world because I had another title now, and that was Father.

I could hear the cooing of Kim. That's what Patricia and I named her, Kim Andrea Gross. I could see her in her crib, and she was covered in a soft pink blanket that matched her gentle, but bubbly personality. Her eyes would shine, and she would smile as if knowing life is great.

Yes, I was a proud father, and I wanted to be the father I knew she needed in every area of her life. It was my goal that she would want for nothing and have access to everything. Walking around in my memory, I remembered too many days of hunger, sadness, and whether I wanted to admit it – neglect. I thought my father could have done a lot more, but the times with his buddies evidently took precedence. I didn't understand it then, and I really didn't understand it now that he was so cavalier about me and my sibling's welfare. As I looked at Kim, I began to wonder why he didn't look at all of us, as I did her, and realize we all had basic needs, and it was his responsibility to make sure they were met. I knew God had put me in a wonderful position here in Washington, D.C., but I did find myself thinking about why we seemingly didn't matter to my father. It was still many years later, but I found myself deeply divided on whether he really wasn't concerned about us or whether he was consumed and controlled by the substances of alcohol.

I continued looking at her, and I dreamed of when she would walk when she would talk, what would be her favorite color, and what was Papa thinking when each of us was born.

****

The December air always had a chill in Washington, D.C. There would be occasions when you could catch a mild day, but this was not one of them. I wasted no time getting from my car to my office, and I had actually planned to have a hot cup of coffee as soon as I arrived.

I got my normal going, looking at my schedule. I also was looking to see if the registrar needed me to talk to any ROTC students. As the mid-morning arrived, I had crossed off many things on my lists, met with students, called Patricia, and heard Kim in the background.

I wanted a second cup of coffee and went down the hall to get it. I stirred clockwise and counterclockwise stirs, blended sugar and cream, making the dark brown tone disappear into shades of light tan. I sipped it, and it was is great. The coffee flows down my throat, and I feel ready for whatever is next on my agenda.

CHAPTER 44 – VIETNAM

I go back to my desk, and my interoffice mail has been delivered. Staff Sergeant William L. Gross, Jr. – I read my name and opened it right away. I held the paper carefully like it's going to fly away. Looking at it, I reread it, making sure I have not made a mistake. I didn't need to read the outside again to see if it was addressed to me, because I saw that first. Breathing deep breaths, I reach for my chair and sit down. My coffee is cooling off, and I have not returned to it. The steam that once revealed that it is hot is now non-existent, and the world as I had known it is no longer.

****

When I turn the key in the apartment door, I pause. I thank God for everything I am and all that he has given me, and no matter what happens in my future.

Patricia and Kim are obviously gone. Maybe they are taking a walk around a couple of blocks. I look at our wedding picture and pictures of our family, and I suddenly wonder, "Why now?"

I go to the refrigerator and pull out a pitcher of water, and fill a glass from the set of collectible glasses from the jelly company. A promotion that keeps everyone buying jelly until they have a full set.

I hear the door open, and I shift my demeanor from somber to normal; at least I'm going to try.

"Hi, Patricia," I said.

"Hi Bill, how was your day?"

I wasn't ready to just go right into the matter. So, I continued to shift as much as possible back to normal.

"Trying to keep the young men on the honor roll," I said as jovial as I could.

"What's my little girl been doing?" I said as I picked Kim up.

Patricia was pulling off her coat and turned to hang it in the closet. I looked at Kim and let the somberness fill my eyes, just for that moment.

Determined to keep a normal demeanor, by the time Patricia turned back around, I was okay.

I wrestled with myself as to when I was going to tell her about my new orders, but I decided that I would wait. For how long, I didn't know. Actually, maybe it would be tonight.

****

I was in the living room after Patricia had put Kim down for the night. I could hear Patricia singing a soothing tune so she would fall asleep.

As I sat on the sofa, I began to pray. This was not the first time, but I called on the Lord a succession of times. Going to God with earnest was all I ever knew how to do, and I began to converse with him each time I didn't felt I understand. Each time I was reminded that this was His will, but my mind was full of complexities. With everything lining up in my life, I had to be honest with my feelings. I understood what God's will means, what God's will can bring, what God's will can teach. However, I wanted to see a clear path if I could with wondering if I would ever get to my desired destination.

I could hear Patricia's footsteps coming toward the living room. If courage had been measured in footsteps, she definitely had more than I had.

"I received my orders today," I began when she sat on the sofa. Her eyes lit up, and I almost decided to reroute the conversation. But what was I going to say? I didn't open them, or would I go to another subject only to have to go back to this one. Patricia knew I had been in Washington, D.C., now for three and a half years, so I could get orders to go to the next duty station anytime.

I swallowed and propelled forward.

"They are sending me to Vietnam."

I wanted to look away. I didn't want to see the pain in her face. I didn't want to see the sadness that had to be present. But that was not what courage would do. I continued looking straight into her eyes.

"Bill, everything is going to be fine."

When I heard those words, I felt like columns of calmness were being erected all around me, as peace was ushered in.

****

The Howard Football Stadium was packed full as usual. I was working at the ticket entrance at the request of Mr. Banks, a man in the Small Business Office Accounts at Howard. He had asked me to work the ticket entrance, and I had been doing so for some time during my station at Howard. It was interesting how things looked once I knew where my next orders were. I enjoyed life and lived it not like I wasn't going to have more, but like I was grateful for it right now, even if I didn't know what tomorrow held. Right at that moment, I saw the Washington Redskins players. I was instructed to let them in at no charge. I saw Charlie Taylor, Bobby Mitchell, Rickie Harris, Sonny Jurgensen, Jerry Smith, and some others, but I was letting them in so quickly. I suppose it was a great outlet for them to see college football, as they were playing in the pros. Also, I guess it was a good look for Howard to have some professional athletes coming to the games.

After the tickets were sold, I took a seat inside and watched the game. I didn't care who was winning. Maybe I did. However, it was just great to be in a place of enjoyment, and I didn't let thoughts of tomorrow invade my space.

****

As the days were going by, I was determined that the time before my departure from Howard University was going to be well spent. Patricia and I were going to see the museums and the sites we could see in Washington. Additionally, I was going to see Kim get a little bigger. She wouldn't be old enough to be walking before I left, but Patricia would fill in all the gaps with pictures, letters, and conversations.

****

I hugged Patricia tightly, and I didn't want to depart. I inhaled the scent of her perfume and allowed it to linger in my mind. Planes overhead were landing and leaving, and I could hear the goodbyes of other people around us. Patricia picked up Kim, bouncing her ever so gently, soothing her.

Maybe a little fretful, soon Kim was looking around, taking in all the things that go on in an airport. People were picking up loved ones, luggage on wheels. We were at Dulles, and this one was probably busier than some since it was close to Washington, D.C., yet not as close as Washington National Airport.

"Well, this is it," I said to Patricia.

"Bill, everything is going to be fine," Patricia returned.

Patricia was always positive. That was one of the reasons I knew my life would be great with her.

I looked at Patricia and Kim and knew I was leaving the largest treasure God had given me.

Patricia and I hugged again, and I hugged Kim, and I couldn't believe what happened. As I walked away, still looking toward both of them, Kim waved "bye-bye." We had been trying to get her to wave for a little while now, but this was the first time. I waved back, and I wanted to go AWOL right then.

****

When I heard the wheels retract under the plane, it was a done deal. I was headed to Vietnam. I actually repeated several times, "I am really going to Vietnam." There was no turning around now. Where my future was going now was up to God. I had made my peace with this decision. If the saying was true that God laughs when he hears your plans, I couldn't help but wonder if he was tickled when I had planned to go to Tuskegee ten years ago.

I thought I had planned a sure-shot not to go to Vietnam, and that was to take the ROTC Program at Howard since I didn't have but twenty months on my time in the military. God laughs again, and my journey is rerouted.

What is my mother thinking? Her youngest child is now off to Vietnam. The sound of each of those syllables made people cringe when they said it. I had seen mothers say they had a son in "... Nam," and something in their faces changed. Blood seemed to leave it, and they wrung their hands without cause, not knowing if they would ever see their sons again. I had seen the look in their eyes. If my mother was not a praying woman, I would think I would have more worry than wonder. But this was the woman who has sent me on my own spiritual journey, and with that, I knew she was not exiting hers. She was probably thinking about why I had to go, and if my tour would be long, and whether I would be sick in another place. Yet, one thing she was comfortable with, I was going to be taken care of, and if I didn't come back, God had better plans for me with Him. That was the kind of certainty she always had. Yet, I still had uncertainty about my journey.

I mostly slept on the plane, wriggled in my seat, and read the whole way to Los Angeles. Then, I got on a plane from Los Angeles to Travis Air Force Base and boarded a plane from there.

I stretched out for the long hall, for this was an eighteen-hour fight. I ate everything that was served and was dozing on and off. Once, when I fell asleep, I dreamt I saw the Cunningham Place. Finally, I got into a position I considered to be peaceful enough to call it to sleep, and before I knew it, we were ready to land.

Before the plane landed, all the elements of war welcomed us, if it could be called welcome. We were approaching Tan Son Nhut Air Force Base, almost ready to land. I had no idea this was what I was going to see my first time in Vietnam. Flashing lights of enemy fire could be seen from the plane, and we could see fire returned.

I could originally hear the lull of conversations from the passengers talking, but a hush fell over the entire cabin, and a chill came forward. This icy reception spoke without words that the reality of war was present. Everything we might have heard and everything we might have read couldn't present exactly what we were seeing. The red tracer lights were US troops fire, and the green tracer lights were enemy fire. This was not a scene narrated by the pilots or the flight attendants, the kind of announcement that is usually made when landing in Honolulu. This was a self-service scene, which required those peering down to move their faith front and center and let fear be on the opposite side.

I kept looking down with the thoughts of wonder. How long would this last? Is this how it was going to be all the time? What did this combat zone even look like in the daytime? This was midnight. The vantage point of the plane made this combat area have a look of mystery, where anywhere could be a fair advantage to attack.

When the wheels on the airplane's landing gear touched the tarmac, the sound seemed to echo. We got our things, and I don't believe there was anyone eager to exit the plane. However, everyone I saw had the posture of bravery, for they were answering their call of duty.

The night seemed to go by fast. We were inside a hooch, a makeshift barrack that had screened wire from mid-level to the roof area around it, yet the air was humid. The air was thick like invisible cotton, and the rain was falling down steadily and no slowing down in sight. This was monsoon season.

I kept my prayers on the tablets of my heart. This was not a time to miscalculate when you were going to pray. I was unsure about the men who didn't have God to call on, or a God of their choice. I just didn't see how they were going to reach an agreement with peace, sanity, and hope in their minds. I was a firm believer that these were areas that only God could issue and perfect.

****

I had heard of Vietnam, and everybody who was in America unless infirmed had also heard as well. But if my eyes had not seen what I saw, no one – and I mean no one – could have described it. Maybe they could have, but the mind could not have possibly perceived the destruction, the desecration, and the devastation of this place.

This was no deception; what I was seeing was real. The question of whether God was here had to come to the mind of anyone who had come to this place. If ever I was thankful for my mother, it was now. She had taught me that God was so real, He was mine, I could have all of Him, including his son, Jesus the Christ, and the Holy Spirit. Because of her, I was not one who wondered if God was there. I knew He was. It didn't matter how it looked. Yet, I couldn't help but question what other men might have thought who may have never heard of God, after seeing such a sight.

****

We checked in at our duty station.

"Sergeant Gross," I heard my name, and I went quickly to the desk. I was issued my uniform, toiletries, and the necessities that we would need for daily living in Vietnam.

I listened to the rain, and it sounded like a thousand men marching in circles on a tin roof, without anywhere to go.

****

Last night was a better night of sleep than the first night since we were in our living quarters. I was indeed glad it was, as I was heading out, reporting to my post for the first time. Being alert and agile was something I always wanted to be in this environment. Making my way there, this was not Howard University. I couldn't hear the sounds of horns bleeping or cars passing by — no students walking across "the yard," as it was called. There was a solemnity that hung in the air that could be self-identified, and it was somberness. Faces were partially grimaced that went by, and I could see some men who looked weary. I was closer to my destination, and I entered the building.

"Good morning, Staff Sergeant Gross, I'm General Harmon Burns. Please have a seat."

I responded, sitting directly across from him. I could still hear the sounds of men marching, as the rain was pouring down.

He was an olive-colored man with sideburns and a thick head of hair. He could have easily been in the movies, where film critics would have adored his profile. His presence was not an intimidating one, but one that felt like a mentor upon his first words. I didn't feel the authoritative arrogance I usually felt from the past. There were those that would let you know who they were and what your position was.

"I look forward to working with you," He said, in a commanding, yet soothing voice.

"Thank you, sir," I responded.

"You will be reporting to me with information that is sensitive. Looking at your records, it is my belief that you could carry this job out in the best interest of our airmen and the United States of America," General Burns continued.

We continued talking about where I would go and where I would have to report. I listened to the intricate details of the duty and knew that this was a job that required me to execute my best skills. I had typed reports when I hadn't even seen a typewriter before, counseled college students in ROTC when I hadn't even been in college before. Now I was going to send communications back and forth, and I hadn't been in a war before. Here I was. Set. Ready. Go. God's order of command. Commands that I would have never rendered myself – ready.

****

I took my job seriously, as I knew that it had everything to do with the lives of men. That night I rerouted what I did in my head and prepared myself the best I could mentally for the night. All night I knew we were subject to hearing shots and sounds from the enemy.

Nothing about Vietnam made me feel like I was getting used to the setting. I felt to even think that meant I was in agreement with being there. I knew this was my journey now, but I couldn't say I was becoming accustomed to my routine. As the days were going by, I prepared myself mentally. Praying. Believing. Expecting. When one day was over, I was closer to my tour of one year being over.

****

I am awakened, and I sit up in my bed. It's not a sound, not a sight. I turn my head from side to side, and I just can't shake this. I leaned forward and looked for my watch, for it is too dark in the barracks to see anything, and I don't want to walk around. Every minute we are wondering when the next round of attacks could happen, so walking around in the night, leisurely like a kid with his Teddy Bear, was not what anyone would want to do. But the air that came around me had temporarily arrested my peace. It took it and held it captive and with everything it had, yet I have to fight to hold onto it.

This would go on night after night until I thought that I would bail out my peace and no longer let it be jailed to this prison that met me at 1:00 am, 2:00 am, and 3 am. I figured if I surrendered to a request, which was coming in my mind, I could get my peace back.

I figured out what it was. It wasn't familiar. I never encountered this before, and I hope I would never experience any such thing again in this lifetime. It was the smell of men who would not sit at their dinner tables again. They were not going to look in their son's and daughter's faces and see their smiles. They had already exited to the end of their journey here on earth but would be routed back to their families for a final goodbye. How many nights would this go on?

****

After your nerves had been frayed and fringed, the words of a loved one were like a balm that soothed your soul. Getting a letter was like getting a million dollars. There were some men who thought that if they read a letter, it meant they would become sensitive and not be ready for combat, but I didn't see it that way. I felt supported like someone was thinking about me, and they were encouraging me with their love. Even if I didn't see them again, their letters brought me the strength to endure.

My wife and mother-in-law sent letters virtually every day. I was told when Kim was turning over by herself and when she was eating solid foods, or pulling up by herself.

"Gross," I heard my name for the mail.

"Yeah, I know he got something good," I heard a voice say.

I chuckled inside. It was the time we were the most jovial. Vietnam was no pool hall or some juke joint. It was a cesspool of madness with no real cause or reason, in my opinion. Men were dying, and it didn't make sense.

I opened my package, and I could smell a hint of lemon. I didn't know what followed, but my nose was ready for the challenge. Unwrapping it was like a gift I wished I had gotten for Christmas when I was young, but I had gotten it right on time. Upon further inspection, it was a Lemon Cake that looked like it was waiting to be devoured. My eyes weren't the only eyes upon it. The men in my unit were waiting for a slice. I think had it been up to them; they would have gotten a piece with their fingers, breaking it off like some churches served communion.

I could taste virtually every ingredient in the cake. I had licked enough bowls and spoons when Mama made a cake to distinguish between flavors, but this time, lemon was spectacular. This was more than just lemon flavoring in the bottle. It seemed like it was a lemon that came from a grove that had a destination to Vietnam to brighten our day while satisfying our palettes and lifting our spirits out of a doleful woe.

At the first bite, I felt an exhilaration within my taste buds that burst forth with flavor that would forever be unmatched. The men in the unit were silent, telling the story that this cake required a salute of silence, meaning it was excellent.

These were peaceful times in Vietnam.

****

The rain was falling, and it didn't seem it was going to stop today. I didn't understand what was going on. Why were we tearing down a perfectly good bunker that could give us protection from the enemy? We were moving bags of sands that were piled high, weighing upward of 30-50 lbs. These bunkers were as sophisticated as they could possibly me. Some were made like a rectangular-shaped shelter. I couldn't believe what was happening.

"I don't understand why we are doing this!" one airman said.

He used a number of expletives, and I had to admit some of the same words were forming in my head; I just didn't let them out.

"Here it is, we are getting hit, and we don't know when we might be attacked, and we are tearing this down."

I think every man took a shot at saying the same thing, and how stupid this idea was to tear down what could save our lives.

The rain was shooting in our eyes, and I thought of how we were touching these sandbags. I remember the chemical Agent Orange was sprayed in Vietnam to kill all the trees so the enemy would have no place to hide during combat. Here we were, experiencing the same thing, like the protection that surrounded us was being snatched away, as we were left defenseless.

I had another thought of how we might be contaminated with this Agent Orange product. No chemical, when sprayed in the atmosphere, was just going directly to its intended destination and only engaged with that subject and not go further. I really was wondering about this. With us moving wet sandbags, I thought this was a resurrection of that chemical that was getting on our hands as we were handling the sandbags. Since I was from the farm, I knew about drifts from crops.

Now, if tearing down the bunker wasn't enough, now we were going to be horticulturalists.

"You all are going to plant flowers now. This is Base Beautification. We are going to put Rhododendrons, Azaleas, Camellias, and Gardenias in the place of the bunker. I understand there was some marijuana growing near some of the bunkers, and we are not going to have that."

I thought I heard something wrong until I heard a voice.

"Sir, you mean we are tearing down a bunker because marijuana was found?"

I didn't really know what was going to happen next.

"That's what I said. We are not going to tolerate drugs over here in our unit."

I studied the look on the guy's face that was brave enough to ask the question. I was glad he didn't pursue more to the Colonel's response. There was a possibility that it could have done more harm than good. I knew this Airman had a point, but honestly, I didn't know if it would add more work to our detail.

I had a few thoughts of my own about this duty. No Colonel should have been allowed to make us take out protection down. He should have been disciplined for this. This was not what I perceived a (superior officer); a full colonel should do. This route of decision-making was perhaps what someone would do in basic training, because of some inspection, but definitely not in Vietnam. This was war, and the lives of men were on the line. Maybe he came to Vietnam and lost all feelings and lost touch with humanity and reality. Maybe he felt this marijuana offense required discipline that was beyond the normal realm. The Colonel's logic was out of reason for the season, and even though I tried to think about his logic, I couldn't really agree with it. What it all boiled down, out of all the things I thought I would be doing in Vietnam, planting flowers was definitely not one of them.

When the day ended, I thought about how the colonel made a decision today that wasn't anywhere near the interests of the unit. I was halfway around the world, maybe even further, but I was still close to the journey of my goals. The colonel may have made decisions about "beautification," but so could I about my life. It was evident that there were some things I couldn't control, but I was going to keep going toward my goals.

I decided to write Tuskegee. I couldn't forget Booker T. Washington's statue and seeing him lift the "Veil of Ignorance" so that a young man could see that there was something else he could experience other than what he knew.

I wrote Tuskegee, requesting an application. I imagined myself on the campus, studying what I felt was the path to my calling. After being an Academic Counselor for the men at Howard University, I saw the coursework and the commitment it took to get a degree. It was truly my belief that this was something I could do after all the conversations I had with students and counseling them to keep their grades up.

I knew what I wanted to say. It didn't' require an autobiography just to ask for an application, yet I still wanted to be professional. I got everything together, and I finally got the words to say precisely what I wanted.

I put the letter inside the envelope and carefully put the stamp on it. I pressed it, patting it down, all while praying for a great response. But this wasn't going to be all. When the application arrived, I would have to send it to Tuskegee with the hope of being accepted. Today was easy. Tomorrow was another story, but I would have to give it my best. The steps I took to mail this letter felt as if I was taking a walk to my destiny.

****

"Take cover! Move it!" I heard shouting, as the sounds of rockets were exploding. Men were running to safety, turning into a chaotic scene that I had only seen captured on a cinematic reel. Only this time, this was real. Far more real than what the human mind could comprehend. Men were running so fast, as the rockets were falling, seeking protective cover as close as possible. Shrapnel, fire, shouting, and smoke were creating a hedge of disaster alone. Everything that was happening was etching upon the memories of all of us, and it was uncertain if we would even live to remember all that was happening. Everything was happening so fast, and I couldn't focus on the past or future, but the right now was more than troublesome.

Smoke was rising as rockets rained down. Then we heard a boom that had the sound of a thousand trains crashing into each other, where the mayhem would be too overwhelming for the human sight or the mind to comprehend.

"The chapel was hit." I heard an airman say. He shouted it repeatedly, while obviously feeling this was the one place he thought would have been exempt. I couldn't explain what I was seeing, but it was, at the least, horrific. Flames from the chapel could be seen from afar like a raging demon was inside. This was no scene anyone could pen; this was something that war produced, and it was the worst I had ever experienced.

My head was pounding, spinning, and all I could think about was how we had torn the bunkers down, as that could have been an additional protective shelter for the airmen to take cover. It was all a terrible experience to see with the naked eye and made for the most maddening scene one could witness. That colonel who obviously had no compassion, no judgment, or no concern, didn't see how those bunkers would have saved the lives of some men.

Every one of my five senses was activated, even taste. There was an acid taste in the air, and to inhale, it meant you could taste it. Someplace that had been hit was hot to the touch, even the next day. The smell was always troubling, but to mix it with all the sounds and horror was simply more than any human should have ever experienced.

We lost six men in that attack. All I can think about is how they could have been saved if the colonel had not ordered that the bunkers be torn down.

The scenes kept playing in my head all night. I could see men running, the sounds of men yelling, the rockets exploding, and the unspeakable disasters of humans and buildings torn apart.

I can't rest. I can't sleep. I stare into space, straight ahead, and gaze into this somewhere, hoping to find something that resembles peace. Everything my mother taught me is within me ... orbiting ... yet my mind is in a spin. I call on the Lord, and I know He is present, but my entire being is sore, including my thoughts, and they are constantly on rewind over and over again.

I recite the 23rd Psalm over and over. I find it fitting to say. Quite honestly, it's the first thing I remember, and when I say the words, "Valley of Death," it is as if the speaker of this Psalm and I are in the same place.

My mind cries out, wishing I could be beside green pastures. What I would give to be beside stills waters, and only see the clarity of it and my reflection. I began to wonder what I could do in exchange for a "restored soul." There is such a fragility within me that I wish God would outright tell me how many times I needed to cry out to him. I would love a formula. How many prayers do I need to pray? How many promises to do good do I need to make this pain go away?

****

I don't know when I fell asleep. I wake up to that smell that comes about 2 or 3 o'clock in the morning. It had a more profound presence, like an intentional visit it is making for just me. I'm beginning to wonder if it is only me, or can everyone smell the dead bodies of these men who will not return home. I wipe my forehead, shaking it like I can shake the thoughts of this reality out of it.

It's important I balance myself. I can't do it within my strength, for I take it to God. As I put my thoughts into God's thoughts, I try hard to surrender to His being. I wish I could just reach out and touch Him. I wish I could audibly hear His voice.

I close my eyes and travel back to the walnut tree, where I prayed to God for understanding. I go back to Antioch, where I am at the Mourner's bench, calling upon God's name. I travel to my mother's arms, the thermostat that cooled me when hot and warmed me when cold. All I really want now is a thermostat that would fix me and regulate my wild emotions running from longitude to latitude. I attempt to count the miracles of Christ, and I remember that God stated that nothing is too hard for Him.

Again, I don't know when I dozed off, but it is morning, and there is an idea that is sitting within my thoughts. It's like an arrow is pointing to it in my mind. This ideal would be absurd to some, but for me, I know this is God's doing. These are His thoughts, for He loves me so much that He wants me right beside those green pastures that I so dearly want to be beside.

****

"Young man, what could I do for you here?"

I thought about what I was getting ready to ask, and wondered if it was going to sound strange to the man, but I couldn't risk my still waters.

"Could I please come in ..."

I could tell this man wasn't sure where I was going, but he didn't give a judgmental crease to his forehead. He was stoic, almost statue-like, as I began to address my question.

"... to just look around and see what this final destination looks like. I just want to see what happens when the men come here."

I could feel the weight leaving my chest. My mind was beginning to be freed of so many twists and turns in that moment. I really didn't know how this man was going to respond. However, I knew I was in the right direction. I was beside the still water, and how God chose this for the restoration of my emotions, proved He was the all-wise, and all-knowing God, and not me.

I took off my hat as the mortician escorted me throughout the morgue. All those who wished to visit were welcome, but there was one condition, you had to take off your hat. I understood because these men deserved respect. As I walked around, the sight saddened me, as much as it strengthened me. All of the nights, I experienced the aroma of death that had come from this building. I knew I had to see what this place was about and retrace the story of these men. They were more than bodies. They were more than decomposition. They were more than just a place for rigor mortis to set in. These were men! These were men! I found myself screaming inside. The scent of them had haunted me in my sleep, as the wind carried it to me, awaking me night after night. And yes, this scent only an obedient act that comes from the decomposition of tissues and ligaments. However, I couldn't accept that this shouldn't be the last thing we remember that came from them. I wanted more for these men. No, I didn't know them personally, and I couldn't speak on their behalf, but I felt if I could see them, I would have closure. Perhaps, if I could see them, the last chapter of their journey in Vietnam, then I could at least acknowledge their worth.

This one-story building, where nothing was intricate, but the presence of these men made it a stately building. These men had given their lives for their country, and in Vietnam, their lives had ended. Some looked incredibly young, and I wondered what their dreams were. Did some want to be fathers or firemen? I wondered had they planned to be teachers or politicians. Those that were fathers, what now?

"Do you want to go on," the mortician asked.

I had paused for a moment without knowing. These questions had surrounded me, and even though I couldn't answer them, the fact that they were coming was just as important as viewing them. I could see a complete picture of what a young man could possibly be if he did not come to war. I knew I had dreams because I had had them since the time I was at Talladega County Training School.

"Yes, sir," I said.

For a moment, I questioned how dreams are born. Did everyone's dream come from the desire to do better because they didn't have the necessities of life? Or, did people just want to be greater, even if they started great?

I realized I was still standing in the same spot as I was before, but the mortician was patient. I looked at a young man again and knew that every man had to have dreams beyond Vietnam.

I saw men who were in aluminum steel caskets. In a few days, they would be back home. I whispered prayers to myself when I saw these men while praying for the peace that only God could give their families.

I could see men on tables, who had not been dressed. They were waiting ... for their turn.

The scent that I smelled at night seemed not to be present. Maybe seeing these men and assigning a life that I thought they were living before made me see that they would be remembered for their duty in Vietnam.

I saw areas where there were parts from bodies. I paused again. This was hard. Deep breaths filled the cavity of my chest. I look and then I looked away. I folded my lips on the inside of my mouth, holding every emotion I could keep within. The mortician knew what I felt, for I had told him how I had cried every time I passed the morgue.

He didn't rush me, but let me have a minute. Within this time of viewing, I chose to believe that if there were those who returned to their families by route of just their name alone, that bravery, courage, and valor preceded them.

****

When I received the mail, I felt some anxiousness leave my body. It was a letter from Patricia, and I felt the sun was coming out in the ever so rainy Vietnam. It appeared Washington, D.C. was still holding rallies and marches because people were honestly tired of being mistreated, overlooked, and seen as less than. It appeared to be a time that rights were desired and needed for lots of populations. But most of all, I loved hearing about Kim and all the new things she was doing.

Patricia could describe how Kim was progressing with a crisp descriptive pen. I could see her bouncing Kim up and down, just as I saw her last in Dulles Airport. She told me Kim was a little fussy these days. She didn't know the reason, but maybe it was because Kim now had some table food. Kim was now forming a few words and was walking up and down the hall, holding the walls. She had put the crawling adventures behind her and was now actually running.

I smiled and could not have been happier that Patricia was doing well with Kim while I was gone. It had to be strenuous to have a child and do everything alone, from the bathing to the feeding, from the diaper changes to the lifting, and from the rocking to the soothing. If it weren't for being in Vietnam, I would be right there, doing what a father ought to do.

I had much respect for Patricia. She sent letters to me like she was receiving a salary. They were informative, comforting and gave me a great outlook on living. It was a day-by-day event in Vietnam. No one could predict the future, and even if God would make a deal and reveal it, I wondered who would want to know. I didn't, and would rather walk by faith.

****

The earth beneath us seems to shake violently. Rockets were raining down again. Even though I had seen this before, it was still just as new as the first time. How do you prepare for battle and safety all at the same time? The haunting of "Hows" kept warming my head. I began to hear men shouting, over and over again. I could hear an officer telling men where to go and take cover quickly. This time we were not over by the "Beautification Side" of the base; we could run into a bunker. Being next to someone was no problem. There was no such thing as "going to the back" of the bunker. We were brothers. We were a team. There was no such thing as color. The "such thing" was called survival.

More rockets poured down, and each one rang louder and more thunderous than the last. I could hear men saying, "Oh God," and "take cover," "Get in there." But there were some indistinguishable sounds that were muddied, yet everyone knew what they were actually saying. "We gonna die, we gonna die!" and this was not an indictment against their military training or values. This was their brutal truth. It was their raw honesty. Fear was no doubt at the forefront, and when it was in that position, mortality was the only thing that could be thought about.

I honestly didn't know how the men in war could even process it without knowing God. Who did they call out to? Who did they cast their cares upon? Where did they really run to in these times? No one could protect themselves. There was no self-reliance in Vietnam, and if there was, it would never stand up to the airstrikes, artillery strikes, rockets, and other unexpected ammo.

We had been hit with 106 rounds of 122-millimeter Russian-made rockets when the chapel burned down, and hearing these rockets, I can determine how many we are getting right now. I began to repeat, "Lord helps us, Lord helps us," with the mind I had left. I was saying this silently, but my heart was carrying all my prayers to the Lord out loud. I closed my eyes and prayed this would be over soon, and the rockets would not find us.

I managed to remember the old people from Antioch who stand up and testify. The recall of those words alone sent moments of peace to cover me: "Let the words of my mouth and the meditation of my heart be acceptable in thy sight. O Lord, my strength and my redeemer."

****

There was no such thing as normal in Vietnam, but working with General Burns made life as normal as it could get. I couldn't quite figure out if working on duty with him was better for my mental well-being during the day, or whether things were better when I was in bed at night, the time most people relax. However, there was no such thing as relaxing in Vietnam. When walking in the halls at work, it was no surprise to see the South Vietnamese employed on the base. This was an agreement between the United States Government and the South Vietnam Government to house U.S. troops on their base in exchange for jobs for local people working there. This must have been some win-win situation between the two. I'm sure this boosted their economy, and at the same time, it enlarged our cemeteries in the U.S.

As we worked with the South Vietnamese on the base, we never knew who these men really were. We could not tell if these men held grudges against the U.S. for fighting them in their country, or whether they stood on the grounds of neutrality.

How could the U.S. send men to war like this? Here in Vietnam, we are surrounded by the natives who could kill us at any minute, being that we are so close to them. Then, there were the North Vietnamese enemies from the outside, who would no sooner pick us off like a target in target practice when the time was right.

After a quiet reminiscence, I concluded that it was just about normal with General Burns. It was evident he was a man who was effective, efficient, but never arrogant.

I had work that I sometimes would seek his advice about its proper disposition.

"Sergeant Gross, I hired you feeling well assured that you can decide to handle this mission in the way you feel it should be handled."

I got ready to speak, but he was not finished.

"I've seen your file, and I have the highest confidence in you. You don't have to ask me about the steps in executing an order; I have complete trust in you that it will be done properly."

I know I said thank you, but my mind was so in the midst of an enchantment that a general was fully trusting my judgment. It was not often that I would meet people in authority who didn't want to fully reign over the "How's of Execution." This conversation allowed me to know who he truly was, as he was one of humility, compassion, and didn't need to make all the decisions to feel important.

****

I thought of home after meeting with General Burns, my childhood home of Alabama, and Mama in particular. I could feel her prayers, knowing she was constantly partitioning God's love and protection to be around me. I wanted her to let her know that I was in full appreciation of her love and prayers, so I thought I would write to her. Working under a general like General Harmon Burns was an indication that God had given me favor, and I felt the prayers from my mother, Patricia, and everyone who was praying for me played a part in me having this favor.

As night came, if it could be called settling down, I picked up my pen and paper and projected my thoughts to Mama.

Dear Mama,

I already know that your prayers are here with me. Every day I wake up, I realize that because of the God you taught me to listen to and hear His voice for myself, I am able to rest under the shadow of the Almighty. Our days here are still rainy, and each day is unpredictable as expected, but I am casting my cares upon Him.

How are you and everyone back in Talladega? I know that's a lot of people to think about in one sentence, but I'm certain you know who I might be thinking about. How's Papa, Janet, and Thomas? Please tell them all I send my love.

Patricia tells me that Kim is growing like a weed. I can't wait to see them when I return, and see what kinds of differences a year can make.

I don't remember when I went to sleep, but the peace of God was upon me. When I awakened, the letter and pen were still in my hand, and I had written pages and pages but had not given a closing. I signed, 'Love, Junior,' and placed it in an envelope and backed it with the address. I got ready to fall asleep again, but I could hear rockets falling, leaving me wondering if my letter would ever get home.

****

The sound of rockets falling caused anxiety to run high, while thoughts of horrid fear tend to exceed the courage everyone believes they have. This is now the third attack, and still, I could not prepare for the rumbling, the running, and rage that the rockets seem to have as they come down. I could hear those terrible screams again of men running to the safest place they could find. It is almost like everyone is stripped of their mental faculties.

Everyone needs someone to believe in now, and it is not just themselves, not just family, not just friends. I'm huddled into this area of protection, and it is painfully hard to remember the shadow of the Almighty. I do, however, remember it, but every time you hear a rocket fall, your mind believes it could be the last. There is the thought where life, as you know it, is fading away, leaving, and you have to hold on tightly to God's unchanging hand. I wonder if the other men actually have a God to call upon.

These rounds had started up at about ten o'clock at night, and then there was silence. But I knew we were not "out of the woods" yet. We stayed in place, searching in every corner of our mind for what the possible outcome could be. Time seemed to crawl, and everything that made a noise made us tense up and made our hearts beat like a drum. There were a certain number of rounds that would come and then silence, like the calm after a storm. As soon as you settled into sleep for a couple of hours, then by one or two o'clock in the morning, the rockets started again. We were in between the two-hour period, so I knew it would be time again soon.

The book of Psalms made for great comfort because all I could do right in these moments was to "lift my eyes unto the hills, whence cometh my help." In sixty minutes, this could be the end. No one spoke about it. There was no dialogue, but you could tell if you look into the eyes of fellow airmen, they were thinking about the same thing.

The angst on their face could speak a thousand words. The deep breaths they took and the pauses were the scenic stops along with their thoughts. We were all wondering would we see our loved ones as well as the dreams and goals we had.

I began to pray silently. That was the beauty of a God that we could speak to without ever opening our mouths. Whenever you needed to be silent, God could still hear our pleas.

"NOOOOOOOOO!!!...Oh, God...NOOOOOOOO!!!!" came from the mouths of the airmen. A rocket had fallen, and the shouts from the men fell openly. Some of the men were shouting non-stop.

Just like clockwork, every two hours, the rockets fell, and over and over again, we were frantic and emotionally fragile, wondering what was going to happen next.

When the artillery strike was over, we tried to put ourselves back together. I saw airmen with cigarettes, holding them with two fingers looking down on the ground. There was no writing there, but I could tell they were in search of something other than the unknown. They continued to look as if they were in chapters two and three of a novel. Their thumbs and forefingers met as they were drawing on them like children trying to get the last part of the milkshake in a cup. Whether some were smoking or just thinking, we were all looking for the message that this whole ordeal was over and we could go back to our normal lives.

Some of the guys had finished their tour, and the next stop for them was to return home. We were glad for those who were leaving, and we would be glad when our turn came also, but we had heard the news that made us all sad. Two guys were ready to return to the U.S., packing to leave, but a rocket fell. It exploded and landed right beside them and blew their legs off. A deep breath and bad news was seemingly all we could get while in Vietnam.

CHAPTER 45 – LOOKING TOWARD THE FUTURE

I held the envelope in my hand. I could feel the adrenalin running through my body. It was like the feeling of fuel being poured inside me, revving me up to drive freely down the highway of life. It was the address that made me imagine myself on the journey of my dreams. No destination, disaster, or devastation was going to annihilate them. The words Tuskegee Institute rose to my eyes. A happy feeling met me, and once again, outside receiving letters from Patricia and home, this was a peaceful time in Vietnam. When I opened it, I saw the letter thanking me for my interests, and then the application. I looked at it carefully and saw the things that I had to fill out. My strategy was to write my answers on a separate sheet of paper and then and later transfer the answers to the application. I was a candidate who had a General Equivalency Diploma, formerly an Academic Advisor to students at Howard University, and currently serving in the Air Force and currently on tour in Vietnam. I thought of all the things that I was that could perhaps show I would be a serious student at Tuskegee.

I remembered Tuskegee Institute was known as the Black Harvard. Surely, my application would be screened and observed closely. I imagined a panel of people who would read every line and make a decision toward my fate.

There was no need to wonder or imagine what the selection process was going to actually include. I needed to present myself on the application as exactly who I was, and in a way where I would be seen as the ultimate candidate.

I saw students at Howard, and I had seen their records. There were courses they had taken in high schools that I hadn't taken. I had seen Calculus, Algebra II, and Human Anatomy. However, I had not taken any courses like that at Talladega County Training School, partly because I left two years early, but the classes I did have, I still deemed those enriching.

Thinking and thinking into the night, I wrote down a list of courses I took, which I thought prepared me for college. Of course, Mr. Armstrong's Vocational Agricultural class was the first to come to mind. This class had science, math, a world of calculation, and exploration. It was designed to cultivate young men to be prepared for the world. Whether we wanted to be farmers, factory workers, businessmen, or others, Mr. Armstrong had a curriculum that no one under him could depart from it. We learned how to manipulate problems in ways whereby we could increase the production of a product and increase profit.

I added to the list with things I had done. Remembering my peanut farm was something to include. This was a small undertaking. I had to plant, maintain, and harvest the crop, and to see how what one puts in something directly affects what comes out, was an even bigger lesson.

I had work to do. It was up to me to show who I was and let Tuskegee Institute know I was worthy of being a student on its campus. I continue to make lists, groups, ideas. There was no need to fear this process. Everything I could be fearful of had already happened to me. Knowing I might never get back to Patricia, Kim, and my family alive, was already the most haunting fear. Thusly, the lines on the application, and the anticipation of whether I would state the right things and be seen as a model candidate was not fear to me.

Like anything else, I was going to have to put this in front of God, and ask Him to guide my thoughts, my words, and the application process. In actuality, I believed it was Him that invoked the strong feelings within me at the Booker T. Washington statue.

****

A little time had gone by since I received the application from Tuskegee, yet I used it wisely. There had been no intense artillery strikes. That alone gave my awareness of being a sense of calm. However, even when I had a little downtime, I was thinking. I had nothing else to do but pray that I would leave Vietnam and be reunited with all my loved ones, and pray I would get back to Tuskegee Institute. All the lists I made and many ways I thought I would present myself to Tuskegee was forming in my mind, creating a tapestry of tangles. But then, like a thread hanging from a cloth, if you pulled the right one, the whole thing would unravel. That's what I needed. My thoughts to unravel, so I could lay all my ideas out end-to-end and then put them back together to form the perfect application.

So, I asked myself some questions, the same ones I thought perhaps might be asked. Why do you want to attend Tuskegee? What is it that you want to study? I thought that was a different question, or was it? Yes, it was because I could want to study a subject, but not at certain colleges. Now, I was getting somewhere. The first thought that came to my mind was Booker T. Washington. I thought of his walk to Hampton University and his deep drive to be an educated man. Then there was Washington at the Tuskegee building, where his students were making their own bricks out of straw and mortar. His ambitions seemed to be everywhere when I was on the campus, and that was even if the statue of him and the slave was not there. It was simply evident that someone thought about how education should be. All things produced right on the campus, from the produce to the milk. Why would I not want to study on campus such as this one, one that taught the importance of self-sustaining?

And then there was George Washington Carver. Why did he work at Tuskegee when he originally intended to stay for a couple of years, and he later stayed over four decades? I had read about him, and I theorized that he saw Washington's mission for Tuskegee, and how he, too, had a mission of research that had benefited Tuskegee and the world. Accordingly, he was invested in this institution, where he would have concerts, traveling, and playing the piano to raise funds for the school.

That covered one question, but I suppose the question, "What do you want to study?" would be a valid one.

I knew myself well enough that I wanted a science-related major. Along with the application, I had the catalog of studies, and when I saw the Veterinary School, that was where my interest pooled. I loved nature from the time I could even remember, and all science that comes with it. But I was interested in research with animals, especially after seeing animals when I visited in 1956. It appeared that the Vet School would provide me an experience of learning that would challenge me to want to learn everything from its foundation. Additionally, I would be able to speak about the origin of anything scientific, as well as its purpose.

I knew there were more questions I needed to focus on, and they're probably about my strengths and weaknesses. How was I going to answer those? As I began to write down what I thought, I was very candid with myself. It was important for me to very honest with myself, even where I thought the shortcomings were. This was the time for me to be my own academic counselor and seek to move the weaknesses to the strength column. I knew, perhaps, they couldn't be there overnight. But I challenged myself just as I counseled the students at Howard, to get help from those who could tutor them in the area they needed until they could understand the concept or subject matter.

I continued with my questions, and I believed I knew myself better than I ever had before.

****

I was on my way to the incinerator right on the base's perimeter. It was evident that this place was designed to be close by, but not too far to handle official business. An armed guard always accompanied me to this destination, and that alone told the seriousness of this mission. There were classified materials that I had to declassify, by route of having them burned in this incinerator. I could see the smoke from a distance before we arrived, and yet it made me wonder how many secrets/strategic operations were actually turned into the traces of smoke. How many were most effective? How many would be repeated? Which ones were actually the best? Strategic operations and plans that were created were now little pieces of carbon, along with other particles, a black cloud that trailed or loomed in the air depending upon the wind. This information couldn't even be filed under lock and key. It was far too sensitive and far too revealing. It was important that the enemy knew no plan of action or any avenues that would give them an edge. In this war, we didn't know who our enemy was; therefore, no stone could be left unturned.

This was a war where we didn't know who the enemy was. This made it mentally detaining. That was one of the reasons we had to burn classified materials. We worked with the Vietnamese on the base, and the same eyes that looked at us with a smile could very well be the same ones that could kill us later. This war was a mental fight, as well as a physical fight — a fight with a person in or out of uniform. Quite simply, you could be standing next to the person that could cut your throat. One of the reasons I didn't get a haircut on base was that I didn't trust a Vietnamese behind me using a razor, where I would be held captive, even if it were in my own mind. When I first got to Vietnam, I did go. However, the thoughts of what could happen were far too haunting. One night, the Vietcong breached the perimeter that same night we were hit. They first hit us with mortars, and then machine guns, AK-47s. Our guards didn't back down or move to let them take over, but that night 32 men were killed. There was another step that the U.S. troops could do, and it was customary. The enemies killed on the base would be laid out on the base prostrate, side-by-side, to see if anyone could identify them. I looked at all the men, taking a closer look, and what I saw next solidified all my theories. There lay three men that were from the barbershop, and right there, I experienced a feeling that was beyond eerie, simply because I recognized them, and they were working on the base.

We were getting closer to the incinerator, and the smoke was streaming out as if it were glad to rid the secrets that had been devised to either kill the Vietcong and North Vietnamese or save the U.S. troops.

I had a job to do, and I had to burn these classified materials. Looking around, I could see the armed guard with his M-16. That was comforting to have that protection, but I had a memory of the time when the U.S. had killed 5,000 North Vietnamese, and there was a mass grave dug with bulldozers. All the bodies were dumped and buried in this same area on the perimeter of the base. This was a big field that was turned into a mass grave. This was unnerving to me. But it was no time to ponder; I completed my mission and left. After this time, I no longer wanted to go there. Consequently, it did not help matters that an enemy soldier slipped by on the mass grave at night. His motive could only be imagined. This was the night right after the troops had dug the grave, so this enemy must have been waiting for more U.S. troops to come back to see what or who he could find. This must have been masterfully planned on his part, but again, who was our enemy? Who could we trust? This enemy was one that was outside, but what about the ones that we're right on the same base with us and looking at us in the eye?

The stench of Vietnam continued to linger all around. It wasn't only the bodies of men; it was the scent of rain. This was not the scent of rain, where the promise of revival was in the midst, but this was the aroma of mold and land decaying and something that just wasn't as it should be.

This was not a place that was currently designed for anyone to be, whether passing through or stationed for a season. This place was a devastation that honestly didn't have to be. The United States didn't need to be here. This was a war that didn't have to be. Yes, I was a part of the military, and it didn't make me less dedicated or unpatriotic to think this. As a matter of fact, many of us serving actively or reserve, or in direct combat or not, these were our thoughts. We were no less committed, but thousands of troops were dying, and what was really going to be the end result for fighting?

I had to pull myself back from these thoughts. Even in the midst of this war zone, I chose to find the hope that propelled me forward. That hope was first, my Lord, as I remembered the song, "My hope is built on nothing less than Jesus' blood and righteousness." For a moment, I wondered how some of the troops coped with things that happened. Had they "subscribed" to the God I knew? Who did they turn to? I thought of this often, for I wondered myself, who would I turn to if I did not know Christ, himself?

Vietnam was a place of just as many mental complexities as there were physical ones. To navigate around them was not anything I would want to do alone, and with my own might. This was when you needed the Almighty.

As I was "banking and building hope," I found the letters from Patricia and my mother truly sustaining. All the new things about Kim and the happenings in Washington, D.C., along with Talladega, gave me a sense of harmony, even though I was surrounded by discord.

But there was another thing that kept me wading in hope. I had mailed my application to Tuskegee Institute. I believed that the application represented me to the capacity that I could be picked out of a crowd. I was sincere, honest, revealing my strengths, weaknesses, my desires beyond college, and what I wanted to contribute to my society, my people, my community. All I could do in the meantime was wait patiently. I didn't choose to consider a Plan B if I wasn't accepted to Tuskegee. Not at this time anyway. I was between "The Valley of the Shadows of Death" and the possibility of going to the Tuskegee Institute. So, I thought it would be deemed appropriate if I could just focus on surviving and winning.

****

"Gross!"

I moved to the middle to get the mail. I had a few letters, and I felt sorry for them. They didn't get any mail. It did, however, seem that some men got more than others. I didn't know the reason, but I knew that some of us share our news with each other, which seemingly helps the spirits of others.

"You got a business envelope," someone yelled out.

Actually, this fellow soldier had seen it before I had. I had all the mail in my hand with my concentration on a letter from Patricia.

"He probably wrote someone to send him something," another soldier said.

"What are you requesting anyway?"

The questions kept coming, but I was opening Patricia's letter and answering at the same time.

"Sometimes I want information about a college or about some college courses," I responded.

"I don't see why you would want to even go to college. You've done alright thus far," was the response.

"There's a world we got to compete in after Vietnam."

"Oh, here he goes, talking about college."

I put the rest of the mail in my hand into my bag and concentrated even more on the letter from Patricia. I had to realize that everybody didn't share my thoughts on education, and I didn't need a show of hands to decide what I should do with my life.

****

Certainty Meets Me in the Bowels of Hell

I gazed at the envelope. My heart picked up multiple beats when I saw the words, Tuskegee Institute. I thought for a moment. Do I tear into this envelope, or do I just sit here and guess what I think the outcome is? I began to think, if I didn't get accepted, surely there was another path to the journey that God would direct. Would it be Howard? Well, I had been there, not as a student, but I knew enough about the campus and the academic side of things that I would navigate through it well. Actually, I would have applied to Howard, but I have to first honor my promise to myself to go back to Tuskegee as a student. That statue with Booker T. Washington and the slave had an impact when I saw it that stayed with me throughout the years. I could not put it aside or put it to the back of my mind. Somedays, even the vision in my mind got stronger. Washington is lifting the veil of ignorance from the slave so he would see that he simply could when all of his life, he thought he couldn't. No amount of despair that had crossed my path, no kind of trial and not even war could change my mind about applying to Tuskegee. Going there would mean a new expense, along with a new baby and wife. But, I didn't see it as an expense. This was an investment toward my future that no one could take away.

I looked at the envelope while holding it this time, and looking at how it was sealed on the back. Behind this seal was an acceptance that could put me on my desired way, or it was a denial that would cause me to reassess my steps to my future.

Before I opened the envelope, I wanted to make sure I was going to be alright. If I didn't get into Tuskegee, was I going to be okay with the idea and apply somewhere else? Could I? Would I be able to apply again at a later date? What if they wanted me to take some courses and then have me to re-apply? I entertained all of these ideas, and again, I wanted to be certain that I could face the true reality of either outcome. I knew where I was academically throughout the years. There were some strengths I have, but I had some challenges. I was college-prepared because I knew how to read for what I needed, ask for what I didn't know, and present what I needed to show. In my best thoughts, all my experiences prepared me for academic life on the campus of Tuskegee.

I looked at the letter again, and my heart was ready. I was going to be okay, whichever way it was. God was the author and finisher of my life, and if he had another path for me, I was going to be okay with it. What I was proud of most was that I had gone through the application process, and to analyze who I was as a student was rewarding in itself.

I slid my fingers under the seal and lifted it gently. There was no reason to tear it open like a wild man. I figured I would save this as a souvenir and look at it 60 plus years later.

Unfolding the letter, I felt a sense of calm that surrounded me. The extra heartbeats that were once in my chest had moved to normal.

Dear...

I stopped reading and decided to look for just the words that meant yes or no.

I scanned the letter up and down, and I don't know when I stopped. The smile on my face just couldn't be moved. My cheeks were virtually under my eyes and couldn't come down. When I saw the words that I was accepted, I couldn't imagine the happiness that filled my heart. I immediately thanked God for this opportunity and promised Him that I would do my very best and make the most of a college education.

****

Who was I going to tell first that I had been accepted to Tuskegee Institute? I could not contain my happiness.

The expression on my face must have had a glow, so much that the guys in the unit wanted to know more.

"It's about that envelope, isn't it?" someone said.

I waited to see what everyone was going to say next, and just like I thought, the murmurs were coming.

"It's that college you want to go to, isn't it? I don't know why you would want to be going?" another voice chimed in.

I let the men have the discussion all by themselves. Proving to them why I wanted to better my life was not at the top of my priority list. If they wanted a seminar on how to get to college, this wasn't the setting for it. The atmosphere that was set up here was one that was for joking and having fun at my expense. Actually, according to the experiences we were having in Vietnam, if they wanted to take shots and say whatever it was they wanted, I was mature enough to let it happen. If these were moments that were giving them relief from the unknown, where rockets were falling, and the questions of whether death would be a visitor, I chose to let this be a stage of reprieve.

I think I heard the laughter and the thoughts of these men go on and on, which seemed like hours. If education was not what they wanted to pursue, I held no judgment about it.

I found my pen and paper and began sharing this good news with Patricia and Mama. I could only imagine what they would think when they read the actual lines. Patricia would be happy and overjoyed. She had long known my dream to attend Tuskegee. I surmised that Mama, however, would go all the way back to the day I fished with a bucket, catching a number of Bluegill fish at six-years-old. She would connect that if I had the ingenuity to fish at that age, lowering a bucket to let the fish come in, I would be able to do many more things each stage of my life.

I was so glad to have such an encouraging mother. She was always inspiring and giving me hope for the things that I did from the time I was a little boy. I wanted to make sure to tell her that in the letter I was preparing to write. As much as she would be glad to hear from me and wanted to know I was still alive, I thought she should hear about how encouraging she was to me and how I credited her for all of the successful moments I had experienced.

****

A new year had come in, and it was finally January 1968, and I had just four months to get back to the United States. Each day I longed to be back with Patricia and Kim and just be back in the land that carried a sense of normality. All the things that happened when I was in the U.S. that were not ideal were absolutely no big deal to me now. I felt I could navigate through the most powerful of storms because what I had experienced here in Vietnam was absolutely no match for the world as I had known it.

Clouds were moving across the sun rays, which made for what could be called a beautiful day in Vietnam. It was the God made gifts that were beautiful here, and if you really looked for them, they existed. If you allowed the devastation of war to surround the mind, no beauty could permeate the mind. Additionally, as I sat outside, I also reviewed all the pleasantries that I had in my mind. I had been a blessed man where God had bestowed upon me two great things; good health and the desires of my heart.

I decided to join the men outside who were smoking, right outside where we worked.

"It's a pretty nice day out here," a man said.

"Yeah, it sure is," another one replied.

"We don't get many of these," I stated, "and if we do, we got to bring the sunshine ourselves in our minds."

I remembered so much rain, day I and day out when I first arrived in Vietnam. It was so much like men marching over and over.

Our conversations continued, but I felt something. There was a stillness in the air that I couldn't explain. I could hear the silence that stood out even through the conversation. This feeling did not leave, and I couldn't shake this perception.

I had the feeling to go back inside and leave this area. The others followed. It was evident that we had a good break, with rays of sunshine and a conversation that energized us to finish the day strong.

I reached for a file and proceeded to work on the assignment General Burns had given me.

As soon as I had the file in my hand, I couldn't believe what I heard next. There was a whistling sound that rushed by, like a rocket taking off. The sound eventually became distant and faint, and when it was silent, there was a boom with an echo like I had never heard before. It sounded like a tragedy rode along with it, and devastation was going to closely follow. I saw men getting down, crawling, and the fear in their eyes told what they were feeling.

There was a thunder and lightning sound that could be magnified a thousand times, and I still could not accurately tell the horror of the sound. We had been under what I called three significant attacks, but this one had a sound that one would imagine coming from the fury of Hell. How anyone could think during this time had to be dependent on a lot of things. The Air Force had trained us for combat, but the mental preparation of what was happening at this moment made me wonder if it had been enough. I called on the name of the Lord, but for a moment, I had a "but" that filled the inside of my mind. The rockets from this artillery strike poured down like the rain that I had seen so often in Vietnam. That "but" stayed in my head, and I continued to pray. I was looking for relief or refuge, anything that would make this whole thing stop. With every strike that came down, my mind was like a machine that was moving at a fast pace; trying to have a linear thought was difficult. I couldn't think of anything but whether I would survive in the next ten seconds. Nothing was promised, and nothing really mattered. I was in a state of mind of just being there in one location, in a state of helplessness, and you wait and wonder with thoughts that travel, and there's no way to keep up with them. They keep moving and moving, and all the questions, "When will this be over?" continuously comes to the mind.

My human mind and my human eyes could not see the end of the "man-made storm." I breathe and breathe, and I couldn't feel my breath. I couldn't hear anything but rockets falling, and I felt like the very next one could fall right on our bunker; the sound was so close. Then, finally, I did something that I didn't question whether it was right or wrong, appropriate, or inappropriate.

I opened my mouth and spoke.

"Lord, you are the father of the most high, and the one that I trust. God, I believe that you are the one who can help us in the midst of these times."

I said this prayer out loud. I was not embarrassed, nor did I worry about what anyone was thinking. Like a fountain with water that springs forth, this is what my prayer did. It rose and came forward, effortlessly. Yet, it was not poetic, nor was I trying to make it that way. I wanted peace, solitude, and refuge. I wanted God to hear my cry, and quite honestly, I felt that if I didn't say it out loud, I wasn't sure God could hear me.

I was lying on my abdomen, and I prayed for what seemed like hours. I had no method by which to measure, nor did I need one because I was talking with the Most High. Nothing seemed real, yet the reality of what was happening made me wonder if anything in my life would be the same. I wondered what God was thinking. Did God feel I had betrayed Him for trading my silent prayers for a thunderous one because I felt He could not hear my prayers in the midst of rockets falling that seemed to destroy the base along with my perception?

The rockets finally stopped. All of us were silent, but we could almost hear what we all were thinking. There was anguish on the faces of the men that was not going to leave any time soon, and nor would it be leaving their minds.

The next day came, and we truly didn't know when it arrived. We were still at the scene of the artillery strike. If sadness had been tangible, we would have been able to measure it, as well as carry it by the bucket full.

"I don't want any men working today," the voice of General Harmon Burn announced.

Some men didn't know if they had heard him right, because they were sure what he meant. He was not the average General that one would encounter. He was sympathetic, compassionate, and knew we needed to be soothed in a manner that would keep our sanity.

"Go and order steaks and beer, and the only thing I want these men to do today is to eat and drink all they want today," General Burns said to an assistant.

All of our minds were numb. We could barely comprehend the happenings of the day, and General Burns knew it. That's why he wanted us to have a day of rest, where we could retreat and not dwell in the agonizing memory of what had happened.

"I know why we didn't die last night, Sgt. Gross," one of my fellow airmen said to me. "It was because you prayed, and we heard you praying."

I heard him, and I wondered whether this was providentially arranged all along that I would pray out loud, so someone else could hear and testify on behalf of the glory of God. I continued to listen to him as he talked about how he could feel the heat of the rockets when they had hit the next building over.

When I felt God couldn't hear me, I had to also recognize that this was an absolute admission of human frailty. How could the God who could hear me ever so lovingly around the walnut tree, not be able to hear me now? Did I allow the fear to come and take over my spiritual constitution completely and not let me have faith to know that when I prayed silently, in the quiet whispers, that He could answer? I realized that even if I did feel this way, God was still able to answer prayers of mine to help the minds of someone else. When I was praying, surely, I didn't know anyone else was listening in such a chaotic time, but it was evident that God did.

As the day went on, I never saw so many men crying in one place. The more we ate and drank, the more the tears came. It was a time when we were so fragile within our emotions, and our thoughts had patterns that were choppy like ships in a stormy sea. We were thankful that we had survived and that God had heard my prayers. I was also thankful that I had been assigned to work for General Burns, who saw the shape of our emotional being while realizing we needed some time to recover.

****

For just a little while, we couldn't see Vietnam for what it was – a war zone. General Burns had ordered a detail to hang parachute material up, where briefly we could have a shady respite from the blistering sun, if only for a brief time, so we could heal.

The next day the tears were still coming, some were slowing down, and then there were those that had stopped but had not dried. That's how it was with tears from Vietnam, there were so many, and they seemed to join in with all the raindrops that came in Vietnam. There seemed to be something that could sadden the very existence in these parts.

I saw the sun shining, and it shone like it was on assignment to shine brightly in spite of what was happening in Vietnam. I thought about this for a moment. If the sun was on assignment, doing what it had been called to do, and the sounds, fire, dust, and all manner of devastation did not stop it, then I was going to move forward in spite of how I felt.

The news traveling about the airstrike seemed to continue throughout the day. It was evident the narrative was going to tint the very memory of everyone who heard. We had heard that one man was sleeping, and he never woke up when he was hit. I wanted to believe that was the best way to go. He had no memory of what happened. Then, there was a man who was split from his chest down to his stomach, and on his way to the hospital, he died calling his mother, and I wondered if his mother somehow intuitively heard him. Was she at the line hanging out clothes, was she baking biscuits, or wherever she was, did she hear his voice? The unit rushed fervently to get him to the hospital down the street, but it would be too late.

The part that played over and over in my mind was that his mother was going to see an unknown car turn into her lane. I wondered what she was going to be doing at the time. The words that these men would deliver would echo in her mind all the days she would live.

As the news continued coming, I saw a man whom I knew laugh and laugh and couldn't stop during the artillery strikes. What was going through his mind is one that we couldn't calculate. Finally, he was pulled to safety, but we wondered what was happening to him. Was he in shock? We didn't know the answer; we just felt that fear had a way of bringing emotions out that no one understood. Just as prayer was my way of dealing with all of this chaos, somehow laughter was his. Some men in the troop didn't understand why these phenomenons happened, but it was obvious that they were coping mechanisms.

When we left the sanctuary that General Burns created for us, there was still a heaviness that was on the minds and shoulders of us all. Even though it's the next day, we are actually still in yesterday's shadow.

I looked toward the sun again. Its rays were bright and seemingly reaching toward land. I supposed that I would be just as determined as the beams coming down and put one foot forward to the next assignment.

I prayed that somehow my memory of this active devastation would all be a blur and that it would not last in the clear, crisp form as it was today. Maybe someday in my life, I would be able to calculate and tally the purpose of why Vietnam was a part of my journey and why I had to see the things I saw during this period of my life.

My prayers were answers, and I was indeed thankful to be able to survive the terrifying moment I had yet experienced in Vietnam. When the next one would come, I did not know, and nor was I anxiously waiting for it to come.

****

CHAPTER 46 – COMING HOME FROM WAR

My time in Vietnam had come to an end, and this had been the longest year I had ever experienced. I had missed a year in Patricia's and Kim's life, and I wondered if I had missed anything in my own life. What I was really thinking was whether I would have been different had I never come to Vietnam. Yet, I stopped my thoughts in their tracks. I had to understand that Vietnam was a chapter in my journey that was supposed to be there. I was blessed and very fortunate. Actually, I had my life, and I was leaving Vietnam with it.

I got on the plane with an uneasy feeling that hung close to me like some predicted omen, determined to loom around uninvited. My mind was racing, yet I had not gone into the state of fidgeting. No matter what I did, I could not get satisfied. I shifted my weight to one side, then back to the other and no relief. It was about 9:00 in the morning, and we were waiting for takeoff. This wait resembled the agony of the man in hell, asking Abraham to send Lazarus to dip the tip of his finger in cool water to cool his tongue – waiting for relief, but no relief coming.

I was glad to be leaving Vietnam, but the wait was like some exaggerated expression that couldn't be paused. It went on and on, and I wished to find the off switch. Everything I had seen, experienced, smelled, stepped over, or moved across, was sitting right at the base of my mind.

Finally, when the plane took off, I lost all sense of my anxiety. It flew away. The omen that seemed as if it was ordered to be with me was now gone, and I realized then that it was simply Vietnam that had carved this feeling into my being. This was a place that should have been off-limits to decent people but was instead ravished by greedy and dirty people with an agenda. There were too many deaths, too many useless deaths, and there was no way I could possibly believe that death was useful. Perhaps I could have defended this war if this had been ordered by God, but I knew that this was no “God ordered” war.

When we were over a body of water, I felt a sense of peace that had risen up within me. My body moved to a relaxed state when I saw the coast of Vietnam as the plane was leaving the land.

I knew I had been right. It was this place, Vietnam, that had given me this sense of continuous anxiety. If the plane had fallen into the water, and I had died right then, I would have been at peace with it, because I just didn't want to die in Vietnam. Everything pointed to this being a God-forsaken place ... that should have been off-limits to humankind. Why would I ever want my body left in such a place?

As were boarding, I knew no men on the plane. I saw men getting off ready to come into Vietnam, trading the duties I had done, or better stated, trading tragedies. Their minds were getting ready to be memory cells, loaded with memories that would regrettably last a lifetime, and that’s if they would be chosen to go back home. They would see what war really was like, and how only God could place them on a path that would be their salvation against the utter chaos they would face. I had a sense of pity for them, for I had lived what they were about the face.

Our first stop was the Philippines. We didn't even get off the plane: next stop, Guam. We got off and were able to walk around and eat. However, if we wanted spirits, we weren’t allowed to take spirits from Guam. But the spirits were packaged in the form of a suitcase that could be taken on the plane.

Still, I saw no one I knew on the next stop, Travis Air force Base in California. We stayed in the air for sixteen hours, and the hospitality never stopped coming. The flight attendants fed us all the way, with endless foods of all kinds. We were treated really nicely, with the comforts of home, as we were given little booties as souvenirs. Something made me feel I was going to keep these for years.

****

When I got to Washington, D.C., everything looked different. What I had to consider was that I had been in the jungle for one whole year, and I probably saw everything differently. I could blink a thousand times, thinking my vision would present something I remembered, but most everything was different. What was the same was Patricia and Kim, and I was so glad to be back in D.C. with my family.

However, I was so rest broken that I basically found myself sleepy all the time, while being so sensitive to all noises I heard. Even when Patricia put dishes in the sink, I was jumpy. When the water ran in the bathroom, it reminded me of the rain from Vietnam.

Vietnam had a way of still presenting itself by route of any noise I heard. I quickly reminded myself of where I was and that I was surrounded by my family. I played with Kim, and she laughed and grinned every time I picked her up. I remembered the first time she waved bye to me when I was off to Vietnam. I was so fortunate that God had allowed me to come back and see her again. I believed that now that I was back in the United States, I had a chance to see her grow up, whereas when I was in Vietnam, there were days I was not so sure.

"Patricia, this is a good breakfast," I said

"Thank you, Bill," Patricia said.

Kim was in her high chair, eating her food. I realized I had missed so much, yet I was grateful I was going to see much more.

"Oh Patricia, I want to tell you, I enjoyed the lemon cakes you sent."

"I was so glad you enjoyed them, Bill. Vietnam couldn't have been an easy place to be, and I just wanted to add something that would make it a lot sweeter," Patricia said.

Kim joined in with a string of yea, yea, yea's, just like she knew what we were talking about.

"Patricia, since I have 30 days leave, we can go to Alabama."

"That sounds good. I know your family would love to see Kim, and this would be such a good time," Patricia replied.

Kim was still making happy sounds.

"Let's leave in a couple of days," I said, picking up my sausage.

"I'll start packing Kim's things, and packing our things," Patricia said.

"You don't have to start right this minute," I said.

Before I could leave the table, I found myself nodding off. This sleepy feeling was still upon me, even though it was only a few hours since I had gotten up.

"Bill, go back to bed if you need to."

I yawned right that minute.

I thought about doing just that, but I figured I would look and see what kind of shape my car was in. However, before I left the table, I began moving the dishes off the table.

"Bill, I'll get this, go on and go back to bed."

"I'll go later."

I went outside to my car. When Patricia's brother, George, picked me up at the airport, I was impressed with what I saw. It was one of the few things that looked the same as I remembered it. Patricia had taken good care of it, and I just wanted to get it ready for the road. I walked around the car, looking at the tires. They could use some air. Before I started the car, I wanted to check the oil. I opened the hood, and it could use a quart. I proceeded to crank it up, and when I did, it sounded just like I remembered. In less than 48 hours, we, the Grosses, were going to be on the highway to Talladega, Alabama, and I wanted to make sure everything was ready when we took off.

****

I could hear the motor purr when we turned out of D.C and got on the highway headed toward Alabama. Just like I had played with the wind when I was riding with Mr. Armstrong to Tuskegee twelve years ago, I did the same thing on the way. The wind was moving through my fingers, and I actually "pushed" it, as it pushed back, driving down the road.

I glimpsed at Patricia and Kim. Every now and then, I noticed that they had nodded off, sometimes Patricia, sometimes Kim, or both at the same time. The closer we got to Alabama, the more I thought about Tuskegee. I was finally going to fulfill the promise I kept to myself to one day go back to Tuskegee Institute.

I could hear Kim making sounds in the back. Patricia heard her also and looked back at her to see if she wanted a cracker. I continued to look in the rearview mirror, and I could see Kim chewing the cracker.

This was one of the most peaceful moments I had experienced. If there had been a million cars on the highway, and we could only move an inch at the time, there would have been a satisfaction that captured my heart to be there with Patricia and Kim, headed to see my family in Alabama. Right where I was at this moment was the Norman Rockwell Painting of my life.

"Bill, are you excited?" Patricia asked.

"Yes, I can't wait to get home," I replied.

"No, are you excited to be starting Tuskegee?"

"How did you know I was thinking about that?" I said.

"I know that's been your dream, and traveling back down to Alabama has got to have you thinking," she said.

"Do your mother and father know you were accepted?" she continued.

"Yes, I told them in a letter," I said. "Mama was happy, but I think Mama was taking one thing at the time and was glad I was out of Vietnam."

"Bill, I was too. You out of Vietnam was the first of all priorities. I wanted you to follow your dreams, but I wanted you to be alive to get there."

I had never heard Patricia so vividly state her thoughts about me being alive, yet I always knew she was thinking it. Anybody who had a husband, son, grandson, uncle or cousin in Vietnam was always thinking about their mortality. Vietnam became the synonym of the word "death."

"As you know, Patricia, when we return, and my leave is up, I will be assigned to Andrews Air Force Base, and I will be there until the end of this year."

"Yes, and I'm so glad you will still be in Washington, D.C., and I think it is great that after you finish there, you'll be going to Tuskegee."

"I thought so as well. I hate that I'll be gone again, leaving you and Kim..."

I didn't finish before Patricia continued.

"Bill, as long as you are out of Vietnam, I can handle being apart from you until you complete whatever you are working on, be it a degree or work," Patricia said passionately.

I found myself in another Norman Rockwell moment. I was so fortunate to have found someone who understood me and knew where I wanted to go in life.

It was evident that Kim wanted something else. Patricia reached into a bag and got some other little vegetables, and Kim reached for them contentedly.

"Bill, could we stop for some drinks?"

"I'll look for a place to stop."

I remember Mr. Armstrong's stance about stopping at stores, and even though this was twelve years later, I continued to be cautious. These were still racially trying times, so we had to be careful.

I saw a store that looked "friendly" enough and took the opportunity to gas up. I stretched, and Patricia checked on Kim. Even though things appeared okay, I didn't linger. I got what we needed and got back to the car.

We were in for a long ride to Alabama, and our conversations were like endless circles that looped into each other. Occasionally, the motor seemed to join in and purr like a perfect backdrop to our ride heading south.

****

When we pulled up to my parents' house, a warm glow fell upon me that seemed to be all over me. It beamed from me toward outside, yet it seemed to remain on the inside. I saw memories of all I had done on the farm. When I parked the car, I got Kim out of the back, unbuckling the seat belts, and started walking around to Patricia's door to open it. I stood with Kim for a moment and gazed around. I literally turned 360 degrees, examining the total landscape. I smiled and could feel the gentle breeze as it passed my face. Now the

Alabama sun wasn't shy, it was beaming in full blast, but I was still in a satisfying moment.

"Bill, I'll take Kim."

I guess it was obvious to Patricia that I was in a moment – just me and Alabama, my home. Just standing here was providing me with such a calming effect. At no other time had I returned home and had been so far away. I couldn't perceive going anywhere else that would be as far as Vietnam. I didn't know whether the distance had given me a panoramic view of things, but I could see things that I wasn't even looking directly toward, like birds on a power line. Also, I could hear things that I wasn't even listening to. There was that one bird that seemed to sing. This was not Vietnam. If it had not been so out of order, I could have run around and danced in the freedom of it all.

I don't know how long I was outside; it couldn't have been lengthy. Patricia and Kim were talking to Mama, and they had been hugging for what seemed like minutes. For just a few seconds, I wanted to bask in the simplicity of peace and familiarity.

When I reached Mama, we embraced each other so tightly that it felt like all the anxieties that I ever had melted all at once. These were the same arms that were my personal thermostat from as far back as I could remember.

"Thank you, Lord. Thank you, Lord. I can't thank you enough for bringing my son home. Junior, it's so good to see you. It's so good to see you and Patricia and Kim," Mama said, only the way a mother could say it.

It seemed as if we hugged for an hour.

"Junior, I'm so glad you are home." Mama stood and looked at me. She still held me by the hand.

"I got some hoecakes you like so much on the stove," Mama said.

I didn't miss a beat to go get them. I didn't need to run and slide under a dresser to get them this time. Mama was reaching for Kim when I left.

"Patricia, what is she eating now? She sure is growing."

I heard Patricia answer, and I stood watching my mother, wife, and Kim. If time had frozen right at that moment, this could have been another Norman Rockwell painting.

I heard the screen door open, and the thuds of steps were coming. I knew all too well who was coming. Even though I had heard his boots a thousand times, this time, it was more comforting than I had ever heard. The distance I had spent away from home had its way toward mending things that were torn and cauterizing things that were once apart.

****

I felt Papa's hands pat me on the back as soon as we reached to embrace each other. It had been twelve years since I left for the military, and for a moment, I was right on the day we were fishing. Had I allowed myself, I would have dwelled in thought, wondering why so many moments with him were not like those all along. But I had to treasure the day he took off work and fished all day with me, which totaled to the sum of his best effort. He had functioned in the best way he knew at the time.

"Son, I'm so glad to see you. This, this ..." Papa said, still patting me on the back.

I could tell there was something he wanted to get out. "What a year," he continued.

When my father said this, I realized that my year in Vietnam had shaped something in his mind as well. He had lost James, and I guess to lose another son must have entered his mind.

"Son, you looking good!" he said with booming strength in his voice. He was still patting my back and resting his hand on my shoulder.

"What's been going on around here?" I asked.

"Everything is about the same," he said.

"Where's everybody else?" he asked.

I knew he was talking about Patricia and Kim. "They are right in here," I said, pointing to the living room.

Papa walked toward Patricia and Kim and gave them a big hug.

"Kim is getting so big," Papa said. "I got something I know she wants to see."

I wondered what it was, yet I had no idea.

Mama and Papa were like perfect hosts to us. I was aware they were my parents, and of course, I would expect this hospitality; it was great to have them catered to us with food, stories, and so much attentiveness.

I guess what I realized is that this was the second time I had been home as an adult with my family, and it was far different from when I was a child. Perhaps Papa was so happy I had a family of my own. Then, I also recognized that after the year away in Vietnam could make anyone thankful to be alive and surrounded by serenity.

"Look, look!" Kim said.

It was the surprise Papa had for her.

He had some puppies outside that fascinated her to no end. She ran behind them, and some let her pet them. It was another moment for Mr. Rockwell to get his camera out.

I took another opportunity to inhale the air and just enjoy the moment that I was enjoying.

The farm looked somewhat smaller than I remembered. Things happened to be like that. The older you are, the smaller your former surroundings seem. I thought of Talladega County Training School. How large or small did the school look now? I wondered if any of the same teachers were there. Maybe I would take a drive up there and take a tour of the building.

"Junior, how's life treating you?" Papa said with a deeper inquiry.

"I'm just glad to be back here in the United States," I responded.

"You don't have to go into any of it," he said.

I knew what he meant. He didn't want me to relive the devastation. Yet he wanted to know how I was.

"You have a beautiful family, and that is really all that matters," he said.

"Thank you, Papa. I'm so thankful for them and just thankful for all that God has done for me."

Papa and I continued talking.

"You know, I never had to give you a whupping, because you were the only child that never lied."

I think, at that moment, I realized even more that family and friends had their share of stresses that shaped and affected them in some way when they have someone they love serving in Vietnam.

I felt that this year had obviously affected Papa in some way, yet I hadn't known exactly how. He seemed smoother in his temperament, not as rigid and not mixed with as much grout as I remembered as a child.

****

Our time in Alabama went fast, and during the whole visit, I felt recharged and revived about life. Yet, I still found myself tired and sleepy when not actively moving around. This was happening all the time, even after I had just gotten up after sleeping all night.

Driving back to Washington, my thoughts were on my next stops in life. I was getting closer to the statue where Booker T. Washington was lifting the veil of ignorance from the slave.

We stopped a few times on the way back to Washington, and once we arrived, it was time for me to prepare to report to Andrew Air Force Base. I had a few days before I had to go, and it gave me a wonderful time to be with Patricia and Kim. I got a chance to see the daily duties and everything it took to be around an active toddler. I could see the sweat forming on my brow, but I wouldn't have traded these moments for anything.

Settling back in Washington, D.C., and working now at Andrews was very predictable, and I was grateful for that. I had experienced a year of unpredictability in Vietnam, and this was exactly what I needed. Sometimes, when I heard loud noises or noises that made screeching sounds, I felt uneasy. I was glad this didn't happen often, but when it did, I immediately asked God to help the anxiousness subside.

I had a classified job and was pretty much in a routine that I could easily navigate. However, I was encountering an issue.

I was at my desk and was nodding off, and I couldn't seem to keep my eyes open.

"Staff Sergeant Gross."

"Yes, sir," I responded."

"I'm going to send you to be seen by one of our physicians," my Commander stated.

I was glad he had known the journey from which I had come. It seemed like I was carrying Vietnam with me all around. I could hear it, sometimes see it mentally, but I was still tired from it also.

"I want you to go over there and let them examine you to see what is wrong."

"Yes, sir," I said.

****

When I got to the 's office, I waited for a few moments, and I was called to go straight to the back. I went through the normal routine of being weighed, pressure taken, and throat observed with a tongue depressor.

"Staff Sergeant Gross, as I am examining you, I'm not finding anything initially that is out of the ordinary," the doctor said.

"Taking into consideration that you have just returned from Vietnam, I think it is safe to say that you are simply rest broken. Try to increase your hours of sleeping, and improve your quality of sleeping – dark room, no noise, no light. Just those simple things can make a difference. If things don't improve, come back, and we will try a different strategy. I don't think you need a prescription to sleep yet."

"Thank you, sir."

"Do you have any questions for me?" the doctor asked.

"No, sir, I'm going to just get more rest."

I left with the thoughts that at least it was just rest I needed and not anything more. I would rearrange some things, but not cut out anything that had to do with seeing Kim grow up. Now that I was home, I was dedicated to seeing her grow each little bit because, in a few months, I would be headed out again – this time, Tuskegee, Alabama, to Tuskegee Institute.

****

My time at Andrews Air Force Base passed by relatively quickly. The duties I had there were not arduous or nerve-wracking. These were the types of duty I couldn't talk about, and maybe that was a contributing factor. When they were finished, that was it. Also, I believe I was propelled forward with my mind headed down south.

I had to make a checklist in my head, leaving Patricia and Kim in as close to a normal state as possible. In just a few days, I would be in Alabama, but everything had to be in place for my family.

I first made sure the car was in top shape. Patricia had kept it in good shape, and I wanted it to remain that way. She and Kim would need reliable transportation, and there was no way I was leaving them to catch the bus or rely on catching rides, just because I was going to Tuskegee to get an education. If anybody was going to walk, it would be me.

I went to the BX or Base Exchange to grab a few things that I thought I would need for my studies that I could take along. I would be riding the bus, so I didn't need to take a lot, but just things that I figured I could get more reasonably priced at the Base Exchange than in Alabama.

As I looked at each aisle, I saw something that I knew I was going to buy.

There it was; a Samsonite Briefcase. I began dreaming about what I was going to learn and what books I was going to put inside. I looked at it and examined it closely, and noticed it was a brownish-grey color.

Opening the briefcase, I looked inside, trying to see all the features inside. I saw a section where I was able to put my completed homework. I had a feeling I was going to have this briefcase a long time. I closed it back up, and I had pretty much made up my mind.

I gathered all of the things I had chosen and headed to the front to make the purchase.

Walking back to my car, I continued preparing my mental list of all the things I needed. Driving around Washington, D.C., I took a closer inspection of the city that had really played a major part in my life. This was the city that allowed me to see what students really needed, as I was an Academic Advisor at Howard University. Me, of all people, chosen to help college students, when I had not even been a college student myself. This had to be a divinely arranged act, where only God would put me in a position to see how I needed to perform as a student.

Then there was Patricia. Meeting her put my life in alignment, a balance, an equation, where everything equaled to a total sum of happiness. I had a wife, a life partner, a confidant whom we could build a life where we could accommodate each other's dreams.

From our union was the little sunshine of my life; my daughter Kim. She was absolutely the crown that adorned my heart. I had dreams all along as I could remember that I wanted to fulfill, but seeing Kim made me want to truly fulfill those dreams, and more, I had not thought even about.

CHAPTER 47 – TUSKEGEE INSTITUTE AT LAST!!

I heard the brakes release, and the bus was ready to move forward. I was sitting in between the same excitement when I went to Tuskegee with Mr. Armstrong and a surrealistic joy that escorted me to what this day would actually feel like. The wheels of the bus were carrying me forward to Tuskegee. I could see Patricia and Kim wave as the bus pushed off. We had said our goodbyes and promised to meet in a few months. As we had weathered a year of Vietnam apart, we could weather one semester apart, now that I would be at Tuskegee Institute.

I had dressed warmly, but this wasn't the first thing on my mind. It wasn't until I looked out of the window as we traveled that I saw some of the same scenes that Mr. Armstrong and I had seen twelve and a half years ago in 1956. Only this time, I saw smoke coming out of the chimney. Children were running around in the yard, probably playing with their toys from Christmas.

My mind suddenly went back to Christmas. It was the first time I was with both Patricia and Kim. It wasn't Kim's first Christmas, but my first Christmas with her. Just like she was so happy with Papa's bird dogs, she was equally as happy with her toys. Patricia had the apartment merry and bright, and it was a heartwarming moment. The whole apartment smelled of baked goods, ham, and greens, and I couldn't have been happier at any other place at that time.

We weren't quite out of Virginia, and I was getting a little restless in my seat. This was going to be approximately a fifteen-hour ride, with well over seven hundred miles to go. I would be glad when our first stop to stretch took place.

Patricia had fixed me a big bag of goodies. There was chicken, grapes, cheese and crackers, and canned drinks. We well knew the possibilities of not being able to be served everywhere.

It was apparent that it would be miles before we stopped, so I decided to read the Ebony Magazine, January 1969 edition that I had with me. The cover itself was interesting, and it posed some interesting questions. "What Can Blacks Expect from Nixon?" "The Natural Look – Is It Here to Stay?" and "Are Black Americans Welcome in Africa?" For a moment, I asked myself these questions, predicting the answers these articles would actually reveal. I pretended for a moment that if I was given each one of these questions in a classroom, how I would answer them. As I examined them closely, none of them could be satisfied with just a "yes" or "no" answer. Two actually could, but there still needed to be support to explain those answers.

Was I actually ready for class? Was I ready to write arguments where I defended my side of the issues, as I saw students do at Howard? Maybe I was. I was ready for anything that was going to prepare me to stay the course and do well at Tuskegee.

My promise to myself to return to Tuskegee was just a few hours away. Even if those hours were going to be a hundred thousand, it was still in the view of "few." I knew when this bus stopped, I would be back to where I promised myself twelve years ago. I was okay knowing this wasn't going to be an easy course to chart, but that was going to be the good part. Whatever happened, I was going to come out better. Actually, I was going to come out greater.

As I heard the bus tires hum, I continuously thought about my life at Tuskegee. I wasn't going there to play. This was a mission for me, and I wasn't going there to fail. My goal was to work hard, bring Patricia and Kim to Tuskegee, and complete all my coursework to have a degree.

****

I was apprehensive right up the last minute as the bus pulled into the city of Tuskegee. I didn't really know where the other travelers were going, but I did know where I was going. This was not just a day trip or a visit for me; it was a destination where I had been waiting to arrive for twelve years. It was a climb up a sliding board, rung by rung, and now it was time to slide down into reality. I had done a lot of things and covered a lot of ground, but attending college at Tuskegee Institute, as I planned, was finally here.

A rush came over me that felt like the feeling of being overwhelmed, but not so much that it would overtake me. I just had to stand where I was and take it all in for a second. I didn't believe my life would have been as rich, or as full as it had been, had I not quit school and go into the Air Force. It wasn't a route I would recommend, but it was the only route I felt was best for me. There was no money for college, no opportunities after high school, just jobs around Talladega, and I couldn't see a linear future for myself without leaving high school.

I was now thirty-two years old. I didn't know anyone here in Tuskegee. I didn't even know if I was prepared to take on such a monumental task like college if it were contingent upon the preparation I had from high school. Even though I had obtained lots of skills and even tutoring in the military, I still had to ask myself if I was ready for this task. However, ready or not, I was going to dive headfirst into it.

The first thing I had to do was look for housing. As soon as I got to campus, I went to the Dorothy Hall Guest House. This is where I had stayed when I competed at the oratorical contest. I decided to go inside to inquire about a room. Looking at the Dorothy Hall, I saw they had expanded to a larger hotel conference center. Part of Dorothy Hall was built by Booker T. Washington's students. There was still some of the straw in the bricks that could be seen that students used to make them from years ago, a testament to the hard work and dedication the students used to get the job done.

"Good afternoon, I'm looking to get a room here for a little while until I can find somewhere to stay for the semester."

"Good afternoon, I can help you," a very friendly young man responded. "We do have a room here. Where are you coming from?" he asked.

"Washington, D.C.," I said.

"So, you are going to start here this semester?" he said.

"Yes, I am finally here."

"I stay at a rooming house that I'm sure has room. If you want, we can meet and go over there tomorrow. My name is Edward Jackson."

"I thank you so much; I'm William Gross."

"Here's your key, and we will meet tomorrow," Edward said, and I proceeded to my room.

I couldn't exactly explain what had just happened, nor could I have predicted it. This was a blessing that had opened up right on the spot. I was expecting to have to search for at least the first two weeks before I was able to find appropriate housing. This was God who was seamlessly bringing things together right on day one.

My first night reminded me a lot of where I stayed just twelve years earlier. I looked around the room, and some of the things were similar. The décor had slightly changed. The colors were different and different pictures were on the wall. There was a welcoming warmth that wasn't overpowering, making my night comfortable.

****

Edward Jackson and I met as promised, and I was able to room right with him. This was such a smooth transition. I was able to knock out the task on my list. I had to get ready to get in the saddle to take the College Aptitude Test. I wondered about it, but I didn't believe God had gotten me so far as to come from places I never thought I would go, only to get to Tuskegee and fail. I wasn't sure I was going to pass this test, but I was going to give it my all.

The next day after taking the Entrance Exams, I met with Dr. Sinai, a professor who would be my advisor.

"Young man, you are mature, and you know what you want and what you are supposed to do. You have passed the Entrance Exams, so I know you are a fit for Tuskegee. I'm not going to give you too much advice on the courses that you are supposed to take, but don't take over 12 hours the first semester."

This was a joy and gladness to my mind. Knowing I had passed was a big relief, but I didn't know if I had to pass with a certain numerical score in order to take certain classes. And, I was unsure if I had to take any remedial courses.

Since I didn't hear Dr. Sinai mention anything, I took his advice and took twelve credit hours. I was happy to know that I would get credit for what I would be exempt from taking. Surprisingly, it was Freshman English. My eyes closed with my hand over my chest in relief. That would not be the only class I would exempt from. Also, since I had military experience, I would be exempt from Physical Education.

I left with Dr. Sinai's suggestions and registered for my classes. I felt as if I was setting sail toward my academic direction. My schedule would be Biology, Botany, Animal Science, and Qualitative Analytical Chemistry and Western Civilization.

****

Walking over to collect my schedule had the same importance as if I was receiving a diploma. There was no Pomp and Circumstance music, but I felt as if it was playing. I felt nothing but good feelings, and I felt absolutely great. This was the beginning of the first school diploma I would receive. I graduated from Boot Camp, the first graduation, and I was determined that wouldn't be my last. God had seen me through abject poverty, troubled school days, Vietnam, and why wouldn't God see me through these college years?

I was near the building to get my classes. I was even expecting a long line. I filled out papers and waited.

"My name is William Gross," I said to the lady at the counter who handed me my schedule. I couldn't wait to see the list of classes and in what order I would take them. I already wondered what kind of supplies I would need, and what kind of books I would have to buy. I wondered whether I needed three-ring notebooks or tablets with spirals on the side. I thought I would wait to go to class and see what was actually requested.

"Here you are, Mr. Gross."

"Thank you," I said with a smile that seemed to be permanent, locked and frozen in nothing but pure gratefulness.

When I took the schedule and I couldn't be sure, but I felt a vibration. It had a thunderous feel upon reaching for it, as if a gravitational pull, right to my future. There was almost an energizing shock that indicated, "You are going all the way."

On the schedule, it read the following classes there was Freshman Biology, Botany, Animal Science, Qualitative Analytical Chemistry, and World Civilization. I knew one thing, this was what I always wanted, and I was ready to actively embrace it. Running from it was not even in my imagination. None of these sciences were going to frighten me. No matter what, I knew that I was going to make it.

I could do nothing by depositing stares into the paper, and tears came briefly. I walked out and felt just as accomplished as the day I was admitted into the military. This was like the second part of my life, second behind the military, now college. I really wanted to pinch myself to see if this was really happening.

I turned, open the door, and looked ahead. I examined the students that had converged upon this campus. Some had on vintage style clothes, some had on more stylish, updated clothes, and some had on only what their parents could afford. I certainly knew what that was about. This was not a put-down, but an observation. Everybody had to get where they were going and in whatever they had.

I had fourteen years on most of these students. Where the traditional students had lived almost two decades, I had lived a little over three, and my three decades had shown me already enough that would last me a lifetime, yet I knew I had more time within a lifetime, and it would not be over before I completed this Tuskegee curriculum.

As I saw students walking by holding schedules, trying to find their way, the real path was evident. We all had one common goal; we wanted to make something out of ourselves because the south, the world, and justice were yet to be on our side.

****

As the weeks went by, I could tell that Chemistry was going to be challenging, but I was okay with the Qualitative analysis part in Chemistry. There were lots of things we had to mix, boil, and blend. As far as the Freshman Biology with Dr. Sinai, I enjoyed the live specimens like frogs and mice. That fell right into my line of interest. Also, Botany with Dr. Yumachagi was a subject that fell right into my lap, for with my interests in plants, I thought it was very interesting. Then there my Animal Science Classes with Dr. Manning. When I thought about the three of these classes, it was as if I stepped back to Talladega and got an advanced ticket of knowledge about plants, living things, and livestock.

****

I could hear the footsteps of Dr. Yumachagi, and my heart was beating even louder. It was loud enough to make me think others could hear it. From a distance, I could see other students receive their exam papers, and I tried to interpret their expression. Some looked and had poker faces, some were clearly disappointed, but when I saw mine, I could hardly contain my enthusiasm. When I saw that I had made an 80 something, I didn't even focus on the second number afterward. The fact that I had answered 80 percent of the test questions correctly gave me the confidence that I could keep continue on. I told God immediately, "Thank You for helping to pass this exam." That was the beauty of a relationship with God; I could thank Him without interrupting the class and still continue the flow of acknowledging Him right on the spot.

I also felt that Dr. Yumachagi had a style of teaching that made me remember the material in Botany. It was said that he had a style like that of George Washington Carver. If we had a question about an area, he would have us do research and go through a maze of self-discovery first. If we then had questions, he would explain further to you.

One of the areas I enjoyed was Dr. Yumachagi's teaching on Primitive Plants, which was quite fascinating. We actually walked to an area on campus where we could view Primitive plants (mosses, ferns, mushrooms, etc.), and how they could be identified as their seeds grow outside of the cone. One example we saw was the Magnolia Tree. I had seen magnolia trees before but had not ever seen them combined with the knowledge that we gained that day.

As I continued to examine my test paper, I looked at the questions I didn't get right and focused my attention on them. "Did I miss a step, interpret the question wrong, or not understand the question?" Whatever it was, I decided I wanted to later ask Dr. Yumachigi, so I wouldn't continue making the same mistakes.

****

All of my classes were very interesting, and I was grateful that I didn't have the difficulty I thought I would have with them. I was way ahead of the freshmen that were just getting to college right after high school. Surprisingly, I was making A's and B's, and the incoming, younger freshmen were making C's and D's. Actually, I thought this is where I would have been since it was a long time since I had been in an academic setting for classes. I was very proud of myself that I was able to even do this level of work. I attributed this to four things. 1. God, 2. Teachers at Talladega Training County School, and 3. The time I spent reading, anything from politics to science, in all the libraries that were on base when I was in the Air Force and 4. My current professors.

When I got back to the rooming house where I stayed, Edward Jackson was there. We were roommates, and to think of how he offered information about the room made me wonder how God linked everything together for me, truly amazing.

"William, how are you liking Tuskegee?" Edward asked.

"Edward, I know you are not aware of this, but it has always been a dream for me to come to Tuskegee. If all the classes were meeting outside, I probably wouldn't object. I just simply wanted an education at Tuskegee, where Booker T. Washington poured his heart and soul into making education something we could obtain."

"I understand, William. Tuskegee has been a great school for me and good for me. I was able to have a work-study program to get me through school. You know, where we met," Edward responded.

"I could use a work-study program in the future myself," I said.

"I can help you with that, and how to find one in your area of study," Edward said.

"Are you finished for the day at Dorothy Hall?" I inquired

"Yes, I've finished for the day," he said.

We talked a little while until it was time for us to go back to our studies. It was evident he had a good work ethic and was able to juggle school and his work-study assignment. Edward was neat and was respectful, and I was glad I had been paired with someone of his character.

****

My semester was moving along, and I was studying and enjoying what I was learning. I was not performing the method of cramming and memorizing, for I had long established that style of studying wasn't learning. "Actual learning" was application, meaning to apply it where it would be remembered for a lifetime.

Along with the curriculum that I was learning, I was beginning to see how real teaching was influential in a student's life. In Organic Chemistry, I could see the style of Dr. Raymond Bararras. I was already wondering how I was going to navigate through Organic Chemistry, but Dr. Bararras put that mystery in simplistic terms. As he lectured, he did not let any of us write any notes. What this allowed us to do was focus on the concept and not be disturbed or distracted by the writing. I liked this because sometimes I might be unsure what to write down exactly. Notetaking was not just something anybody could do, for I found out this was a process too. At the beginning of the lecture, Dr. Bararras would give us a written copy of the lecture, and from there, I had a good idea what he wanted us to know, and how I could take notes for other classes.

Overall, I was pretty happy about my pursuit to enroll in the Veterinary School. I knew it might be challenging, but I didn't mind that. With the experiences I had in Vietnam, which were the most unpredictable of my life, there somedays, I didn't see how I could come out on the other side. So, by declaring this as my major was not going to overtake me.

One reason I thought that this was the area for me as I had seen cattle farmers with big farms who seemed to amass an abundance of wealth. I couldn't imagine how I could do better than this life. Formerly, all I thought I could do well was play baseball, but that dream ended when an Air Force recruiter lied and said I could play semi-pro baseball in the Air Force. However, I always felt if there had been such a league, I was good enough to play and be successful.

Right now, I was going to take all my energies and put them in one place right now, and that was here at Tuskegee. After reviewing all the tests that I had taken, I was pleased that I was still keeping my A/B average.

My one class that was different from the rest was my Western Civilization class. This wasn't a surprise to me, because I knew it wasn't like the sciences I was taking in my other classes; it was more like History. I was learning about societal civilizations, cultural civilizations, and infrastructural civilizations and the introductions. Now I was interested and was committed to working just as hard in this class as my others, but I quickly ran into a snag.

My teacher, Mrs. Brown, assigned something that I did not agree with, and that was participating in a demonstration against the U.S. Draft Board. I stood where I was, and I was not going to cross over into her decision about this topic. I wasn't coarse or non-compliant or uncooperative. I was standing up – not only what I believed in – but where I had actually been. Mrs. Brown decided that students were required to participate in the demonstration to march against the draft board. When I heard this, it was all too familiar, but I believed people really didn't understand.

"Everybody who does not participate in this march, you might as well know you are going to fail this course."

I didn't flinch or wrinkle my forehead, nor did I get loud.

"You might as well give me my grade now," I said with direct authority, but with respect, "because I'm not going. If you all understood what you were doing, I don't think you would go, and you wouldn't let the rest of these students go."

She looked at me real funny — a look that didn't detest what I had said, but one that caught her off guard.

We parted company, and I went on to the library and then to my other class, and the students went downtown and marched.

I could not demonstrate against my brothers, who were lying down in trenches and dying every day. To march as she required was a march against them and what I saw.

A few days later, Miss Brown found me at one of my other classes and apologized.

I was quite comforted when Miss Brown retracted her stance about me participating in the demonstration. It was my belief that she saw me in a different light, and that I had a responsibility to remember those men who I left in Vietnam, and those still being shipped off daily. There was actually a community of us who were here at Tuskegee, and some parts of our voices were not heard.

****

The semester was coming to an end soon, but I had a few more weeks before exams. Grades were on my mind, but I also was thinking about housing. I was looking for housing for me, Patricia and Kim. I walked searching, asking if there were any places, and I had a few leads, but I didn't know if any were affordable. Having the summer before classes started did add a little buffer to the concern because it wasn't like it was I needed to find a place by next week.

My next class was in Dr. Manning's Animal Science class, and we had a few minutes before class started. I got the idea I should just ask some students in the class.

"Do you know anywhere I could rent a place for my family and me," I directed to the students that were in my vicinity. I didn't know if my question would come back void, but I didn't think asking couldn't hurt. Time wasn't slowing down, so I had to make every minute count.

"Well, we live out in Chehaw, and we are going to move after the semester is over, so you can rent that place." This was a girl and her boyfriend who responded.

I thanked them immediately, and later they took me out there and showed it to me, and introduced me to Mr. Beasley, who was the overseer of the property. I liked what I saw and thought this was going to be the place I would rent.

With one semester down, I could really tell what existed in the college life of a student. I had no complaints, and I was so glad of the opportunity that God allowed me to attend Tuskegee Institute. I often think that if I had enlisted in the military two years before I did, I would have never participated in the New Farmer's Speaking Contest, where Mr. Armstrong chose me to be a contestant. I would have never seen Tuskegee's campus, and never had a thought to attend this school. As a matter of fact, I had never set foot on a college campus ever. I often think that if when I was at Tuskegee the first time and had only seen the "The Lifting the Veil of Ignorance Monument," and just where I had to speak for the contest, I would have still been impacted to return to Tuskegee. I saw the Carver Museum and all of the campus, but there was just an anointing impact that set the sail within me to return.

This past semester had been a "strike" in my book. I felt I bowled a perfect game. I didn't make all A's but felt I had accomplished more than I had ever planned, and for that I was grateful.

I was looking forward to this new semester because academically, I felt like I had my feet on the ground. But more than anything, Patricia and Kim would be in Tuskegee with me. This was going to add a more determining angle to my life because although I considered myself determined, having my family near was going to give me even more motivation to do well in my studies.

****

The military owed me one move during my time with them, and I never needed to use it. I was so fortunate that the military arranged for packers and movers to get everything ready and have it shipped from Washington, D.C. to Tuskegee, Alabama.

Mr. Beasley became our landlord, and he was a nice man – much more than a landlord. He lived across the road from the property and was an activist within his own right. He worked so hard on voter registration to get Black people to vote. He was a real soldier, and he became the Tax Collector of Macon County, an elected official. His wife, Mrs. Beasley, was a school teacher who could cook anything, especially cakes.

This was another God-directed place for my family and me to stay that no one could have orchestrated but Him. First, a place with Edward Jackson, and now a place at the leading of two Ag Students, overseen by Mr. Beasley.

Now that Patricia and Kim and I were reunited, life had a balance just as I thought it would have. Kim was in full bloom, and I was met with many home-cooked meals by Patricia. This made my college life a tad different from my contemporaries. I guess both of us had never experienced what the other had. I didn't really know what it was to be in college without a family, and they didn't know what it was to be in college with one. What I did know was that I had everything, and God had blessed me tremendously.

This was my first summer in Tuskegee, and I had the good fortune to get a job coaching a sports summer program at the Recreational Center. This was a wonderful opportunity that gave me a chance to see Tuskegee through the eyes of the children who were ages K through 12, where they were able to play basketball and baseball in intramural teams.

Patricia and Kim would occasionally get a chance to come and watch some of the sports when the teams would compete as well as have fun. One of the things we wanted the kids to know is the rules of the games, good sportsmanship, and have a great time playing the sport.

As much as I enjoyed being there, I really couldn't wait to see what the new semester had to offer, and as quickly as two days, I was going to have my wish very soon.

Kim was almost three now, and I was able to spend time with her and see what some of her developing interests we're going to be. I see her playing with dolls and emulating things that Patricia would do around the house, but I would hear her hum and sing certain songs where I could hear the tunes exactly on key.

During this time, we also had time to attend some area churches, see some of the downtown areas, and explore more Tuskegee.

****

It was here, and I really couldn't wait. I was like a child waiting for Christmas morning. My second semester had arrived, and I saw all the classes.

I was able to predict much of what was going to happen because all of my professors were the same but one. I could tell this second semester was going to take on a similar complexion to the first. All the classes were virtually part 2 of the first, Biology Part 2 with a Physiology concentration: Dr. Sinai, Quantitative Analytical Chemistry: Dr. Larry Ludwick, Botany: Dr. Yumachagi, but one professor that was new: Beef Cattle Science taught by Dr. Durdle.

"Patricia, I'm gone."

"Ok, Bill. Have a great day. See you tonight."

I got to campus with a little time to spare. I vividly remembered just how cold it was my first day of the first semester, but now this was a warm change. I was a little lighter with no heavy coat and could freely move around, without the stiffness that I had with gloves and hats.

Instead of Animal Science as I had the first time, which explored all the animals on the farm, Beef and Dairy Cattle, this Beef Cattle Science was concentrated totally on Beef Cattle.

"Welcome to Beef Cattle Science; I'm Dr. Durdle."

I could tell by the greeting I was going to like this class. He had an authoritative pitch in his voice. I didn't discern arrogance at the centerpiece of this authority; what I discerned seemed like knowledge coming forth.

"You will be learning how to select good breeding stock, and choose a good heifer that would be a good mother," Dr. Durdle said.

This took me right back to the New Farmers of America's Conference when we had our clipboards and checklist ready to grade the cattle.

If I could have shouted openly and not disturbed the class, I would have. I was moved for the moment, standing right here, seeing how God orchestrated my life to "make certain" I would get here.

I was really taken by this class with Dr. Durdle. My other classes were essentially part two my last semester, so I knew what to expect. But this Beef Cattle Science class seemed to confirm just why and how my destiny was tied to coming to Tuskegee.

"Good morning, we're going on a little tour today. Bring your papers and pencils, and we are going to take a look at some of the cattle," Dr. Durdle said enthusiastically.

It was evident he enjoyed what he was doing as a professor. We all got up and met him on the Ag side of the campus. Here I was going to the same place when Mr. Armstrong had taken me 14 years ago. Here I am, back where my desires began, wear a veil would be lifted, as Booker T Washington did for the slave. I really could have cried again, but I didn't. I kept going and saying thank you, God, to the count of what I believed was a million times.

We had arrived. While this was not the first time I had been here since I returned to Tuskegee, I felt something penetrate my being when Dr. Durdle said the word, "select." I felt the warm reminiscence of my time with Mr. Armstrong and how we graded the livestock.

"Look at those hips," Dr. Durdle said.

I thought I heard some giggles, and I did see some heads spin around. However so, I knew exactly where Dr. Durdle was going with this

"You see how those hind legs are structured?"

He went on with his process of discussing the cattle. I could tell the students were enjoying this presentation, as well. Some seemed a bit startled, probably those who were not from farms, or those who were expecting strict terminology to be a part of the process.

"Look at the way this bull's head is structured; his hind legs; he doesn't have post nor sickled hocks. This bull has some great genes. This is our Blue-Ribbon black Angus bull, and he was donated by Bob Hope and other celebrities at the price of $500,000. This is why you have to know the right kind of bull with the right kind of genes ... if they don't come into the world looking like this, then they're not going to be a blue-ribbon bull. You have to be born with it. This is the kind of bull that you want to breed your cows too. No matter what the breed, you want them to have good genes, which dictates good confirmation."

All the students were intrigued and enlightened at the same time.

"What happens to those cattle that don't make the cut?" a student questioned.

"The only thing you can do is prepare that animal for food. For instance, this Herford bull calf has too much white on one of its ears; therefore, he cannot be registered. Just one blemish is enough to stop this bull from being registered."

We returned to the classroom, and Dr. Durdle brought the class to an end with any further questions.

Before I knew it, we were getting closer toward fall break, and Patricia, Kim, and I decided we would take a ride up to Talladega. We hadn't seen Mom and Papa for a long time, so we thought we would just make a quick day trip. It wasn't quite fall break yet, or I would have had the time to stay the entire time. Patricia didn't have time off from her job, so we were glad to go just for the quick weekend.

The closer we got to Talladega, all the memories of being there were coming back to me. I had to save these; they were memories that I could use as a measuring stick to show just how far I had gone. I was grateful to be a college student and not a farmhand. I was grateful to be getting an education and not have to be scared to get it as I was under Maude Barnett. I was grateful to have a family that I provided for and protected, and they could feel much more secure than when I was growing up.

As soon as we drove up, I saw Papa in the yard. Mama was probably in the house making some hoecakes, and I sure hope she was making some rabbit gravy, but I couldn't be certain about that. I knew she was going to be surprised to see us.

"Junior," I hear my father say when I pulled up.

"Papa, how are you?" I said toward him as I was reached to hug him.

It seems like it was a long time, but it had not been as long as some of my tours away when I was in the military

"You be looking good," Papa said.

"Thank you, thank you. Patricia does a pretty good job of keeping me up," I said, winking at Patricia.

She threw back a look at was half confirming, and I wasn't sure about the other half. However, she knew I was teasing about the "pretty good" job part, and that she was, indeed, supportive of me in all areas.

"How's Tuskegee?" Papa asked.

Before I could answer, Mama came out of the house. Mama was always a vision I could see a thousand times a thousand, and still, that wouldn't be enough.

"Junior!" Just the call of my name made me want to stand still and hear it over and over. It was like rain to my soul. She had been a spiritual leader that prayed for me from birth to this very day I was standing, and I was so glad to see her.

We hugged, and if I had any troubles, they melted away. She went towards Patricia and Kim, and the day felt like yet another Norman Rockwell painting.

****

"It's important to know that when cattle are not chosen to be breeders, they are put on a feeding and finishing program, and they are then raised to be sold for food," Dr. Durdle stated.

All my other classes had me running on all cylinders, and I was spending a lot of time in the Huntington and Armstrong buildings. If I wasn't studying plants, I was studying cells, or I was analyzing chemical compounds. But if I had to reveal my truth, the most enjoyable class that I was having during this semester was beef cattle science, which stayed somewhat within my being, day-to-day. Mainly, it was at this juncture I knew 'certainty' had joined my journey.

CHAPTER 48 – ME, A SPOKESPERSON

It was 1970, and I couldn't believe I had been in Tuskegee, Alabama, for one whole year. I stepped outside and looked around, and as far as my eyes could see, I thanked God for everything in this 360-degree view, while I turned around and stretched out my arms with thanks. If even this day was my last day on earth, I was still thankful for everything: my wife, Kim, and my life. About a year and a half had passed since I had left Vietnam, where I couldn't forecast day-to-day what was going to happen. I could now at least feel the comfort of my surroundings.

I could see my breath in front of my face, a steady stream of white fog, but I had no complaint about this. Thirty-degree temperatures were no strangers to me. I had spent many cold days in Talladega, where the houses we had lived had so many cracks and leaks, where, in comparison, a day like today was a summer day. I grabbed my bag and headed to campus.

There was a fight that was headed my way that I didn't see coming. With one whole year down, I had a lot of people to thank. Edward Jackson, the guy who I met, seemingly by chance, allowed me to room with him, where we bonded in many ways. He had served in Vietnam, yet we didn't talk about details. It was like it was an understood code of action. Yet we formed a veteran's club where it grew to 150 students. It was evident that everyone didn't understand our needs, but of course, we were there to support each other. Our dilemma was funding. The school did not want to give us financial aid.

College life was now allowing me to be in areas that were not only academic for me but were turning into social activism. I didn't shirk it; I actually embraced it because there was a cause that truly needed attention. As the Vietnam Veterans were converging on the campus of

Tuskegee, there were those professors or those in personnel who didn't quite understand our plight.

The college did not want to give veterans assistance like they gave other students. We immediately felt this wrong, and we invited the President of Tuskegee to one of our meetings to address our needs to him.

I had been voted spokesperson for the Veteran's Club to do the administrative work. I wondered why I was chosen, but maybe it was because I had always been rather vocal during the meetings about my concerns.

Vietnam had given me an additional dose of courage that made me see things in a linear process. After being down in a bunker and hearing thunderous sounds, perceptions change. Not really knowing whether death would be waiting on the other side, perceptions change. If I was knowingly safe, with a mind to do what was purposeful, I didn't see why I shouldn't go forward for good.

When it was time to speak to the President of Tuskegee, I stated, "Sir, you are giving the rest of the students some assistance, why are you treating us differently?"

"Because you all get the G.I. Bill," the President said emphatically.

In my head, I thought, *What does that have to do with it?*

A lot of us were married and had families, and that little money we were getting from the VA was not going far.

It was evident President Foster wasn't too pleased with us for bringing this matter to his attention. So, he got up and left the meeting.

So, that night we all agreed to draft a letter to the Secretary of the Department of Health, Education, and Welfare and started a petition.

The members of the Veterans Club wanted me to write it. I stated in the petition that if Tuskegee could not treat the veterans at the Institute as they did other students that had financial needs, then we requested that the Department withdraw all Federal funds from Tuskegee.

We also requested that Health, Education, and Welfare investigate how the money was distributed among students.

After I drafted the final copy of the letter, I thought it only right to give Dr. Foster a courtesy copy.

"Good afternoon, Dr. ------, I wanted to give you this copy that I am sending to the Secretary of the Department of Health, Education, and Welfare," I said.

He took it and read it right there at the moment. "You are still going to send this letter?" he asked.

I replied, "Just as soon as I leave your office. I'm going to the Post Office." My attempt was not to be smart but to let him know I was adamant about this mission.

He quickly replied, "Here."

He gave it back to me with a brashness.

I could tell he was hoping that question alone would persuade me not to do it. Maybe he wanted me to ask myself the same question, but I was continuing as planned. I loved Tuskegee, the campus and curriculum, and although I had gotten here, I realized some would not have even made this stand because it could have been a risk to me, but I understood that right was right and too many people were riding on this outcome as well. If our stance was going to get us blacklisted in some manner, then I well understood that God could select another place for all of us.

I turned and left the President's office. From there, I went to the Post Office and then went to a class in the Agriculture Building at three o'clock.

When I arrived, there was a big red notice on the Ag Department's Bulletin Board reading Bill Gross; please see Dr. ------ right away. I proceeded to go back to Dr. ------'s office to see what the urgency was all about. When I arrived at his office, I noticed he had a rather interesting look upon his face.

"Good afternoon again, Dr. ------, I saw on the bulletin board, you wanted to see me?" I said.

"You don't need any assistance," Dr. ------ said flippantly.

I looked at him rather perplexed, wondering how he could come up with such a theory. And, how did he come to such a conclusion from the time I left his office?

"Why do you say that?" I asked him.

"Your wife works at the VA."

I guess he thought about matters after I left and decided to find out everything he could about me.

"So does your wife," I volleyed back to him.

He didn't know I knew that, for I had known that Patricia knew his wife.

"Just take it on over then," Dr. ------ said, meaning the letter. "Because I know you are going to mail it anyway."

I could tell he was upset, and it was unfortunate that this matter made him upset because I liked him as Tuskegee's President, and I didn't allow this to make me see him differently.

With this dilemma out of the way, I could at least see my way clearly ... hopefully ... if just for a little while.

****

I had arrived and was settled into my seat, easing my bag down.

"Here is a bag of bones." I wasn't quite sure what we were doing or where this was going, but I was attentive, just the same. I was there to learn. I glanced around the room to see if anyone else had an expression on their face like the one that I probably was hiding on mine. Puzzled looks are all around, so I thought it best to predict a totally different look on my face, knowing full well I felt the same as others.

We had to learn the skeletal system, the humerus, the arms, the ulna and radius, bones and arms by the hands. I saw this go on for the entire class. Students were parading around the room, feeling the bones of the skeletal system. We touched them, making mental notes because that's what we were told that we were going to have to do, learn by feel knowing which ones were what.

I could hear myself screaming on the inside as Dr.-------- was teaching Gross Anatomy like this. Certainly, there could be another way of teaching this. I was just simply having a hard time figuring it out. How was the lab part of learning going to help us learn the skeletal system better or, might I say, learn the function of the bones? Actually, I could have drawn a stick figure, added more bones, and labeled what each part was.

This just didn't cut it. Yet there was nothing I could do about it but follow along and see where the lesson was going. Soon the class was out, and I could tell that some students had the same amount of frustration. However, I was older than the mainstream group, so some of them may not have found this as frustrating as I did. I thought I needed to be lectured, but this professor let it be clearly known that he did not believe in lectures. I had come from such a background where I wanted knowledge; I wanted to know more about each bone. Each thing I could count on, whether they had been a class on what I still wanted to know the difference between the west wind and the east wind. This was just not an ideal way of getting to know the skeletal system, at least for me.

I wasn't sure what to make of my next class, but I wasn't going to hold that one class hostage, letting it color what I would be going to next.

****

I didn't let that bag of bones depress me because I was a third-semester student and I knew it was time for the rubber to hit the road, and I was really getting into my biology and chemistry classes, and believe it or not, I dropped in on a physics class that really took me over the edge. I did not find that I understood the principles in physics so well, but it was fascinating. Motion was one of the things that had always fascinated me. Maybe that's why I enjoyed seeing the airplanes when I was younger, and Marguerite would always call me to let me know one was outside. When we discussed the flight of an object at 180,000 miles per second, I was sitting there trying to figure out how long it took the Sun to get around the Earth, and there is a war 93 billion miles away; that was an interesting concept to me.

Perhaps I was ready for something else to take place in Gross Anatomy, but Physics made me realize that God does everything in his time, as it always amazed me how he made different planets and put them in orbit with a perfect speed according to his will. So I settled my feelings and said to myself, *I'm okay for now, hoping for a lecture the next day.* Well, the next day was here, and it was a bag of bones this time, a cadaver. Well, I said, “Let's see where this is going.”

When I went to Biochemistry, a familiarity was waiting for me. I saw the structure of chemical molecules that was interesting because I really didn't learn to appreciate Biochemistry until I understood the theory of motion. In order for me to get the theory, I needed to see the motion. Basically, in chemistry, there was the structure in the molecule and the sugars. For example, sugars were in the liver, glycogen, and also in the muscles. Then in Physiological Chemistry was the place where I saw the actual motion, where I started to appreciate Chemistry.

My time at Tuskegee led me to run into interesting professors that I didn't even have classes under. One was Dr. Judkins. It wasn't often I met people who had a kindred spirit and with the same ambitions to be at Tuskegee. We had made similar promises to ourselves about being at Tuskegee, and this alone was something I found to be unique.

Having George Washington Carver as an instructor, he had established a deeper interest in plants, even though he was studying to be a veterinarian, and became a professor in the Vet School. Upon talking to him about class, he was willing to share his knowledge of anatomy, plants, and other areas freely with students.

While spending time with Dr. Judkins, he realized that I had an interest in plants that went back to my childhood in Talladega. I told him the plants I saw on the farms and how those that were poisonous had a definitive look that differed from those that were non-poisonous.

Before coming to Tuskegee, Dr. Judkins was offered a position at Colorado State University, where he received his Master in Anatomy. The university was so adamant about him accepting a position at their university; they offered him to write down any price. Colorado State was willing to give him any amount, yet he decided against it. As I had made my promise to return to Tuskegee, he had promised himself to go back to Tuskegee and support his Tuskegee, the institute, the students, and the community. He was one of the few natives, and he was born and raised right in Macon County. At the time I attended Tuskegee, he was the only professor there who had been taught by George Washington Carver.

Dr. Judkins had been a late bloomer because his life had been temporarily altered by a car accident before his preteen years. This caused him to enter high school later, but he was no doubt well-read due to the times he was recovering. His community meant a great deal to him, as he was nurtured during his recovery, and saw how Macon County had helped him develop as a young boy, student, and adult. This was the reason for his deep desire to return to Tuskegee.

After talking with him, we discussed a poisonous plant garden, and he asked if I would be willing to work on one. I thought I had won the "Botany Lottery" and I obliged.

This poisonous plant garden had become almost a second home to me. Dr. Judkins and I conferred about many different plants because, as a child, I saw so many things, that even from childhood, I knew they were not good for human consumption. For instance, the castor bean seed reminds me of a pinto bean seed in color but looks like an engorged tick in shape. Consequently, "do not eat." The plant also produces the deadly chemical ricin.

When Dr. Judkins and I created the poisonous plant garden, he would ask me if I could identify certain poisonous plants in the wild. He would show me a picture of the plant in a book, and I knew where they grew in nature. He and his wife used to go to the Botanical Society meeting every summer. This meeting was important to him because he taught a poisonous course to Tuskegee's sophomore vet students each year after teaching a required course on poisonous plants to second-year vet students. He asks if I could find him a specimen of the plant, water hemlock. I got him a specimen, and he propagated it, and on their next trip to the Botanical Society meeting, he took this specimen with him and had society key it out. The Society found that it was a strain of water hemlock that not been identified. Little did I know, Dr. and Mrs. Judkins had the Society name it the 'Bill Gross Strand of Water Hemlock.' It was so toxic you cannot handle it with your bare hands without getting intoxicated, and it is related to the celery family.

****

I did have an interesting experience with an Organic Chemistry lab. As irony would have it, I would have Dr. Ludwick's wife for Organic Chemistry Lab while he taught the Qualitative Analysis Chemistry course.

"Mr. Gross, I would like for you to make sure you are really looking at these chemicals by their shapes of how they look because that's going to be the real way of making that determination."

I "yes ma'amed" her, with the appearance to be in total agreement; however, each time I used my nose, I was proven to be correct in my identification of the chemicals.

****

"Home early, Bill?" Patricia said, pulling off her shoes.

"Yes, I am. They closed Tuskegee for today. You know what happened, don't you?"

"I heard, and I can see why they closed early with a shooting on campus. You definitely don't know if any of the protesters might hurt, or even a student," Patricia replied.

At this moment, the nightly news was reporting on the Kent State shooting, where four unarmed students were killed by the Ohio National Guard during a protest against the bombing of Cambodia by the U.S.

****
***

Well, the semester was ending, and I couldn't believe how I was going to take my Gross Anatomy test. I heard it was going to be a really hard class, but when we had the exam, there was a bag arranged on the table and what we had to do was put our hands on it and feel for the femur, for the humerus, or for the patella. I didn't bother to look around to see the faces. I have seen them before, but I surely thought that this was going to be different. I will talk about this with somebody, maybe Dr. Judkins would be the one to listen to me and to mention to tell Dr. W. of my concerns for a lecture in Gross Anatomy.

Larry Ludwick's wife made an intriguing opposite. She taught Organic Chemistry Lab. I enjoyed everything that we did in this class. We learned how organic chemicals react under certain conditions. At the end of the semester, each student was given an "unknown" organic chemical that we had to identify by subjecting it to a given set of tests, including the "smell test." I circumvented most of the tests by depending on my sense of smell to identify the class of chemicals that my unknown was in. After I took my final exam, I entered Dr. Ludwick's office, confident that an A or B awaited me. I could smell each one of these chemicals virtually a mile away if I had to; there was just a distinction that I had down to a science. I went through all the stations that she set up with each chemical. At each chemical, I wrote the appropriate information and felt great when I left.

Smelling these chemicals all depended on the class of the chemicals. There were aldehydes, ketones, and amines. Aldehydes had a musky/sweet-like smell, like musk oil and perfume contain. Ketones have a sweetish swell, and the Amines had a biting odor, like green peanut vines.

Mr. Gross, I want to congratulate you and tell you that you made an A. However, I'm giving you a B because you relied on your nose too much."

I laughed, and I couldn't even get mad with Dr. Ludwick because deep down inside, I knew I deviated from the proper and assigned method. I knew the science side of it, but I guess the reliance on my nose made for a great backup that I simply chose to use.

****

I was back at the Poisonous Plant Garden, and Dr. Judkins would ask me if I knew what a certain plant was called. He would show me a picture of the plant in a book, and I could identify it in nature. One day, when we were in the garden, he asked me if I could identify the plant, Water Hemlock. He asked me I could get him a specimen on my next fishing trip. I did, and he started propagating it in his Poisonous Plants Garden. Dr. Judkins and Mrs. Judkins were members of the Botanical Society and attended their annual meetings. One year the Judkins took a specimen of the Hemlock that I gave to him to the annual meetings, after the Society keyed out the specimen, they determined that it was a strain of Hemlock that had not been named. They asked the Society to name it in my honor: "The Bill Gross Strain of Water Hemlock."

Certainty Pulls Me to the Side

I knew I shouldn't have taken an Ecology Graduate class this new semester, but I figured it couldn't hurt. As I was moving along in my course work with biology and chemistry, I was doing rather well. I wanted to learn all I could; for one day, I saw my life as a scientist. Taking the first exam was challenging, but I felt prepared. I answered every question with everything I had, and I awaited the results.

When I saw my grade of 65, I felt the floor sink in under me. A dizzying sway seemed to take hold of me, and I couldn't process anything else for that moment. 65!!! Wait a minute! I studied. I did not neglect my notes and reading, so what happened? I wasn't trusting this method again, for I didn't see any other way to do this. I made a decision – writing everything down on 3x5 index cards. Here is where all my answers would be. I decided to write them very small, with all the terms and formulas. I was going to be very careful, move slowly, and take them out during the next Ecology exam.

As I was writing the information, I wrote it as clearly as I could and was careful the way I put everything down. Reading it over and over again, I wanted to be sure I was familiar with this "Pony" – this cheat sheet. Everything was on it, and I was rather pleased. I was quite fond of my work.

The next morning came, and I jumped up, shaved, bathed, and headed to class.

"Alright, everybody, sit down and let's get ready to start. I believe everybody is going to do well. Just take some deep breaths, and let's get ready to do this."

The test hit my desk, and it felt warm like it had come off some machine. I couldn't prove that maybe it had been sitting in the sun by the window.

When I saw the exam, I read every question before answering. I was going to be okay because I "prepared." After the test was over, I felt terrible, and there was someone I needed to call.

My hand was on the back of my neck, and I was walking in the Armstrong building. Pacing back and forth, I felt terrible, convicted, like something felt as if I had a hollowness inside of me. Why did I feel so empty when I had known I had passed the Ecology Test?

Something I couldn't explain made me feel absolutely odd. I would have rolled around on the floor and probably groaned had no one been present. This feeling would not leave me, and I just felt as if a virus set in.

I saw students walking by. They were happy, talking, and walking by doing things that students do on campus, laughing, and talking about their studies. Some even running and tossing a ball.

Then, I saw it. A realization had hit me. I kept looking at the students walking by. Everyone was here at Tuskegee as a student and here to learn. Now what kind of student was up to each person.

How could I have let the thought of cheating come to my mind? Did I not think of the thought of jeopardizing my college education? Why did I let a 65, two numbers, cause me to prepare to cheat? But mostly, how could I not let God be God to me?

God had been with me from the beginning, even when the journey was so uncertain. I didn't know how I was going to make it out of the first grade with Miss Maude Barnett, but God chose Ruth and Claudia to get me out. Then, there was the time where I almost slipped into the rushing water with Mama. There waiting was a root that caught me, saving Mama and me, because she would have risked her life to keep me from drowning.

I recognized God was chauffeuring my mind around to areas of my life where major circumstances had been present, and the outcome could have been very different. Once I was playing and backed into a number 10 tub filled with water. I fell backward, and Velma was looking out of the window while she was washing dishes. She saw me and ran to rescue me when I fell in the tub.

Then there was probably more I didn't even know, but the major one was Vietnam. How could I have forgotten how God kept me? All the artillery strikes that sent many men back home in a box, God allowed me to live.

I wanted to cry out aloud, but I didn't. I couldn't. Yes, I could, but I didn't – not with students passing by.

"God, forgive me! Forgive me for not remembering. Thank you for showing me where you brought me from. I recognize I could have put everything in jeopardy, as I prepared not to consult or trust you."

I felt my balance coming back to me. The virus that was seemingly trying to set in was now subsiding. My vision that was once clouded with some apprehensive purpose was returning, and I could see that I could have been kicked out of Tuskegee had I used that Pony cheat sheet.

I was thankful to be convicted. Even though I did not use the "Pony," I had planned to use it, and it was evident that God had a way of showing me my weakness.

Only God could turn a thing like this into a time of remembrance.

When I opened the test, I knew every question.

I had not only written answers on my cheat sheet, but I had also written them in my brain. Never did I take the sheet out or use it. I didn't have a need for cheating.

I had so meticulously prepared, copying notes, and reading the notes over and over, I was learning the material.

All the effort I was using to cheat, I was actually creating a style of studying for myself.

No test would have been worth getting kicked out of Tuskegee and risking the future I left Talladega to seek. I had learned my lesson: "In all thy way acknowledge Him, and He will direct thy paths."

CHAPTER 49 - CERTAINTY ACCELERATES

I had the good fortune to have Dr. Steve Goldsberry in two of my biological science classes (Neuro Anatomy and Histology). I was still in thought about a question he had on an exam from Neuro-Anatomy; Dr. Goldsberry was willing to give us ten extra points on our exam if we could give the function of a structure in a dog's tongue called a Lysa. I left the answer blank, because I didn't know, and was not going to guess.

I never asked him about it after the class. In this class, we were involved heavily with tissues in Histology. He, again, gave us lectures, which displayed his keen knowledge of his subject matter, for it was more than evident he knew his business. We got another box of slides, and we had to study and distinguish between normal tissue and pathological tissue. I knew the routine all too well, and I was glad I did. I knew how to prepare and how to "ready, set, go."

He would give us a slide with tissue from a heart. It helped us distinguish the difference between pathological and normal tissue. He would give us cardiac tissue from a person who had experienced a heart attack, as well as tissue from a healthy heart. As we examined the slides, we could distinguish the pathological tissue from the normal tissue because of breaks in the cells.

Heart tissue was made up of striated muscle, the same as skeletal muscle. Students were asked to distinguish between the two types of muscle tissue. If you studied the two types carefully, cardiac tissue always has a "give-a-way" feature called an intercalated disk, a little black band across the fibers at unpredictable intervals. And if we were not careful and we didn't study the structure in tissues, we would be lost, because there were tell-tell signs.

I was learning many styles of learning from the professors at Tuskegee. My Microbiology class with Dr. Williamson set me up for immediate success. Even though I was just encountering him, I could have used his tip from day one. His advice to us was to take his notes, and as soon as we had a break in our schedule from classes, we should go to the library and read them over. Rewrite them or make notes from them to become even more familiar with the material. This seemed simple enough, yet I had not been doing this. I would review my notes later at the end of the day or the night. This tip alone put me much further ahead, not just for Dr. Williamson's class, but the other ones for the semester.

****

I wasn't taught by George Washington Carver, but to be his "grand student," as he taught Dr. Judkins, was equally as pleasing.

Time was moving at a rapid pace, and along with classes, I had a new surprise.

****

I was looking at one of the most beautiful people I had seen in my life. He was not a thing, but he was my son. Patricia had just had him, and I was excited that I had a son. I couldn't explain what was in my chest, but it was like a peppermint that filled my chest.

I looked at him often, where I seemingly couldn't take my eyes off him. He was agile, and I could see that in his moments after his birth. I could see his feistiness at first sight when his lungs seemed to be in high function when he first started crying. Everything I had ever done and made sure I was putting into place proved to be all worth it when I saw Karlton.

Patricia was doing fine, just a little tired and somewhat sleepy. We talked briefly, but she was dozing in and out. I left the hospital and went back home to pick up a few things.

On my way, I thought of all the questions Kim might have and would want to know about her new brother. Now I had two children, and I considered myself blessed. Actually, looking at my life, I was tracing the whole thing as I did when I first got to Washington, D.C. Looking at the entire journey, it was one the I found rewarding. I could feel the proudness in my being, not that it came from me, but that God had made it possible. It was God who had navigated this journey, and I am able to see the benefits of His navigation. Before I knew it, there was a full matinee playing in my head.

"Daddy, where's the baby," Kim said.

"He's in the hospital," I said. Kim was now five, and her birthday was just two days ago.

"I still have some cake he can have," Kim said happily.

"I don't think that he can have a cake yet," I said.

"He can't?" Kim said inquisitively.

"No, he's baby, and he needs milk," I said.

"He can have some with it," Kim said.

"He has to have all milk for a little while until his system is ready for food."

"Why is that?" Kim asked with wonder on her face.

"Babies need milk until they have matured. He's so small, and he can't digest that food as you can. See, when you were a baby, we gave you milk. Now that you are older, you can eat birthday cake, but then you couldn't."

I imagined Kim with a startling look on her face. I knew she thought he could eat it and still couldn't really understand why, but I knew she would eventually understand.

"Can I see him? Can I see him?" Kim said, jumping up and down.

"We are going to see him soon," I said.

I walked inside the house and gathered a few things for Patricia that I knew she wanted, and look around for a moment.

In a few days, I would be bringing a son home, someone who would one day take my name and keep the lineage going. He would be the next male who had the name, which was originally "Groce," but with the spelling "Gross." There were now four "Grosses;" me, Patricia, Kim, and now Karlton.

I looked around again and wondered how different things would be when Karlton came home — looking for things that would sharp or pointy crossed my mind. Of course, I knew he couldn't walk, but when he would be walking, I wanted to have an idea for what I needed to change.

My mind was back at the matinee. I could hear Kim singing a tune, which made me know she was happier than two pigs in the sunshine. I didn't know what she was singing, but I could tell that contentment was all over her. She was going to see her baby brother for the first time, and that was going to make her world go around a revolution or two. I already knew it would because the world had already gone around at the speed of sound.

****

When Kim did meet Karlton, Patricia was holding Karlton when we walked into the hospital room. Kim was wide-eyed, looking directly at Karlton.

Karlton was having a bottle and looking around, seeing all the world had to offer. His eyes were opened wide, and he was filling them with sights coming from the voices that he heard.

The matinee of Kim was playing in my head again.

"I want to hold him," Kim said.

"You will have to be very careful with him," Patricia said. "I will let you hold him a little later when he gets a little older."

"That sounds like that will be a long time," Kim said.

"It won't be as long as you think," Patricia said.

I reached to hug Patricia as this dialogue between Patricia and Kim ended the matinee. I saw that Karlton was drinking from a bottle while taking in a little more than five ounces.

****

It was my senior year here, and I was now really coasting. I had taken so many classes that I was above my 124 hours and was around 161. Karlton's presence gave our home a new and completed feeling. Giving him a bottle and looking at my notes had become natural. With the help of Kim, having her be a big sister, made a lot of things easier.

This year I had Neuroanatomy, Chemistry, Genetics, and Microbiology. These classes were sort of a repeat of the second semester, and they were equally fulfilling as the ones

I had already taken. What I found in my senior year was that I loved what I was learning and really didn't want to stop taking classes, but I knew the time had to come to an end for me to move forward.

Looking at my time at Tuskegee, I felt much fulfillment.

There were a few teachers that really made me stop and reflect on who were true role models at Tuskegee were.

Dr. Steve Goldsberry

I had the good fortune to have Dr. Steve Goldsberry even in the next semester for Histology. I was still in thought about a question he had on an exam. In NeuroAnatomy, Dr. Goldsberry was willing to give us ten extra points on our exam if we could answer explain how the tissue Lysa in a dog's tongue actually functioned. I left the answer blank because I didn't know. Nothing in any of my readings and reviews stated anything about Lysa in a dog's tongue.

I never asked him about it after the class. In this class, we were involved heavily with tissues in Histology. He again gave us lectures, which was my preferred way of learning and remembering. We got another box of slides, and we had to look and distinguish between normal tissue and pathological tissue. I knew the routine all too well, and I was glad I did. I knew how to prepare and how to "ready, set, go."

He would give us a slide with tissue from a heart. It helped us to distinguish the difference between pathological and normal tissue. He would then give us cardiac tissue from a person who had experienced a heart attack. As we examined the slide, we could tell that this was pathological tissue because it had a lot of breaks in it. This was not normal tissue.

Heart tissue was made up of skeletal type muscle with strident cells that sort of look like it had stripes. He could fool us with heart tissue on a slide, asking us where did this tissue come from? And if we were not careful and we didn't study the structure in tissues, we would be lost, because there were tell-tell signs. It was the intercalated discs that gave the clues. It had a little black ban across the stripes, indicating that this tissue was indeed pathological.

Dr. Williamson

I was learning many styles of learning from the professors at Tuskegee. My Microbiology class with Dr. Williamson set me up for immediate success. Even though I was just encountering him, I could have used his tip from day one. His advice to us was to take his notes, and as soon as we had a break in our schedule from classes, we should go to the library and read them over. Rewrite them or make notes from them to become even more familiar with the material. This seemed simple enough, yet I had not been doing this. I would review my notes about later on at the end of the day or the night. This tip alone put me much further ahead, not just for Dr. Williamson's class, but the other ones for the semester.

George Washington Carver

I was a little firmer in my footing when it came to my confidence in my studies. Enjoying the breeze upon the campus even felt different when it blew. I took in the structure of the buildings, and I even thought I would go inside the Carver Research Center to review his work. The Research Center is where he worked tirelessly with all his findings based on peanuts and sweet potatoes. For a man who decided to just stay in Tuskegee for a couple of years, his desire to stay forty-three years proved to give the world more than was imaginable. Those additional decades must have given him an insight into not only his work but to observe the students and what they needed to succeed. Also, playing the piano to help fund projects for the school tells a story of its own, where he was deeply committed to the cause of teaching, discovery, and scholarship.

Dr. Judkins

It wasn't often I met people who had a kindred spirit and with the same ambitions to be at Tuskegee. Dr. Judkins, my Anatomy professor, was one of those people. We had made similar promises to ourselves about being at Tuskegee, and this alone was something I found to be unique.

Having George Washington Carver as an instructor, he had established a deeper interest in plants, even though he was studying to be a veterinarian. He was a professor at the Vet School, where he was my Anatomy teacher. Upon talking to him about class, he was willing to share his knowledge of anatomy, plants, and other areas freely with students.

Spending time with Dr. Judkins, he found I had an interest in plants that went back to my childhood in Talladega. I told him the plants I saw on the farms and how those that were poisonous had a definitive look that differed from those that were not.

Before coming to Tuskegee, Dr. Judkins was offered a position at Colorado State University, where he received his Master's in Anatomy. The university was so adamant about him coming to their university; they offered him to write down any price. Colorado State was willing to give him any amount that he asked for, yet he decided against it. They offered this to him in the 1960s. As I had made my promise to return to Tuskegee, he had promised himself to go back to Tuskegee and support his Tuskegee, the Institute, the students, and the community. He was one of the few natives and was born and raised right in Macon County. At the time I attended Tuskegee, he was the only professor there who had been taught by George Washington Carver.

Dr. Judkins had been a late bloomer because his life had been temporarily altered by a car accident before his preteen years. This was caused him to enter high school later, but it was no doubt well read, due to the times he was recovering. His community meant a great deal to him, as he was nurtured during his recovery, and saw how Macon County had help him develop as a young boy, student, and adult. This was the reason for his deep desire to return to his home town.

I wasn't taught by George Washington Carver, but to be his "grand student" as he taught Dr. Judkins was equally as pleasing.

I was the one who was fortunate to have all my professors give much of themselves for my education.

CHAPTER 50 - CERTAINTY APPLAUDS

My graduation day was here, and I thought about the song, "If it had not been for the Lord on my side, tell me where would I be, where would I be." God had personally brought me to this day, and this is where He wanted me to be.

I thought of all the teachers at Talladega Training High School who had a wonderful helping hand getting me here. I had to circle Mr. Armstrong in big red ink, for had he not chosen me to be a speaker at the New Farmers Convention, I would have never had the desire to go to Tuskegee Institute.

Papa gave me a white shirt and one hundred dollars. I was overcome by this generosity. It spoke volumes, where he couldn't speak. It spoke in the past tense, when I wondered, "why?" At that moment, I think he answered, and I was fine with his dialogue.

Mama was proud of me. I remembered her spelling tests and hoecakes. Actually, if I had the time to cry and reminisce for a moment, I would have. There was no greater person in the world that my mom. She was my advocate every step of the way. I was glad she was here in Tuskegee to see me graduate.

Patricia, who had been with me basically throughout adulthood thus far, from the ride starting from Washington, D.C., helped me with my graduation regalia. She had been a strong tower, confidant, and the apple of my eye. I was exceedingly glad she entered into my life when she did.

"William L. Gross, Jr." I proceeded across the stage. I'm really not sure I walked. Perhaps I levitated or gracefully glided. This was a dream that came into fruition, and God had made it all happen at this appointed time.

CHAPTER 51 - CERTAINTY REVEALED

"Welcome to the Celebration of Mr. William L. Gross." We are excited to have Mr. Gross's family and friends speak on his behalf and talk about his contributions. Where did thirty years go? We would like to thank you, sincerely, for your 30-year service with the Environmental Protection Agency."

The crowd applauded with a thunderous response. I let the sound pebble over me as I basted within it for a moment. I could have only wished that my mother and father had been here at this moment. My father said I was the only child he never spanked because I had never lied to him; therefore, he said he trusted me and knew me. Perhaps, this night would let him and my mother finally see why I decided to quit school, leave Talladega, and see that I was not only succeeding in life, I was thriving.

My leaving Talladega was a desire to stand on my own two feet with confidence, knowing I could make it. I wanted more than just to be piddling around in Talladega, but to one day rise to become someone respectable, raise a family, and help others within my community.

I would have loved my parents to see that I had gone far, not just in the distance, but I had traveled as far as I could in desire — the desire to simply be somebody better, and better than I was the day before.

When I left for the military, I didn't know where I would go exactly, but as I look around the room today, it wasn't too bad of a distance at all.

At that moment, I turn my head and saw my wife Patricia, my daughter, Kim, my son, Karlton, and my mother-in-law, Mrs. Elizabeth Turner.

There were lots of speakers who were coming forth to speak on my behalf. I imagine some would be humorous and maybe some with embarrassing moments, nevertheless coming, I knew it was all in the name of celebration.

When the first speaker was up, I traveled back to the day I had gotten my Master's Degree. I was happy, and I had turned my tassel to the other side. The world didn't look any different, but I knew I would be making a difference in my world. I was equipped with more knowledge and more experience and was on a journey that whatever happened, no one could take my education away.

My road to getting a Master's took place when I was looking for a job.

I happened to be on Tuskegee's campus right after graduating, and I ran into one of my favorite professors, and my Major Professor, Dr. Raji Sinai.

"What are you doing over here?" Dr. Sinai said.

"I'm over here looking for a job," I responded.

"Well, I want to talk to you about something?"

I was hoping he had a lead or two where I would be able to put my Biology degree and passion in the same place.

"Have you thought about going to grad school?" he said.

I had to take a deep breath and think. This wouldn't be a bad thing, I thought.

"Chevron has a fellowship. and I would like for you to apply."

I listened intently.

"They are looking to give a Black student this Fellowship to be trained as an Entomologist. You will be trained at Auburn University, meaning you will have classes here on Tuskegee's campus and at Auburn."

I could find no hesitation in my being. Science always did have a way of holding me captive, for it had been a way of life for me that kept me from age six to the present, even if it was just examining a leaf.

****

I had discussed going back to school with Patricia, and she was very supportive. Karlton was now five, and Kim was ten, so the kids were in a place of self-sufficiency, not toddlers, and it seemed that all the "needles" were pointing to go.

The application process was different. I was not in a war zone this time but in the comfort of the home that Patricia has made for us. I didn't have to worry about artillery strikes or the unexpected, and I could concentrate just a little better. As for the requirements, that was the same, requesting transcripts and statements of intent. I knew what I wanted to say, yet I wanted it to be concise and to the point. My statement of intention was simple. I saw Biology as the bridge to all knowledge that continuously contributes to our communities.

****

"Bill, you got a phone call."

I had experienced that before, and I was hoping for the same results. There was no need for me to wait to answer the phone. It was Dr. Sinai, and I didn't know what I was going to hear. Courage was the inertia that moved me forward, and it was no need to not activate it now. I wasn't sure I was qualified, but I felt I had a variety of classes beyond what I needed for Biology to at least be considered.

"You have been chosen to receive the Chevron Oil Fellowship."

I heard the words "chosen to receive," and they echoed. I was thankful and grateful that God had allowed me to be chosen for this fellowship, and like most good things that come. The devil was at the door. Life from here took on a kaleidoscope of change, and it was the first time I had been called a name based on the color of my skin in the classroom.

****

Who would have known that the roads Mr. Armstrong were traveling would be the same roads that I would be traveling again at the age of 39? I was passing my future the whole time and didn't even know. I had seen the road signs, Auburn 20 miles, but nothing registered to me that I would have any business there. Once I arrived on the campus of the Tuskegee Institute, my intentions were solely to be a student and contribute to my community. Little did I know that God was going to give me an extended plan. After letting me become a student at Tuskegee, He obviously had more for me at Auburn University.

My arrival must have been stunning for those at Auburn. Upon arrival, I could feel an icy reception. The looks that came my way were like daggers, and the thoughts in the minds of some were almost audible. However, there were audible words, and surprisingly not from my contemporaries. Never did I have students call me any racial slurs, but the professors used the word nigger like it was running out of a faucet.

"I'm going to the test so hard for you that you can't pass it," I was told by Professor B.

"You mean you are going to make one to flunk the rest of the class because I'm going to pass your test," I quickly refuted.

"Nigger..." Whatever he said next really didn't register with me, but I saw the eyes of the students and their disbelief, throwing a glare at him. I didn't lose my composure, but continued my stance, ready to hear the rest of the lesson. The students didn't go back immediately to their notes. Some dropped their heads; others *shook them in disbelief. What I found interesting there was never a student who* spoke to me indignantly.

This professor didn't stop here. He wanted me to fraternize with the students. He actually asked me when a girl walked past me as her breasts accidentally rubbed my back, "What are you going to do about that?"

I gave him no reply, for I knew he wanted to have something over me that would possibly get me to sabotage my education.

Professor B. didn't get what he wanted; instead, I served Auburn with my master's thesis in just a few years as I studied insect pests and insecticides. However, my Master's degree was conferred by the Tuskegee Institute. Unsure which day God said, "Let there be Soybean research for William," I take pride in knowing there was such an expression, long before I was in the womb.

****

God didn't need to configure things within any ironic framework, yet if he wanted to, He could, for He is the author and finisher of all things. I thought of how I grew up on a farm, where fields of rows are ever-present; however, when I studied my graduate course work, there I was again in the midst of rows of plants again. Man may call it irony or maybe coincidental. But God, without apology, called it into being, and it was just like the way He did things – equally scientific, equally spiritual – during the days of creation. It was His divine order to do whatever He wanted and just the way He chooses.

I was now at a place where George Washington Carver's fascination had placed him, and I was in a place where my fascination had placed me. Carver's research had been primarily with peanuts and sweet potatoes, along with other things, but these two plants he studied would go on to bring multiple uses. How was it that I would fall right onto the same grounds that Carver had walked upon? How was it that I, too, would bring my own fascination with soybeans, something that I would see my father plant, move its way through the course of my graduate work.

It was clear, this was not irony, but a divine arrangement that would allow me to access the same grounds, same research atmosphere, and same ambitions as Carver, as I would deposit my research to the world.

I had always had a fascination with soybeans and insects, and the marriage of the two steered the passion of my coursework.

Only God could put these two fascinations together, and nobody could change this in my mind. Although my respect for science will always exist, science couldn't predict it, yet my professors and I had already discussed it, but the heart and mind of God had already appointed it. I was going to be able to do my research on soybeans and insects, something that, as a child, would have been beyond my comprehension.

My work began.

CHAPTER 52 – A CULMINATION OF HIS LIFE'S JOURNEY

EXCERPTS OF MASTER'S WORK

When I was sampling my experimental soybean plots, I saw something that caught my attention but was not on the route of my scheduled research. I was truly in a learning process at this very moment. I was sampling the soybeans, I identified several soybean pests, including a copper-colored Mexican bean beetle that was being attacked by a predatory stink bug, a spined soldier bug, that was quite interesting. Both predator and prey have hard coverings on their bodies. However, the spined soldier was patient enough to wait until the Mexican bean opened its hard hind wing covering, then inserted it's piercing and sucking beak into the bean beetle's soft tissue to feed. I continued to record my findings while examining other places within the plots.

As I furthered my investigation into the plots, I saw differences between two treatment formulations of the same chemical. Where I had treated plots 72A with the emulsifiable concentrate spray, there were lots of leaf-feeding pests. However, plot 72B I treated with the granular formulation had no signs of leaf-feeding pests. However, there were many insects with piercing and sucking mouthparts. Because this insecticide also has nematicidal properties, it controlled nematodes; these are little microscopic worms that feed on plant roots and get into the plant roots and damage them. This chemical was controlling nematodes too. I didn't have any of this in mind when I started my research, but this is why I call it discovery.

ANOTHER DISCOVERY

That same summer, I had planned to gather a lot of data on plants and infestation. Especially worms, green clover worms, velvet bean caterpillar, and corn earworms. It just so happens that when summer started, the amount of rain and the humidity was high. I got a lot of help in my soybean plots, without knowing the weather was going to "help" me. The humidity brought about a fungus, and it was the fungus that attracted worms. As a result, it just wiped the whole worm population out. I didn't know it was attacking until all of them were dead. Usually, when a worm gets sick from a parasite attack, shortly before it dies, it climbs to the highest peak on the plant, and then they die, and that's what those worms had done. When it stopped raining, it was like they were a piece of chalk up there. If you touched one of them, you could see the spores of the fungi being released from those dead bodies of worms. Had it not rained, we wouldn't have experienced the fungal parasite that attacked the Green clover worm, Soybean Luper, and the Cabbage Luper. This was wonderful additional data for a thesis.

This period of rain was steady, and it lasted for about a week, with the accompaniment of high humidity, the worms could survive. This brought unexpected things into my research. You don't expect what you have not predicted. Most of the time, you don't know if a parasite is around or which one is going to appear, and you have to record it. You got to make a note of it and how it has changed the nature of your predicted results.

I had good professors, and many let you know that the results may differ from your predictions while letting students know that all results are needed.

Most people think negative results are bad when this is far from the truth and the heart of science. Negative results can be as good as positive results because they both tell a story, and you have to record the story.

MORE FINDINGS

So far as my collection of data was going, there was an insect that came on the scene that we had not seen before. It was around, but this was the first time it had been discovered as a pest. It was an immature form of a skipper, which is related to butterflies and moths.

Following my observation of the differences in the emulsifiable concentrate spray versus the granular formulation, I had in my mind what was happening. I needed to take Dr. Sinai to the field to see what I was talking about. He rode in my truck, and he looked at it. Once we looked at the difference in the plot ... with the ground applied vs. that which was sprayed, we went to his office and discussed the findings, and I asked him to contact my sponsor at Chevron to ask if they could make me a sample of the chemical tagged with radioactive carbon 14. He did, and they called back said, "We'll make it." It was $16,000 for just a 10-milligram sample. This sample looked like a tiny piece of cheese stored in vials. It didn't have to be frozen, just diluted with alcohol, and stored in cabinets labeled appropriately.

I knew within my own mind that something was going on in the plant, and I wanted to verify what I thought.

I had taken plant physiology, so I knew about the translocation of chemicals in plants up and down the plant, the translocation streams, xylem, and phloem. Xylem ... takes water up the plant from the roots all the way up to the growing part of the plant.

Phloem, its translocation pattern, takes it up and down the plant because what it does, it takes the sugars and other substances up the plant, and it redistributes it. If you take it to the first set of leaves on the plant, it will take sugars there. As the plant grows and manufactures sugars and nutrients, it will redistribute to the upper growing plant leaves. This is commonly referred to as: from source to sink. A manufactured substance by the upper leaves, and transported in a downward direction is carried by the phloem. This downward transported substance ultimately winds up in the roots where it is stored.

I knew the same principle would apply to the soybeans as soon as I received the Chevron sample, and I couldn't wait to explore my hypothesis.

God fixed it right. The environment took care of me, and when God made this earth, I am convinced that He had me in mind. He knew that when He made me, I was going to enjoy this earth. That's why he molded me for it. I'm going to fix this boy and give him a mind so that he can wrap his mind around my creation.

DEFENDING MY THESIS

A nervousness somehow crept into my being, where I found myself pacing back and forth. The beginning of sweat beads was coming forth, standing at attention on my forehead, as if by invitation. The temperature inside didn't invite them, no physical activity had caused them to come near, but I guess my angst had summoned them.

It was a Saturday morning, where I could hear lawns being cut, the grass is thrown from the blades of the mower, as they were turning clockwise. I could hear birds chirping distinctively on pitch, and I was imaging children all over watching cartoons. As a matter of fact, that's what Kim and Karlton were doing. My mind was playing a dodging game between where I was going and what was actually happening all around me.

I couldn't settle. I was in orbit, in some frantic moment. I felt like I was in a galaxy, but not just sitting. Turning ... moving ... with my mind moving as fast as the winds on Neptune. In a matter of moments, I would have to defend my thesis, "Studies on the Control of Major Insect Pests of Soybeans with Systemic Insecticides." A panel of people would be there to ask me questions, and I just couldn't help being preoccupied with a case of "Whats and Hows." What will this process be like? How will I do it? What will the outcome be?

It was time for me to leave, and I gathered my things and myself, but that was easier in thought than in reality.

I had been in the Carver Research Foundation hundreds of times, but this time seemed like the more I went toward it, the more I was being repelled mentally. I never remembered another time that I hadn't looked forward to going. It was just like Carver himself was there, and I could bask in all of his works while hoping that he would be proud of what I had done with my studies.

I had arrived. I had an urn of coffee in one hand and a cake in the other, and if I had the luxury of spinning like a spinning top, I would have. On the walls would have been coffee spattered with cake, where I would have been in the midst of this centrifugal force, in a dizzying drunken daze, caused by my own dismal anticipation.

I had managed to work myself into a frenzy. I was pacing up and down like a caged tiger. Somehow, I didn't see the cage as containment of fear, but it was a barrier to the freedom of my thoughts. I knew I needed to be out! I walked faster, pacing. I hadn't heard the heels of shoes so clearly, since I was in the recruiter's office almost eighteen years before. I could hear the click, the clack, almost an incessant stomp, and drag across the floor. And then I stood. A stillness came — a silence that seemed to hold back all the peripheral sounds. And then, I could hear. I clearly heard the words, "Stop and pray." The words were placed on my heart and then on my tongue, Lord, I have done all I can, now you take over. A calmness came and took me by the hand and carried me into a peace where nervousness and anxiousness could not enter.

It was my time to go inside and see the panel of people that would be asking questions about my thesis. I stepped inside, relieved from the frazzles that I had entered. I placed the urn and cake on a table in the hallway.

A certain certainty was present.

The questions began. I answered. Before I knew it, the session was over. I had answered each question as accurately and honestly as I could, where I even had to give an "I cannot recall."

Even with that response, certainty was still present.

"Mr. Gross, please step outside."

I left, and a calmness came over me.

Even though the name of a chemical had escaped me as I was asked, and I had responded with a simple, I don't know/I cannot recall," I was no longer worried.

I was called back inside.

"Mr. Gross, you passed with flying colors."

I called my wife with the good news, and she wanted to know if I wanted a ride.

"No, I'll walk," I said.

I graciously walked home. Giving time to commune with God, I saw that all I had to do was honor Him, and He presided over the panel. I took in the scenes of the nature of

Tuskegee, as it would be some of the last times I would see it. I remembered the six years of growth that I had experienced as a student.

As I arrived home, my wife's famous yellow cake was waiting, and the only thing anxious this time were my taste buds.

MASTER'S DELIVERED

The drums were beating with a steady beat and at a syncopated pace. The bicentennial year was a time where America was engaged in their freedom from England, and here she stood independently two-hundred years later. All the efforts of George Washington heading up the Continental Army was now on display, and America could see all they had fought for.

This was America in her glory. Red, white, and blue was the year's décor.

But no amount of tapping on drums with a patriotic beat, or flutes that blew with the sounds of symphonic waves could overshadow the accomplishments of my newly minted thesis. I was not ready to receive my Master's Degree.

I handed my thesis to Dean Zubi Metcalf. I took my thesis for him to sign. As Dean of the Graduate School, it was required for him to sign, and I didn't want to make matters impersonal. I wanted to take it to him personally. He was a nice guy, and for a moment, we sat down and talked a while. I knew this would be one of my last times in the office, for my graduate work was done.

As I sat there, I saw the degrees on the wall, along with a picture of Booker T. Washington. Many professors did have his picture on the wall, those that had offices. But being a Dean of a college came with a big office. It was a beautiful office with a big chair and all the oak fixtures that one would expect. Even though I enjoyed my research, I was glad it was over. Now was time to go out into the world, and I would be doing it without the six years covering Tuskegee.

I didn't receive just my Master's that day, but an apology, which was accompanied by revelation, which was a far cry from day one.

The day I received this Master's, Dr. B.'s eyes moistened. These weren't tears of joy or sorrow, but tears of reflection. This man had wronged me horribly on that day, he had a tearful speech of admittance, "It's how I grew up."

I heard another applause, and it was more thunderous than the last. It was time for the next speaker. I found myself reflecting back on life after my master's.

From the time I received my master's, I had three jobs where each one presented something that was seemingly inevitable. All three felt like I was experiencing a test, and maybe I was. Maybe it was character building, or maybe it was to test me, to prepare me to withstand opposition. Whatever His plan was for me, it appeared I got a lot of it.

It just seemed like the devil met me at the entrance of each door. There were no horns, a tail, or a visible pitchfork, but the actions and language which was so freely spoken to me were from a fork-tongued and dark heart, designed to let me know who I was and who I wasn't.

After being under "attack" in Vietnam so often, allowing words to penetrate my being was not going to happen. If God allowed me to survive Vietnam, He also had the power to shield me from a direct and even a carefully designed insult.

UNIROYAL

On the other side of the "tassel" was my first job after my Master's 1976 at Uniroyal. This company had requested students from Tuskegee for employment. We, as students, were eager and excited, and actually thought we were going to get a chance to have jobs where we would incorporate our science degrees, applying scientific practices.

I decided I would go and put in my application, for it seemed that everything was going to line up. I told Patricia I would be working at Uniroyal, and I felt great about bringing in "full-time" money to the family after all my years of studying. I didn't know what kind of job responsibilities I would have, but I loved science and felt it could be applied in any capacity when a hypothesis is raised and a result is needed.

That night I slept just as good as most people do when they anticipated a good thing, as excitement peers closer and is all around.

Morning came quickly, and I arrived at Uniroyal, where I was taken on a short tour.

"This is where you all will be." I looked around, and I did not see what I thought I would see.

"Is this it?" I felt like stating out loudly, but I didn't. I was expecting to see a science lab, with test tubes and Bunsen Burners, but I was expecting something that said, "science." The lab didn't have to be like Carver's Research Center, but I expected something else. Maybe there was something science-related, and I just didn't see it.

I was not prepared for what was coming. I was moving tires and manually handling them. I saw nothing wrong with an honest job of this nature, but was this really what Uniroyal was contacting the Department Heads at Tuskegee about? They wanted Tuskegee graduates to apply with them? I was actually appalled, and I really couldn't believe this. Here we were, graduates in various scientific studies, and we were not going to be testing rubber or steel for its strength for distance. We were not going to be measuring or hypothesizing. This did not seem right. This seemed like this was some setup and a mockery deliberately designed to show male graduates of Tuskegee what Uniroyal thought of us.

There was only one thing to do, and that was to prepare and prepare graciously. I wasn't going to "raise Cain," nor was I going to do things that were destructive to me and my wife and children to harm our reputation. I didn't let this stop me, as I continued what I was doing in the community of Tuskegee. I coached baseball, mentored students, and stayed in regular attendance of church services. I got a chance to see the Dixie Hummingbirds and treasured their music, and all of this added to the dimension of who I was.

I relished the time with my children, Kim and Karlton, and they were growing like weeds. This was most important, for I would never be able to get this quality time back.

However, I was faced with a new pleat in fatherhood duties when Karlton was pushed down and fought back. The principal made a decision to punish him, and I vehemently objected. Things may not have been exactly like I wanted them in my life at Uniroyal, but I was going to make sure things were in line for Karlton.

Karlton, born with achondroplasia, was sometimes susceptible to bullying. Yet, he could respond with the fierceness of kids who were considered normal size. I found out that the principal spanked him for pushing a boy down because this boy had pushed Karlton down. I felt my blood percolating within me. Not a vile anger, but a violation of principles that I had taught Karlton. This was going to require a conversation. Not a blowout, mind you but requesting that the principal used different measures when someone was aggressive with Karlton. When the day came, the two of us sat down. The office was a standard office with file cabinets and some across his large desk. It seemed that everything was perpendicular to whatever was around it, leaving me with the feeling that there may be some form of "anal retentiveness" present. I wondered how this might affect the reception of my presentation, as I explained to him that I did not want him disciplined for standing up for himself. I wanted Karlton to have a right to defend himself respectfully and not be punished for it.

He understood, we shook hands, and we continued with the day.

As for my time at Uniroyal, I would continue to handle tires, and additionally, do what I was used to doing. Planning and moving forward, and that is what I did. However, I began to not be able to sleep. Physically, something was wrong. My back was giving me problems, and it was not letting up.

An examination proved I needed Cervical Fusion surgery in my L5 and L6, and this wasn't going to be as easy as I would like for it to be. I became numb on one side and couldn't really dress myself. Time went by, and I was not as nimble as I wanted to be. Yet, in spite of all this, I was going to pursue other interests in a career I felt was suited for me. Later a cleared me to fly to Asheville, North Carolina, and interview for what would be my next job.

I was massively appalled about my stay at Uniroyal. My Workmen's Comp was cut. When I wanted to pursue legal matters, a local attorney stated to me, "I haven't won a case in Lee County, and I am not going to take your case. You ought to shut your mouth and go back the work."

I refrained from what I wanted to call him.

FISH AND WILDLIFE

I didn't accept my fate in that matter; I just accepted that God was going to take it from here. That's exactly what happened. I was headed out of not only this tire business but out of the state of Alabama.

I vividly remembered the drive down and the reception I received on the first day at the Fish and Wildlife Refuge. I unfolded the map that was sixteenths and plotted my course from Tuskegee, Alabama, to Hyde County, North Carolina. I examined the scales of miles and noted that it would take about twelve hours from departure to arrival. My destination: Swan Quarter, North Carolina. I was off to my first job as a Biologist and a Manager of the Young Adult Conservation Corps. I surmised this was an opportunity where I would apply all of my Tuskegee Biology studies and give back to the environment as it had so kindly given to me. The environment deserved to be livable, breathable, and beautiful for all. Water, air, soil, animal, plant, animal testing – any that was needed – and I was ready to roll up my sleeves and delve into any matters that made the environment its best Aquatic and wildlife self. I saw endless possibilities of protecting and servicing the environment.

My wife prepared my food for the trip: sandwiches made with bologna and cheese and liverwurst sandwiches, not the ring around it, but the one that is round. I made reservations in my mind that I would stop for occasional snacks, soft drinks, and coffee.

My travels would take me through 85 to Raleigh 264, as I peer closer. From experience with Mr. Armstrong, I made sure to "fill her up" the night before. Since my truck was red, I was always cautioned that I could be seen in the distance. I had to take into consideration that I would be traveling through towns that I had never encountered, and I couldn't be certain that "in-towners" were going to be friendly to out-of-towners. I figured my pick up would give me the benefit of going at least 8 hours off of a full tank.

The morning air gave my lungs a kick, like a puff of air from a nebulizer. I stretched and loaded my bags into the pick-up, and it was the first time my luggage would ride shotgun for a long career assignment. I put my trunk on the truck bed. I started the truck and could hear the ignition turn with rapidity. It didn't need a choke or pat on the pedal, for it zoomed with exuberance as soon as I hit it. The Chevrolet Silverado started as promised by its design. I let it warm up for a few minutes, as the oil went to all its extended paths, and soon I would be heading toward northeast Georgia, South Carolina, and then North Carolina.

It was when I first signaled and could hear the audible ticking of the signal lights, that reality really began to sink in, that I would be leaving for a new adventure in life. This time it didn't include pursuing a degree, it didn't include the campus of Tuskegee, and sadly it didn't include my family in Alabama. I was going to Eastern, North Carolina, and I had not a family member, distant relative, or even a known friend there.

Before I knew it, I was on Highway 81 to 85, crooning to a tune from the Dixie Humming Birds in my head. I had just seen the Dixie Humming Birds at my daughter, Kim's, old high school.

For miles, I forgot to turn on the radio. I tuned to the station of my songs and my own wondering. Although I had seen pictures, I wondered if Lake Mattamuskett was as placid as defined in the brochure. Was the picture shot from the best side? Would there be two worlds that I would have to merge mentally? The reality and the perceived? What would the personnel be like? How would my daily work performance be viewed? I didn't want to muddle myself down with too many questions at once. Before I realized it, I had not even turned on the radio. I had been entertained by my meditative thoughts, and prayers of proclamation, as I called those things that be not as though they were.

The sun was not ready to rise yet, and I had covered many miles in two hours. Starting at four o'clock in the morning, I began with a little fog, but nothing terribly serious. I decided to turn on the radio, and a hot political topic about Jimmy Carter was on. The men were calling him the "Peanut Man" from Georgia. For a moment, it seemed they couldn't see beyond his association with soil and peanuts to see that he was also an intelligent man who had graduated from the Naval Academy. Actually, it was my opinion; I felt his association with the soil had probably given him a distinctive insight on how things actually would work. I'm sure Carter saw how the deliberate process of sowing and nurturing had an effect on the harvest. There was no way he could have become president without looking at such a thing with an eye of complexity in the midst of what everyone else dismissed as simplistic. I could see my own life from the soil, and I could see Jimmy's and how the process of germination, fertilization, and pollination had made for an interesting comparison with a human's life and a plant's life.

I remembered how the fields and trees entertained me for hours, where I could determine what was poisonous and what was not, and how this led me to help Dr. Judkins create a poisonous plant garden leading me to my scientific dreams. Carter's life on his farm brought him closer to the black kids, sons, and daughters of the farmhands, and this led him to his political dreams. Even though his father was pro-segregation, he allowed him to befriend these children.

It was time for me to stop, but the show was so interesting, I thought I would extend the drive until it was over. I stopped at a convenience store and got a Pepsi, and drank it right there on the spot. It didn't seem the Silverado was near ready to be refilled at the halfway point as I preferred, so I just enjoyed the break, soft drink, and a little stretching.

When I returned to the road, my mind fell on Kim and Karlton. Kim was now going into the sixth grade, and Karlton was second grade. In just a few days, they would be going back to school for the new year. Thus far, they had no experiences like mine when I was in school and were afraid to learn. They were eager to go to school, full of energy, and were always engaged.

****

Many people were taught that a firm handshake can speak volumes and even foretell the character of the person by the firmness. It can sometimes strengthen the faith in the agreement and give flight to any unsettling feelings.

When the refuge manager greeted me, we extended each other our hands, and his handshake was like a wet fish coming up from the water. Limp and languid, he extended it just enough to say he had shaken my hand. Even a dying fish would have had a more aggressive response, with jumping and pulsations, indicating the desire to live. Not here. I immediately read the message. It was a cold message, and it was just the opposite of the firm handshake. My employment was not the desired agreement; it was not a deal. I was seen as some agent that was coming to expose or uncover something about the refuge, and packaged in the skin I was in; this was cause for a distant moment.

At the end of this "reception," the assistant to the Refuge Manager wanted to discuss something with me, and without any introduction, he spoke.

"We need to fire some of these kids."

I responded as deliberately as the dialogue began.

"I don't think so," I responded equally as deliberate.

I could tell this was not what he was expecting. He was expecting a pause because his face turned red, and he looked down.

He didn't say, "I don't understand what you are saying," or an "I'm sorry, I didn't hear you." He cleared his throat as if to prepare to clarify his statement since he thought I needed to hear it again.

I proceeded to my statement.

"We don't need to fire anybody."

His hand went to the back of his neck — a movement that indicated that he was going to volley his next comment, and it was going to be understood why some of the kids had to be fired. Before he could bring it forth, I began.

"If any of these kids are going to be fired, it will be my decision."

He had a Goliath stance with a spear. I had a stone. I saw the spear come my way.

"I can see we are not going to get along very well," he said as if he was going to add some other words at the end.

I got out my "smooth stone" and launched it.

"We are going to get along very well, and it will happen when you come to the realization that I am in charge of this program."

I had been hired by Fish and Wildlife as a Biologist and Director of the Young Adult Conservation Corps.

A glazed stare came to his face, which it was evident he would have like to participate in longer, but he had to cut it off. The longer he stared, the more he looked like the loser.

I knew that I had to stand firm with these Refuge Managers. If it was left up to them, they would have gotten rid of all of the kids right then, and these kids needed jobs, hope, and a future for their tomorrow.

Although I was met with a hollow reception at the job, there was warmth waiting for me in the community.

I found a place to stay, as I rented a house and found myself in just as much warmth as I was in a cloud of suspicion. There were whispers that I was FBI, looking for something within the Fish and Wildlife or something within the local area. Perhaps there were those who had whispered couldn't accept that I had a budget over $100,000 to use as I saw fit to improve the areas within the Fish and Wildlife and the YACC.

When word made its way around that equipment was purchased, and Fish and Wildlife benefited from it, the whispers began to subside.

As the months were passing, I noticed that even though I was officially hired as a Biologist and Youth Director, I had been utilized more for the Youth Director and not a Biologist. Meetings that were concerning the animals and their welfare with chemicals left me absent in attendance until there was one nobody knew. Then there was a moment with urgency to get me to the meetings to present findings of the effects on green head ducks to make the agency look good.

The thought of me making decisions in those areas left the Refuge Managers in worlds of disdain. It was a similar theme to Uniroyal, where it appeared that being Black meant there was a category. It wasn't decision-making, administrative, or in the leadership of any kind, but some subservient positioning.

When it was all said and done, my time at the Fish and Wildlife served the young women and boys working on the YACC. I resolved within myself that it was these young people who needed me because they had no advocates there. These young people had homes headed by single parents who were doing all they could to make ends meet.

I looked around the room, and some of the people who started with me at the Environmental Protection Agency were no longer here. One of my supervisors, whom I truly believed might have been here, had passed.

When it came to moving on to the Environmental Protection Agency, I was really on the up and up because there was no other way it could be. I was offered a job, a federal job at that, at Auburn University in the Parasitology Lab. I often thought about it and then looking back, maybe I should have taken it. What was unbelievable was the fact that they weren't going to pay me as much as I would have made at Uniroyal. However, I did want to do research on parasites, but I later believed that the USDA had a job also at Auburn, and they wanted me to be the animal caretaker. That really wasn't going to cut it.

The EPA had pulled my name off the Federal Register because I had filled out a Standard Form 171. EPA decided they wanted to hire me as an Entomologist. I was going to do the emergency exemption for pesticides because sometimes farmers cannot control a certain pest with currently registered chemicals. Therefore, they request a chemical not registered on the crop in question. I had to examine the requested chemical and make sure that it would have no adverse effect on beneficials.

****

Return to Auburn University as a Faculty Member

After two years with the Environmental Protection Agency (EPA), I returned to Auburn University as a Faculty Member on an Intergovernmental Personnel Agreement (IPA). It was apparent to me, that my work as a graduate student at Auburn University made me worthy to be accepted as a

Faculty Member to engage in research on insect pheromones or 'insect sex attractants.'

The Dean of Agricultural Sciences even requested that the EPA allow me to remain at Auburn past my two-year assignment to complete work on a Ph.D., at no cost to the EPA in excess of my salary. The cost of all academics would be covered by Auburn. However, the request was denied under the pretense that my presence at the EPA was indispensable, although the Agency stressed higher education.

****

EPA Service of Thirty Years

Waking up to my birthday was no ordinary day in 1979. As I was getting ready, it was a morning full of wishes and wonder.

"Bill, what do you want for breakfast?" I could only imagine my wife asking.

"I think I'll just have a little coffee and a strip of bacon and one egg," I pretended to answer in my mind.

Even in my imagination, I knew the excitement of a new job, and a big breakfast was not going to mix well together. I was going to take the Metro bus in, a new way of transportation different from any job I had ever had.

My wife and children were still in Alabama, and I moved to Washington, D.C., to begin my life as a scientist and researcher with the Environmental Protection Agency.

I stood in my closet and quickly decided what I was going to wear. Basically, I had prepared mentally what I might wear the night before.

I chose a sport coat, trousers and a dress shirt, and a tie that would complement my look and express that I was serious about research. I was sharp as a tack ... I was dressed appropriately.

This birthday turned out to be a birthday and the beginning of a thirty-year anniversary all into one. Three decades of working for the mission to protect the environment against all kinds of chemicals in water, air, food, and also in wildlife, yet there was no protection against my thoughts or feelings on the first day.

The ride to Crystal City from Washington, D.C., was a fast one. I could see the beginning of new highways and office buildings, and people like me going to another day of work. Some looked happy, maybe content, and some looked like they were counting down to retirement.

It was time to get off, and I could see my destination. I walked into the building.

"Good morning, you must be William L. Gross."

"Yes, sir, I am. It's a pleasure to meet you," I said as we shook hands. "You must be my supervisor."

"Great to meet you as well," he replied, but something in his posture made me feel that perhaps he felt slightly different. His red face looked like a red bruised tomato, and it seemed to take a full presence over the conversation.

"Let me show you around and give you a tour of the office."

I walked around, seeing some faces without the eagerness I anticipated. Some people spoke with a welcoming voice, even if it was just congeniality.

I made notes where my route was as I would be traveling. Soon we were back to the office of my supervisor. He gave me a briefing on my job, on my duties, and my responsibilities, and then what would have been the benediction until I spoke.

"You know there were many other people who were more qualified than you, but we had to hire you because you were black." That was a hot poker that went through my skull. That's how angry I got with him because it was so insulting.

I cocked the trigger of my words back, and I pulled it point-blank. This was no reckless act or some random rattling of my emotions, but it was a statement that he had to hear. A statement that told the truth and my qualification, as preparing for them for the last ten years.

"Wait, let's hold up here a minute, I feel I am just as qualified as you and any other scientist in this field. If you don't believe me or find this truthful, try me. Try me out for yourself."

There was a look of surprise on his face. He had a clay face, stoic look as if the wind had shifted, and it had frozen solid for a moment. He turned an ashy white. That tomato left, he said it without the privilege of trying to mince his words.

"You ain't got no business here."

That's the kind of greeting that I had and received wherever I went. It was evident that he didn't expect me to respond this way. I knew one thing, yes, this was the Environmental Protection Agency, but this department was not going to protect me as a person or my feelings. This declaration made by this man to me was by every standard a dirty statement to any person. It was horrible because he didn't care. I recognized it for what it was. He was fresh out of South Africa, and he brought his racial prejudices across a couple of continents with him.

I was at the Environment Protection Agency for thirty years, and just like a movie has a soundtrack of songs, my time here was pitched to the tune of chemicals, chaos, and creative racism. These thirty years seemed like a medley of dissonance, but like my time at Uniroyal, I focused on things outside the job that propelled me forward to whom God wanted me to be.

My first chemical was carbofuran. A chemical that the agency obviously wanted to rule out. I had used this product at Tuskegee and Auburn, so I knew this was not a chemical of horrendous harm, as was reported by some at EPA. Submitting my findings proved to fall upon deaf ears and avenues of dislike. It was hard to remember that I was still receiving my salary even though my findings were being objected to. What was hard to believe was that people with no science backgrounds were making determinations about chemicals with minimal research. Nevertheless, it was apparent that my work was deemed to be objected, for after a time of statements, questions, and outright objections, I was taken off the "Carbofuran Committee."

Another memorable chemical was Malathion. The approach was different from this chemical. I was buddied up with a gentleman who was to present his findings, and I was to present mine. This was common because with people doing research, it always helps to have several findings to cross-reference.

I went through pages of information, books that were pulled from the registrar. I wrote endless drafts before I submitted my final. Upon finishing, I gave a copy of my findings to my research partner, and what happened next, I couldn't believe it. He took my paper, critiqued it up and down, pointed out all that was wrong about the use of the chemical, yet he did not even submit one. What made matters even worse, he gave it to his supervisor for this supervisor to contact mine, resulting in him questioning me.

I took a cab from Crystal City, VA to Manassas, VA: Destination home. My blood was boiling and probably passed 212 degrees. It would seem that my supervisor would have stopped the matter and did not even let it get off the ground. Here's another employee at the same level critiquing me. My supervisor should have stopped this. He didn't.

Time would move on, and I would be assigned to fumigants and their effects. With fumigants, it was important to have those that would treat pests and yet not harms humans. I would travel with a team to Carolinas, North, to be exact, to a tobacco warehouse. Upon observations, there was nothing that was apparently wrong, but a warehouse manager reveals a type of fumigant that was used. As the team met, I spoke candidly about how workers who are around this chemical needed to actively wear masks. They weren't any offensive objections initially. However, there were some questions. It wasn't until I got back to Virginia when my supervisor mentions something strange.

"Bill, I understand you appropriately dressed at the sites."

I did not understand what this was about.

"I don't understand what you mean?"

"I was told you had on a tank top at the warehouse."

This was unbelievable since I was the only one on the team with objections, this is what happened. I didn't want to believe it, but perhaps the chemicals that came through the EPA were already predestined to be or not to be, depending upon who wanted it promoted or demoted, no matter the effects.

More chemicals were assigned, and I received the same kind of icy reception. This was the chemical pirate. This was an insecticide used to preserve cotton crops. Having a chemistry minor, I knew this chemical and what it could kill. It was killing the cotton leafworm, and with it, it was going to kill the birds. I didn't know why placidity was surrounding this chemical, but I was getting some peace. What I suggested was received, things I spoke about were heard, and I submitted findings that I knew supported my theory.

I spoke with a manager to hear the ramifications.

"If you allow this chemical to be registered, it is a detriment to the environment, killing birds, and non-targeted organisms that need to exist."

All was silent for a while, and I didn't hear anything.

Then suddenly, I got a call profusely thanking me for my insight about the long-term effects of this chemical. That was one of my shining moments. I guess the EPA let me have this one.

They also allowed me to submit a feed ration formula that is currently used for animals for proper nutrition and weight gain.

But there was ugliness waiting in the wings.

****

It was a normal beginning of the day at work, or at least I thought until I stumbled on a poster. There was this image, who was black with three big balls in its mouth. It was accompanied by a saying, "A Brain is a terrible thing to waste, that's why niggers don't have any."

This was one of the most despicable displays of racism I had ever seen. The employee that did this thought it was just a joke. This kind of thing hurt me, and I wanted to make sure EPA understood this wasn't right. I asked my supervisor to give that employee a letter of reprimand — the action taken: None.

As I had already told myself, I had other areas outside the EPA. I would give my knowledge and skills to other areas.

There was a major opportunity that caught my attention in the midst of this "brainless" matter; however, I knew it was going to take all the brains God gave me to do it.

More applause were coming and more speakers. As much as I enjoyed the speaker, I thought about the time I was able to attend be chosen for the NCO Academy.

NCO ACADEMY

I can't say I woke up, and it was staring me in my face, but like many of my ambitious desires, I had read about the opportunities. I always remembered the day Kim waved goodbye to me when I left for Tuskegee. I knew that day there would be ambitions I didn't know I had but would come forward. I felt the same way when Karlton was born; there would be places I would want to go but didn't know where. I did know the names of these places, but "further" would cover all bases.

I saw something that was of interest to me. It was an application to the Noncommissioned Officer Academy. I had experienced lots of challenges that weren't tied to a dilemma, delinquency, or dismissal, and a challenge like the NCO Academy was a good place where I would be able to select.

Something quickened within me, and I wanted to go to Non-Commission Officer's Academy.

I had been blessed to be chosen for a few things: ROTC Duty, Court Reporting, and Embassy Duty. However, I thought this new area would be something I was interested in. Upon reading it, I heard the word 'rigor.' I knew that. If it had anything to do with the Air Force, rigor was going to be a part of it. Being in the reserves after being in Active Duty taught me how to prepare for whatever I needed to do.

The process of filling out an application took me back to the Chevron Grant process. Only now, it had been over ten years. There was nothing to fear, just something to face.

I got a call saying I had been accepted. I was thrilled, especially after I had been served a poster on my desk working at the EPA, which was obviously meant for me to see. "A brain is a terrible thing to waste, that's why niggers don't have any." I should have known by now that God replenishes when the adversary wishes to tear down. I had been down this road before, and with God, I prevailed.

I was on my way to Air University at Maxwell Air Force Base in Montgomery, Alabama. It was much to the EPA's chagrin. They did not want to grant my leave, but they had no other choice. I was officially in the Air Force Reserves, and this was a duty.

When I got to Alabama, it was far from the familiarities of home, and that was a good thing. I recognized I was there to fulfill a duty for both the Air Force and myself.

I had been met with challenges, but these challenges were different. It was academically rigorous, but it wasn't impossible. There were times when everything looked like it was turned backward and upside down, and you had to make sense of it all.

Shortly after settling, I vividly remember the class 'Creative Problem Solving.'

"I'm giving everyone index card, and I want you to write down a problem," the instructor said. He had a voice that was authoritative, not soothing, a little unpredictable. I couldn't quite determine what kind of personality he had.

I put the card in front of me on the desk, but I didn't write anything on it.

Footsteps were coming towards me.

"I don't see you writing a problem," the Instructor said.

"That's because I don't have one," I responded.

I could feel the other students looking around toward me with curiosity.

"I don't understand. You mean you don't have a problem," he said. "I have never met anyone who doesn't have a problem."

I didn't feel threatened when he said it, nor did it come across in that manner. There was a sincerity in his voice.

"Let me explain why I don't have a problem. If I can solve what I perceive to be a problem, it's not a problem."

I could hear the students turning around in their seats.

The instructor didn't respond. He continued to wait as if I had more to say, and I did.

"If I can't solve it, I turn it over to a higher power, so it's still not a problem."

The instructor looked at me and shook his head.

The students were engaged and wondered what would be said next. I waited, for I wondered what his verbal response would be.

"I wish I had some of what you got."

"You can. It's given out freely every day," I responded.

I didn't realize I would be having an evangelical moment, but when was I ever going to be ashamed of the Gospel?

As time went on, even after my personal confession in Creative Problem Solving, I was feeling a little worn down. This program was coming with a punch, but this was different. No one was telling me I wasn't qualified and had to choose me because I was black. It wasn't that kind of punch, and I was grateful. I could appreciate being seen for my own merit. However, I was feeling ground down.

The NCO Academy assigned our own personal library of resources that made studying accessible to us. This was a true gift with resources nearby. We all had a project that we had to present, which was the central theme for our being at the academy. After a few weeks, we had to develop what we were going to do.

Classes preceded, and it was like a vice grip on the back of my neck. I muddled through, passing God my index card. Lord, help me.

I thought I would have a conversation with the Comandante.

"Sir, I find that I'm ..."

I was in front of the Comandante, kicking some ideas around about the program.

"Look, it's hard. It's rigorous. I hear these conversations all the time. Let me just say this to you. If you are thinking about quitting, you will be paying the $16,500 that the Air Force Paid for you to be here. And, please note, if you quit, you are sending the Air Force a message that you don't want another promotion."

I gathered myself on the way out, immediately after saying, "Thank you, sir."

****

"Hello, Patricia."

"Hi Bill, how are you?"

"Well ... Everything is alright," I said hesitantly, but still, what I thought was believable.

"What's going on, Bill?"

"This is a different ball of wax here. Like I've never seen before," I said. I wasn't looking for sympathy, but I just needed to get the frustration off my chest.

"Bill, I can't imagine it being any harder than anything else you have been up against," Patricia said effortlessly. She didn't seem to have to think up the words or think about what she was going to say.

"If you don't finish, don't bother coming back home."

I guess I just wanted a soft spot to land. Instead, I landed on a springboard.

****

Patricia didn't let me in wallow around in all of my processed thoughts of pity. Patricia was right. Life at the NCO Academy wasn't harder than anything else I had been up against. I was grateful for her confidence and did a forward march.

Before I arose the next day, I began to reflect on a trip to Langley Airforce Base with some cadets. We saw lots of combat-ready fuel tanks that were stored underground. As a Biologist, I knew this was a disaster waiting to happen. The tanks were rusty and corroding, and the Air Force was attempting to get companies to move them, but it wasn't happening. These companies felt it was too dangerous and were afraid of explosions.

I felt a light bulb come on. This was the project for me. This was everything I had seen from the age of six. The fish I pulled up with the bucket, the nature I so enjoyed, the Biology I studied, the Chemistry I minored in, the Entomology I studied. How did this fit in with some old fuel tanks underground? If these tanks exploded, look at what would happen to all the aquatic life, the insects, the soil, and so much more. What about the six-year-olds who might be counting on the environment to carry them into a self-exploration journey as the environment had carried me.

It was clear that this was going to be my project. I could create a sealant that could be poured around the tanks that would seal off any areas that could potentially explode.

****

It was almost that time – Graduation. I was so happy the end was about to be near.

My name was submitted to do the benediction for the graduation after I told an instructor I would be willing to do it since the academy was looking for volunteers. I just needed to have an interview.

When I got to the interview, I saw a rather stoic-looking man — another hard-to-read gentleman.

"Why should you do the benediction?" he asked.

"Number one, I'm a Christian, and two, I'm a deacon."

"When you pray, you don't want to insult anyone by invoking the name of Jesus."

I knew where this was going, and I proceeded into my explanation with no shame.

"There is only one man that walked this earth who told people how to pray. Being that he saved me, anytime I pray, I'm going to invoke his name. Tell you the truth, if anybody is there at the exercises, when I'm praying, they ought to be uttering their own prayer. I figure they invoke whose ever name they want."

When I said that, I don't even know when my lips moved. It was as if it fell out of my mouth without me having to even form the sentences.

This man looked at me and laughed. The stoic look he had recessed, and he was quite jovial.

He didn't further the conversation into anything deeper.

He told me, "I'll let you know if you are chosen."

The graduation was a memorable sight where everyone graduated with the exception of two people; one who was sick, who had the opportunity to return, and one who didn't quite meet the requirements. There was something else missing. I was not on the program for the benediction. Was I surprised? Not at all.

Now that I have finished the NCO Academy, I was back in the arms of Patricia as she welcomed me home.

"I knew you could do it," she said.

Life, at that moment, was great!

This was another experience where God taught me; he had ordered my steps so I would be prepared for the next journey.

****

When I arrived back at the EPA, I knew what I had to do. Since no letter of reprimand was going to be sent to the employee who sent me the "brainless" memo-poster, I was going to file a suit against EPA for this action. The EPA thought because they approved me to go to the academy, I would perhaps forget I had begun to pursue this before I left, and actually, with all the hours of blood, sweat, and tears I experienced at the Academy, I was reminded of just how much I needed to continue with this egregious matter.

The EPA sent a gentleman out to investigate the matter. He was a Black gentleman, and I wondered if they thought because he was Black, this was going to put me at ease, perhaps change my mind. I felt this gentleman was already informed of how to handle this situation. The line of questioning didn't offer objectivity, and I thought it would. It appeared slanted. I let him know how the EPA called a meeting and had an unusual request of me.

My supervisor and the man's supervisor wanted to meet, and when I arrived, the perpetrator was with them. They actually were there to suggest I apologize to him for sharing this with the supervisors and co-workers, and I jumped straight up and hit the table so hard, I could have knocked a hole in it. Before I knew it, I dropped an expletive right there, stating I didn't owe anybody anything.

I didn't expect a miracle, nor I didn't get one. Although the case was dismissed, it sent the message that I was not taking anything sitting down without my side being heard.

****

I held on to what I believed and what I chose for myself. There was life outside of my job at the EPA.

"Bill, I want you to go on the Mission Trip with us to Kenya."

"Miss Rozelle, I don't know anything about being a missionary."

"Pray about it."

Normally, that would have been a flimsy promise in passing. I would have said 'yes' and somehow forgot about it, but this promise I would need to follow through.

"Lord, is this what you want me to do? Fix me up and prepare me for it."

God didn't come back to me in a loud voice. The passport, visa, and immunization worked out so smoothly. However, a sudden twist came. I couldn't really explain it.

The closer I got to the date of departure, the more excuses I came up with why I shouldn't go. Why have I had a sudden fear of insects and diseases? Yet God still compelled me to go. I was sure God was sitting on his throne, laughing at me.

Bill, I have anointed you to be a biologist. You are going to tell me you are afraid of insects and diseases, and more specifically, I anointed you to be an Entomologist.

At first, I didn't understand until I got to Kenya and some things I understood before I arrived at how powerful my God is.

Like most things in my life, there was an unexpected presentation waiting for me. Leaving for Kenya wasn't uneventful. I was sitting across from the pastor's wife, and the airplane proceeded to shake violently. I thought the plane was going to fall to pieces, hit the desert, and life as I knew it would be over. Never had I experienced turbulence like this before.

I didn't believe God had brought me all the way into the air to let me fall and never testify about his goodness, so I began to pray. "Lord, this is your universe, and you made this universe and everything that is in it. You made this airplane. In the name of Jesus, take this plane out of this turbulence."

What happened next surprised me, but at the same time, it didn't surprise me. There was a stillness that moved over me and that airplane. There was a smooth, quiet glide in the air; the airplane's flight had become smooth in an incomprehensible way.

"God is powerful, isn't He," Mrs. Bradley said.

"Yes, He is," I responded with agreeance.

God was showing us how powerful He was, letting me know He could do all things. I can do anything you ask me.

The rest of the flight remained quiet and reflective. I still didn't fully understand why God was compelling me to go to Kenya until I fully got there.

Having been a Vietnam Veteran, I thought I knew death, sorrow, and infinite hurting. Yet, there was more to come when I got to Africa. When I saw the children's orphanage, I saw human catastrophe from another perspective.

It hit me right there. All of these hurting kids that were there, helpless, without parents, some ill with diseases. I suddenly understood and realized that the poor in the U.S. were rich compared to them. It was unbelievable.

Consequently, out of all their sorrows, the faith they had was unbelievable.

One Sunday morning, the streets were full on the roadside to and from the church. They were grateful for all that they had.

I believe God wanted me to go to Kenya to make me a better person, make me more humble, more forgiving, to make me more disciplined in my life, and make me more appreciative of things the that I have, and to not whine and complain about things I didn't have.

It was always evident that the Kenyans were grateful for the little things, like a small piece of bread.

I was taught a lot about faith when a man approached me at a souvenir barn that had multiple levels. He was sitting at the foot of the stairs and asked as I was going by could I help him. At the time, I had no money in his denomination since I hadn't exchanged it, so I told him I would come back later on. To my amazement, this man had actually waited hours, believing I would return as I had mentioned. There was something in his eyes that told me he had executed what he had the most, and that was faith.

This scene reminded me of the story in the Bible of the man at the Beautiful Gate in the Book of Acts.

Had I not gone on the missionary trip, I would not have realized this man had such faith in another human being. People would usually dismiss this man and keep going.

However, he expected something from me, and I gave it to him. What I gave him in return was probably the equivalent to helping him for a year.

Additionally, there was a girl at the orphanage that I almost considered adopting who was around eight-years-old. Her name was Martha, and she was very smart and would have been a well-rounded addition to our family. Her obedient mannerism, as well as the other children, made her very delightful. I thought she would enjoy science and nature and would rave over the various subjects.

Often, I think about how she is doing to this day. I really became attached to the children at the orphanage. They had diseases and many kinds of afflictions and infirmities. These children's parents didn't just abandon them; they left the children there with the hope that they would be taken care of, where they would have three meals a day.

This trip was in far contrast to what I saw in Vietnam. I saw sorrow, I heard sorrow, and I could smell sorrow due to combat. I had finally accepted that the dead didn't hurt anymore – only their survivors. However, in Africa, people were alive yet hurting at the same time because much of what they needed, they didn't have.

I was grateful to be able to travel and let God show me who I was on this missionary trip, and how I was to go on continuously, giving and remembering the less fortunate with humility.

This had been a wonderful night filled with my retirement memories as I listened throughout the night. I continued to thank God for the journey He had given me, whether it was bumpy, smooth, or a mixture. Either way, I knew that as I drew near to Him, He would lead me to many more paths that would let His light so shine that men would see His good works. This journey made me who I am and taught me. "All things are possible to those who believe."

William Louis Gross

IT IS WITH CERTAINTY THAT . . .

The voice of my daughter, Kim, will move mountains and the mountains of mankind. Just as Christ made Peter and Andrew fishers of men, Kim will penetrate the minds of men, where she will absorb the nutrients of necessity to walk among the nation, departing goodness, fairness, and equality. Her voice, when necessary, will shatter the exterior shell of those where time, circumstance, or perception has formed, and like the scales that fell off Saul's eyes in Acts Chapter 9, they will see and begin their life as Saul's changed on "Straight Street."

Reciting a poem at six-years-old, when her mother momentarily forgot the words, was one of her introductions to the spotlight. As years went on, she commanded the microphone with a combination of speeches or song, where, in song, she has the ability to turn a church into an amphitheater, as her voice melodically turns into the songstress she is. Her voice has and will affect change and lift people to the standards in which they were called.

It is with certainty that my son Karlton will forever be a phenomenon, for, at first sight, he has Achondroplasia, which makes him a little person in stature, yet he possesses a powerful tower in spirit. In that tower is a beacon of light that continuously guides others around him, and just as God's word is a lamp unto our feet and a light into our path, so is Karlton who leads the way. He has led the way bravely as a son, husband, father, and friend.

Now it is with certainty that my granddaughter Mya Simone will take up a cause and affect the change that awaits her. She is who I call "The Sugar Plum," as I am reminded of a reference where Jesus is sweeter than the honey in the honeycomb. It is evident that God has indeed made her into His own image, where she embodies the image of delightfulness. I do not know what she will contribute to society by profession, yet I would love to see that she continues to discover, explore, question, hypothesize, and make the world greater than she found it.

CERTAINTY PROGNOSTICATES

When I look back over my life, there is one thing for sure; uncertainty was seemingly wandering around. I couldn't always shake him. He would leave for a bit, but it appeared we were on a journey together. As time would venture further, His brother, Certainty visited, while making himself more of a familiar companion in what seemed was the darkest times in my life. In the midst of this deserted and desecrated time was my one year stay in Vietnam. Certainty introduced himself. He was venerable, applicable, protective, and assuring, as he let me know his purpose. He really was the answer to the silent monologue swirling around in my head most times. However, Uncertainty, his brother, was in my head, fueling the questions, "Why?" It was clearly Uncertainty, when I wondered, "How?" and when I didn't necessarily know if I could make it beyond was happening next ...

Nevertheless, in Vietnam, in a place where no one would want to be, I understand why Certainty came. He let me know when I believed God was at the rudder of my life, turning the wheel against the forces of a storm, and the questions would become silenced. As loud and frightening as it was, I could hear God better than I had ever before. Uncertainty wasn't wrong to be in my life; he had a job to do as well. His presence allowed me to recognize that trusting God was going to get me to Certainty.

Now, as I listen and as I go to God, I believe all things are possible. Certainty is no longer a guest, for he is a conduit and sits within me, bringing assurance to what I have asked God. Certainty brings hope, that mysterious thing that God made for us to carry forth, and to get going when the way looks dim.

As a result of Certainty, He reminds me that I will lead, as I will continue to follow God. I will teach, as I will continue to follow the teachings of Christ. I will minister, as I will continue to follow the ministries of the Gospel, and I will experience new encounters, as I will continue to encounter the work of our God.

EPILOGUE

"Hate corrodes the container it's carried in."
– Alan Simpson

Forgiving Miss Maude Barnett

As I look out over my life, God has been with me at every turn. From the time the egg and sperm united that created me, and even before that, God had orchestrated my whole life. He was not just waving a stick as a musical conductor, letting the violin section know when to come in or telling the cello section when to play; He had created everything from the musicians, instruments, and even the sound. God knew where I would come in within the song, and where he wanted me to go, as the music "crescendoed." Would there be a soft beat or an untimely clamor in the midst of the song?

Yet, there were days when I could not comprehend where my encounter with my first-grade teacher could fit inside the composition of my life. How could this encounter make the song of my life better? How could putting on that musty black dress strengthen me to be a part of this song God was playing? How could her beating me be an act that would add to the tempo of my life? I saw it as discordant, dissenting, not a smooth sound at all, but a scathing, scratchy sound that went against every chord that was beautiful. My swollen eyes were a constant reminder, telling a story of its own, so how could this play a part in the symphony in my life?

I had to ponder this throughout the years of my life, and each time, it was beginning to appear that the clouds of Miss Maude Burnett had loomed over my life for over seven decades and were not moving. This was not a daily reminder, but a periodic remembrance of her harsh prejudice and deliberate treatment of students she didn't like because they were dark-skinned Black students or poor.

Those beatings I received were far beyond the meaning of corporal punishment but have long entered the corridors of abuse. Even by yesterday's and today's standards combined, any court would have ruled that child abuse was present. I had resigned myself to the thought that I am never going to be over this memory of Maude Burnett.

But then there was God with his baton. His stick raised again. Ready to compose in my mind a peace that would surpass all understanding as He always had promised.

God had me enter a dream after my verbal confession that I would always see Miss Barnett in this dark light, forever burning into my memory. I had ultimately decided she was going to stay there. But this dream began with God placing me on assignment, as I worked with his own time signature. Just like Maude Barnett had beat me, God was keeping the beats of this composition, and in this symphony, He would conduct this arrangement, and he would give all the answers. There I was, responsible for a young minister's arrival time and his clothing for this trial sermon. This young man would preach the word of God, and I was, by some means, assigned to him to make sure he arrived at his pulpit destination on time and with the right clothes.

I didn't foresee any problems ahead in this task. I readily made my plans to care for this up and coming preacher and had clothes ready for him. I delivered the clothing, and now there was nothing to do but have them put them on and be ready to deliver to this waiting audience, filled with family and friends. But when he puts them on, they are too big.

I awakened in a panic, almost a cold sweat. I knew I had entered a nightmare. It became a nightmare as soon as I saw this young preacher in clothing that did not fit. I knew what this meant. God's baton was over my head, playing a tune that sounded like it was designed just for me. Just as I recognized the clothes did not fit, I knew God was not in the midst, and those clothes were not "fit" for him and not the ones God originally planned. Also, I knew that my comments about Maude Barnett were not those that God originally planned for the composition He had been orchestrating for my life. The sounds that I had added were those of clamor, like a gong to the movements he had thoughtfully, and with effort, created for me. I quickly realized that this was God's time signature, His baton, and His creation of this symphony that was written for me to be present, faultless before the father, and I would be ready to present the pieces of the puzzle of my life back to Him, acceptable in His sight.